God Has Spoken

Volume II:

Seeing Christ in the New Testament

GOD HAS SPOKEN

Vol. II:

Seeing Christ in the New Testament

STEPHEN KAUNG

CHRISTIAN FELLOWSHIP PUBLISHERS, INC.
NEW YORK

GOD HAS SPOKEN, VOLUME II:
SEEING CHRIST IN THE NEW TESTAMENT

ISBN 13: 978-0-935008-95-1
ISBN 10: 0-935008-95-0

Available from the Publishers at:
11515 Allecingie Parkway
Richmond, Virginia 23235
www.c-f-p.com

Printed in the United States of America

Contents - - Volume II

Unless otherwise indicated,
Scripture quotations are from the
New Translation by J. N. Darby

Introduction*

II Timothy 3:16-17—Every scripture is divinely inspired, and profitable for teaching, for conviction, for correction, for instruction in righteousness; that the man of God may be complete, fully fitted to every good work.

John 1:17-18—For the law was given by Moses; grace and truth subsist through Jesus Christ. No one has seen God at any time; the only-begotten Son, who is in the bosom of the Father, he hath declared him.

Revelation 1:3—Blessed is he that reads, and they that hear the words of the prophecy, and keep the things written in it; for the time is near.

Let us pray:

Dear heavenly Father, we thank Thee for the privilege of being gathered together in the name of Thy beloved Son, the Lord Jesus Christ. We thank Thee for the assurance of His presence with us. We thank Thee for "Thou will make known to me the path of life: thy countenance is fullness of joy; at thy right hand are pleasures for evermore." We look to Thee to reveal Thy Son to us through Thy precious word. We believe that Thy word is living and life-giving. We trust Thy Holy Spirit to bring us to Christ and bring Christ to us. "As the hart panteth after the water-brooks, so panteth my soul, after thee, O God." Hear our cry. For we ask in the name of Thy precious Son, the Lord Jesus Christ. Amen.

The Holy Scriptures, the Bible, is the foundation of our faith. It is God-breathed. It gives us the full knowledge of Him and of His Son. "This is the eternal life, that they should know thee, the only true God, and Jesus Christ whom thou hast sent"

(John 17:3). God's word gives us eternal life through faith in Christ Jesus. It makes us men and women of God. It is most profitable for our spiritual life, for it teaches us, convicts us, corrects us, and instructs us in righteousness. Thus, we are made complete and fully equipped to do God's will.

A special blessing is given by God to those who read, hear and keep His word. It behooves us, therefore, to diligently search the Scriptures. How can we escape if we have been negligent of so great salvation, which having had its commencement by being spoken of by God himself through the prophets of old, has been confirmed to us by God's own Son and the apostles (see Hebrews 2:3). The Holy Spirit himself bears witness to its truthfulness all through the centuries. Dear saints of old gave their lives for its preservation. How dare we today neglect it, and thus incur untold loss!

The Bible is a compilation of sixty-six books. These are generally divided into the Old Testament and the New Testament. The Old Testament contains thirty-nine books, while the New Testament has twenty-seven. They are so divided because of time and content. The Old Testament contains books of the early age, while the New Testament books are of a later age. The Old Testament was compiled before the time of Christ. The New Testament was composed after the ascension of Christ. Testament means covenant. The Old Covenant is that of law whereas the New Covenant is none other than that of grace. "For the law was given by Moses; grace and truth subsist through Jesus Christ" (John 1:17). The Old Covenant was preparation, but the New Covenant is fulfillment. Law demands, but grace supplies. Both are closely related. They are distinguishable though not isolated; for law leads to grace, Moses leads to Christ.

This collection of twenty-seven books of the New Testament came into existence during the second half of the first century A.D. The early Christians depended on the writings of the Old Testament and the oral tradition delivered to them by the apostles and those who knew the Lord Jesus in His earthly days. Gradually, by common usage and consent, writings of the apostles and those who were intimate with the apostles were recognized as being inspired by the Holy Spirit. Twenty-seven books were universally accepted as God-breathed. These formed the New Testament that we now have.

These twenty-seven books may be divided into three parts: (1) the Historical—which includes the four Gospels and Acts, (2) the Epistles—which includes the Pauline epistles and the catholic or general epistles, and (3) the Prophetic—which is the book of Revelation.

If God wills, we shall go through the New Testament book by book on each Lord's day. It cannot be an exhaustive study. As a matter of fact, the Holy Bible is God-breathed. It is infinite as God is infinite. Men may only touch the surface. Its depth and riches are beyond comparison. Our purpose is to simply give a taste of the sweet word of God so as to induce us to search His word more diligently. May He draw us deeper into His word so that we may be drawn deeper into Him.

** As was indicated in the Foreword in Volume I, some twenty-five years ago the author had begun delivering a series of messages on all sixty-six books of the Bible, with the messages of the New Testament books having commenced being presented, in 1983, on each Lord's day (followed three years later by his beginning to deliver the messages on each of the Old Testament books). This opening chapter represents the author's opening message delivered in his series of messages on the New Testament books.*

MATTHEW

Seeing Christ as Our King

Matthew 1:1—Book of the generation of Jesus Christ, Son of David, Son of Abraham.

Matthew 5:3—Blessed are the poor in spirit, for theirs is the kingdom of the heavens.

Matthew 11:12—But from the days of John the baptist until now, the kingdom of the heavens is taken by violence, and the violent seize on it.

Matthew 28:18-20—And Jesus coming up spoke to them, saying, All power has been given me in heaven and upon earth. Go therefore and make disciples of all the nations, baptising them to the name of the Father, and of the Son, and of the Holy Spirit; teaching them to observe all things whatsoever I have enjoined you. And behold, I am with you all the days, until the completion of the age.

Let us pray:

Dear heavenly Father, how we do praise and thank Thee for giving us the privilege of gathering in Thy presence, worshiping Thee, and remembering what Thy Son, our Lord Jesus, has done for us. Our Father, we do thank Thee that we may continue in Thy presence to read Thy word. We ask that Thou wilt bless Thy word and make Thy word living and operative in each of our lives so that Thou mayest get all the glory. We commit this time into Thy hands and trust Thy blessing. In the name of our Lord Jesus. Amen.

Revelation of Christ

When we open the New Testament, we find that the first four books are called the Gospels: the Gospel according to Matthew, the Gospel according to Mark, the Gospel according to Luke, and the Gospel according to John. These four books tell us the story of our Lord Jesus. They are historical in nature; they are biographical. As we read these four Gospels, we come to a knowledge of our Lord Jesus—His life and His ministry. However, one thing we need to remember: the Bible is given to us as a revelation. In other words, the Bible is to reveal Christ to us. Whether it is given to us in the form of history, biography, poetry, prophecy, or allegory, in whatever form it may be presented to us, the purpose is one: to reveal Christ Jesus to us. Therefore, we will find that the Bible is not only historical, it is also spiritual.

As we approach the word of God, on the one hand, we need to read, to study and to know what is written there. Such knowledge is important. However, if that is all we get from the Bible, then we miss the very reason why the word of God is given to man. It is given to us as a revelation—it is to reveal Christ. Because it is given to us as a revelation, it has to be received as a revelation. It is not enough just to receive the book as history, or poetry, or teaching, or doctrine, or ceremony, or ritual. We have to receive the word of God as a revelation. We need to know the story, the history, the teaching, the doctrine and so on; but beyond these we have to see Christ Jesus. If we do not see Him and all we know is story, if we do not see Him and all we have is teaching, then we miss the very purpose for which the word of God is given.

Therefore, as we approach the word of God, we need to ask the Lord to give us the spirit of wisdom and revelation that we may truly know Him. In other words, the Bible is given as a revelation, and it has to be received as such. Revelation means that God reveals Christ, and through this Book we are to see

Christ in our spirit.

When a revelation is given, it results in fellowship. If it is not revelation, there is no fellowship. Fellowship means having things in common. If there is revelation, then we have fellowship with what is revealed. Therefore, we find that the *logos* of God has to become *rhema* to us. *Logos* is the fact, the truth, the story, the word once spoken and given by God as revelation. *Rhema* is when the Holy Spirit breathes once more upon the word that was given and makes it living, present, real, experiential to each one of us. That is the reason why we need to receive the word of God as a revelation. Only then is there fellowship, and the result of fellowship is transformation. We will be transformed by the word, by what is revealed or Who is revealed and thus be transformed and conformed to the image of God's Son. This is what the word of God, the Bible, is really for. May the Lord help us approach His word as a revelation and receive it as such and, by revelation, have a sight of Christ.

The first four books of the New Testament are histories. Yet even though they are books of biography of the life of our Lord Jesus, God's purpose is that we not only know the story but we truly see Jesus—that we may know Him. This is the purpose of God's word.

We would like to begin with the first book, Matthew. Chronologically speaking, that is, according to time, Matthew was not the first gospel written. Most commentators agree that the first gospel written was Mark; yet in God's sovereignty (and we do believe there is sovereignty there), as we open the New Testament, the Gospel according to Matthew is put first.

From a human standpoint, we would place the Gospel according to Luke first, because this is the gospel of grace for the remission of our sins. We are conscious of our sins. We know we are sinners. We need forgiveness. We need the grace of God, and the gospel of Jesus Christ is the gospel of grace. Through grace by faith we are forgiven and we receive eternal life. So from the human standpoint, we would say the Gospel according to Luke should be placed first. But from the divine viewpoint the Gospel of Matthew appears first because the first thing which we need to see and to know is Christ as our King. The gospel of the kingdom is *God's* viewpoint of the gospel; the gospel of grace is *our* viewpoint of the gospel. Of course, it is both, but we humans usually begin from ourselves. We are so self-centered, we want grace for ourselves—for our enjoyment—and sometimes we forget that we need to be God-centered, that we need to see the gospel from His viewpoint. What is it that God wants us to know about the Lord Jesus in the first place? He wants us to know Him as our King.

One of the reasons Christian lives are so weak and Christian testimony is so ineffective is that we receive the Lord Jesus as our Savior, we see Him as our Redeemer, but we fail to see Him and to recognize Him as our Lord and as our King. We receive the gospel for our personal good, but we do not obey the gospel in order for God's purpose to be fulfilled. Therefore, as we open the New Testament, the first thing God wants us to see is His Son, the Lord Jesus Christ, as King. The whole Bible is to reveal Christ, but the first thing which needs to be revealed to us—which needs to be *received* by us—is to see the Lord Jesus as King. And, again I say, this requires revelation. The Holy Spirit has to reveal this to us in our spirit. It is written there in the Gospel according to Matthew, but what is written there has to be quickened to our heart by the Holy Spirit so that we may truly see Jesus as King.

In our opening the Gospel according to Matthew, the first verse tells us this: "Book of the generation of Jesus Christ, the Son of David, the Son of Abraham." There are only two places in the whole Bible where we find somewhat the same formula—"Book of the generation ..." One is found in Genesis 5:1: "This is the book of the generation of Adam" (ASV 1901). The other is here in Matthew 1:l. This is because there are only two men in God's eyes. The first man is Adam, including every one who comes out of Adam; and we know that "in Adam all die." The second Man is Christ; and we know that "in Christ all shall be made alive" (I Corinthians 15:22).

What is the history of the generation of Jesus Christ? "The Son of David, the Son of Abraham." In other words, from the very beginning of this Gospel, God is testifying who this Jesus Christ is and His history. Who is the son of David? Solomon. Yet Solomon is only a shadow; the real Son of David is Jesus Christ. God told David: "Thy Son will build My house, and His throne in the kingdom shall never end" (see II Samuel 7:13).

Solomon built a temple, but it was just a physical temple. Solomon did reign, but the throne did not last forever. So we know that Solomon is simply a shadow or a type of Christ. There is *the* Son of David, who is greater than David, and by Him the true house of God shall be built. Christ declared: "On this rock I will build my assembly, and hades' gates shall not prevail against it" (Matthew 16:18b). It is in this Son of David that His throne shall never end. He shall reign forever and forever.

He is also the Son of Abraham. Now who was the son of Abraham? Historically, it was Isaac; yet God promised Abraham this, as recorded in Genesis 22: "In thy seed shall all the nations of the earth bless themselves" (see v. 18a). We know that Isaac is just a type or a shadow. The reality is Jesus Christ, because truly in Christ Jesus all the nations shall be blessed. Here at the very outset, God is presenting Jesus to us as the King. He is the promised King. He is the promised Son of David and the promised Son of Abraham in whom all the nations shall be blessed.

Rejection of the King

However, as we read the Gospel according to Matthew, we learn something very interesting there. On the one hand, God is bearing witness all the time to Jesus as His Son and as His appointed King. Yet at the same time, it is recorded that the people rejected Jesus as King continually. We see a conflict there. Why is it that people fail to see the Lord Jesus as King?

As a matter of fact, out of all the nations God chose a people, and He prepared that people over a long period for one reason—that the Messiah could come forth from their midst. That is to say, God prepared the children of Israel from the day of Abraham up to the day of Christ for only one reason, that in the fullness of time the King, the Messiah, should come. But strangely, when the Messiah and King arrived, the people of Israel failed to recognize Him as King. They rejected Him because the concept of a king had been so distorted in human history. The concept of a king in human understanding was so different from that of a king according to the divine understanding. When the King finally arrived, very few recognized Him.

The Jews at that time were disappointed in Jesus. They were expecting Him as King in the beginning and they thought probably He was the King. They were waiting for Him to present himself as such: to overthrow the Roman Empire, cast off its iron yoke, and make Israel the head of the nations. But He did not do that, and so they were disappointed in Him. He was not a king according to their thought. Therefore, even though He claimed himself to be King and was born to be King, they rejected Him. He did not fit their concept.

Only a few of all the children of Israel at that time received Jesus as King, those such as Mary, Joseph, Zechariah, Elizabeth, John the Baptist, Simeon, Anna, a few shepherds. (These, by the way, were probably very special shepherds, not ordinary ones. Scholars today believe they were shepherds of the temple; they kept the sheep that had been set apart to be sacrificed on the altar.) Also, a few of the disciples of John the Baptist received Him through revelation.

The human concept is in such contrast to the divine concept of a king that it needs revelation to see Jesus as King. This was not only true in the first century when the Lord Jesus came upon this earth in a human body, but it has always been such and is still true today. Do you think you can really see Jesus as King without revelation? As you read the Gospel according to Matthew, you will probably have a conflict within yourself, because even though Jesus is presented to you as King, you do not see too much of His kingly nature, of His kingly manner, of His kingship there. You will most likely take the same position as the Jews did in olden days: "He is not much of a king. What has He done?" It requires revelation.

We really need an unveiling by the Holy Spirit in our heart as we read the Gospel of Matthew. God has to open our eyes to see that Jesus is truly a king, but not a king according to human thought. He is a king in accordance with God's thought and we must receive Him as such, as truly our King.

The King is Born

In Galatians we are told that "in the fullness of time" Jesus was born (see Galatians 4:4). He was born of a woman and born under law that He might deliver us from the curse of the law and bring us into adoption—that is, sonship (see 4:5). For God, the time was right for the Lord Jesus to come as a king. But if you are aware of the history of that day, you will probably say that this was *not* the right time, because when Christ Jesus was born, Herod the Idumean was on the throne of the nation of Judea. It was not a Jew, not a son of David, but an Idumean (that is, an Edomite) who was on the throne of the kingdom of Judah. And who was on the throne of the world empire? Augustus Caesar. We would say this was not an auspicious time; yet from God's viewpoint, it was the fullness of time for His Son to come as King.

When Christ was born, He was not born in Jerusalem. We would expect a king, a prince, to be born in the capital of the nation, but He was not born there. He was born in a little town called Bethlehem. At His birth, nobody was aware of it except for a few wise men from the East—magi. They looked at the stars; they detected a tremendously brilliant star, and their interpretation of this was: "A king is born." Being Gentiles, they probably had some knowledge of the prophecy by Balaam, who was a Gentile prophet and had prophesied about the star and the scepter. So they thought there must be a king born in the area of Judea. Naturally, they went to Jerusalem because that was where this new king should have been, but he was not there.

Herod was disturbed because he was king; and yet, another king had apparently been born. He called all the Pharisees and scribes together to learn from them where this king was to be born. These Pharisees and scribes were truly Bible scholars. They did not have to go back and refer to their concordance; they themselves were living concordances. When Herod asked them where the King of the Jews would be born, immediately they said, "He will be born in Bethlehem of Judea." How did they know? There was a little word which came from one of the Minor Jewish Prophets—not a major prophet—indeed, from Micah 5:2: "(And thou, Bethlehem Ephratah, little to be among the thousands of Judah, out of thee shall he come forth unto me who is to be Ruler in Israel: whose goings forth are from of old, from the days of eternity.)"

These scribes and Pharisees knew the word of God by heart. Today, if I asked you to find Micah, I do not know how many of you could find it; but they did not have to look it up, they knew it by heart. Oh, they truly had the knowledge, but did they themselves go to seek the King? No. On the contrary, they remained where they were, greatly disturbed. Even though they had the knowledge, they did not seek Him out that they might have the King.

Is not the same thing true today? Mentally, you may say Jesus is King, but spiritually, do you seek after Him as your King in reality? Do you yield your life to Him and let Him rule over your life? There is a great difference to be seen here.

This King was reared in Nazareth, a town in the upper part of Galilee in the hilly country. He was in that place for about thirty years. He was not raised in a palace. He had never been to school, that is, to a rabbinical school. He did not have a theological degree; yet He was in the school of God His Father.

When the day came that Jesus was about thirty years old, He was to be presented to the world, as it were. And He presented himself to the world not on the occasion of a royal banquet but by going to the River Jordan and being baptized by John the Baptist.

The King is Baptized

The baptism of John the Baptist is the baptism of repentance: Repent, change your mind, turn around 180 degrees, turn about-face. The way you are going is entirely wrong. Indeed, you are very religious—you have the temple, the sacrifices, the priesthood; you have the synagogue, the Old Testament, the five books of Moses, the Torah, the Prophets, the Psalms. You seem to be doing all the right things. But not so; therefore, repent! Turn about-face. You are traveling completely in the wrong direction because the kingdom of the heavens has drawn nigh. The King is coming! Being *religious* will not help you. You need to repent of being religious, as well as of being *irreligious*, all because the King is coming. It is time for repentance.

The King himself came to be baptized, although He had absolutely nothing of which to repent. Our Lord Jesus and the Father are One. He always pleases the Father. Yet here, in presenting himself to the nation, He took the baptism of John. He offered himself as a sacrifice for the sins of the nation, for the sins of the world. That was His presentation. He is the King of love. He gave himself as a sacrifice for us. That is His credential; that is His qualification; that is the proof that He is King. His kingship is not proven by fanfare and pomp; it is proven by His being a sacrifice. As He went down into the water to be baptized by John the Baptist, He identified himself with the sinful world, offering himself as a sacrifice. The Bible says that when He came up out of the water, the Holy Spirit came upon Him as a dove, and not only came *upon* Him, but also dwelt in Him.

Do you know what a dove is? The dove is an offering of the poor. The poor cannot afford to offer a bullock or even a lamb; they can only offer a dove. Our Lord Jesus offered himself spotless to God as a dove—the offering of the poor. This was the way He presented himself as King.

Then He was led by the Holy Spirit to a desolate wilderness to be tempted of the devil for forty days and nights. There He overcame the Enemy. In the beautiful Garden of Eden, that is to say, in the best of circumstances—the first man, Adam, fell before the Tempter. Here, though, in the worst of circumstances, out in the desert fasting for forty days and nights, the Lord Jesus overcame. It is just like the way King David was presented to the nation of Israel. The first time King David was presented to the Israelites was when he slew Goliath; and by slaying Goliath, everybody knew he was a king. Here, our Lord Jesus, being tempted in the wilderness forty days and nights, overcame the Enemy. The Enemy could not do anything to Him; he had no place in His life. The victory of the Lord Jesus over the Enemy proved to the world that He is the King.

The Call to Discipleship

When John the Baptist was in prison, the Lord Jesus began to preach in earnest. As He was walking by the Lake of Galilee, He began to call disciples. He saw Simon Peter and Andrew casting nets into the lake, and He said, "Come after Me, and I will make you fishers of men." So they left everything and followed the Lord. Then He went a little distance farther and saw the two sons of Zebedee mending their nets, and the Lord said, "Come, follow Me" (see Matthew 4). They left the nets, they left their father, they left the boat and everything, and followed the Lord. It is the calling of the disciples.

Today, you may have heard much about discipleship, but what is really meant by discipleship? The Lord called people to be *His* disciples: "Come, follow after Me." He is calling for disciples. That means those people who responded to His call gave up everything to be with Him. They put themselves under His kingship and let Him transform them and conform them to His image. This is what discipleship really means. The call of discipleship is the call of the kingdom; it is the call of the King. The King is calling His people to put themselves under His kingship, His rulership, so that He might transform them and truly make them His kingdom. That is the call of discipleship.

If this is what the call of discipleship is, can you be discipled to any man? Does any man have the qualification to call you to be his disciple? No. We are only discipled to Christ, not to anybody else. People may help us in the discipleship, but they are not our masters. We have only one Master; we have only one King. We do not have two kings; we do not have the Lord Jesus and Caesar. We have but one King, the Lord Jesus.

The call of discipleship is the call of the King to come into this kingdom to be His subjects. It is the call to submit ourselves wholly to Him. That is why every time the call of discipleship comes, the response has to be to leave all and follow Him. If you still try to look back and cling to something, the Lord says, "You are not worthy to be My disciples." Let go of everything. Let go of yourself and let Him do what He wants with your life and in your life. If you hold on to yourself, you make a mess; but if you let go of yourself and let *Him* take care of you, He will make you a son of the kingdom. He will transform you and let His kingly character be wrought in you so that you may truly be kings and priests unto God. We are not only being washed by the precious blood but we are also made kings and priests unto God (see Revelation 5:10). Do you know you are a king, potentially? And He has called you to be His disciple so that He truly can make you a king.

What is our concept of a king? Oh, how different is God's concept from man's! We may think: "If He calls me to be king, I will sit high up and give commands, and let everybody serve me. Now that is a king." But no, that is not the type of king our Lord Jesus is. As we have already mentioned, *His* kingship is so divine, so different. He calls us to be His disciples, and as we come to be His disciples, He is going to disciple us, to discipline us, to train us.

I believe we all are familiar with the Sermon on the Mount. The Lord Jesus gathered His disciples, He then went up a small mountain with them, and there He opened His mouth and began to speak. Remember that Matthew 5, 6, and 7 are not words spoken to the world, even though many people on the periphery heard them. These words were spoken directly to His disciples. They had already placed themselves under His kingship and had allowed Him to have absolute sway over their lives, and so, this is what the Lord Jesus shared with them: "Blessed are the poor in spirit, for theirs is the kingdom of the heavens" (Matthew 5:3).

In the Sermon on the Mount the Lord Jesus described His kingdom. His kingdom is not of the world. We know what the kingdom of the world is like, but we do not know what His kingdom is like. He is describing to us the nature of His kingdom, and as a matter of fact, His kingdom is just like Him, the King. This is what He is, and because this is what He is, therefore, this is what His kingdom is like; this is what those who are in the kingdom are like. It is not law—it is grace; that is to say, this is what He is able to do and to make of us.

Characteristics of the King

"Blessed are the poor in spirit, for theirs is the kingdom of the heavens" (Matthew 5:3). What is meant by being poor in spirit? It does not mean that you are spiritually poor. On the contrary, because you are spiritually rich, you can be made poor in spirit.

Let us contemplate the Lord himself: He who is equal with God; and yet, divinity for Him was not something to be held onto or grasped after; and that is what He is, essentially, eternally (see Philippians 2). He is equal with God. He is in the form of God, and the word *form* there means "the inward character." Whatever God is, that is what He is. He is rich; spiritually, He is full. As we find in the letter to the Colossians, all the fullness of the Godhead makes its home permanently in Him. That is how rich He is, how full He is; and because He is so rich and so full, therefore, He is able and willing to empty himself and become poor. Actually, there is not much for us to empty of ourselves, because we *are* empty. We do not have anything, but we think we have a lot. The Lord Jesus is rich—all the fullness of the Godhead resides in Him. Can we imagine the fullness of the Godhead? That is something beyond our understanding. Everything that God is, and His fullness, all such dwells in Christ, bodily. They all make their permanent home in Him; not just a momentary flash, but permanently.

"But [He] emptied himself." Oh, what an emptying it was! Of course, He cannot empty himself of His deity; that is impossible. He emptied himself of all the things that are connected with deity—His glory, His honor, His worship. He took the form of a slave—not just the form of a man but a slave. Inwardly, He became a slave, a love slave to God, His Father. He, who is equal with God, took an inferior place to God to such an extent that He became a slave, a love slave to God. Outwardly, He took upon himself the fashion of a man; He put on flesh, the likeness of sinful flesh but without sin. He took the form of a man; and being found as a man, He humbled Himself. He took His place as a created being before the Creator. He humbled himself, becoming obedient to God, obedient even unto death, and that, the death of the cross. That is being poor in spirit. In other words, *poor in spirit* simply means "humility."

What is humility? The brethren in Laodicea, as mentioned in Revelation 3, boast of themselves and say, "We are rich, we have everything, we lack in nothing." Yet God says, "You are poor, you are miserable, you are naked, you are blind."

Oh! How arrogant we are! How self-assertive we are! How self-confident we are! How self-sufficient we are! We think we know everything, have everything, that we are lacking in nothing. Yet the Bible says, "Pride goes before a fall." If we are proud, we will fall; but the man whom God looks upon is the one who is of a poor and contrite spirit and who trembles at His word (see Isaiah 66:2).

Naturally, we are all proud and arrogant. We assert ourselves; we are self-sufficient. We think it is a shame if we have to look up to somebody else. Naturally, that is what we are; but as we come to be disciples of Christ, as we answer the call to the kingdom of the heavens, the first quality of His own character which the King will work in our lives is humility. He has to transform us from thinking: "I am somebody, I have everything, I can do all things by myself," into saying: "I am nothing, I can do nothing, I have nothing. Therefore, He has to be everything to me." This is the first quality of a king according to the divine concept.

According to the human concept, the last quality of a king is humility. If you are a king, you cannot afford to be humble. You have to assert yourself. You have to be authoritative. You have to be proud—just like Louis XIV who said, "I am the State." Oh, no! A king, in the divine sense, is so opposite. The first quality of a king in the divine sense is humility. Are you a king in God's thought? Do you have that kingly quality in you? Is that humility in you? If there is humility in you, then the Bible says that God looks upon you favorably.

There were only twelve disciples of our Lord Jesus, and these twelve did not come from very noble backgrounds. They were fishermen, a publican, and so forth; yet we observe one particular thing among them: they argued and struggled and strove with each other throughout the years they were following the Lord. Think of that! They were following the Lord. They were His disciples. They were to be transformed by Him, and yet there was something in them which seemed to nag at them, to haunt them, that seemed to trouble them, even to the very end. What was it? "Who was the greatest?" Their whole mentality was akin to the worldly concept of a king, wherein everyone seeks to position himself on the highest seat. If he can assume that position, then he can look down upon the others and the others will have to serve him. That mentality was very deeply entrenched in the thinking of the disciples, and again and again the Lord had to teach them otherwise.

As recorded in Matthew 18, the disciples were struggling and striving against each other and saying, "Who is the greatest?" The Lord took a child and showed them that unless one is converted and becomes like a little child, he cannot enter the kingdom of the heavens. Who is the greatest in the kingdom? He that is humble as a little child is the greatest in the kingdom of the heavens because a little child has nothing, knows nothing, and has to look up to everyone. That is the spirit of a child. Hence, God wants us to be very childlike, but not childish.

Then as noted in Matthew 20, when the Lord was going to Jerusalem for the last time, all the disciples thought it was the time the King was to be crowned and that they would sit on His right and left. The two disciples, the sons of Zebedee, came to the Lord Jesus with their mother. Humanly speaking, their mother stood as the aunt of the Lord Jesus and thus the word of an aunt would have weight. The mother seemed to be very selfless, wanting nothing for herself, but only for her sons. She came with her two sons to the Lord Jesus and said, "We want to ask You something; promise that You will grant it." Yet they did not say what they wanted; perhaps they were too ashamed to say that. Inwardly they knew something was not too right, so they simply presented the Lord with a blank check and said, "Please sign."

Now we know that the Lord never signs a blank check; instead He said to them, "What do you want? Speak out; be honest, do not be subtle."

So the mother blurted out with: "Let my two sons sit, one on Your right and one on Your left, in Your kingdom." That is the worldly concept of a kingdom. But the Lord Jesus responded as follows: "Are you able to drink the cup which I am going to drink? Are you able to be baptized with the baptism which I am going to be baptized with?" (see Mark 10:38)

The two sons of Zebedee (that is, the Sons of Thunder) did not really know what the cup was or what the baptism meant, but they wanted the right and left positions in the kingdom so much that they would do anything which was required of them. Ignorantly they said, "We are able." And the Lord replied, "You must; but whether you sit on My right or left is not for Me to give, it is for My heavenly Father to give." In other words, kingship in the heavenly kingdom is not a matter of position; kingship is determined by whether or not one drinks the cup and is baptized with the baptism. That is where kingly character is revealed.

The Will of God and Cross-Bearing

What is the cup? The cup in the Scripture here stands for the will of the Father. In the garden of Gethsemane, the Lord prayed, "If it is possible, let this cup be removed from Me; but not My will, Thy will be done" (see Matthew 26:39). And finally the Lord said, "This is the cup that My Father has given me—the will of God." Whether the will of God is bitter or sweet, it does not matter. *It is the will of God.*

The baptism spoken of here is the cross which the Lord would be baptized with. It is through doing the will of God and by taking up the cross that the kingly nature, the kingly character, the kingly power and energy is to be released. The Lord said, "In the world those who are rulers, who are high up, rule over people and issue commands to people. But in your midst, it is to be different. In the kingdom of God, it is different. He that is the greatest among you should be the smallest. He who would be great should serve as a slave to the others" (see Matthew 20:25-27).

Our Lord Jesus is truly King, but what kind of King is He? What is His kingly character? How do we know He is King? We cannot judge Him by the human viewpoint; if so, we will be disappointed. We must see Him from the divine viewpoint. Oh, let us see His humility, meekness, purity, gentleness and lowliness. Let us see how He does the will of God, how He goes to the cross. It is by all these things that He reveals himself as the King.

When our Lord Jesus was crucified on the cross, Pilate actually wanted to mock the Jews. So he had the crime of which Jesus was accused written over the cross, and it read: "The King of the Jews." He did that as a means of mocking the Jews. It was put there in three languages—in Latin, Greek and Hebrew. That was for the whole world to know. But unknowingly, Pilate was doing God's will because, there on the cross, Christ was declared to the whole world to truly be the King. There is no time nor place in the life of Jesus wherein His kingship was made clearer than at the time He was crucified on Golgotha's Hill. Behold the cross and you shall see the King. How different it is indeed from the world.

The Mark of the Cross

Do you see the cross? If you see the cross, can you fail to see Christ Jesus as your King? Has He not conquered you with His love? Are you not being constrained by the love of Christ, noting that "One died for all, therefore all died and that now you live for Him who died and lives for you?" (see II

Corinthians 5:14-15). Can you live for yourself anymore? Do you not recognize the King? If you receive the cross, can you reject the King? If you receive the cross, you have to recognize the One who has been crucified on the cross as your King. He has a claim upon you. He has bought you with His price; you therefore belong to Him. He is going to transform you, to make you a king, because He is the King of kings. He is going to build His own character into your very life, the kingly character—humility, meekness, purity of heart, lowliness, gentleness, selflessness. "Deny yourself, take up your cross, and follow Me," declares the Lord (see Matthew 16:24).

"From the days of John the Baptist until now, the kingdom of the heavens is taken by violence" (Matthew 11:12a). We do not like the word *violence* because it has such a bad connotation today; but actually, the word itself is neutral. The word *violence* there simply means "force." "Take it by force and the forceful seize upon it." What does it mean? It does not mean that you do violence to other people; rather, you do violence to yourself. You deny yourself, take up the cross, and follow the Lord. That is doing violence to yourself.

Whenever we see the mark of the cross in a person, we know he is a king in God's kingdom. Remember Paul. He once told the Galatians, "Do not bother me; I have the brand-marks of Jesus upon me" (see 6:19). It was the mark of the cross in his life. Do we have the mark of the cross in our life? What is the mark of the cross? It is the crucifying of self in order that Christ may be all in our life. That is the mark of a king.

Finally, we learn that our Lord Jesus was raised from the dead and appeared to the disciples for forty days. Before He left this world, He said this, "All power has been given me in heaven and upon earth" (Matthew 28:18b).

How did He come into all power? He came into it all through the cross, through emptying himself. He proved himself to be truly a king; therefore, He is fit, He is qualified to handle all power and authority in heaven and on earth.

Let me inquire of you, If a little power is given to you today, can you handle it? Power and authority are so abused and misused in this world because people are just not fit or qualified to use them. All power was given to the Lord Jesus because He had proven himself capable to handle it.

He then said, "Go therefore and make disciples of all the nations." Let us bear in mind that the great commission is not simply evangelizing all nations; it is much more than that. Of course, evangelizing is included and is essential. But the great commission is to disciple all nations. We are not only to bring them to Christ that they may be saved, but also to bring them to Christ that they may submit their lives to Him. They are to accept Christ not only as their Savior but also as their King. This is the great commission: that we disciple all nations; bring all nations to Christ that the kingdom of this world will one day become the kingdom of our God and of His Christ.

And next, the Lord Jesus said this: "Baptizing them to the name of the Father, and of the Son, and of the Holy Spirit." Why do we baptize them? Baptism is merely an outward testimony to an inward reality; which is, that everything in the past is now dead and buried. From this moment forward, everything is new, everything is Christ.

He then added: "Teaching them to observe all things whatsoever I have enjoined you." That is building them up. And the Lord ended by saying: "I am with you all the days until the completion of the age." This is the Gospel according to Matthew.

Shall we pray:

Dear heavenly Father, we do praise and thank Thee because Thou dost present Thy Son to us as Thy King. Yet how different He is from the kings and the concept of a king that we know! Oh, do change and renew our minds that we may truly see Christ as King, that we may admire His kingly character, that we may give ourselves to Him and let Him disciple us and transform us and build that kingly character in us, so that truly one day we may rule and reign with Christ. Lord, we ask that these may not just be words passing through our minds. We ask that Thy Holy Spirit will open our spirits and reveal Christ to us so that we may truly take Him as our King and let Him make us kings unto Him, the King of kings and the Lord of lords. We ask in the name of our Lord Jesus. Amen.

MARK

Seeing Christ as God's Servant

Mark 1:1—Beginning of the glad tidings of Jesus Christ, Son of God.

Mark 10:45—For also the Son of man did not come to be ministered to, but to minister, and give his life a ransom for many.

Mark 16:19-20—The Lord therefore, after he had spoken to them, was taken up into heaven, and sat at the right hand of God. And they, going forth, preached everywhere, the Lord working with them, and confirming the word by the signs following upon it.

Let us pray:

Dear heavenly Father, how we do praise and thank Thee for giving us Thy Son, our Lord Jesus Christ. Oh, how we do enjoy Him, how we do appreciate Him, how we do love Him, how we do worship Him. And now, Father, we pray that Thou wilt again, by Thy Holy Spirit, reveal Thy Son further to us that we may know Him more, love Him more, and let Him have us more. And to Thee be all the praise and glory. In the name of our Lord Jesus. Amen.

Every Scripture is divinely inspired or, literally, every Scripture is God-breathed. The purpose of all the Scriptures is one—to reveal the Lord Jesus Christ. Whether the form of the Scriptures is biographical, historical, prophetic, poetic or whatever it may be, it is for that one and only purpose—to reveal Jesus Christ. Therefore, as we touch the Scriptures, we must touch the Lord Jesus. If we read the Scriptures and do not touch the living Word, our Lord Jesus, then we will miss the whole purpose of the Scriptures.

We have mentioned that the Gospel according to Matthew is biographical; it gives us the story of our Lord Jesus. However, it is more than biographical, it is spiritual. It is not only historical, it is a revelation to us of the Lord Jesus. In Matthew we find the Lord Jesus is the King, God's King, and how different is God's King from man's concept of kingship. He is King because He is humble; He is King because He died on the cross. He is calling us into His kingdom that we too may partake of His kingly nature.

Now we will consider together the Gospel according to Mark. Of the four Gospels, most probably the Gospel according to Mark was the first one written. However, in God's sovereignty, it has been placed second and the Gospel according to Matthew is placed first because, from God's standpoint, He wants us to see Jesus as King so that we may give Him obedience, allegiance and worship. The Gospel according to Mark, on the other hand, reveals the Lord Jesus as the servant of God. The word *servant* is actually to be translated as "bondslave" and, from the human understanding, king and bondslave stand on two opposite sides. We humans cannot put these two together: for when we think of a king, he is high up, full of authority, giving orders, and obeyed by people; but when we think of a bondslave, a servant, he is someone way down below having no right of his own—he is simply to serve and to obey. In short, we cannot conceive of these two aspects—kingship and servanthood—as being united into one. But according to divine understanding, these two are in fact complementary; or we may say, they are one.

The Lord Jesus said, "In the world, those who rule exercise lordship over others; they exercise authority over other people, but this is not to be so among you. If you want to be great, you must learn to be a servant. If you want to be the first, then you must learn to be the bondslave of all" (see Mark 10:42-44). The Lord Jesus also said, "I came not to be served, but to serve and to give my life a ransom for many" (see 10:45). He who serves is the King; the King serves. This is the divine concept and, of course, in the life of the Lord Jesus, we find indeed the model servant.

When you open the Gospel according to Mark the first sentence is: "Beginning of the glad tidings of Jesus Christ, Son of God." You do not find any record here of His genealogy nor His birth as you find in Matthew. No genealogy, no birth is mentioned because who cares about the genealogy and the birth of a slave? A slave is nothing, a nobody, and that is the reason why in the Gospel according to Mark there is no such record. The first sentence—"Beginning of the gospel of Jesus Christ"—is the gospel of Jesus Christ as the servant of God. But immediately afterwards there is added the words, "Son of God." Now that is a strange combination. This Gospel is to reveal Jesus to us as the bondslave of God. Yet it says that He who is the bondslave of God is also the Son of God. A bondslave is a nobody, but the Son of God is above everybody; and yet here we find the bondslave of God is none other than the Son of God. Now how can that be?

We know it is so because of what we read in Philippians 2. He who is equal with God, who is in the very nature of God, because He *is* God; nevertheless, for Christ Jesus the Son of God it was not something for Him to grasp at or hold on to but He emptied himself. He made himself nothing. He poured out himself. Of course, He could not pour out concerning His deity; that is impossible because He is God; nevertheless, He poured out all the glory, honor, majesty and worship that are connected with deity. He emptied himself in order to become nothing, and then He took upon himself the form of a servant, a bondslave. He took the very nature of a slave and, being in the likeness of man, He humbled himself, becoming obedient to God even unto death, and that, the death of the cross (see

vv. 5-8). The Son of God, who is equal with God, voluntarily made himself nothing and took upon himself the very nature of a slave for the sake of God's plan being realized. He put himself under the rule of God His Father, and He was obedient even unto death, the death of the cross. In sum, Jesus became the Son-Servant.

In Mark 12 there is recorded a parable told by Jesus of a man who owned a vineyard. He fixed up the vineyard and then he lent it out to several husbandmen. At the time of harvest, the owner sent some servants to go and collect, but the husbandmen drove these servants away. He sent another group of servants; in response they killed them. He sent more servants to them, but they rejected all of them. Finally, the owner said, "I will send my only begotten son; maybe they will respect him." And, of course, we know how the story ends. But God sent His Son into this world as His servant because the Son is the servant of God. This is the very person of God's servant, the Son of God.

Before we go on, I would just like to apply this principle of son-servant to ourselves. No one can serve God, no service is acceptable by God unless it is served by the life of His Son. If we want to serve God, if we want to be His servants, we cannot do it with our natural life, this fallen Adamic life. Even with the best of our knowledge, the best of our intention, the best of our experience, the best of our energy, if we try to serve God out from ourselves, or with our self-life, we will be utterly rejected. God will not and cannot accept such service.

Many today are trying to serve God in their own wisdom and strength. They think they are doing Him a service, but we know they do Him a disservice. As a matter of fact, God will not and cannot accept such service. It is only when we serve God with the life of Christ in us, with the energy of the Holy Spirit, and with the mind of Christ that God is well pleased. So there is a basic principle here—it is the principle of being a son-servant. It is not just a servant doing something, but we must be a son who has the very life and mind to serve the God whom we serve today.

Before God's servant, the Lord Jesus, came into this world, it was prophesied in Psalm 40:6-8: "Sacrifice and oblation thou didst not desire: ears hast thou prepared me. Burnt-offering and sin-offering hast thou not demanded; Then said I, Behold, I come, in the volume of the book it is written of me—To do thy good pleasure, my God, is my delight, and thy law is within my heart."

"Sacrifice and oblation thou didst not desire." This is strange in one sense, because for the Old Testament people, sacrifice and oblation are what God demanded of them. Instead of sacrifice and oblation, it is "ears hast thou prepared me." In the original, it signifies a pierced ear, a hollowed-out ear, a digged ear. According to the Old Testament period, when the ear was digged through, or pierced through, it meant a love-slave was present. He did not want to go out free; so the master would take that slave to the door and pierce, dig through or hollow-out his ear and he thus became a slave for life—a love-slave. This is what is mentioned here. God does not desire oblation or sacrifice. What He really desires is an ear that has been pierced.

"Then said I, Behold, I come, in the volume of the book [that is, in the Bible] it is written of me [it is prophesied of me]—To do thy good pleasure, my God, is my delight." The delight of our Lord Jesus, as the pierced-eared servant of God, is to do the will of God because His law is within Jesus' heart. This prophecy is fully fulfilled in the life of our Lord Jesus. And in Hebrews 10 this same prophecy is quoted as signifying a fulfillment of it in the life of the Lord Jesus.

The Nature of Service

The Lord Jesus is the Servant of God. He came to do God's will, and when we read the Gospels, we find that while He was on earth He was busily occupied with many things. He preached, healed, cast out demons, and comforted people. He uttered many words, He did many deeds, He traveled here and there, and lived a very busy life. He supplied the needs of the people, which was His life and His service; but let us remember one thing: even though He was busily occupied with doing many things and saying many words, as the Servant of God, He did not do all these things merely because there were such needs. He did all these things according to the will of God.

What governed His life? What governed His movements, His actions? It was not need, nor people, nor environment, nor work. What really governed His actions was the will of the Father. As the Servant of God, He came to do the will of His Father. That is the nature of His service. No one could push Him into any work. No one could say, "Lord, here is a need; do it." No. It is true, He supplies the need, but He is not governed by needs. He is governed by the will of the Father. "Lo, I come to do Your will, O God." This is the very nature of His service.

Now if this is the nature of His service, what should be the nature of our service to God? In a sense, we are all saved to serve. In I Thessalonians we learn how God delivered the believers at Thessalonica and they turned away from idols to serve the living God. Every one of us is to serve God, but how do we serve? What is the nature of our service?

The Lord Jesus said, "Take my yoke upon you, and learn from me; for I am meek and lowly in heart; and ye shall find rest to your souls; for my yoke is easy, and my burden is light" (Matthew 11:29-30).

The Lord Jesus wants us to be yoked with Him. It is said in Numbers 19 that when the children of Israel were in the wilderness, God provided for them a way of purification. They would take a red heifer which had never been under a yoke and burn it completely into ashes, which were then mingled with water to purify those who were defiled. The Lord Jesus is like that red heifer. He had never been under any yoke of sin. We have all been under the iron yoke of sin, but no such yoke had ever come upon the Lord Jesus. He was completely free; and yet, He willingly put His neck under one yoke—the yoke of the Father's will. It is within this context that He said, "Take my yoke upon you."

In the olden days farmers did not have tractors, so they used an ox or horse or donkey to till the ground. They would take an ox or horse and put it under a yoke. The yoke represented the will of the farmer because when an ox was under the yoke, it was under the will of its master. The yoke was placed on the neck or shoulder of the animal and then it was connected with the plow. The farmer would hold onto the plow and drive the animal in order to till the ground.

Sometimes, in order to do the work more effectively, the farmer would use two oxen or two horses instead of one. The yoke is one bar with two curves, and on the one side would be an ox or a horse that had been tamed; one that had been disciplined, broken, and knew the farmer's will. In order to break in a new animal, the farmer would put it under the other curve. These two animals were then yoked together. One was tamed, disciplined, broken, obedient, following the farmer's will. The other one was unbroken, raw, strange, having its own will. As the farmer began to plow the field and direct the animals, the animal that had been tamed and broken would follow the farmer's will completely, but the other one was impatient and wanted to go its own way. As it tried to go its own way, the one that had been tamed was stronger than the untamed one and would pull it back, naturally against its will. But gradually, gradually, the unbroken animal would learn from the broken one.

That is what the Lord Jesus meant when He said, "Take my yoke upon you." If you want to serve God, there is only one way—you have to take the yoke of our Lord Jesus upon you. He is on the one side and you have to put your neck on the other side. That is the only way of entrance into God's service.

"Be not diversely yoked with unbelievers" (II Corinthians

6:14). Do not be unequally yoked with unbelievers because what is there between righteousness and lawlessness, between light and darkness, between Christ and Belial, between believers and unbelievers, between the temple of God and idols? There is no agreement, there is no participation, no fellowship; and hence, we should not be yoked diversely or unequally with unbelievers.

Unfortunately, today, many believers are unequally yoked with the world. But the Lord Jesus says, "Do not do that. Be yoked with Me. Take My yoke upon you." It is true, when the yoke is put upon us, we feel it. We want to be free: "Give me liberty or give me death." But if we are given that kind of liberty, death is given to us. May I underline this matter again. If we really want to serve God there is but one way—*we have to take the yoke of Christ upon ourselves since the yoke of Christ is the will of God.*

You have to be yoked to God's will, not to a work. You are not to be yoked with a need. Yes, you will supply a need, you will do a work, but you are not yoked to the work or need. Many of God's servants are yoked to the work; therefore, they want the work to be a success and they will do anything to make it successful, even compromising the will of God. Why? It is because they are yoked to a work; they are not yoked to the will of God. We have to be yoked to God's will, and then His work can be done. But there is much we have to learn. Naturally, we will rebel against the yoke. Naturally, we will fight against it; but thank God, on the other side there is the Lord Jesus. As we are struggling and striving and just looking at the Lord, gradually, we are being broken and tamed, and thus we are being broken into the will of God. The nature of service is the will of God—not the work itself.

The Character of the Servant

For a man to serve God in his work there is one thing which

is of utmost importance, and that is, character. Discipleship means the making of a king. That is, when you respond to the call of discipleship, you are actually placing yourself under the discipline of the Lord; and then, His kingly character will begin to be built up in you. At the same time, discipleship is also the training of the servant. Under discipleship, you are being trained to be a servant of the Lord, and the servant character will be built into you.

Let me read a paragraph to you from Watchman Nee's book, *The Normal Christian Worker*:

> *The daily life of a Christian worker is intimately related to his work. To qualify for spiritual service a man must not only have a certain amount of spiritual experience but he must have a certain kind of character. A worker's character must be suited to the character of the work. And the development of a man's character does not take place in a day. If a worker is to possess those qualities that are necessary to make him of service to the Lord then many practical matters relating to his daily life will have to come under review. Old habits will have to be shed and new habits formed through a process of discipline, and fundamental adjustment will have to take place in the life to bring it into harmony with the work.*

How important it is that the character of the servant be suited to the character of the service. If we want to serve God and do His will, then we will find there is a certain character which needs to be developed in our life. Yet, for such character to be developed, it must be a daily matter. It has to be gradually developed and there will be many adjustments. Old habits have to be shed; new habits have to be formed; and there must be transformation going on within us in order that we may have that servant character necessary to do the servant work.

In the case of the Lord Jesus, it is perfect. His servant character suits the character of His work completely and perfectly, because He is the model servant. And in a sense, this kind of servant character has to be built within us. Can we imagine a person doing a work of God without there being that servant character built into him? What will happen to the work? It is impossible. Therefore, in the Gospel according to Mark the servant character of our Lord Jesus is very evident. We will simply mention here a few qualities of this servant character; but if we read through this Gospel, we will find many more.

Diligence

One of the important characteristics of a servant is diligence. As we read the Gospel according to Mark, one word is repeated many, many times; as a matter of fact, thirty-seven times. What is that word? *Immediately, straightway, at once*—it depends on the translation, but the original Greek is the same word in all instances. The Gospel according to Mark is to reveal to us Christ as the Servant of God, and we shall find that as the Servant of God He is most diligent. He is diligently doing the work of God. He does not say, "Well, tomorrow." On the contrary, with Jesus it is a matter of: "Immediately, straightway, at once."

Mark 1:10: "And straightway going up from the water, he saw the heavens parting asunder, and the Spirit as a dove, descending upon him." (Straightway)

v.12: "And immediately the Spirit drives him out into the wilderness." (Immediately)

v.21: "And they go into Capernaum. And straightway on the Sabbath he entered into the synagogue and taught." (Straightway)

Mark 2:8-10: "And straightway Jesus, knowing in his spirit that they are reasoning thus within themselves, said to them, Why reason ye these things in your hearts? Which is easier, to say to the paralytic, Thy sins are forgiven thee; or to say, Arise, and take up thy couch and walk? But that ye may know that the

Son of man has power on earth to forgive sins." (Straightway)

Mark 5:36: "But Jesus immediately, having heard the word spoken, says to the ruler of the synagogue, Fear not; only believe." (Immediately)

The servant came and said [to the ruler], "Do not bother the teacher because your daughter has just died," but the Lord immediately comforted the father and said, "Fear not, only believe." (Immediately)

Mark 6:50: (The Lord was walking on the water.) "For all saw him and were troubled. And immediately he spoke with them, and says to them, Be of good courage: it is I; be not afraid." (Immediately)

These are just a few illustrations, but throughout the Gospel according to Mark, this word is repeated thirty-seven times. It shows us a most important servant characteristic. God can never use a lazy person, and I think it was D.L. Moody who said, "God never saves a lazy person." He is too lazy to be saved. Everyone that has been or is being used by God is a diligent person, not a lazy one, because a lazy person will spoil God's work. The Lord Jesus is the most diligent of all men, and this trait has to be developed in us.

Naturally, we like to put things off—till tomorrow. We will do it, but tomorrow. We need to be disciplined. If it is the will of God, and if He has revealed His will to you, and it is something He wants you to do, then do it. Do not put it off.

Probably, we will say, "Is there not a contradiction between this matter of diligence and that of waiting upon God? Are we not supposed to wait on Him?" Of course, we should wait on God. If we do not know what His will is, then let us not rush ahead and do it, because we do not know what we are doing. We will be like Peter. Oftentimes Peter, not knowing what he was saying, just blurted it out; not knowing what he was doing, he simply did it. That was Peter, and because he did it, he was disciplined. We need to wait on God, but let us not make it an excuse. If we are not sure of God's will, then we should wait on God. Even if it means we have to wait for a whole year, wait for a whole year. But once God's will is made known, then let us do it ... immediately ... straightway ... at once. Let us not delay, let us not make excuses anymore, and let us not try to push it off till another day.

Actually, these two aspects of service are not contradictory; they work together. In the life of the Lord Jesus, we can discern how this is true. Recall the scene in Gethsemane: He waited upon God; but once He knew it was the will of God, then straightway there was no looking back. So as God's servants, we need to have that diligence worked into our lives—diligence in doing His will.

Compassion

In the Gospel according to Mark, we discover another characteristic of the servant of God, and that is, compassion. A servant of God is not called merely to do something or to say something. We may do something out of duty or say something out of obligation, yet there is no heart there; there is no compassion there; there is no feeling or sensitivity within us. If we are merely laboring for the Lord like that, we are a hireling. We are being hired like a hireling and we are not a real shepherd, a real servant of God.

The Lord Jesus is full of compassion. Whatever He says, He says so out of His heart; whatever He does, He does so out of His heart. He is not merely trying to fulfill a duty, an obligation; He is full of love and compassion. We may remember how a leper came to Him and said, "Lord, if You will, cleanse me." Here the Bible says, "Jesus moved with compassion ..." He not only said, "I will," but He also stretched out His hand and *touched* the leper. Anyone who touched a leper became unclean, but the Lord Jesus stretched forth His hand to touch that leper and made him clean because He is full of compassion. He wanted to be identified with him.

On another occasion noted in Mark 6, the Lord Jesus was stepping out of a boat and, seeing all of the people there, He was full of compassion. He beheld them as sheep without a shepherd and how they were terribly harassed.

Again, in chapter 8, we learn that these same people had followed Jesus, listening to Him for three days. They had nothing to eat, and the disciples came and said to Him, "Send them away." But the Lord was full of compassion towards them and said, "Give them to eat." The Lord Jesus is a person who is full of compassion. When He is doing God's work, when He is doing God's will, He does it with His heart full. Oh, how we need to be filled with His compassion!

However, even though the Lord Jesus is full of compassion, this does not mean He is blind. We think of compassion as an emotional thing, and it is. But compassion is more than an emotion; it is also character. An emotion is something that will flare up or something that will be stirred up. When you see some very pitiful scene, it stirs up your compassion. That is why missionaries, when they come back to this country and try to gather support for their missionary work, always present the worst picture. They show you a picture of a child who is without food and dirty, or a Chinese with the pigtail, in order to stir up your compassion. Such compassion will come and go. For when you do not see the picture, you have no compassion. It is nothing more than an emotion. But compassion in the Bible has about it character as well, which is deep-rooted within a person. It does not depend upon outside influence. It comes out from within, and it touches those who are outside. It is not something which is stirred up by what is outside; rather, it is something which comes from within; and therefore, compassion is not blind.

There is another incident told of in Mark 7. One day the Lord Jesus was at the borderland, and a Syrophoenician woman came and cried out to Him, "Son of David, have mercy on me, because my child is demon-possessed." Yet the Lord Jesus just walked on as if He had not heard, but the woman followed and repeatedly said, "Son of David, have mercy on me; Son of David, have mercy on me," until His disciples became troubled.

It seems as though the disciples had more compassion than the Lord. They could not stand it any longer and said, "Lord, do something or send her away. You cannot let her follow You, crying all the time, and not give an answer. Do something, say something."

But the Lord said, "You do not give the food of the children to the dogs." This appears to be a very harsh saying; nevertheless, the Lord had been sent by God to the children of Israel. And this woman, being a Syrophoenician woman, had no part in the Commonwealth of Israel. She had no claim upon the Lord as the Son of David because, as the Son of David, He came for the children of Israel only. She had mistakenly addressed Him. She had called Him the Son of David and it thus bound the hands of the Lord. The Lord could not do anything towards her, so He did not answer her. The Lord was not blind but very clear, and under the urge of the disciples, the Lord opened up to the woman a backdoor. He said, "One cannot give the food of the children to the dogs;" this was because the Jews considered themselves as God's children but viewed the Gentiles as dogs. Yet, actually, what the Lord Jesus was employing here was a special word: *pet dogs* or *domestic dogs*—and it thus provided that woman with a handle of faith. Immediately she responded with: "Yes, I am a pet dog; but even a pet dog can receive the crumbs cast under the table; so I have a right, a claim, upon You." And the Lord said, "Your faith is great;" and the child was healed.

The Lord is full of compassion, but it is compassion tempered by discretion. Sometimes, we are full of compassion but we are not at all discreet; on the other hand, we may be so discreet that we have no compassion. With us, too often our heart is warm and our head is warm, but our Lord's heart is warm and His head is cold. That is our Lord, because He is here to do God's will. Hence, we need to have this characteristic developed in us: we need to have compassion with discretion.

Selflessness

The Gospel according to Mark reveals to us Christ, the Servant of God, as One who is absolutely selfless. Selflessness is the character of a servant. A servant should never think of himself. If a servant is *self*-interested He cannot serve his *master's* interest. A servant has to be so selfless that he can be wholly occupied with his master's concern. This is what the Lord Jesus said as recorded in Mark 10:45: "For also the Son of man did not come to be ministered to, but to minister, and give his life a ransom for many."

That is the key verse in the entire Gospel according to Mark. Think of the disciples. They were supposed to be learning service from the Lord; yet all the time these twelve were quarreling among themselves: "Who will be the greatest? Who will have the highest place?" They were full of self-concern, self-interest, self-centeredness. No wonder the Lord had to bear with them and instruct them again and again, telling them that this was not to be the case with them, that they should not conduct themselves like that.

When the Lord told them He was going to Jerusalem to die and be raised on the third day, Peter even took hold of Him and said, "No, no, not so!" This compelled the Lord Jesus to say in response: "You are mindful of the things of man, not the things of God." The Lord has absolutely no self-interest. He is totally selfless. Let us all realize that for us to have that kind of character developed in us takes a long time. Oh, how the cross has to cut deeper and deeper and deeper into us because we are so self-centered! By contrast, the Lord is completely selfless.

Gentleness

Another characteristic of a servant is gentleness. Our Lord is so gentle. It is prophesied of Him in Isaiah 42: "My Servant does not raise His voice on the street. A bruised reed He will not break, and a smoking flame He will not quench." He is full of gentleness.

The gentleness of the Lord can be seen in the way He deals with children. People came to Him with their children and the disciples said, "Our Master is a big man. He has no time for children; go away, go away." But the Lord said, "Suffer [permit] the little children to come unto Me, for theirs is the kingdom of God" (Mark 10:14). The Lord had time for children; He took them into His arms and He blessed them. That is gentleness.

Mark 16 tells us that after His resurrection Jesus sent the women to the disciples to tell them that He had resurrected and was going to meet with them. Through an angel He said to these women: "Tell my brethren and Peter." *And Peter*. He was so gentle and considerate towards one who had denied Him three times.

But this gentleness does not in any way mean weakness. If it is our gentleness, it is weakness; but divine gentleness is strength. It is because Jesus is so strong, therefore, He can be gentle. Recall the time told of in Mark chapter 3 when the Lord came into the synagogue and everybody was watching Him. There was a man there with a withered hand, and they wanted to see whether He—against Jewish law—would heal on the Sabbath. The Lord asked the man to stand up and then He challenged the people in the synagogue by asking: "Is it all right to do good on the Sabbath day?" Nobody dared to answer, and so the Lord Jesus was full of indignation. He asked the man to stretch out his arm and be healed—that demonstrated His strength. The Lord Jesus denounced the hypocrisy of the Pharisees and scribes. He was not being weak in any way, but was gentle nonetheless.

In II Timothy Paul writes to Timothy that the servant of the Lord should not contend but always be gentle. Gentleness is a characteristic of the Lord's servant. To be gentle does not reflect weakness. It does not signify that because you are gentle you therefore compromise, that you therefore give in. Not so.

Gentleness is a characteristic of the servant of God.

Confidence in God

Finally, we find that the Lord Jesus has full confidence in God. As a servant, we have to have confidence in our Master. If we have no confidence in our Master, how can we serve Him? How can we serve His purpose? In chapter 11 of the Gospel according to Mark the Lord is quoted as saying: "Have faith in God." He walked on the water; He calmed the sea. He had full faith in God even unto death because He knew there would be resurrection. He had full confidence in God. We, too, need to have that kind of faith.

I just love the way Mark concludes his Gospel. In essence he was saying that the servant is now the Lord when he wrote: "The Lord therefore, after He had spoken to them, was taken up into heaven, and sat at the right hand of God" (Mark 16:19).

Jesus came to earth as a servant and He returned to heaven as the Lord of all. God has anointed Him Lord and Christ because He had served God's purpose completely. And now He is sitting at the right hand of God as King. The Servant is now Lord and King. He has served well and has thus proven himself to be qualified to sit on the throne. This is indeed the way to the throne. And then, speaking of the disciples, Mark's Gospel concludes by adding: "And they, going forth, preached everywhere, the Lord working with them" (v.20a).

The disciples became servants and they began to serve, the Lord working with them. Think of that! Jesus today is seated at the right hand of the Father as Lord and King, yet by His Spirit He is still working with us. His Servant-character, His Servant-life is in us, and it is still working together with us.

"And confirming the word by the signs following upon it" (v.20b). So here we find both the Son-Servant and Servant-Son as well as Servant-King and King-Servant. These are all one, they are not divided. May God help us that we may see Christ as the Servant of God in this Gospel according to Mark.

We mentioned before that if there is revelation, there is bound to be transformation. If there is revelation there has to be fellowship. We cannot see Christ as the Servant of God and yet have no fellowship—no participation—with Him in His servanthood. We cannot say we see the Lord as the Servant of God if we ourselves are not being transformed to have the same character within us. Stated conversely: if there is no fellowship with Christ as God's Servant, if there is no transformation in us in having that Servant-character built into us, then we have not seen Christ as the Servant of God. Hence, may God have mercy on us.

Shall we pray:

Dear heavenly Father, how we do praise and thank Thee that Thou hast revealed to us Thy perfect Servant, Thy Son, the Servant of God. Our Father, Thou hast called us into Thy service. We acknowledge that in ourselves we are not fit to serve, but we do praise and thank Thee because this Servant-life, the Son-life, is in us. We do pray that by Thy Holy Spirit there will be transformation, that this will be developed in us and brought out from us, so that we too may serve Thee diligently, serve Thee absolutely, serve Thee unselfishly, and serve Thee with gentleness and with faith. In the name of our Lord Jesus. Amen.

LUKE

SEEING CHRIST AS THE SON OF MAN

Luke 1:1-4 — Forasmuch as many have undertaken to draw up a relation concerning the matters fully believed among us, as those who from the beginning were eye-witnesses of and attendants on the Word have delivered them to us, it has seemed good to me also, accurately acquainted from the origin with all things, to write to thee with method, most excellent Theophilus, that thou mightest know the certainty of those things in which thou hast been instructed.

Luke 19:10 — For the Son of man has come to seek and to save that which is lost.

Luke 24:50-53 — And he [that is, our Lord] led them out as far as Bethany, and having lifted up his hands, he blessed them. And it came to pass as he was blessing them, he was separated from them and was carried up into heaven. And they, having done him homage, returned to Jerusalem with great joy, and were continually in the temple praising and blessing God.

May we look to the Lord in prayer:

Dear heavenly Father, how we do praise and thank Thee for the privilege of knowing Thy Son, of knowing Thee, because knowing Thee is eternal life. Father, we do praise and thank Thee that we could gather together to worship and to remember what Thy Son has done for us. And now Father, as we continue in Thy presence, we do pray that Thou wilt open Thy word to us, open our eyes to Thy word that we may really see Thy Son, our Lord Jesus Christ. We ask in the name of our Lord Jesus. Amen.

We know that Luke was a Greek, and he was a physician by profession, and therefore, you will find that he was very much interested in human beings, in man. He tells us that even though he was not an eyewitness of what had happened, yet he had investigated it accurately. Out of Luke's investigation came his desire to write what he had found to Theophilus, that Theophilus might understand that all he had believed was reliable.

We do not know who Theophilus was. Probably he was a nobleman of that time because it was the custom whenever a writer was writing something to dedicate it to a nobleman or to a patron. Whether Theophilus was a nobleman at that time or not really does not make much difference, because we know the name Theophilus in Greek means "lover of God." And to this one who is a lover of God, this Gospel was presented that he might know more fully the Jesus in whom he believed.

Is it not true that in one sense, we are all Theophiluses, we are all lovers of God, and if we love God, then we need to have a revelation of who Jesus is. In the Gospel according to Luke, he found out that Jesus is the perfect Man; that He is the Son of Man; that He is the God-Man. Therefore, he shared what he had understood, and presented the Lord Jesus to his readers as the perfect Man, the Son of Man. God is always interested in man. That is why He created man in the first place.

"For he does not indeed take hold of angels by the hand but He takes hold of the seed of Abraham" (Hebrews 2:16).

Redemption is for the sake of man. Psalm 16, which is a Messianic Psalm, prophesies of our Lord Jesus: "To the saints that are on the earth, and to the excellent thou hast said, In them is all my delight" (Psalm 16:3).

In Proverbs 8, again speaking of our Lord Jesus, it says: "And my delights were with the sons of men" (Proverbs 8:31b).

God is always interested in man. Now sometimes, we make a very serious mistake. We do not want to be human beings;

we want to be angels. But God is more interested in human beings than in angels; He wants us to be true human beings. The problem today is that man is subnormal, abnormal. If only we can be normal, if only we can be the man after God's own heart, then this is what God is really looking for. Sometimes, we think that to be spiritual, we have to be less human, but that is a serious mistake. I remember how our dear brother Watchman Nee used to say, "If you want to be spiritual, you must be human first." If you cannot be human, how can you be spiritual? To be heavenly and not of the world does not mean that you become less human. On the contrary, the salvation of the Lord is to bring us into that humanity God has ordained from the very beginning. Look at the Lord Jesus: He is that perfect Man; He is the Man after God's own heart; He is the Man whom God looks for. Therefore, we find that God's interest is really centered upon man. So let us not try to be angels; let us be human beings.

From the word of God we learn that God's interest in man is very evident. For instance, as mentioned in Genesis 1:26-28, we learn that God created man in His image. In His image He created him; both male and female: "And God blessed them; and God said to them, Be fruitful and multiply, and fill the earth, and subdue it; and have dominion over the fish of the sea, and over the fowl of the heavens, and over every animal that moveth on the earth." That shows how God's interest is in man.

"What is man, that thou are mindful of him? and the son of man, that thou visitest him? Thou hast made him a little lower than the angels, and hast crowned him with glory and splendour. Thou hast made him to rule over the works of thy hands; thou hast put everything under his feet" (Psalm 8:4-6).

We know that Psalm 8 is literally fulfilled—first, basically, in our Lord Jesus, because Hebrews 2:9 says, "We see Jesus, who was made some little inferior to angels on account of the suffering of death, crowned with glory and honour; so that by the grace of God he should taste death for every thing."

In I Corinthians 15 we read that we who have borne the image of the earthly one shall also bear the image of the heavenly One. In other words, our Lord Jesus is actually the second Man. In the eyes of God there are only two men in the whole world through all the centuries. Of course, we see billions of people, but in God's eyes there are only two men. In I Corinthians 15 we are told that the first man was made of earth, of dust—that is, Adam; the second Man is from heaven—that is, Christ. There are only two men in God's sight, and Christ is the beginning of a new mankind, a new race; and as He is, so shall we be who believe in Him. From all these verses we can see that God's interest is really upon mankind, upon human beings. He wants us to be men and women after His own heart.

When one considers the history of man, several things are of great importance: 1) birth, 2) growing up or growth, 3) work, service, or ministry, and 4) death. In the Gospel according to Luke, these four things concerning Jesus are recorded with method. Of all the four Gospels, that according to Luke gives us the most detailed story of the birth of our Lord Jesus. In the Gospel according to Mark His birth was not even mentioned because Mark presents Christ to us as the servant of God or as the slave of God; and who is interested in the birth of a slave? But here in Luke, Christ Jesus is presented to us as man; therefore, His birth is described in detail.

We know that the birth of John the Baptist was supernatural, because his parents were far advanced in age. They had no children and they had no natural way of having children; they had given up hope completely. Yet in a most marvelous way God touched them, and John was born. So John, the forerunner of our Lord Jesus, was born supernaturally. But even though he was born supernaturally, it was naturally supernatural, because he was born of natural parents.

The Birth of the Lord Jesus

When we come to the birth of the Lord Jesus, it is truly unique. It is completely supernatural, because He was born by the overshadowing of the Holy Spirit upon the womb of a virgin, Mary. This is of tremendous importance, because if our Lord had been born of natural, human parents, He would invariably inherit the sinful nature of Adam because Adam, the first man, is the federal head of mankind. Therefore, everyone who comes out of Adam inherits from Adam the sinful nature. If the Lord Jesus had been born of natural parents, He would have inherited that sinful nature and thus could not be our Savior; He could not be our substitute because only the sinless can substitute for the sinful. That is the reason why the incarnation of the Lord Jesus was through the overshadowing of the Holy Spirit. That is the reason why, when the Lord Jesus was born, it is said, He is that holy Seed; He is the holy One of Israel; He is the sinless One. Jesus did not inherit from Adam man's sinful nature: "He who knows no sin," declares the Bible (see II Corinthians 5:21). He has never committed any sin; He does not even have a sinful nature. Jesus does not know what sin is because He was born by the overshadowing of the Holy Spirit upon the virgin, Mary.

When God wanted to use a virgin to bring forth His beloved Son, He chose out of all the tens and hundreds of thousands of women one virgin—Mary. She was the favored one, the blessed one, because God found in her a spiritual suitability. When the angel told her she would bear a son, at first she did not understand how it could be. And when it was explained to her that it was through the overshadowing of the Holy Spirit, she said, "I am the handmaid of the Lord; be it unto me as thou hast said" (see Luke 1:38).

This was most difficult for Mary, in one sense, because what would people say about a virgin carrying a child? What would her fiancé say? According to the custom of the Jews, if any woman should bear a child conceived before marriage, she was deemed an adulteress, and her fiancé should be the first one to throw a stone upon her to kill her. Yet here was a virgin, Mary, who was willing to give herself completely to God so that the Son of God might become the Son of Man. There was a spiritual suitability there.

Christ was born, and in God's eyes, He is the second Man; that is to say, He is the beginning of a new race, the beginning of a new mankind. This is very clearly stated in I Corinthians 15:45-49:

"Thus also it is written, The first man Adam became a living soul; the last Adam a quickening spirit. But that which is spiritual was not first, but that which is natural, then that which is spiritual: the first man out of the earth, made of dust; the second man, out of heaven. Such as he made of dust, such also those made of dust; and such as the heavenly one, such also the heavenly ones. And as we have borne the image of the one made of dust, we shall bear also the image of the heavenly one."

We once came out of Adam, the first man, who was made of dust. We bore the image of Adam, the image of the one made of dust. But thank God, through the Lord Jesus, we now come out of the second Man, and therefore, we shall also bear the image of the heavenly One. This is the gospel and this is the reason why we must be born again. Once we were born through natural parents, through the seed of Adam. We were born out of Adam, and we were made of dust; we inherited the sinful nature in us. We were sinners when we were born. Oftentimes we think that we become sinners after we have committed sin, but according to the word of God, we are told that by the unrighteousness and rebellion of one man, many were constituted sinners (see Romans 5). In other words, because of the rebellion of our father Adam, we have all been made sinners. When we were born, we were already sinners even before we committed any sin. We have inherited that sinful nature in us; but thank God, even though once we were born of Adam and were sinners and were made of the dust, yet, when we repent and believe in the Lord Jesus, we are born from above. "That which is born of the flesh is flesh; and that which is born of the Spirit is spirit" (John 3:6). We are born of the Spirit into the family of God. We receive a new life of the second Man, which is a heavenly life, and that is what we are today by the gospel and the grace of God. So if there is anyone today who has not been born again, no matter how moral you are, no matter how good you are, remember, if you are of Adam, then "in Adam all die;" but "in Christ all shall be made alive" (see I Corinthians 15:22). How important it is that we be found in the second Man—Christ.

The Growth of the Lord Jesus

The second thing that is important in the life of a man is his growth. Of the four Gospels, only the Gospel according to Luke gives us some history regarding the growth of the Lord Jesus. After Jesus was born, He was circumcised on the eighth day. This brought in His covenant relationship with God. God made a covenant with Abraham that every male child born of him must be circumcised on the eighth day, and circumcision is a sign of His covenant with the children of Israel. If any child of Israel was not circumcised, he was not considered as belonging to the Commonwealth of Israel, he is excluded from the covenant of God.

Now on the day of His circumcision, He was given the name Jesus, which is a name given to Him by the angel. But of course, we know it was given by God. It means: "He shall save us from our sins" (see Matthew 1:21).

After Jesus was circumcised on the eighth day, His parents went to the temple to present Him to God (see Luke 2), because according to Jewish law, the first-born belongs to God. He was brought to the temple to be presented to God that He might have a divine relationship with God, not only a covenant relationship but also a divine relationship with Him. Jesus was offered to God. In a sense, He was sacrificed.

Then Jesus went to Nazareth. Now there is but one sentence telling us what happened during His childhood.

"And the child grew and waxed strong in spirit, filled with wisdom, and God's grace was upon him" (Luke 2:40).

After Jesus was born, circumcised and offered to God, His parents brought Him back to Nazareth. There He grew up, and it is said that He "waxed strong;" physically, He was getting stronger. And He was "filled with wisdom;" so mentally, He was developing. "God's grace was upon Him;" spiritually, He had the grace of God. He had a most normal growth. When we think of a normal growth, we must think of three sides to it—the physical, the mental, and the spiritual. With a child, the physical naturally comes first; so the Bible says, He "waxed strong." Physically, He grew stronger and bigger. The second is mental: He was "filled with wisdom." And the third is: "God's grace was upon Him." It was a perfect growth in Jesus' childhood.

Thereafter, we do not know anything about Him until He reached the age of twelve, and again the only place where this is recorded is in the Gospel according to Luke. When He was twelve years old, He was brought by His parents to Jerusalem to the temple to worship. And we know during those ancient days that when a Jewish boy grew to the age of twelve, he was to be made a son of the law—that is to say, he experienced Bar-mitzvah. Today, among the Orthodox Jews, their Bar-mitzvah is at age thirteen, but at that time, it was at the age of twelve. So evidently, when Jesus was at the age of twelve, His parents brought Him to the temple and there He was made a son of the law.

What does it mean by "a son of the law"? It means that before the law He was now a true member of the synagogue. He now had the right to read the oracles of God; He now had the right to ask questions; He now had the right to answer questions. He had become a full-fledged member of the temple and of the synagogue of God.

The Lord Jesus was made a son of the law at the age of

twelve, and then something happened. When they went to Jerusalem to worship the Lord, after the feast was over, everyone went home. Those who came from Nazareth usually traveled together, and as they were going home, the adults would travel together, talking together, and the children would also travel together. So the parents thought that Jesus must be with the other children of His same age, and it was not until night that they discovered He was not there. Returning to Jerusalem, it took them three days to finally find Him—in the temple. In other words, His parents had gone home, but He had remained in the temple. His mother said, "Child, why have you done such a thing to us? See how sorrowful we are?" The Lord Jesus replied: "Why are you worried? Do you not know that I must be occupied with My Father's business?"

We know that the Lord Jesus is God, but He is also Man. He is perfect God; but He is also perfect Man. From the human standpoint, we would probably say that as a child gradually growing up, an increasing consciousness was developing within Him of His divine relationship with God, a consciousness that He is God's Son. This consciousness grew increasingly until at the age of twelve, He was made a son of the law; and I think that that really sealed it. In other words, He was fully conscious of His relationship with God His Father, and because of this, He must be occupied with His Father's business. He had stayed behind in the temple; nevertheless, He was still a minor. Though He was fully conscious of His divine relationship with God the Father, He is also a perfect Man. Therefore, as a minor, He obeyed His parents and went back with them to Nazareth. What a balance between humanity and divinity!

From twelve years of age to about thirty years of age, He remained hidden in that hilly village of Nazareth, out of the way. He had never been to school, that is, to the rabbinical school, and yet, He was in the school of God His Father. As a human, He learned the trade of a carpenter. He must have been a tremendous one since they called Him the carpenter. He lived a perfect normal life as a perfect human being; yet during those hidden years, He was trained in the school of God. We do not really know what happened during those formative years, but the Bible does give us a one-sentence clue: "And Jesus advanced in wisdom and stature, and in favour with God and men" (Luke 2:52).

As you grow from babyhood to childhood, the most evident growth is physical. However, when you grow up into a teenager, the most evident development from twelve to thirty should be mental—growing in wisdom. His mind grew—"He advanced in wisdom"—but Jesus also advanced in stature. You grow until you are thirty. (After thirty, I don't know whether you are still growing or are "de-growing.") He was likewise "in favor with God and man" during all those years, until He was thirty years old; then He stepped forth.

When Jesus stepped forth, the first thing He did was to be baptized by John the Baptist. The baptism of John the Baptist was the baptism of repentance; yet here was a man, indeed, the perfect Man, who had nothing to repent of. Is there anyone in the whole world who has nothing of which to repent? I am afraid we all have too many things to repent of. There are many things we have forgotten of which we should repent, but the Lord Jesus is the perfect Man. He had nothing to repent of; yet He came to be baptized by John.

At first John wanted to prohibit Him because he sensed there was something in that Man which was so perfect, so noble. He said, "No, no. I should be baptized by You. How could it be that You would be baptized by me?" But the Lord said, "Let us do it for the sake of righteousness." In other words, the Lord Jesus identified himself with those repentant souls. God is calling for man to repent and here is this perfect Man who had nothing of which to repent, but He identified himself with those who do repent in order that He might offer himself as their sacrifice.

Therefore, after He was baptized, the Holy Spirit came down upon Him as a dove and abode in Him. The dove in the Scriptures is the sacrifice of the poor. When a poor man cannot afford a lamb or a bullock, then his sacrifice is a dove. The Lord Jesus offered himself to God by the eternal Spirit, spotless as a dove, as a sacrifice for the poor. Thank God for the Lord Jesus. Such was His growth.

In our union with Christ we also need to have such growth. After we are born again, there should be an increasing awareness, an increasing consciousness, of our relationship with God. We are now children of God, and shouldn't we be occupied with our Father's business? I do believe that in our union with Christ, as we grow in Him, there should be an increasing sense that we belong to God, that we are here for His sake. We are not here just to live for ourselves; we are not here to be occupied with our own business; but we are His, and we are here to do the Father's will, to be occupied with the Father's business. Because of that, how we need to commit ourselves to Him for that purpose! I believe that there should be an increasing consciousness of this within us.

When He was twelve years old, the Lord Jesus was fully conscious of His relationship with His Father, and He desired to be occupied with His Father's business; but being a minor, He still had His duty to obey His parents, which He fulfilled. Even though we have other duties and obligations, these should not be contradictory to our consciousness that we must serve God. On the contrary, through all these various responsibilities we will grow in a balanced way and we will mature. We will find that as we grow in the Lord we can be occupied with the Father's business even when we are occupied with other things. We begin to realize that the Father's business is our true occupation, and that under His rule and ordering we may be husbands, wives, students, physicians, nurses, teachers, or this or that, yet all of these are but our avocations. Our one vocation is serving our God and Father, and by carrying out these avocations, we fulfill our one vocation. So we need to grow spiritually as did our Lord Jesus, because He is our Head.

THE WORK OF THE LORD JESUS

The third aspect in the history of man is his work, his service. After you have grown up, of course, you need to work, you need to serve, you need to do things. The Lord Jesus, when He was some thirty years old, stepped out into the limelight of the world. The Gospel according to Luke, chapters 4—21, records what He did and what He said. He traveled from village to village and from city to city, preaching the gospel, casting out demons, healing the sick, speaking the word of grace, and doing the deeds of power and authority.

The Lord Jesus did many things. Even though He only labored for some three years, the Gospel according to John nonetheless tells us that if you were to record all which the Lord Jesus did while He was on earth, the whole world could not contain all the books; neither the Library of Congress nor all the libraries of the entire world could contain the innumerable books written about Him. In those three years He did a lot, He said a lot; and the result is that whatever He said is true, whatever He did is grace.

Do let us bear in mind one thing here: in spite of the many things Jesus did, in spite of the many words He spoke, He was not on earth for success or popularity. He said these things and He did these things, because He was doing the will of His Father. Throughout His life, especially during those public years, everything He said and everything He did was not out of himself; it was for the will of His heavenly Father. That was the one thing within Him which governed His whole life—to do the will of the Father.

Another thing you will notice about the Lord Jesus from Luke's Gospel, as we earlier noted, is how He is interested in human beings. He is interested in all men—not only the Jews but also the Gentiles; not only the Pharisees like Nicodemus but also sinners and publicans. He is interested in all of mankind. When He touched people, it was not only with divinity but also with humanity. Such is the work of the Lord Jesus.

In union with the Lord Jesus, we are also to serve. God may use us in many different ways, in doing many different things; but one thing let us always remember: whatever we do, whatever we say, it must be for the glory of God. We are not here working for success; we are not here seeking popularity. We are here to do the will of God, by the power of the Holy Spirit, and through the grace of the Lord Jesus. That should characterize everything we do and everything we say.

The Death of the Lord Jesus

The death of the Lord Jesus is recorded in Luke, chapters 22—24. His death is unique. It is supernatural in one sense. He did not die a natural death. Most people like to die a natural death. He did not even die the death of a martyr. If you read the numerous stories of martyrdom which are found in *Foxe's Book of Martyrs*, you will learn of thousands and thousands of martyrs who died for the Lord Jesus. How they glorified God in the way they died! In the book of Acts we are told about the first martyr, Stephen, who was stoned to death. He saw heaven open and the Son of Man standing there waiting for him, welcoming him. He knelt down and prayed, "Father, forgive them." It was a glorious death. But let us realize that when the Lord Jesus died on the cross, He did not die a martyr's death. Why? Because He cried out: "My God, My God, why hast thou forsaken Me?" Is that a martyr's death? No. He died a death that is substitutionary and vicarious in nature. In other words, He died an atoning death.

"Him who knew not sin he has made sin for us, that we might become God's righteousness in him" (II Corinthians 5:21).

When Jesus was hanging on the cross, during the first three hours He was suffering from the hands of man and the enemies of darkness. But at twelve o'clock, the sun was darkened and He cried out, "My God, My God, why hast Thou forsaken

Me?" In other words, from twelve o'clock to three o'clock, He suffered not from the hands of man nor of the devil; He suffered at the hand of His beloved Father. God crushed Him on the cross; and He became the sinbearer of the world. His death is vicarious, substitutionary, atoning: indeed, a unique death; and because of *His* death, we die no more.

Jesus was raised from the dead after three days, appeared to His disciples, and then He ascended to heaven. There is now a Man in glory. The Gospel according to Luke begins with a baby in a manger and it ends with a Man in glory. In union with Christ we die in His death. In union with Christ we also are raised from the dead in His resurrection. And we also are now seated with Him in the heavenlies in His ascension. Thank God for all He has done for us.

But the most important thing in the life of a person—and even more important than what he says or what he does—is his person, or, we may say, his personality. What kind of person is he? What kind of personality does he leave with the world? I think that is the most important thing, because what an individual says and what an individual does are merely the outward expression of that individual's inward person or personality.

What is personality? Personality is the sum total of character. Throughout the years of our lives we build up our character, and the sum total of our character is our personality. That is what our person is, that is what we are. God never wants to get rid of our individuality, but He certainly does want us to change our personality.

Each one of us is a person, an individual, and God makes us that way. No two persons are exactly alike. Physically speaking, no two persons are exactly alike. Even twins are not a hundred percent alike; there must be something different the one from the other. I always remember what a friend of mine used to tell me: "If you look at the human face, how many features do you see in that small area? Two eyebrows, two eyes, one nose, one mouth, two ears. That is all there is; yet God can put together these few features in a small area, and among billions and billions of people, you will discover no two persons are alike." Isn't that a miracle?

But I believe God does something more than that. Not only are your features different, your temperament, too, is different. God makes our soul-shapes all different. You are of one temperament, I am of another temperament; that makes your and my individuality. You are you, and I am I. It is not God's will that you should be I and I should be you. We like to copy, but let us not copy; for God does not like copying. Each one is to be the first imprint, so be yourself; that is what God wants you to be. He made you that way and that is what you are. This is your individuality and it shall remain until eternity. We are told that even in the New Jerusalem the twelve foundation stones are twelve *different* stones, because one is Peter, one is John, etc. They are vastly different one from the other, because Peter, for example, is an extrovert and, of course, John is an introvert. But thank God, He can use everyone. No matter what your temperament is, God can use it if you let Him control you.

Individuality remains, but personality must be changed. In other words, the character of Christ must be built up in you. You have the fallen character of Adam. You have some combination of his fallen character and I have another combination of his fallen character, but it is all Adam's character and that is not acceptable to God. Our character has to be changed and developed because when we believe in the Lord Jesus this new life in us has a new nature. If we follow that new nature, cultivate that new nature, then we will develop within us a new character, even the character of Christ; and the sum total is Christ. Hence, when people see us, they do not see us but they see Christ. He is expressed through us; His personality is being diffused through our individuality. That is accomplishing something glorious! And this is the purpose of God with mankind; this is what He is interested in.

The Lord Jesus is the perfect Man. God sent Him into the world to be a model, and God says we shall all be remodeled according to the Lord Jesus, transformed and conformed to His image. Of course, Christ is more than a model, because He is our very life. God puts His very life within us, and as His life is allowed to be developed in us He will be formed in us. So the Bible says, "Conformed to His image" and, "Christ formed in you." When we come to this matter of Christ as the perfect Man, we need to know His personality. We need to know what His human character is, the features of that character which God is well pleased with. There are many of these displayed in the Gospel according to Luke, but I think there are a few which stand out above the rest.

A Transparent Life

When we read about the life of Christ as a man, the one thing which strikes us most prominently is that He is transparent. That makes Him real, makes Him true. He is not a person who lives one way privately and another way publicly. He is not a person who lives one way before man and another way behind man. He is not a person who says something in one way and does something in another way. The Lord Jesus is the same within and without. In other words, before God, this is what it is; and before man, this is likewise what it is. Before His enemies, this is what it is; before His friends, this is also what it is. He does not put on anything; there is no facade. On the contrary, He is crystal clear; He is transparent. Oh! Can we find a man more transparent than the Lord Jesus?

Adam and Eve sinned in the Garden, and when they heard the voice of God coming, they hid themselves among the trees. Sin makes us hide ourselves. That is the reason why no person on earth is transparent. We cannot afford to be transparent. If there is an X-ray that could show all that is going on in our minds, we would want to be sunk into the depths of the sea. We are not transparent; we are hiding all the time. We hide from each other because we cannot afford to be open. We cannot afford to be transparent because we know there is too much in us that cannot and must not be known.

But not the Lord Jesus; He is transparent. Even His enemies had to concede this. They came to Him, trying to tempt Him, and said on one occasion, "Master, Rabbi, we know that You teach righteously. You know no person after the flesh and You teach the truth—the way of God by truth. You are that kind of person. You never try to be political, or try to maneuver, or try to be diplomatic, or try to play hands. You are so transparent." Because the Lord Jesus is so transparent, He can see us through and through. Nothing can be hidden from Him. We do not need to say anything to Him because He knows already.

Sometimes we are honest, but most of the time we are not. And even if we are honest, we can be naive. Unfortunately, many honest people are very naive because, even though they are honest, they can be deceived by not being transparent. If we are transparent, we are not only honest, we are real, we are true, we are crystal clear, we see things through. That is the reason why the Bible says the spiritual man discerns all things because he can see through everything (see I Corinthians 2:15).

This is the Lord Jesus—a totally transparent person. He is transparent because He lives by His heart; He lives by the Spirit. There is nothing before and nothing behind. "He is the same yesterday, today, and forever" (see Hebrews 13:8).

This trait of transparency is one characteristic in man that needs to be developed. Oh, how opaque we are; how dark we are! We need the blood of Jesus to cleanse us. We need the cross to purify us that we may develop within us a transparency: always the same before enemies, before friends, before man, before God, in secret, in public—always the same person.

Thank God, one day, when the work of God is done in eternity, the New Jerusalem stands as a city which is transparent. Even the gold is transparent, clear as crystal. We can never find gold on earth that is transparent because there is no such thing. But in eternity, the street is paved with gold which is like crystal—totally transparent—and the spiritual meaning of street is fellowship. The fellowship is in transparency. There is no shadow, no shade, no hiding; it is open, it is clear. That is what the grace of God is able to do in our lives. Oh, may the Lord bring in more transparency!

A Dependent Life

The life the Lord Jesus lived as a human being was a life of dependency. When God created man, He created him to be dependent upon Him. But Adam and Eve said, "We do not need God, we are God ourselves." That is sin. Sin is the declaration of independence towards God. However, the Lord Jesus, the perfect Man, lived a life of utter dependence upon God.

Now dependence does not mean that you are weak, that you have no backbone, that you become very passive. Not at all. The Lord Jesus' life was very dedicated, full of power; yet His power and His dedication was dependent upon God His Father. He said, "I cannot do anything by Myself; I do it because My Father does it. I cannot say anything by Myself; I say it because I heard My Father saying it." In other words, His whole life was dependent upon God. He never acted independently from Him. That is the man whom God desires, because in our dependence upon Him, we find our fulfillment.

How do we know that the Lord Jesus lived such a dependent life? I think there is one sign that is very evident. Of all the four Gospels, in that of Luke's, there are more records of how the Lord Jesus prayed. Now why do we pray? If we are independent, we do not need to ask for anything, we do not need to pray to God for anything, because we are able; we are independent. So, why pray? We pray because we know we are *not* able; we know we have to depend upon Him, we have to look up to Him, we have to wait upon Him. Prayer is an outward sign of our dependence upon God.

From the Gospel according to Luke we can see how the Lord Jesus prayed. We are told in chapter 3 that when He came up out the water of His baptism, He was praying. Before He chose His disciples, He went to the mountain and prayed the whole night. The disciples saw Him praying and asked Him to teach them to pray. He encouraged people to pray and not to faint. He told Peter, "Satan wants to sift you as in a sieve, but I have prayed for you, that after your faith is restored, you will strengthen your brethren." On the Mount of Transfiguration He also prayed; and when He prayed, He was transfigured. In the Garden of Gethsemane, He fervently prayed; and even when He was on the cross, He prayed. The life of the Lord Jesus was a life of prayer, a life of dependence. Oh, how we need to develop that kind of life!

A Large Life

When we read the life of the Lord Jesus as a man, we notice that He was a large man. I do not mean large physically, but large in heart. We say He is a universal man. The Lord Jesus was born in Bethlehem, reared in Nazareth, and when He was about thirty years old, He began to travel. But during His some three years of travel, He never went beyond two hundred miles. Today, two hundred miles is nothing. Many people travel that in a day. But throughout His life, He had never traveled beyond two hundred miles; and yet this Man was so large of heart that He was never affected by the bigotry, the prejudice, or the narrow legalistic system of the time. He was never narrow or small; He was a large man: His heart embraced the whole world. His heart was so big that even children could come to Him. He was so large in heart that even sinners and publicans felt comfortable in His presence.

We often sense how small and petty we are. We are small men and women; our heart is so narrow; our love is so limited; we are full of prejudice. A little something can disturb us. May God deliver us from our smallness and pettiness. May we be delivered so that we may be large in heart. The Lord Jesus is the Universal Man. He embraces us all. May we be large in heart by His grace.

A Single-Minded Life

Finally, the Lord Jesus was single-minded, serious. His life was single-minded; He set His face towards Jerusalem. He was on earth doing one thing only—the Father's will—no matter what happened to Him. And this is the kind of man whom God is looking for.

Oh! May the character of the Lord Jesus, as a perfect man, be formed in us that we may be transparent, that we may be large in heart, that we may be dependent upon God, that we may be single-minded on earth. Today, there is a Man in glory. He is not only God, He is also Man. And this Man in glory guarantees that one day there will be many men and women in glory because He shall lead many sons and daughters into glory (see Hebrews 2:10).

Thank God, we are born again like babes, but if we follow the Lord, He will work in us by His Holy Spirit. He will transform us and conform us to the image of the Lord Jesus so that one day, when He shall return, He may find many like himself. He will be the firstborn among many brethren, and there will be many men and women in glory. May the Lord help us.

Shall we pray:

Dear heavenly Father, how we praise and thank Thee that Thy Son, our Lord Jesus, is not only God but He is Man. We thank Thee that He is the Man after Thine own heart. He is the perfect Man, and Thou art seeking such men in Him. So Father, we do praise and thank Thee that by Thy grace we have been born again, that we are now in Christ. And our desire today is, Lord, work in us until Thy character is fully built within us. Oh, that Christ may be formed in us, that Thou mayest have many sons according to the image of Thy only begotten Son. In the name of our Lord Jesus.

JOHN

Seeing Christ as the Son of God

John 1:1-4 — In the beginning was the Word, and the Word was with God, and the Word was God. He was in the beginning with God. All things received being through him, and without him not one thing received being which has received being. In him was life, and the life was the light of men.

John 1:14-18 — And the Word became flesh, and dwelt among us (and we have contemplated his glory, a glory as of an only-begotten with a father), full of grace and truth; (John bears witness of him, and he has cried, saying, This was he of whom I said, He that comes after me is preferred before me, for he was before me;) for of his fulness we all have received, and grace upon grace. For the law was given by Moses: grace and truth subsists through Jesus Christ. No one has seen God at any time; the only-begotten Son, who is in the bosom of the Father, he hath declared him.

John 10:10b — I am come that they might have life, and might have it abundantly.

John 20:30-31 — Many other signs therefore also Jesus did before his disciples, which are not written in this book; but these are written that ye may believe that Jesus is the Christ, the Son of God, and that believing ye might have life in his name.

Let us pray:

Dear heavenly Father, we do praise and thank Thee

because Thou hast promised us: "If there are two or three gathered together unto My name there am I in the midst of them." We know in our spirit that Thou art here with us and we do pray that we may not only sense it in our spirit but we may truly hear Thy voice through Thy word, that we may see Thee, that we may really know who Thou art and be in fellowship with Thee. We commit this time into Thy hands and ask Thee to bless it. In the name of the Lord Jesus. Amen.

We have mentioned that the first four books in the New Testament are historical books because they record the story of the Lord Jesus. But even though these four Gospels are historical records, they are more than history; they are actually a revelation from above. God does indeed reveal Christ to us through history, but if all we know about the Lord Jesus is just the historical events, we miss the real purpose of these books. In other words, through the knowledge of the history of the Lord Jesus, we are to receive a revelation of who the Lord Jesus really is. It is not simply a mental knowledge; it also has to be a spiritual understanding. And if we do see who the Lord Jesus truly is through history, then we will be drawn into fellowship with Him. Out of such fellowship there is bound to be transformation. We shall be transformed from glory to glory according to His image. So as we approach these historical books in the New Testament, our desire and our prayer is that we may truly see deep in our spirit who Jesus really is.

Today we would like to touch upon the Gospel according to John, which is the last of the four Gospels. In this Gospel John is presenting to us Jesus as God, as the Son of God. This is made very clear from chapter 20, for as he is concluding his Gospel, John tells us himself that these things are being written, these signs are being recorded, in order that we may believe that Jesus is the Christ, the Son of God: and that in believing Him we shall receive eternal life in His name.

LIFE OF THE SON OF GOD

At the outset, we would like to think together about the term, the Son of God. What is meant by Jesus being the Son of God? We mentioned last time that He is also called the Son of Man. As the Son of Man, first, He is man; He is a real man, the perfect Man. Second, as the Son of Man, He is the beginning of a new mankind. But what is meant by Jesus being the Son of God? It simply means that He is God; He is the image of the invisible God. No one has ever seen God, but the One who is in the bosom of the Father, He has declared Him (see John 1:18). The Lord Jesus, being the Son of God, is the image of the invisible God. Image in the Scriptures always speaks of "representation." The Lord Jesus, as the Son of God, is the full representation of what God is. Image also means "manifestation." He is the full manifestation of what God is.

In the Old Testament times we find that God did speak to our fathers through the prophets, but whatever God has revealed of himself through the prophets were pieces and fragments and bits. Such revelations came in parts, not in whole; it came in many ways, but not in totality (see Hebrews 1:1). But when God sent His Son into this world and spoke through the Son, God was fully revealed and fully manifested. The mystery of God has been fully unveiled, because the Lord Jesus is the mystery of God. So when we think of the Son of God, we think of Him as God himself, as the full representation and full manifestation of God. The Lord Jesus said, "If you see Me, you see My Father. If you hear Me, you hear My Father, because I and the Father are one" (see John 14:9; 10:30). That is the meaning of being the Son of God.

There is a secondary meaning, which is just the same as His being the Son of Man. Because He is the Son of God, He is the only begotten of God; He came into this world in order that He may bring many sons into glory. The only begotten Son of God is to be the firstborn among His many brethren that He may lead many sons into glory.

The Gospel according to John begins with: "In the beginning was the Word." We know the term *Word* simply means "speech," "utterance," "expression." The Lord Jesus is the very speech of God; He is the very utterance of God; He is the very expression of God. "In the beginning was the Word." This tells of His eternal pre-existence; He is self-existent in eternity past. "And the Word was with God." This tells of His distinctive person. He is a person. There is a distinctiveness in His person. "And the Word was God." This tells of the essential, eternal unity of the Godhead. So at the very outset we find that the Lord Jesus, as the Son of God, is God's expression. He is with God and He is God himself. All things were created by Him. There is nothing that is not created by Him. "In Him was life, and the life was the light of men."

This Word of God became flesh, the Son incarnate. In the Gospel of John we are not told how He became flesh, but we know from the other Gospels that, through the overshadowing power of the Holy Spirit upon the womb of the virgin Mary, Christ Jesus, the Holy One was born. The Lord Jesus, the Son of God, is the fullness of the Godhead. Colossians 1:19 says: "All the fulness of the Godhead was pleased to dwell in Him." In order for the fullness of the Godhead to come upon this world, for the Godhead to take upon himself the form of a man, even the likeness of sinful flesh, yet without sin—how can it be done? We are given the answer in Philippians: "He [Jesus the Son of God] being equal with God, and that is not something to be grasped at, He emptied himself." For the Son of God to become a man He had to empty himself. The emptying is not meant to be an emptying of His deity—that is impossible. The emptying meant here is for God's Son to empty himself of all the glory, honor, position, majesty and worship which are connected to deity. He emptied himself of everything in order to take upon himself the form of a slave, even the likeness of a man. And being in the likeness of a man, He further humbled himself, becoming obedient to God, even unto death, and that the death of the cross.

One day, two thousand years ago, the Son of God, the Word, became flesh and dwelt among men. In the original Greek the word *dwelt* in Scripture is the same as "tabernacled." "The Word became flesh and tabernacled among men." This brings us back at once into the Old Testament. There we are told that God delivered His children of Israel out of Egypt and brought them to himself at Mount Sinai, and there God revealed His mind to them. He said, "Make Me a tabernacle that I may dwell among you" (see Exodus 25:8).

So let us remember that God's thought is always to dwell among men. God loves to dwell with men; but unfortunately, He had not been able to dwell with them because He is holy and men are sinful. So we see in typology that only after God had delivered the children of Israel out of Egypt could He begin to reveal His mind to them and say: "I want to dwell among you. Make Me a tabernacle." Moreover, in reality, that tabernacle is the Lord Jesus. "The Word became flesh" is the tabernacle. For when the Word became flesh, He tabernacled among men. Now, therefore, God is with men through His Son who is full of grace and truth.

Grace—Love

We know that God is love. Love is His very nature. God always loves and His love does not depend on outward circumstances. By contrast, when we love, our love depends upon, and is influenced greatly by, what is around us. But God being love, it comes from Him unconditionally; it does not depend on environment nor does it depend on condition; love is the very nature of God. Even when He judges, He loves. God is love, and when love is translated into human practical expression, that is grace. So here we have the incarnate Word who is full of grace, because the love of God has now been converted into concrete grace—deeds of grace, works of grace. The Lord Jesus is full of grace and full of truth.

Truth—Light

God is not only love, He is also light. God is light and there is no darkness in Him. And when light is translated into human practical expression or manifestation, that is truth. That is the reason why, when the Word became flesh and tabernacled among men, He—Jesus, the Son of God—is full of grace and truth because He is the very practical expression of what God truly is. And hence, we find in Him the words of truth and the works of grace.

The Gospel according to John is written in such a way that he always writes beginning with an incident—an event. And in this instance, the event is a fact of grace ("The Word became flesh, and dwelt among us."), and then he follows with a teaching: the words of truth. For the Gospel of John then says: "The law comes through Moses" (see John 1:17a). In other words, Moses was the agent through whom the law came to the children of Israel, but grace and truth subsists through Christ Jesus.

What is meant by the phrase "subsists through Christ Jesus"? It means that before the coming of Christ, there was no grace or truth in the world. It was by means of His coming that grace and truth came upon the earth; yet grace and truth are not just things *coming out* from God; grace and truth are the *very essence* of God. When Christ came into the world, grace and truth came upon the earth. And when we receive grace and when we receive truth, we are actually receiving Christ himself. He is imparting himself in the form of grace and in the form of truth.

A great difference is to be seen here. Sometimes we may listen to a teaching, and it may indeed be truth. We say it is truth because it is correct, accurate, and right. But if all that we have received is merely the correct teaching and yet Christ himself is not being received, then it is not truth; it is simply a teaching. When truth is really being received, what you have received is not just a teaching but is also a living Person; it is Christ. For He *is* the truth.

The same thing can be said about grace. We may witness a miracle, we may behold a wonderful work, but if all which we have seen is only a miracle or a wonderful work and Christ is not in it, then we cannot say that this is grace. Grace is the Lord himself that is given to us. So, whatever He does or whatever He teaches is not simply doing something wonderful or simply teaching something wonderful; whatever He does and whatever He teaches is actually also an impartation of himself to us. We cannot simply marvel at the teaching as such, or merely marvel at the work as such. We in addition must see that all His teaching of truth and all His works of grace have no other purpose than that we may receive Christ, that we may have Him as our grace and have Him as our truth.

The Life He Gives Us

The author of the Gospel according to John employs a very special word. When the Lord Jesus was on the earth, He performed many marvelous works, miracles and wonders. Yet John does not use the words wonder and miracle; instead, he always adopted the word "sign." What is a sign? It is a pointer, a guidepost; it points you to something. In other words, a sign is not the thing in itself, it instead points you to something beyond. So all the miracles recorded in the Gospel of John are called signs because God does not want us to be occupied merely with these wonders, however wonderful they are—and they are wonderful. He also wants us to see something beyond these wonders and miracles; He wants us to see Someone. That is the reason why all these signs are recorded. And John, it will be recalled, said there were many other signs which he had not recorded. Even so, he considered that the signs he had recorded were sufficient enough to prove the point that Jesus is the Son of God, and if a person receives Him, he receives life.

There is another thing we should take note of in John's Gospel: the word "life" is very much emphasized. The Lord Jesus said, "I am come that they might have life, and might have it abundantly" (John 10:10b). As a matter of fact, when we put together all His words of truth and all His works of grace, we need use but one word—life. His word of truth is to give us life; His works of grace are also to give us life. Life is what Christ has come to give. He is the Son of God, and being the Son of God, He has life in himself, and He has the power to give His life to whoever believes in Him. Accordingly, the word life is very much emphasized in the Gospel of John, and as we read and consider these various signs, we will find that they are signs of life. Through these signs the Lord is telling us what kind of life He gives to us. We need to recognize the life we have received from the Lord Jesus and what kind of life it truly is.

An Inexhaustible, Satisfied Life

In the Gospel according to John there are altogether eight signs recorded. In chapter 2 we learn that the Lord turned the water into wine at Cana of Galilee during the time of a marriage feast. It is very instructive that the first sign the Lord Jesus presented occurred at a marriage. In fact, the Bible states that this was the first sign He gave to manifest His glory. Why is it that this first sign should happen at a marriage? Because we know from the word of God that, in God's thought, there is to be a marriage. All the marriages which occur upon this earth are but a type or shadow of that marriage between Christ and His church.

In Ephesians 5 Paul teaches about the relationship between the husband and wife, and throughout he says this relationship is a type of Christ and the church. Wrote Paul: "This mystery is great but I speak as to Christ and as to the assembly." All the way back even into eternity past, before God had created man, indeed before God had created anything—there was a marriage in God's thought. His thought always had been: "It is not good for man to be alone." God has His only begotten Son, but His thought continually was: "It is not good for Him to be alone. I want to give Him a life-companion." There will be an eternal marriage between Christ and His people, the church. That is in the very heart of God, and that is the reason why we see that the first sign the Lord Jesus ever performed upon earth happened at a marriage feast. It gives us a hint that this is what God is truly after and that this is what Christ came into the world for.

On this occasion Jesus turned water into wine. In olden days when there was a marriage, there was usually feasting. It is not like modern times when attendees may have just a little snack after a marriage. No, in the old days, according to Jewish tradition at that time, they feasted several *days*. In this regard, I remember that when my oldest brother was married it was still conducted in the old-fashioned way, for all the relatives and friends came and we feasted for three days.

Here in John chapter 2 we find that a young couple was getting married with many guests present—both invited and most likely even uninvited. Probably this couple was popular, so there were far more guests who came than had been expected. The feast continued on day after day, and on the third day all the wine had been exhausted. What a tragedy this was, and what a shame it would bring upon this newly married couple. Here they were almost at the peak of their happiness; and suddenly, there was no more wine. But fortunately, Mary, Jesus' mother, was there. She turned to her Son, and He turned the water into wine.

I am not going to explain this event because that is not my purpose, but what I want to emphasize is this: What is water? Water is flat and tasteless, and actually, the water in the six stone vessels at the entrance of the feast hall was for purification. The Jewish tradition was that whenever guests came into a house they needed to have their feet washed. Since they wore sandals instead of shoes, and they had dirt streets instead of paved streets, they needed to have their feet washed when they came in; otherwise, they would not have felt comfortable to enjoy the feast. Probably, they needed to wash their hands, too, because that was the Jewish tradition. There were six stone vessels of water there—lots of water—but evidently, there were many guests, so the water became less and less. So the Lord Jesus said, "Fill the vessels with water."

Water *here* represents our old life, the life which we receive from our fathers—the Adamic life. That life is flat, tasteless, and is only good for washing oneself outwardly. All which we can do is have an outward appearance of being clean. Some people seem to be very moral, some seem to be very kind, some others seem to be very generous, but this is merely an external facade. So far as the heart is concerned, it is still as wicked as it ever was. Our life can only do something externally, make it appear clean; but so far as our inward heart is concerned, it is wicked above anything else. And furthermore, our heart deceives us as well. Such is what the water of our life in Adam is like, and even *that* is not sufficient. Like the six stone water jars, our Adamic life is becoming less and less. *Our* life is insufficient; indeed it is nothing.

Now the Lord Jesus transformed this water in the stone pots into wine. The very nature of wine and that of water are quite different. You cannot make water into wine if there is not something new coming into it. Actually, when the Lord Jesus turned the water into wine, He put something into the water. This is but a picture—a sign—of what Jesus has put into our life: He has put himself, His very life into our life; and in putting His life into us, we experience a transformation.

Wine is what makes the heart glad. Wine is what makes us forget our sorrows. And there was such an abundance of wine—six stone vessels—that it not only would satisfy all the guests during the remaining days of the marriage feast but also there was most likely much left over for the young couple to enjoy. In other words, it suggests an inexhaustibility. The life which the Lord Jesus has given us is full of taste, is full of joy, and is inexhaustible. Such is the life which the Lord Jesus has offered to those who believe in Him.

I would like to say something about transformation. Transformation does not mean that your flesh is changed into spirit. Not at all. The Bible says: "That which is born of the flesh is flesh, and that which is born of the Spirit is spirit" (John 3:6). It is eternally true. Whatever is born of the flesh is always flesh; you can never change it. You can make it look better, you can wash it externally, but you can never change the basic nature of the flesh; it is always flesh and shall remain so. By the same token, whatever is born of the Spirit is spirit. Whatever comes from the Spirit of God is of God and cannot be changed either. So transformation does not mean your flesh is now changed into spirit. Not at all. It simply means that the life of Christ comes into your life, and this new life displaces the old life in you so that, from now on, it is His life that is being manifested in you. Such is transformation.

May I put it another way? Our soul, which is our self, as an organ, remains. God created us as a living soul, so our soul remains the same. But the problem is, that at the fall of man the *life* of the soul is now the self. Self has become the very life of the human soul and that is the reason why all our thoughts, emotions, intentions, decisions and desires simply express ourselves. It is the flesh—which has become selfish. However, when transformation occurs, there is a new life which comes into our soul and displaces self. Christ now lives in my heart instead of self reigning in me, and the result is, I begin to love as He loves. I begin to know the mind of God, and I begin to will the will of God. That is transformation.

Paul said, "I am crucified with Christ, no longer live, I, but

Christ lives in me" (Galatians 2:20a). In other words, the I is still there; the I as a person remains. It does not mean that when transformation comes, you are no longer there; you are still there. Keep in mind, however, that as a believer even though you are there, it is not you who lives; it is Christ who lives in you. That is the difference. So Paul can say: "For me to live is Christ" (Philippians 1:21). If you look at Paul, it is most certainly Paul; but what comes out of him is no longer Paul; it is Christ. That is transformation.

We have no confidence in our flesh, knowing that our flesh always remains the same. Even if a person believes the Lord for thirty years, his flesh will remain the same. It will not change in the slightest. But thank God, we know that He has given us a life, and if we allow that life to reign in our souls, we shall discover that we are being transformed from glory to glory according to the image of His Son. The Lord Jesus, as the Son of God, gives us a new life, which is His own self, and that life is joyful, satisfying and inexhaustible. Thank God, we have this life!

A Life of Meaning and Strength

The second sign in John's Gospel which the Lord Jesus performed is covered in its chapter 4. There we are told that the Lord Jesus healed a nobleman's son. This man must have been a Roman and of the royal circle. He must have been wealthy and have had honor, position and everything; but unfortunately, his son was sick with a fever and lay dying. What is the use of position, fame, wealth, honor and all such things if your only son is dying? It makes all things vain. Fortunately, this nobleman had heard about the Lord Jesus and so he came from Capernaum to Cana to beg the Lord to come to his home and heal his son. And the Lord said, "You go back, for your son is healed." By faith, believing in the Lord Jesus, he went home. On the way, he met his servants coming, who told him that his son was well. When he asked at what hour this had occurred, it turned out to be the very hour at which the Lord Jesus had told him, "Go home, your son is healed." And he and his whole household believed. This is the second sign which the Lord Jesus performed.

What is the meaning of this sign? I believe it signifies that the Lord, as the Son of God, gives us His life, and that that life gives meaning and strength to us. That child of his had a high fever, and that, of course, made the child lose his mind and lose his sense. Everything was confused, and eventually, it would end in death.

Do we realize that that is what our old life is like? If we contemplate our old life, it is in high fever. We are so hot we do not know what we are doing; we are totally confused. We may do something which is crazy and the result will be death. That is what we are, and we do not know what is the meaning and purpose of life. We are grasping after this and grasping after that, but we are utterly ignorant. But thank God, when the life of the Lord Jesus comes into us, He gives meaning to life and we can sing that life is worth living because of Him. If it is not because of Him, life is not worth living; that is true. But when His life comes into us, it gives new meaning to our life. We know why we are here. We are not here only for ourselves, to enjoy ourselves and enjoy the world. No! We are here to worship the Lord, to enjoy Him, and let Him enjoy us. And He gives us new strength that we may go forward in our life's journey. This is the new life that is given to us.

A Life of Deliverance and Sabbath Rest

The third sign is recorded in chapter 5, and there we are told about a man infirm for thirty-eight years. He was lying by the Pool of Bethesda hoping that when the angel came down and stirred its water, he would be the person who would get in first to be healed. It was very difficult. Being a paralytic man, he could not do it by himself, and yet nobody else there would help him into the pool fast enough to make him the first one. So he had been lying there for thirty-eight long years, and there was absolutely no hope. He had given up hope altogether. Then one day the Lord Jesus came by and said, "Do you want to get well?" The Lord instilled a hope into his heart. He naturally said, "I do;" and the Lord said, "Rise up; take up your couch and go home." Instantly, he was healed. Later the Lord Jesus met him in the temple.

What does this third sign tell us of life? The life which we originally had is an infirm life. We cannot walk the way of righteousness. We are told that this man had been ill because of his sin. It was a judgment from God, and we know that God's judgment is already upon us. We are hopeless. We may have tried before—tried to be good, tried to accumulate merits—but probably, we have given up hope now, because we are simply hopeless. But thank God, as with this infirm man, when Christ comes by, He gives us hope. He gives us His life. The result is that this man at the pool was not only delivered, but we find him later worshiping in the temple. There is rest. For the Lord had done this work of healing on the Sabbath, because the Lord Jesus is our Sabbath. Let us understand that the life which we receive from the Son of God is a Sabbath rest. We have been delivered from the bondage of sin and are now resting in Him. And because we rest in Him, we worship Him. Such is the life which Christ has given us.

An Abundant Life

The fourth sign is presented in chapter 6 of John. There we learn that the Lord Jesus was feeding five thousand with five loaves and two fishes. He said here, "I am the bread of life." He is not only life, He is also the bread of life. Not only does He give His life to us, but continuously He supplies himself to us as bread. How we need to believe in Him; how we need to trust in Him; how we need to take Him in, day after day, day after day, in all our wilderness journey. God rained down manna upon the children of Israel throughout their wilderness journey, and in a sense, we are in the wilderness today. The world is but a wilderness, and how do we have strength to go through this world? By receiving from Him as the Bread of Life. Oh, how He gives himself continuously. He said, "As I live by My Father, you shall live by Me" (see John 6:57).

Have we learned this secret? Or are we still living by ourselves, trusting in our own strength? If so, we will not make it. Do we not know that we have to live by the Lord Jesus? Without Him, we can do nothing. Without Him, we cannot finish our course. We need His life continuously in supplying us as the bread from heaven. Do we feed upon Christ? We not only need to receive Him but we also need to feed upon Him. We have to collect the manna every day before the sun is hot, because once the sun is hot, the dew becomes dried and the manna disappears (see Exodus 16:21). We must come to the Lord Jesus daily to receive Him as our bread for our daily need and for our spiritual support and supply. He is the supplier and He is also the supply.

A Life of Light

The fifth sign which our Lord performed is found in chapter 9 of John. There we are told that the Lord Jesus opened the eyes of a man who had been born blind. The disciples began to try to figure out the reason why this man was blind. Was it because of the sins of his parents? Or was it because of his own sin? How could he have sinned before he was born? When we attempt to theologize about things, we can come up with almost any explanation; and here, we find that Jesus' disciples were natural theologians! They theorized everything conceivable; but the Lord Jesus said, "Don't do all these things. This which has happened to the man born blind is for the glory of God." We cannot see the logic of it, but there is a logic there, nonetheless. The Lord Jesus opened the eyes of the one who was born blind, and so He declared: "I am the light of the world" (John 9:5). "In him was life, and the life was the light of men" (John 1:4).

We all were blind, even born blind. We have never seen. Let us not think we have ever seen and later we became blind. We, none of us, have ever seen the real thing. We have been deceived all our lives. We live in imagination, in supposition. But thank God, when His life comes into us, we begin to see: "In His light we see light" (see Psalm 36:9). What a difference! His light is the light of life, and when the light of life begins to shine upon our path, we know where we are going. "But if we walk in the light as he is in the light, we have fellowship with one another, and the blood of Jesus Christ his Son cleanses us from all sin" (I John 1:7). That is what the life of Christ is.

A Life that Has Overcome Death

The sixth sign is recorded in John chapter 11. There we learn that the Lord Jesus raised up Lazarus, who had died. The wonderful thing was that this family was loved by the Lord Jesus and they loved the Lord. The two sisters in the family had sent word to the Lord Jesus who at that moment was on the other side of Jordan in Perea to where he had retreated because of the opposition of the Jews. They sent to Him and said, "The one whom you love is sick." They believed that that brief word was enough to impel the Lord to rush over and put His hand upon Lazarus and heal him. But when the Lord heard this news, He stayed back until Lazarus had died. Then the Lord Jesus said, "Let us go and call him back from sleep." And the disciples said, "Well, if Lazarus is really asleep, that is good." But the Lord Jesus said, "No, he is dead." So the Lord went, and by the time He arrived, Lazarus had already been in the tomb for four days; and the sister, Martha said, "The decaying process has already begun," thus signifying that

Lazarus was thoroughly dead. Why did Jesus delay? Because the Lord wanted to manifest His glory as the Son of God. He is the resurrection and the life.

You do not know resurrection if there is no death; you can only call it resuscitation. But when there is real death, then there is real resurrection. The Lord Jesus declared: "I am the resurrection and the life." He wants us to leave the old life dead because He is going to give us a life which has gone through death and come out of death. Such is resurrection.

Is it not true that, oftentimes in your experience, or when you are in trouble, or when you have some problem, you cry out: "Lord, hurry, hurry, come and help me. Don't let me die." And sometimes, the Lord stays back and you begin to wonder, you begin to blame Him, and then you begin to murmur and say, "Now, the Lord does not love me anymore." No, He wants you to die so that He may let you experience resurrection. Oh, how often He allows you to go to the end, the very end, before He will come to your rescue. And thank God, when He does come, what glory it is! It is resurrection. It is HE. It is not you. You cannot take any glory from it; it is all His. For He is the resurrection and the life.

A Victorious Life

The seventh sign is the greatest of all signs and that is the resurrection of the Lord Jesus, himself, narrated in chapter 20 of John. The Lord Jesus was placed into the tomb, was buried for three days, and on the third day, He was raised from the dead. Never before or since had there been any man who having entered into real death, was able to come out of it alive. The Lord Jesus voluntarily, willingly and purposefully laid down His life for our sakes. He said, "No one can take My life away from Me, for I lay down My life and I can take it up" (see John 10:18). He went into death; He robbed death of its power; and He came out victoriously. It speaks of victory, the greatest victory in the world. And this is the life He has given to us. It is not a defeated life; it is not a weak life. It is a strong, victorious life. It is able to overcome even death itself. There is nothing that it cannot overcome, and this is the life the Lord Jesus has given us.

A Life of Love and Service

The eighth and final sign is found in John chapter 21 and it occurs after resurrection. Seven of the disciples went fishing, but they caught nothing that night. In the morning, the Lord appeared on the shore and said, "Children, do you have anything to eat? Did you catch anything?" "Nothing." They realized it was the Lord, and then He prepared the breakfast for them. As they were finishing the breakfast, the Lord began to ask Peter, "Do you love Me? Then feed My lambs," and so on. Now what does all this mean? It means that the life the Lord Jesus has given us is a life of love, it is a love-life. And because there is love in that life, there is bound to be service. We cannot think of ourselves alone; we have to feed the lambs. We have to shepherd the sheep; we have to feed the sheep. In other words, the life which we receive from the Lord Jesus is a sacrificial life, a love-life, a life of service. We cannot simply sit here and receive and receive and receive all the time. We have to give, to love, to serve, and to think of the little ones among God's people. We even have to help those who have grown up, and have to take care of those who are sick—spiritually sick. This is the kind of life we have received.

Now through these eight signs the Lord is telling us He is the Son of God. If you believe in the Son of God, you receive life. You receive Him as your life, and when He comes into you as your life, what will happen to you? You have joy and satisfaction. You will find meaning in life, and there is strength there. You are being delivered and you also have Sabbath rest. You not only have life but you have it abundantly, being daily supplied. There is a light within you, shining upon your way so that you know where you are going and what you are to do. If you have done something wrong, when you realize it, the blood of the Lord Jesus will cleanse you. It is a life which has overcome death. We are surrounded with death, yet there is a life that will overcome death. The life of Christ is a victorious life; it is a risen and ascended life; it is a life in heaven, seated in the heavenlies, and yet it is also a life that is on earth being lived out in and through God's people. And that life is therefore a life of love and service.

This, then, is the life which He has given us. It is not simply a matter of reading the Gospel of John as a history; it is seeing and receiving Jesus as the Son of God. And if you truly receive Him as the Son of God, you receive a new life, and this which we have described is the kind of life you receive. No wonder the apostle Paul said, "All the fulness of the Godhead dwells in Him bodily, and you are complete in Him" (see Colossians 2:9-10). Everything is in Him, and He has given himself to you so that you are complete in Him. May the Lord be everything to us. We do not need to go anywhere else to glean, but let us glean in the field of our Boaz (see Ruth 2:22).

Shall we pray:

Dear heavenly Father, we do praise and thank Thee that Thou dost reveal Thy Son to us, the Son of God, and in believing Him, we receive life in His name. We do thank Thee for the life which we have received, but we do pray that Thou wilt open our eyes to see what a life it is, that we will refuse to live anymore by our old corrupted, selfish, self-centered self-life, but we may be willing to let Thy life live in us and reign in us, that Thou mayest be glorified. We ask in the name of the Lord Jesus. Amen.

ACTS

Seeing Christ in the Body

Acts 1:1-8 — I composed the first discourse, O Theophilus, concerning all things which Jesus began both to do and to teach, until that day in which, having by the Holy Spirit charged the apostles whom he had chosen, he was taken up; to whom also he presented himself living, after he had suffered, with many proofs; being seen by them during forty days, and speaking of the things which concern the kingdom of God; and, being assembled with them, commanded them not to depart from Jerusalem, but to await the promise of the Father, which said he ye have heard of me. For John indeed baptised with water, but ye shall be baptised with the Holy Spirit after now not many days. They therefore, being come together, asked him saying, Lord, is it at this time that thou restorest the kingdom to Israel? And he said to them, It is not yours to know times or seasons, which the Father has placed in his own authority; but ye will receive power, the Holy Spirit having come upon you, and ye shall be my witnesses both in Jerusalem, and in all Judea and Samaria, and to the end of the earth.

Acts 28:30-31—And he [Paul] remained two whole years in his own hired lodging, and received all who came to him, preaching the kingdom of God, and teaching the things concerning the Lord Jesus Christ, with all freedom unhinderedly.

Let us pray:

Dear heavenly Father, as we continue in Thy presence, we ask that Thou will open Thy word to us that we may receive revelation from above, that we may truly see Thy Son, the Lord Jesus Christ. We ask in His beloved name. Amen.

The Bible is the revelation of Jesus Christ. It is not only the case that the last book of the Bible is called The Revelation of Jesus Christ, but the whole Bible is the revelation of Jesus Christ. That is why the Bible is given to us. If we know a lot about the Bible and yet we do not know the Lord Jesus Christ, we miss the whole meaning of the word of God.

The Pharisees and the scribes, in the days of the Lord Jesus, knew the Old Testament, their Bible, so well they were able to quote any portion verbatim through memory. Yet they did not come to the Lord Jesus to receive life. The Lord Jesus said to them, "Ye search the scriptures because ye think that in them ye have eternal life, but it is the scriptures that speak of Me; yet ye do not come to Me to receive eternal life" (see John 5:39-40). How important it is, as we read the word of God, that we actually see the Lord Jesus in every book of the Bible because this is the reason why the Bible is given to us. And if we receive revelation of the Lord Jesus, then we will have fellowship with Him and we will be transformed and conformed to His image. So may the Lord help us as we open the word of God that we may really come to a living knowledge of the living Word, the Lord Jesus Christ, through God's written word.

Now we would like to turn to the book of Acts. This book, as in Luke's Gospel, opens up with "O Theophilus." As indicated earlier, we really do not know who this man is, but we know that, in the olden days, as well as even today, when a person writes a book, he often would like to dedicate it to some other person whom he appreciates very much. Most likely, Theophilus was a nobleman at that time and Luke dedicated his book to him. But as was learned earlier, the very name Theophilus means "lover of God." So probably, it is a pseudonym; it is not a real name. This book is therefore dedicated to those who love God, and if we love God, it is dedicated to us.

Probably in your Bible the title of this book is shown as "Acts of the Apostles." However, we know that that is not the title in the original manuscript. Because of this very title by which this book is commonly known, we have misunderstood this historical book for it is not a narrative of the acts of the apostles. How do we know this? Because when Luke, the beloved physician, introduced this book, he said, "I composed the first discourse;" and the first discourse refers back to the Gospel according to Luke.

"I composed the first discourse, O Theophilus, concerning all things which Jesus began both to do and to teach." The Gospel according to Luke was his first discourse, and in that first discourse he wrote concerning all things which Jesus began to do and to teach until the time He was taken up to heaven. Now, though, he is writing the second discourse or the second part, and what is Luke going to write about in this second part? I think a hint of it can be found in that word "began" because he said, "When I wrote the first discourse, I wrote things which Jesus began both to do and to teach." Indeed, in reading through the Gospel according to Luke we find many things which the Lord Jesus did and many words which the Lord Jesus spoke. Whatever He did was wonderful; whatever He said was full of grace. But Luke said, "I previously wrote to you to tell you what the Lord Jesus *began* to do and to teach." In other words, the Gospel according to Luke does not record all the doings and teachings of the Lord Jesus; he only told us what the Lord Jesus began to do and to teach. In this second discourse, called the Acts, he intended to continue with what he had written before and was thus going to tell us what the Lord Jesus *continued* to do and to teach.

Acts of the Risen Lord

The Acts is therefore not an account of the acts of the apostles; although, if a person reads it very superficially, he will think it is certainly the acts of the apostles and especially the acts of the apostles Peter and Paul. The first section of this book of Acts tells us much about Peter and the second section tells us much about Paul. But it is not the acts of Peter and Paul, nor the acts of all the other apostles. It is the acts of the risen Lord through His body on this earth, and this body is the church. It is still the Lord Jesus himself, who is speaking and working, and such acts have no ending. In fact, we shall discover that of all the books in the New Testament, indeed, in the whole Bible, this is the one book which has no ending. At the end, we find Paul in Rome lodged in his hired apartment, where he was free to preach and to talk about the Lord Jesus and His kingdom unhinderedly. But when we do come to that concluding section we want to know more—"What next?" It is not finished because the Lord has not yet finished His working and teaching. For He is still doing His teaching and doing His work even up to our time, and He will continue doing and teaching until He returns. So the book of Acts is really the acts of the risen Lord who is continuing to teach and do through a corporate body, which is the church of God.

When the Lord Jesus came to this world two thousand years ago, how was His physical body formed? In the Gospel according to Luke we are told that the Holy Spirit of God overshadowed the womb of the virgin Mary, and Jesus was born. As the Bible says, "The Word became flesh and tabernacled among us, full of grace and truth."

Jesus is the name of the Lord when He was on earth, and with this physical body that He took upon himself, He was able to do many things and to say many words. Without a body He could neither speak nor do the things which He wanted to do; but with a physical body He was able to do and to teach, and we do thank God for what He has done and what He has taught us. We thank God for the redemption which the Lord Jesus has accomplished for us on Calvary's cross. We thank God for the blood He has shed for the remission of our sins.

We thank God for this body that was broken that we may have life and life eternal. He was crucified, He was buried, but on the third day, He was risen from the dead; and for forty days He appeared to His disciples, teaching them about the kingdom of God. Then He was taken up into heaven. But that is not the end of the Lord Jesus because after He was taken up, the Holy Spirit came down on the day of Pentecost and one hundred and twenty of His disciples were baptized into one body (see Acts 1:15 & Acts 2:1ff). Through this body, the risen Lord, as the Head, continues to do and to teach even up to today.

The Lord Jesus not only has a personal body, He also has a corporate body. Two thousand years ago when He walked upon this earth, He had a personal physical body. After He was taken up into heaven He is still teaching and working on this earth for these twenty centuries and is doing all this in a mystic, corporate body of His, which is the church.

How is the church formed? In one sense, we can say the church is formed through the overshadowing of the Holy Spirit upon the ruptured side of the Lord Jesus. We remember how Adam was created and then how Eve was built. In the beginning God created man. He fashioned a form—a body—with red earth, and then God breathed into the nostrils of that form the breath of life. This man became a living soul—that is, Adam. Then God said, "It is not good for man to be alone. I am going to give him a helpmate, his counterpart." But there was none, so God put him to sleep and took "something" out of his side. Our Bible says "rib," and it could have been a rib; but it could have been something else because in the original it just says "something." God took something out of the side of Adam and "built" around that something, making it into a woman. And the word "built" employed here is the word which is used in architecture. So the woman was built with something which had been taken out of man, and then she was led to Adam. When Adam saw her, he immediately said, "This is me, bone of my bone, flesh of my flesh." Therefore, the woman was joined to the man and they became one flesh.

But this also serves as a type, a picture of the true. For the reality is: God has an only beloved Son. And God said, "It is not good for Him to be alone; I want to give Him a helpmate, a counterpart." Therefore, God, as it were, put Him to sleep on the cross, but it was not as peaceful a sleep as Adam had experienced. It was a violent death because of the sins of the world. If there had been no sin in the world, there would have been no need for the shedding of blood. When God performed that operation on Adam, there was no blood; it was a bloodless operation. But because there is sin upon this earth, the Lord Jesus, the Son of God, had to die a violent death on the cross; blood had to be shed. And you remember what took place after He died. Soldiers came to make sure that Jesus had died. They looked at Him, and then to be sure He was dead, one soldier thrust a spear through His side. The Bible says, "There came out blood and water;" and if we carefully read the Gospel according to John, we will notice that John makes this a point of emphasis. For he writes: "I saw it. I saw blood and water coming out with the spear, and I bear witness to it, and my witness is true because I have seen it." Why does he make such a strong point out of this incident? Medically, we are told that the Lord Jesus died of a broken heart because, when the heart is broken, the blood disintegrates. Hence, we find here that when the last drop of blood in His heart was drawn out, it disintegrated into water and blood. Oh, the love of God!

Then the Holy Spirit used that blood and water, as it were, to build a woman—the church, the body of Christ. It is the blood for the remission of our sins, because the law says, "Without the shedding of blood, there is no remission" (see Hebrews 9:22). So the blood of the Lord Jesus had to be shed for the remission of our sins. But He also poured out His soul like water—that is, His life. He poured out His life, and the Holy Spirit takes hold of both the water and the blood and builds up a body, a woman—the church of God. And when the Lord

Jesus sees His church, He says, "This is Me."

Do you remember how Saul of Tarsus, the great Pharisee, persecuted the Christians—the early believers—in his day? According to the tradition of the fathers, Jesus was considered an impostor of Judaism; and so, because he was a Pharisee Saul persecuted the followers of Jesus. But on the road to Damascus, the risen Lord appeared to him and said, "Saul, Saul, why do you persecute Me? You are persecuting Me because these people are Me. They are My body, members of My own body." Even though the Lord Jesus, who is the Head, is in heaven, He has His body upon this earth. This body has been traveling on this earth for twenty centuries. This body has traveled to every place upon this earth, and thus it can be said that the Lord Jesus continues to do and to teach in and through that body.

The church has no teaching. If the church teaches, it is heresy because the church only teaches what the Lord teaches. It is the Lord who is teaching through the church. The church does nothing. If the church does anything, it is corruption because it is the Lord who is doing through the church. It is the Lord himself who continues to do and to teach. Whenever you hear the church teach, you will know it is heresy. Whenever you see the church do things on its own, you will know it is corruption. The church, as the body of Christ, is to do and to teach whatever the Head does and teaches. Or, to put it another way: It is the Head who is doing and teaching through His body. The book of Acts tells us of the teaching and the doing of the risen Lord through His corporate body, which is the church.

When the Lord Jesus came to this earth two thousand years ago, it was prophesied of Him in Psalm 40: "Sacrifice and oblation, God, You do not want, but You prepared Me a body. Lo, I come to do Thy will, and Thy will is the delight of My heart."

We know this was fulfilled in the life of the Lord Jesus because He took upon himself a human body. God has prepared for Him a body, and in this body of His, He did the will of God even to the point of death, and that, the death of the cross. It was not because He was forced to, but because He loved to. This is the body that He had, and through that body, He was able to do and to teach when He was on earth.

Now in the same manner, we need to recognize that from the time He was risen, and up to our time and up to the time of His return again, He is still speaking and working upon this earth. It is through a corporate body that He is revealed, manifested and known. This is what the church is—to reveal Christ and make Him known. The church should be His revelation. She is not to speak of herself. The church should not draw people to herself. The church is to lift up Christ and to let the world hear what He says and see what He does.

The Teaching of the Apostles

When you read the book of Acts, what do you find the apostles teaching? The three thousand who believed in the Lord Jesus on the day of Pentecost persevered in the teaching of the apostles (see Acts 2:42). What did the apostles teach? There are a number of messages recorded in the book of Acts, which today we would call sermons. These are messages which the apostles gave to whatever audience they could find, and if you read these messages, what do you learn?

For instance, on the day of Pentecost, Peter declared loudly and clearly: "God has raised Jesus Christ from the dead and we are His witnesses. Let all the house of Israel know that the One whom you have crucified God has made both Lord and Christ" (see Acts 2:32, 36).

Then, in the third chapter of Acts we learn that a lame man was healed, and Peter said to the people who crowded around them, "It is in that Name, in His name, that this lame man was healed."

In the seventh chapter we are told that Stephen, in his defense (actually, he was not defending himself; he was defending Christ), concluded his speech by saying: "You have killed the Just One; you murdered Him."

What did Peter say when he was in the house of Cornelius? This is what he declared: God has appointed a Man to judge the living and the dead; the prophets have all spoken about Him, and whoever believes in His name shall have his sins remitted (see Acts 10:42-43).

What did Paul preach when he was in Antioch of Pisidia? The same message came forth: the remission of sins is through that Man whom God has appointed (see Acts 13:38).

When Paul was in Athens he preached the same thing to those philosophers and learned people: God has appointed a Man to judge the world, and to prove it He has raised Him from the dead (see Acts 17:31).

Hence, when you read the book of Acts, you find that whatever sermon or sermons were preached, to whomever it might be, it was the same message—the Lord Jesus. It is no wonder then, that Paul said, "We do not preach ourselves, but we preach Jesus Christ, the Lord" (see II Corinthians 4:5). The early church taught nothing but the Lord Jesus.

Doings of the Early Church

In the early church many miracles were being done. Luke tells us in the third chapter of Acts that one day Peter and John went into the temple to pray, and there was a man there born lame who was sitting at the Gate Beautiful. Isn't that a contrast? The gate is called Beautiful but the scene was not too beautiful that day. This man had been there day after day, day after day, asking for alms; and when Peter and John came by, Peter looked at him and said, "Look at us. Silver and gold have I none; but what I have, I give to you: In the name of the Lord Jesus, rise up and walk." And immediately he rose up and walked. Naturally, people gathered around him wanting to know: "What happened?" And Peter and John said, "Don't look at us, as though it is our faith and piety which has healed this man; not at all. It is that Name that has made this man whole." What they had done was nothing but what Jesus had done. It was not they who did it; it was the Head doing it through the body. There was nothing to boast of so far as these two members of the body were concerned because Peter himself had not performed the miracle but it was the Lord who had done so through this man called Peter.

Again, we find the same thing happening with Paul and Barnabas as they were preaching in Lystra. There was a man there who had been crippled from birth, and they raised him up, and he was made whole. People wanted to offer sacrifices to them, thinking that they were gods. Paul and Barnabas ripped their garments, ran into their midst and said, "Don't do this. We are trying to help you out of this; we are human beings just like you are. We are nothing; we are nobody. It is God who did it" (see Acts 14:8ff).

Let us clearly understand that all the doings recorded in the book of Acts are nothing less than the doings of the Lord Jesus; they are *not* the doings of the apostles. The apostles never took any credit for anything. It is not like so many people today; too many people in our day like to take credit, but not these apostles. They made it clear: "We have not done it, it is the Lord who has."

Within thirty years—a generation—the gospel had been preached from Jerusalem to all Judea to Samaria and to the end of the world, which was the Roman Empire. Rome was considered the center and the end of the world at that time, and Paul was in Rome. What a great and mighty work the apostles had done, but it was not the apostles doing it, nor the early Christians doing it. It was the risen Lord doing all these in and through His corporate body.

Living

Look at the way these early Christians lived. In Acts chapter 2 we find some descriptions of these believers, who had grown in number from a few—one hundred and twenty on the day of Pentecost—to three thousand added by God.

> And they persevered in the teaching and fellowship of the apostles, in breaking of bread and prayers. And fear was upon every soul, and many wonders and signs took place through the apostles' means. And all that believed were together, and had all things common, and sold their possessions and substance, and distributed them to all, according as any one might have need. And every day, being constantly in the temple with one accord, and breaking bread in the house, they received their food with gladness and simplicity of heart, praising God, and having favour with all the people; and the Lord added to the assembly daily those that were to be saved" (vv. 42-47).

Oh, how these people loved one another! They broke bread together, they gave thanks to the Lord together, they supplied the needs for one another. God delivered them from all their sense of self-possessiveness, and they were together and worshiping together. That is the way they lived. How can it be? If it had not been Christ living in them, it would not have been possible. It is difficult for two to live together and yet here we have twenty thousand. In the early church they had about twenty thousand people, and yet they were in such harmony as described because it was not them—it was Christ who lived in them.

> And the heart and soul of the multitude of those that had believed were one, and not one said that anything of what he possessed was his own, but all things were common to them; and with great power did the apostles give witness of the resurrection of the Lord Jesus, and great grace was upon them all. For neither was there any one in want among them; for as many as were owners of lands or houses, selling them, brought the price of what was sold and laid it at the feet of the apostles; and distribution was made to each according as any one might have need" (4:32-35).

They were with one accord and in one mind, because Jesus lived in them; Jesus lived through them. That was their testimony—a body—and in that body, the Lord was able to continue to live on earth.

Suffering and Dying

Let us also take note how these early Christians suffered. Suffering can truly reveal what kind of person you are. Here you learn that when the apostles had been beaten, they came back to their own people, rejoicing, because God had counted them worthy to suffer for the name of Jesus.

Let us also take note of how they died. The first martyr in the church was Stephen, and when his persecutors took him out to stone him to death, he said, "I saw heaven open and the Son of Man standing there welcoming me." And just before he died, he said this: "Lord, do not put this charge upon them; forgive them" (see Acts 7:60). It was like the death of Christ. It was Christ dying in Stephen. And it is the same thing with all the martyrs throughout the ages, because it is not them; it is Christ in them.

Let us inquire: What is the church? What is the body of Christ? Why is the church existing upon this earth? Why are we here? Are we here to teach our own teachings? Or do we teach the teachings of Christ? The teachings of the apostles are none other than the teachings of Christ. They do not teach anything else but Christ. If we read Revelation chapters 2 and 3, we will find that some churches began to teach something other than Christ, and what did they teach? It was the doctrine of the Nicolaitans, the doctrine of Balaam, the teaching of Jezebel. In other words, these are not the teachings of Christ. When the church begins to teach something other than Christ and what Christ teaches, then she is teaching something else. It is heresy.

What are we doing here? Are we here letting Christ do what *He* wants to do in and through us? Or are we here to do something ourselves, even something for Him? Today, there are many works done in the name of the Lord Jesus, but these are works which are done for God, a doing something for Him, but it may not be *His* doing. We can do nothing but what He does. We can only co-operate with what He is doing, and such is God's work. If it is not that, it is trash.

How do we live? Do we each live our own lives, even when we come together? When the Corinthian believers came together for the breaking of bread, which is the most solemn time of remembering the Lord, they each ate their own food. Some got drunk and some were hungry and even starved. Church life is not when we are together in one place, but it is Christ living in a corporate body. It is not limited to time and space. It is the love of the brethren—and not because one is lovely or lovable, but because he or she is a brother or a sister. Such is the body, so that Christ may be expressed.

This is what the church is, and if we can live and die and do and teach in this fashion, then thank God, it is verily written in the book of Acts; for the Holy Spirit has continued to write this book up through the twentieth century and beyond, if Christ should delay His return. The Holy Spirit is still writing, and whatever is of the Lord who does and who teaches, and who lives and suffers and dies, then it is indeed recorded in the Acts. It will be remembered forever. But if it is not such as this, no matter how it may appear in this world, and no matter how successful or prosperous or well-known it may be, such will all be burned and remembered no more. Hence, as we read the book of Acts we need to see Jesus continually, yet not only in the early church, but we also need to see Jesus today in His people.

Seeing the Person

Finally, we need to see the Person through the body. When Christ was upon this earth, He had a physical body, and with that body, He was able to do and to teach. He was full of grace and truth. But the Jews at that time looked down upon Him and said, "Where does the wisdom and power come from to this Man? We know this Man; He is the son of the carpenter. We know His mother, called Mary. We know His brothers: James, Joseph, Simon, Jude. We even know His sisters. Where did all this come from to this Man?" And the Bible says that they were offended in Him. In other words, they saw the body, even this body that had done so many wonderful things, that had uttered so many gracious words; yet they were offended with that body. And why? It was because they had only touched the body; they had not touched the *Person* in that body.

This can similarly happen today. People can see only the church and not see Christ. That, unfortunately, is what Christianity is today. The world knows Christianity, but do they know Christ? We cannot look at the body as though it is everything because the body is *not* everything. The body is simply a means to an end, a channel, a habitation for the Person who dwells in that body. The church is the body of Christ; the church is the holy habitation of God by the Spirit; the church is the vessel to contain the riches of Christ; the church is the channel and the instrument through which God works; but the church is not something in and of itself. It is the Person in that body—Christ. We need to see Christ and not see only the church. It is true that Christ is being expressed through the church because, without a body, how can a head express itself? But it is the Head, it is Christ whom we must see.

So let us see Christ in the church and not just the church. If all we see is the church, then it must be an organization or an institution which we see. It is not Christ. If, however, we see Christ in the body, then we will forget about the body and only see the Person. If the church is what it should be, we will not notice it because all we will see is Christ, all we will hear is Christ. If people should notice us instead of Christ, may God have mercy upon us. When people see only the church and do not see Christ, how frustrated they become with the so-called church. They repudiate it; they want to have nothing to do with it. Oh, if only they could see Christ, then what a difference it would make. Hence, the book of Acts reveals Christ in the body, and may this book be continually written today among God's own people.

Shall we pray:

Dear heavenly Father, we do thank Thee for that physical body the Lord Jesus took upon himself while on earth because, in that body, He has done great things; in that body, He has accomplished the work of redemption for us. Our Father, how we do praise and thank Thee that even though He is now seated at Thy right hand, He does have a body upon this earth, the church. And we do thank Thee for the church, the body of Christ, because in that body of Christ, we are able to see Him, to hear Him, to live and to die for Him. So our Father, do have mercy upon us that as we are here upon this earth, we may truly offer to Thee such a habitation, such an instrument, such a vessel so that the world may see Christ and not us. We ask in Thy precious name. Amen.

ROMANS

Seeing Christ in the Gospel

Romans 1:1-4—Paul, bondman of Jesus Christ, a called apostle, separated to God's glad tidings, (which he had before promised by his prophets in holy writings,) concerning his Son (come of David's seed according to flesh, marked out Son of God in power, according to the Spirit of holiness, by resurrection of the dead) Jesus Christ our Lord.

Romans 1:16-17—For I am not ashamed of the glad tidings; for it is God's power to salvation, to every one that believes, both to Jew first and to Greek: for righteousness of God is revealed therein, on the principle of faith, to faith: according as it is written, But the just shall live by faith.

Romans 16:25-27—Now to him that is able to establish you, according to my glad tidings and the preaching of Jesus Christ, according to the revelation of the mystery, as to which silence has been kept in the times of the ages, but which has now been made manifest, and by prophetic scriptures, according to commandment of the eternal God, made known for obedience of faith to all the nations—the only wise God, through Jesus Christ, to whom be glory for ever. Amen.

Dear heavenly Father, how we do worship Thee. Thou hast been so good, kind, merciful, and gracious to us in giving us Thy Son, our Lord Jesus Christ. Now our Father, as we come to Thee, truly our hearts are filled with gratitude and worship. We ask Thee that at this moment Thou wilt open Thy word to us, that through Thy word we may see more of Thy Son, that we may be more drawn to Thy Son, and Thy Son may be more formed within us; and to Thee be all the praise and glory. In Thy precious name. Amen.

The New Testament is divided into three parts. First are the historical books, next are the letters (the epistles), and finally there is the book of Revelation. The five historical books, which are the four Gospels and the book of Acts, are the history of our Lord Jesus. They give us the fact, the followed by the epistles, and they give us the explanation of these facts. The historical books give us the example and the epistles give us the interpretation. But whether it is the fact, or the explanation of the fact, one thing is sure: it is the revelation of Jesus Christ.

We have seen that in the historical books of the New Testament there is this revelation of Jesus Christ. Whether He is revealed in His Person, in His body which He took upon himself when the Word became flesh, or through that corporate body which He has taken upon himself after His death, resurrection, and ascension, it makes no difference. It is the same Jesus Christ. Whether in His personal body or whether in His corporate body, He is being revealed to us. And how precious He is!

As we come, now, to the letters of the New Testament, the first one we have is the letter to the Romans. Of all the writings of the apostle Paul, this is the one letter that deals with one particular subject, which is the gospel. It is the fullest and most systematic dissertation on that one theme, the gospel of God. At the very beginning of this letter Paul declares he is the bondman of Jesus Christ, a called apostle, separated to God's gospel. So we know that the gospel is what this whole letter deals with.

What is the gospel? In Luke 2 we are told that when Christ was born in Bethlehem, the angel of the Lord appeared to the shepherds in the field of Bethlehem, saying, "I announce to you the glad tidings of great joy, which shall be to all people. For today a Savior has been born to you in David's city, who is Christ the Lord." That is the fact of the gospel. The fact of the gospel is Jesus Christ the Lord. As the apostle Paul begins to write the letter to the Romans, he reestablishes this fact at the very outset. He said, "I am separated to God's gospel ... concerning His Son, Jesus Christ our Lord."

This gospel is concerned with the Son of God, Jesus Christ the Lord. "Separated to God's glad tidings ... concerning His Son, Jesus Christ our Lord." That is the opening statement; and according to this passage's grammatical structure, there are two parenthetical assertions inserted therein. One is: "(which He had before promised by His prophets in holy writings)." In other words, this gospel is not an accident. It had been promised before by God's prophets in their holy writings. That is to say, if one goes back to the Old Testament, he will find that the prophets of old had been prophesying about this gospel. The gospel is not something which just happened; rather it is something which had been prepared by God throughout the ages past.

The second parenthetical insertion is as follows: "(come of David's seed according to flesh, marked out Son of God in power, according to the Spirit of holiness, by resurrection of the dead)." This Son of God, who is verily the gospel of God, is, on the one hand, of the seed of David; He has come to be a man. And yet, on the other hand, He proves himself to be the Son of God by the resurrection from the dead. Accordingly, this gospel of God is concerning the Lord Jesus, who is both Man and God. He has a humanity and He has a divinity. He is the God-Man. And this God-Man *is* the gospel of God.

The gospel of God is a Person. I think that at the very beginning we need to emphasize this fact: the gospel of God is a Person. It is not a teaching; it is not a doctrine; it is not a technique; it is not a formula. It is a Person— God's Son, Jesus Christ the Lord. *That* is the gospel. And hence, it just reaffirms what is made clear in the historical books, that the fact of the gospel is none other than the Lord Jesus.

The apostle Paul likes to explain this fact to us. Further

down in this same introduction to the Roman epistle he said this: "I am not ashamed of the gospel because it is the power of God to salvation, to everyone who believes." There is no difference regardless of one's background. The gospel is God's power to save everyone who believes, whether Jew or Greek, and the gospel is the power of God that saves to the very uttermost. If we truly know this is the gospel, surely—like Paul—we will boast of it and not be ashamed of it. In this very gospel, the righteousness of God is revealed, and this gospel is based upon the principle of faith and unto faith. God has prepared everything in the gospel, and all we need to do is believe; and if we believe, then the righteousness of God comes upon us.

After Paul introduces the theme of his letter (vv.1-17), he then begins to explain it. We can treat the letter to the Romans as being divided into three parts. The first part consists of chapter 1:18 through chapter 8. This part can be termed "the provision of the gospel"—what the gospel has provided for us. The second part is found in chapters 9—11. This covers "the purpose and plan of the gospel." Then finally, the third part from chapters 12—16 is "the power or the product of the gospel"—how the power of the gospel manifests itself upon the earth; or, in other words, what the product of the gospel is. In short, we can say that this is the way the gospel is going to be explained by Paul, and as the apostle explains the gospel in his letter, no matter what he says, the picture painted for his readers throughout is the Lord Jesus Christ.

Provision of the Gospel

Before we know the gospel we know nothing about the righteousness of God, simply because the righteousness of God is revealed in the gospel. Without the gospel nobody can know the righteousness of God. What had we known previously? All we knew was the wrath of God. The wrath of God has been revealed, and it is upon all the ungodliness and unrighteousness of men. We surely know this because we were ungodly; that is, we were not like God. We were made in God's image, we were supposed to be like God, we were supposed to manifest Him and represent Him upon the earth; but unfortunately, we all have sinned: we all have fallen and come short of the glory of God. We have become ungodly, not like God anymore.

More than that, we have not only been ungodly towards God, we have also been unrighteous in all the relationships among ourselves. We have been unrighteous one towards another. We have sinned against one another; we have hurt and harmed one another; we have done many wrong things to one another. And because we were in that kind of situation, all we knew was the wrath of God. We knew in our conscience that the wrath of God was upon us. We knew that we were condemned. That is why religions have been invented, which try to appease the evil conscience and try to appease God somehow. We had tried to do good, to do the works of the law. But we knew that our righteousness, all our righteous acts—that is, according to the law, having done something good by fulfilling the law—are like filthy rags (see Isaiah 64:6).

We needed to realize that our works are unable to cover our nakedness before God, that they are all unclean, dirty, filthy in His sight. That is the reason why no one can be justified by works of the law. If we bring all the works and all the good things which we have done and offer them to God, we will be utterly rejected. It is just like the offerings of Cain, who brought to God the best of his produce upon the earth, which represented his own merits. He brought them to God for His acceptance, but they were completely rejected. Not only were his offerings rejected, his very person was rejected by God. No one can be justified by the works of the law. All are under condemnation; all are under the wrath of God. And I believe we who are believing Christians have all experienced and realized these things.

But thank God we find this in Paul's letter: "But now [being] without law" (this phrase "[being] without law" does not have reference to "lawlessness;" it simply means "[being] outside of law") the "righteousness of God is manifested, borne witness to by the law and the prophets; righteousness of God by faith of Jesus Christ towards all, and upon all who believe: for there is no difference" (Romans 3:21-22).

The righteousness of God is being manifested to us in the gospel. Yet how does the righteousness of God come to us who believe? For the sake of clarity, let us say that there are actually three aspects mentioned in Romans chapters 1—8 which the gospel has provided for us. In chapters 3:1—5:12 we find justification. From chapters 5:13—8:17 there is discussed the matter of sanctification. And from chapter 8:18-30 we learn about glorification. This is God's three-fold provision for us in the gospel.

Justification

What is justification? We often hear people say that justification means "just as if" we had never sinned. We have sinned, but now being justified, we are before God as if we had never sinned. But actually, justification is more than that. Not only will God consider us as if we have never sinned and are just, but justification means that we are now being accepted in the Beloved. Justification means that we have been reconciled to God. It means that we now have a standing in His presence. Formerly, we could not approach God; we could not stand before Him. If we were to stand before God, we would be judged, condemned, executed, and dead. But thank God, through justification, today we can stand before Him with holy boldness. We are no longer afraid of the wrath of God because His righteousness is upon us. So, justification actually includes all these thoughts. We are justified as though we had never sinned; that is, all our sins have been forgiven. And they have not only been forgiven, they are forgotten, because if they are not forgotten, then we cannot say we are justified as though we had never sinned. We have sinned, but now all is forgiven and forgotten. God has forgotten; therefore, we are justified. We have been reconciled to God; we are no longer enemies of God. He has received us and accepted us in His beloved Son, and now we can stand before God in holy boldness. That is justification.

How are we justified? It is an age-old question. That question was put forth in the first book in the Bible (first, historically speaking), the book of Job. This book was the first one written, even before Genesis, because Genesis was written by Moses, but Job had lived in the age of the patriarchs well before Moses' time. Even in that book, in its ninth chapter, Job is recorded as having asked this question: "How can man be just with God?" Given this fact that man is unjust and a sinner, how can he be made just before God? He is a just God. How, therefore, can He justify unjust people? If God should justify unjust people without any compensation, that would make Him unjust. That would compromise His righteousness, but God cannot do that. God loves sinners, but He hates sin. But thank God, that is where the gospel comes in. The gospel is this: that God loved the world so much that He gave His only begotten Son to the world. His Son came into this world as a man, Jesus; and He took our sins upon himself and died on the cross as our substitute. He shed His blood for our sins, and His blood satisfies the justice and righteousness of God. His blood purifies our hearts from an evil conscience, and that is the reason why today we are justified before God. In other words, we are indeed justified, but not by ourselves.

Oftentimes we try to justify ourselves, but no matter how we try to do so, we are not justified. *God* has to justify us. He justifies us through the blood of His beloved Son, and because the blood is shed, sins are remitted. Therefore, God can justly justify us. And His righteousness comes to us.

"Him who knew not sin he [God] has made sin for us, that we might become God's righteousness in him" (II Corinthians 5:21).

It is interesting to note that not only does God justify us

but also, through our receiving the gospel, we justify God. We become the righteousness of God. We say that He is just in justifying us. It is a mutual thing.

How are we made righteous before God? Today God looks upon us and declares: "I see no iniquity in them." You may remember that in the Old Testament time Balaam, the Gentile prophet, had tried to curse the children of Israel but God turned the curse into a blessing and said, "I see no iniquity in Israel." And thus it is the same thing with us. Today God says, "I see no sin in them." We are justified in Christ Jesus. God does not see any sin in us. Instead, He sees us as righteous.

How, though, is this possible? Among God's people there are different understandings on this matter, and some actually demonstrate a *lack* of understanding. Some people think that if we believe in the Lord Jesus, then we are made righteous. That is true, for in Romans 5:18-20 Paul has written: "As [it was] by one offence towards all men to condemnation, so by one righteousness towards all men for justification of life. For as indeed by the disobedience of the one man the many have been constituted sinners, so also by the obedience of the one the many will be constituted righteous."

We have indeed been made righteous, but *how* are we made righteous? Some people think that when you believe in the Lord Jesus, God has immediately changed you from sin to righteousness. In other words, formerly you were a sinner; formerly you knew nothing except to sin. But after you believe in the Lord Jesus, a change instantly comes over you. You no longer sin but are made righteous; that is, everything you do is now righteous before God because a change has come upon you. That is certainly one way of looking at it, but have you truly been changed? It is true that when you first believe in the Lord Jesus—perhaps during the first few days or perhaps the first few months—it seems that you have changed. It seems that way but then, when the excitement and the thrill of your initial salvation begins to subside, you begin to revert back to your former conduct, and you realize that actually you can still sin. You are not as righteous as you think you are. In other words, you have not changed. It does not mean you are not saved; you are saved. A new life has come into you, that is true. You have received eternal life; but so far as you yourself are concerned, you have not changed. You are still the same old person but, thank God, you have a new life.

Someone else may theorize on this matter as follows: "Well, when you believe in the Lord Jesus, and though you have not changed, God nonetheless imparts the righteousness of Christ to you. His merits become your virtues. Therefore, when God looks at you, He sees that you are full of virtues—full of righteousness—because the righteousness of Jesus Christ has become yours." That seems to be closer, but not yet close enough.

The phrase "righteousness of Jesus Christ" is only mentioned once in the whole New Testament. (I leave it with you to find out where it is.) The righteousness of Jesus Christ means that when the Lord Jesus was on earth He was righteous in every way. Even today He is the righteous One seated at the right hand of the Father. There is no one righteous, but Jesus Christ is righteous. He is the *only* righteous One because He pleased the Father *in all things*. And that was and is His righteousness. But do you realize that His righteousness will not justify you? On the contrary, His righteousness will condemn you because He is so righteous and you are so unrighteous. The more righteous He is the more unrighteous you appear to be. Therefore, you are the more condemned.

Suppose you are a very loose person and you meet a person who is very controlled. The more controlled he is, the more loose you become because there is such a contrast there. Let us not forget that John 16:10 tells us: "Of righteousness because I go away to my Father." When the Holy Spirit comes, He will condemn the world. In what sense? Jesus said, "Of righteousness because I go away to my Father." Why does righteousness condemn us because Christ goes to the Father? Jesus is the only One on earth who *could* return to God. He is the only *One* who can stand before Him. Jesus is the only One who can live before Him. He is the only righteous One whom God can accept. Therefore, because Jesus has gone to the Father, it proves that Christ's righteousness is perfect. He can go to the Father, and that righteousness condemns us because we cannot go to the Father. In fact, we dare *not* go; for if we go we will be smitten to death. That is righteousness.

Let us understand that the personal righteousness of Jesus Christ does not and cannot justify us. The righteousness of Jesus Christ qualifies Him to be our substitute before God because He is without sin. Therefore, He can be made sin for us. If He were not righteous, He could not be our substitute. He would instead die for His own sin. But thank God, He is all righteous and He can thus be made sin for us so that the righteousness of God may come upon us. His righteousness qualifies Him to be our Savior, our substitute, but His own personal righteousness is not something that is imparted to us to be our righteousness.

Some other people have said that not only our Lord Jesus has all the merits and all the righteousness to impart to people, but that in this world there are even some saints who have been canonized. That is to say, that when they die, they have enough merit for themselves to go straight to heaven without needing to go first to what has been called purgatory; and that they arrive in heaven with some merit to spare. Consequently, if you pray to one of these saints, the latter can impart some merit to you by which to lift you out of purgatory into heaven. That is impartation. But the gospel of justification by faith is not that. It is not that Christ, who is so full of personal righteousness, takes out from himself some of His righteousness and puts it on you, so that now you are made righteous. Not at all. We are made righteous because God has given us His beloved Son, Christ Jesus. He himself is made our righteousness.

"But of him [God] are ye in Christ Jesus, who has been

made to us wisdom from God, and righteousness, and holiness, and redemption" (I Corinthians 1:30).

God has made Christ our righteousness. It is not a matter of His personal righteousness being imparted to us, but God has given us Christ His Son, and accordingly we are clothed with Christ. It is in union with Christ that we are made righteous. Today, as we stand before God, He sees not us but Christ, because we are clothed with Christ.

Oh do let us see that this is the way we are justified; that this is the way we are made righteous. We have not changed. God has not imparted to us some of Christ's merits, but He has clothed us with Christ himself. Today, we are in union with Christ. Therefore, when we stand before God, He does not see you and me; God sees His beloved Son and He declares: "You are justified as though you had never sinned; you are accepted; there is now peace."

Justification or righteousness is not a teaching, a doctrine, a method, a formula or a technique. It is a Person, and that Person is Jesus Christ. When you have Him, you are justified. If you do not have Jesus Christ, and even if you know the doctrine of justification by faith, you are not justified. People may accept the doctrine of justification by faith, but if they do not believe in the Lord Jesus, they are not justified. People may use this teaching as a formula, but it does not work until you believe in the Lord Jesus. And then, thank God, you are justified. You are righteous before God because Jesus Christ has been made righteousness to you. He himself is your righteousness. That is the gospel.

I recall the story about John Bunyan, who wrote *Pilgrim's Progress*, which is well known. (If you have not read it, I hope you will, because it is not just for children, it is for everybody.) When John Bunyan was a young man, sometimes he was deeply convicted of his sins and he tried to reform. Most of the time he lived a very loose life, but from time to time he was convicted, and then he tried to reform. He tried to stop swearing and go to church and do all kinds of "good" things to reform himself. It happened again and again, but it did not work.

One day, John Bunyan was once again under deep conviction and in a period of trying to reform himself. He was walking in the fields thinking about this matter. How can I be justified? How can I be made righteous before God? I have no righteousness, how can I be made righteous? What should I do? As he was walking in the field, suddenly he heard a voice: "My righteousness is in heaven." Now that is a revelation. He thought his righteousness was in him, that he had to do something in order to be made righteous. Then he heard that voice: "My righteousness is in heaven."

Righteousness is not in you; it is in Christ Jesus. He is your righteousness, and if you have Him, then you are made righteous before God. If you have Jesus Christ, then you are justified. As brother Watchman Nee once said, "You may change, and you will change, but your righteousness never changes because it is Jesus Christ." No matter how you may change, your righteousness never changes. That is the first part of the gospel as is described for us by Paul in his letter to the Romans, and it is Jesus Christ. It is not a teaching, not a method, not some thing which God has given to you, but it is Christ who is given to you.

Sanctification

The second aspect of the gospel is sanctification. This is a big word, but it simply means, a "setting apart for God." In practical terms, sanctification means to live a godly and holy life, overcoming temptations and the power of sin, and to live a victorious life. That is sanctification. In Luke 1:75 there is a prayer offered up which says that we may walk before God in holiness and righteousness all our days.

It is true that after we have been justified, after we are saved, we ought to live before God and walk before Him in a godly manner (that is, like God) and in righteousness all our days. It is not expected of a Christian, a true believer, to continue in sin or to fail in the face of temptation. It is expected of a Christian to live like Christ lived upon this earth, overcoming the power of sin and living a holy life. "Be ye holy because I am holy" (see Leviticus 19:2). This is not only an exhortation, it is a command. God commands you and me to be holy. *Holy* simply means "uncommon." It means that we should live in a manner uncommon to how the world lives. We should be different because we have been set apart for God. We are here on earth to represent God, to express and manifest Him—His glory. That is what we are here for. And such is sanctification.

How can we be holy? How can we live such an overcoming life? We know we should live such a life, but can we live it? In Romans 7 Paul said, "In my heart I know, in my renewed mind I know. I know I should keep the commandments of God, and I am willing to do that. I try to do that, but the more I try, the more I fail. To will is in me, but to do is not in me. Oh wretched man that I am, who can deliver me from this body of death?"

Is this not the experience of many Christians today? You are justified before God, you are saved, reconciled to God, and you have His life in you; yet somehow you cannot overcome the power of sin. Somehow, and though the willingness is in you, the strength is just not there. You try and try and try, but you are defeated and defeated and defeated. You live a miserable Christian life. That is certainly not the gospel.

The gospel is not only for sinners; the gospel is also for believers. That part of the gospel for believers is: "Do you not know you were crucified with Christ?" (see Romans 6:6). In other words, for our justification it is the *blood* of the Lord Jesus; but for our sanctification, it is the *cross* of our Lord Jesus.

When the Lord Jesus went to the cross, He took all your and my sins upon himself. He has borne our sins in His body on the tree, and there He died for our sins. Therefore, if we believe in Him, our sins are forgiven. In the same manner, when Christ Jesus went to the cross, He took you and me with Him. Thank God, Christ has not only taken our sins but He has taken us with Him to the cross, and there He died as us—not only *for* us but *as* us. This is because when the Lord Jesus died on the cross, He not only became our substitute to pay the penalty of sin for us but He also became our representative. He represents us on the cross: that is to say, when He died, we died in Him and with Him. When He was raised from the dead, we were raised from the dead together with Him. That is why Paul declared elsewhere: "I am crucified with Christ, and no longer live, I, but Christ lives in me; but in that I now live in flesh, I live by faith, the faith of the Son of God, who has loved me and given himself for me" (Galatians 2:20).

Do we know experientially what sanctification is? Yes, sanctification requires that we live a holy life, but who can live such a holy life? Neither you nor I can live such a holy life by ourselves. Even though we are saved, if we try to live holy lives by our own wills, by our own efforts, we will fail because we have not changed. There is only one Man who can live such a holy life and that Man is Jesus Christ. He is the only One who can live such a life, and do you not know that He lives in you? He is in you, but you do not allow Him to live through you. You are still living by your own strength, and that is why you cannot live a holy life. If only you would step aside, as it were, and let Christ live, then it is no problem to live godly and righteously before God all your days because He has himself lived that life on earth two thousand years ago. He just relives it in and through you and me. Remember this: sanctification is not a changed life; sanctification is an *exchanged* life. You have not changed, but there is an exchange. It is no longer you; it is Christ who lives in you.

A classic illustration of this is Hudson Taylor, the founder of the China Inland Mission. He loved the Lord, and went to China as a missionary. He was used by God mightily, but when he was in China, he realized that even though he was preaching to the Chinese, he found his own life was a failure. He discovered that there were many things he could not overcome. He got worried, grew concerned so easily, was touched by small things; and so he looked to the Lord for a life that could really overcome, a life that is glorious and would glorify the Lord. He prayed and prayed. He read the Bible and fasted. He asked God to give him faith, and he did everything he could. But finally, God simply showed him that it is an exchanged life. "It is not you, Hudson Taylor, who can make it, but I am in you, and I will live such a life. Just relax and let Me do it." And he found his whole life was revolutionized. This is sanctification.

Sanctification is not in the first instance a doctrine; and it is not a second blessing. There are people today who believe in the notion of a second blessing. They say the first blessing is that you get saved, and then the second blessing is that you become sanctified. And how? Well, the root of sin is eradicated, it is yanked out of you. Then you cannot sin anymore.

Now, I have to confess that I was saved among the holiness people who believed in the eradication of sin. I was saved in their midst in a conference. Unfortunately, during the conference, the founder of that mission lost her temper. Sin is not eradicated. Sin will remain in you as long as you live, but thank God, *you* are eradicated. Not sin—you. The cross has taken you out. Therefore, it is sanctification by faith.

John Wesley preached sanctification by faith. It is not only justification by faith, but also sanctification by faith. Why is it justification by faith? It is because everything is already done for you. All you therefore need to do is believe and receive it, and it is yours. The same thing is true with sanctification. Christ is *the* sanctification. Therefore, when you believe in Him, you are sanctified. It is that simple. Just believe and take Him as your sanctification. Is it not in I Corinthians 1:30 that we read: "God has made Him our righteousness and sanctification"? Sanctification is not something which God gives to you. Sanctification is a Person—even Christ. Christ himself is given to you. *He* is your sanctification. And that is the gospel of God.

Glorification

Many believers think that because we are justified we will not go to hell but go to heaven, and that that is good enough. There are some other believers who think that such thinking is not good enough. It is not good enough to simply believe that in the future they can go to heaven and not to hell, for these believers truly want to live a godly life, a holy life on earth. Thank God for such believers. But if you should be one of these who think that that is good enough, God says that even *this* is not good enough for Him. The gospel has to fully satisfy God's heart. It is not only to satisfy you; the gospel has to satisfy God, and He is not even satisfied with both justifying you and sanctifying you. God says, "No, I am going to do something far more; I am going to *glorify* you."

What is glorification? Glorification simply means that God wants to transform you from glory to glory and to conform you to the image of His beloved Son. "Whom He has foreknown, He has also predestinated to be conformed to the image of His Son, so that he should be the firstborn among many brethren. But whom he has predestinated, these also he has called; and whom he has called, these also he has justified; but whom he has justified, these also he has glorified" (Romans 8:29-30).

Glorification does not mean that your natural man is glorified, is changed. No, *you* do not change, for "that which is born of the flesh is flesh" and "that which is born of the Spirit is spirit" (John 3:6). Being transformed simply means that the Holy Spirit will so work in your life that He will take away your self-life, and will add to you Christ until Christ is fully formed in you, and that you are conformed to His image. That is glory. We are shameful; only Christ is glorious. So when Christ is formed in you, there is glory there. In other words, glory means God is being seen, expressed and known.

Whenever you see God, you see glory. This is His purpose. He will not only justify you and sanctify you, He also wants to glorify you. He also wants Christ to be fully formed in you so that you may be conformed to His image.

How is God going to do that? God the Holy Spirit is responsible for this beautiful work. The Holy Spirit is like an embroiderer. He is stitching stitches, needlework by needlework, in your life so as to weave, as it were, Christ into you. And as He is doing that, you will be clothed with a garment of embroidery. You will be fit to be the bride of Christ. By this process, what is stitched in you, constituted in you, is nothing less than Christ. Christ is our redemption, and the redemption is towards sonship; that is to say, looking towards the placing of a son. You will have grown up by then and you will have become sons of God. That is glorification. And again, it is not merely a teaching; it is not merely a doctrine. Glorification is first and foremost Christ. When you see Christ, there is glory, and this is the work of the Holy Spirit.

The apostle Paul concludes the first part of his epistle with a shout of victory, and that is found in chapter 8:31-39. If you look into that passage, you will read that God has not spared His own Son but has delivered Him up for us all. And if that be true, how shall He not also with Him grant us all things? It is God who justifies, and He has justified us. It is Christ who has died, and He has also been raised up. Moreover, it is Christ who is at the right hand of God interceding for us. God justifies us; Christ delivers us; and then the Holy Spirit works Christ into us until we are conformed to the image of God's beloved Son. This is the provision of the gospel.

The Plan and Purpose of the Gospel

I will merely mention the last two parts of Romans without explaining them too much. The first of these two concluding parts, chapters 9-11, are beautiful chapters. Very often, while reading Romans and you come upon these three chapters, you end up getting stuck in them. They are too hard. Indeed you do not know what to make out of this section; but actually, chapters 9-11 are most beautiful because they show us the plan and the purpose of the gospel. It is the sovereign will of God to save us. That is why He shut us all up in sin that we may be shut up to Christ. Such action taken was first towards the Jews, then towards the nations, and will then turn back towards the Jews again. It is not by our will or by our running, but it is by the mercies of God (see Romans 9:16). Yet, through it all, you will discern that it is simply this: "whosoever believes in [or calls on] Him shall be saved" (Romans 10:9-13). In other words, you discover the beautiful arrangement by God in order that everyone will have a chance to come to the Lord Jesus. His ways are unsearchable, but His purpose is clear. He wants Christ to be all and in all, for unto Him be the glory. "Of Him, through Him, and to Him"—that is the purpose of the gospel. The purpose of the gospel is Christ glorified, that is to say, Christ having the first place in all things.

The Power and Product of the Gospel

The last part of Romans concerns the product of the gospel. There in the concluding section to this epistle you find a body of believers, a body of the redeemed. They become one body, and this one body is on earth to express the Head, Christ. It is on earth to glorify Christ. In this body they love one another and receive one another, they care for one another and build up one another, and they become a testimony of Jesus in this world. That is the product—the end result—of the gospel.

The last three verses are a fitting conclusion to this letter. There are three "accordings" mentioned there. "Now to him that is able to establish you, according to my glad tidings and the preaching of Jesus Christ." That is the provision of the gospel, which is a reference back to the very first part of the epistle.

Next, "according to the revelation of the mystery, as to which silence has been kept in the times of the ages, but which has now been made manifest, and by prophetic scriptures." That is the purpose of the gospel, which refers back to the epistle's second part.

And finally, "according to commandment of the eternal God, made known for obedience of faith to all the nations." That is the power or product of the gospel, which is a reference back to the third part.

"The only wise God, through Jesus Christ, to whom be glory for ever. Amen."

We see Jesus in the gospel because He *is* the gospel. What you receive is Jesus Christ—not a teaching, not a method, not a formula, but Jesus Christ. He is himself our gospel.

Dear heavenly Father, do reveal Thy Son to us and in us that we may see Him as the gospel, the glad tidings which we have received and believed. We pray, oh Lord, that Thou wilt open our eyes so that we may see Him as our justification, our sanctification and our glorification. We ask that Thou wilt open our eyes to see that He is the purpose of the gospel, that He may have the preeminence in all things. We pray that we may be on this earth a corporate expression of what Thou art. To Thee be the glory. In the name of our Lord Jesus. Amen.

I CORINTHIANS

Seeing Christ through Problems

I Corinthians 1:1-9—Paul, a called apostle of Jesus Christ, by God's will, and Sosthenes the brother, to the assembly of God which is in Corinth, to those sanctified in Christ Jesus, called saints, with all that in every place call on the name of our Lord Jesus Christ, both theirs and ours: Grace to you and peace from God our Father, and the Lord Jesus Christ. I thank my God always about you, in respect of the grace of God given to you in Christ Jesus; that in everything ye have been enriched in him, in all word of doctrine, and all knowledge, (according as the testimony of the Christ has been confirmed in you,) so that ye come short in no gift, awaiting the revelation of our Lord Jesus Christ; who shall also confirm you to the end, unimpeachable in the day of our Lord Jesus Christ. God is faithful, by whom ye have been called into the fellowship of his Son Jesus Christ our Lord.

I Corinthians 2:1-2—And I, when I came to you, brethren, came not in excellency of word, or wisdom, announcing to you the testimony of God. For I did not judge it well to know anything among you save Jesus Christ, and him crucified.

I Corinthians 16:22-24—If any one love not the Lord Jesus Christ let him be Anathema Maranatha. The grace of the Lord Jesus Christ be with you. My love be with you all in Christ Jesus. Amen.

Dear heavenly Father, we are in Thy presence, and we trust Thy Holy Spirit to open Thy word to us and open us to Thy word that we may see Christ, that we may be conformed to His image, that we may be to the praise of His glory. In Thy precious name. Amen.

We mentioned before that the Bible is the revelation of Jesus Christ. God gives us the Bible for one purpose, that we may know the Lord Jesus Christ. God reveals His Son through the Bible, and we need to ask God to give us the Spirit of wisdom and revelation that we may truly see the Lord Jesus in His word.

In I Corinthians we are given to see the Lord Jesus through problems. This letter was written by the apostle Paul to the church in Corinth. However, it was not only written to the church in Corinth, but to all those in every place who call upon the name of the Lord Jesus. Therefore, this letter is addressed to us, too, because we are those here who call upon the name of the Lord Jesus. So let us not treat this letter to the Corinthians as though it were written to somebody else, a church that existed about two thousand years ago; that their problems are not our problems, and their solution is not our solution. Let us therefore bear in mind that this first letter to the Corinthians is addressed to us. The problems we find in that church we often find to be our problems. And the solution which Paul gives in this letter shows us the way to solve our problems today.

The church in Corinth had a wonderful beginning. If you read the book of Acts, you will learn in chapter 18 that Paul had come to Corinth after being in Athens. While he was at Corinth he was pressed in his spirit in respect of the word of God. He preached to the Jews, then to the Gentiles, and many came to the Lord. But there was much opposition, too, and the Lord appeared to him in a vision, saying, "Do not be afraid but speak; do not be silent. I am with you; nobody can hurt you because I have many people in this city." So Paul stayed in Corinth for a year and six months, and many came to the Lord.

After Paul left, another great servant of God arrived in that city—Apollos. Apollos was a very eloquent man, a very learned man, who was deeply taught in the word of God. And through his labor, many believers there were built up. We do not know if Peter had ever been in Corinth. But we do know that his influence was felt there because in this first letter to the Corinthians some people there are recorded as having said, "I am of Paul," because Paul had been there; others there said, "I am of Apollos," because Apollos had also been there. And still other people there had said, "I am of Cephas" (Peter). So whether Peter had even been there or whether just his influence was there, we do not know; but we do know that Peter was influential in the church in Corinth. Think of that! If a church had the labor of the great apostle Paul, the great teacher Apollos, and the great apostle Peter, what privilege that church must have had! Because of these various labors, Paul was moved to mention in the first chapter of his letter that they were truly enriched. They were enriched in the word of doctrine, in knowledge, and they were not short of any gift.

We would probably say, "Well, if this is the church and if this should happen here with us, how glorious that would be!" But unfortunately, even though they were rich in the word of doctrine, in knowledge, and were not short of any spiritual gift, these things did not seem to help them grow spiritually. On the contrary, these things seemed to be a hindrance to their growth. They remained as "babes in Christ" (I Corinthians 3:1b), and they were full of problems. I think this should be a warning to us. Let us not think that because we are rich in the word, in knowledge and in gifts, therefore, we are bound to be spiritual, and that the church must surely be a spiritual church. Not always. Sometimes it is just the opposite, because people become contented with all these things and lose sight of the one thing that is necessary, and that is, the Lord himself.

The church in Corinth had many problems. It was not a perfect church. In fact through the twenty centuries, we do not find any perfect church on earth. Can we find any person or church that has no problems? If we can find people who have no problems, then the church, being the gathering of God's people, will have no problems either. But there is no one who does not have problems; even little children have problems.

The more we grow up, the more problems we have. How can we expect any church on earth to be without problems? I think only a dead person has no problems: indeed, all his problems are over! And probably it is a dead church that has no problems. If the church is living, it is bound to have problems. Let us not be afraid of them. How often we try to hide our problems or evade them. How often we try to deceive ourselves into thinking that we have no problems. If problems come, let us face them. Let us not be afraid of them, because problems are opportunities. If problems are solved in the proper way, it will mean spiritual growth. Of course, if we allow the problems to remain, it will be damaging. But no problem needs to remain forever, because there *is* a solution.

When we have a problem, how do we face it? Do we merely attempt to solve the particular problem we have at that particular moment? If this is the way that we try to solve our problems, then after one problem is solved another one will pop up. There will be no ending to our problems. Therefore, when a problem arises, the secret is to go to the root. Let us find out the cause of this or that or all problems and then deal with the root of the problem. What is the root of most of the problems? Actually, the root is the self, it is the flesh. If we learn to deal with the flesh through the cross of the Lord Jesus, then we find it is the solution to most, if not all, our problems.

Problems in the Church

As we read this first letter to the Corinthians, we discover that this church had many problems. For instance, from chapters 1—4 the problem is division—a party spirit. Let us first bear in mind that all these people in the Corinthian church had been called into the fellowship of God's Son, Jesus Christ, and what a wonderful fellowship that is.

Just think for a moment. We were enemies of God. We had no hope, no God. We were dead in sins and transgressions. We were under condemnation. We could not face God because if we did, we would die. But now, by the grace of God in Jesus Christ, we are called into the fellowship of God's Son. We are called into a fellowship, and *fellowship* simply means "having in common." We are to share with the Lord Jesus all that He is. We are called into such a wonderful fellowship.

Unfortunately, the church in Corinth was divided. Although they were all called into the fellowship of God's Son, they were divided among themselves. They had different opinions and different ideas. Some said, "I am of Paul because Paul led me to the Lord. I belong to Paul." Some others said, "I am of Apollos because Apollos built me up with the word of God." And still others said, "I am of Cephas because Cephas is one of the original twelve apostles. I go back to the root." And some even said in a sectarian way, "Well, if you are of Paul, and you are of Apollos, and you are of Cephas, I am greater; I am of Christ." There was division, a party spirit, that was breaking up the fellowship of God's Son, Jesus Christ. That is a big problem.

In chapter 5 the problem there was identified as sin. Some of them had fallen into grievous sin, even incest. This was something which was rare even among unbelievers. And the church was so insensitive as to have allowed this issue to continue on without having dealt with it.

In chapter 6 we are told that they had another problem. One brother had sued another brother in the law court of the world. Instead of loving one another, instead of being willing to be defrauded, they defrauded one another. They went to the court of the Gentiles, suing one another. That happened in the church in Corinth.

In chapter 7 we find that these Corinthian believers had marriage problems of all kinds.

In chapters 8—10 we learn about their various social problems. There were some people among the believers in Corinth who went to the temple of idols to eat and drink because in those days social activities were carried on in the temple. If a person did not go to the idol temple, then he would not be able to enjoy all the social functions. And some Christians were so greedy that they greatly craved after such social activity. Without thinking, they just went into the temple to eat and drink, but when they did that, they caused the weak to stumble.

In chapter 11 we see that they had problems over the matter of head covering. Should sisters have their heads covered? And that does not mean the sisters only, but should the brothers themselves be covered before God? Who really is the head?

They also had problems with the Lord's Table (or Communion) because when they came to eat and to drink at the Lord's Table some would get drunk beforehand. In those olden days, they usually had a love feast before the Lord's Table because when the Lord Jesus had first given us the Lord's Supper, He had been eating the Passover Feast with His disciples. Towards the end of that Passover Feast, He gave us this Lord's Supper. So the practice of the early church was that they usually gathered to eat first and then have the Lord's Supper. Unfortunately, some who were rich ate rich food and some who were poor were starved. They did not share with each other, and after that they came to break the bread at the Lord's Table. What is that? Where is the unity? Where is the love? Where is the oneness?

In chapters 12—14 we are told that they also had problems with spiritual gifts. They were rich in spiritual gifts. We would say that if they were rich in spiritual gifts, certainly, the whole church would be built up quickly. But unfortunately, they tore down the church because, instead of using the gifts to build up the body, they used such gifts to display themselves, to make a show of themselves.

In chapter 15 we discover that they even had problems with doctrine. Some of them did not believe in resurrection. Doubting questions arose among these believers. How could people be resurrected? When a person dies, the body is buried; it is corrupted and disappears. How, then, could that person be resurrected? Where does that person take up his body again? They did not believe in resurrection.

In chapter 16 we can discover that they also had problems over the issue of giving. Christians are supposed to give, but those at Corinth were very, very slow in giving. They not only had problems with giving but they likewise had problems with submission. How could they submit to those who led them, who helped them? They were failing to submit. Finally, the Corinthian believers had that big problem of love. Love one another and love the Lord Jesus. They had lost their first love.

Is that not a contradiction? On the one hand, these people were rich in the word and in knowledge and in gifts; yet simultaneously, they had all these problems. These problems were very basic. These problems were very great. These problems were even breaking up the fellowship.

Do we have problems, individually and collectively? We may not have all of the problems which we have just mentioned that affected the church in Corinth, but certainly we have some of them, and perhaps we may have some others which they did not have. Regardless, life is full of problems, both individually and together. Yet what was the root cause of all these problems? Why should these problems exist in the church at Corinth? The apostle Paul, inspired by the Holy Spirit, gave the diagnosis: "Are ye not carnal, and walk according to man?" (I Corinthians 3:3b)

Spiritual Conditions

In relation to spiritual conditions the Bible divides mankind into three groups: (1) the natural man, (2) the carnal man and (3) the spiritual man. Let us briefly take up each one of these conditions.

The natural man refers to a person who lives by his natural life without the teaching and the leading of the Holy Spirit. "But the natural man does not receive the things of the Spirit of God, for they are folly to him; and he cannot know them because they are spiritually discerned" (I Corinthians 2:14).

This natural man is man in the natural state. Of course, we know when we are talking about man's natural state, that actually, it is already *un*natural, because at the beginning when God created man, he was without sin. He was created with a spirit, and soul, and body; but because of sin, man's spirit became dead. Even though we are still very active in our soul and in our body, yet before God we were dead in sins and transgressions, which means our spirit was dead. The scientific definition of death is the cessation of communication with its proper environment. Our spirit's environment is God, but when we lost that communication with Him, our spirit was considered as dead. Therefore, a natural man is a person whose spirit is dead towards God; there is no communication with Him. You may be very clever, you may be very healthy, but when God is mentioned, there is a blank, a block. There is no communication because you are a natural man. The natural man does not receive the things of the Spirit because he considers them as folly. Which is really foolish, however, the natural man or the things of God? Of course, we know that the natural man is foolish in the sense that he does not receive the things of God, nor can he receive. There is no ability to receive spiritual things. Such is the natural man.

Then the Bible tells us of the carnal man. Who is the carnal man? Such a person is not an unbeliever. The carnal man is one who has been saved. Unfortunately, he still lives by his flesh instead of by the Spirit. "For ye are yet carnal. For whereas there are among you emulation and strife, are ye not carnal, and walk according to man?" (I Corinthians 3:3)

These Corinthian believers were justified, set apart by God, and called saints; yet, they are still carnal. They still walk according to man. Even though they are saved, they are no different from the natural man. The only difference is they have the life of God in them, but they still walk according to man, doing what everybody out in the world is doing. There does not seem to be any difference because they walk after the flesh. They have the Holy Spirit. The Holy Spirit has indeed quickened their spirit and dwells in their spirit, but they do not walk according to the Spirit. They still walk according to the flesh, and because of that, they walk like the world. That is the carnal man.

Finally, the Bible speaks of the spiritual man. "But the spiritual discerns all things, and he is discerned of no one" (I Corinthians 2:15).

Who is the spiritual man? The spiritual man is actually what a believer ought to be, what God has intended us to be who are saved. He is a man who walks according to the Spirit. The Holy Spirit, who dwells in his spirit, has control over his life, and because of that he is a spiritual man and is able to discern all things.

The Scripture divides mankind into these three groups. If you are the Lord's, you are not the natural man. You will be either the carnal man or the spiritual man. God's will is that we be the spiritual man, but it is possible for you to be the carnal man. Which one are you?

The Corinthian believers were still carnal, and because of their carnality, problems arose in their midst just as is found in the world. The root of their problem was carnality.

The Remedy for All Problems

Under the searchlight of the Spirit of God you will find that the problems in your life are mainly, if not totally, due to carnality. If you look at the church, you shall find the same thing. The reason why you find all these problems in the church is because the people therein are carnal. They do not walk according to the Spirit. But what is the solution? Paul not only gives the diagnosis, he likewise provides the remedy. The remedy to all their problems is but one: Christ Jesus.

And I, when I came to you, brethren, came not in excellency

> of word, or wisdom, announcing to you the testimony of God. For I did not judge it well to know anything among you save Jesus Christ, and him crucified (I Corinthians 2:1-2).

During the first century Corinth was a city of culture and a center of civilization. It was a corrupted, wicked city; but, strangely, in history you can come across a saying that if you are very eloquent and able to present things in a logical and excellent way, it is said to be the Corinthian way of speaking. Then again, it is likewise said that if you live a dissolute, dissipated, depraved life, you are living like a Corinthian. Is it not strange that these two things often co-exist in the same place or among the same people? You may think that the more cultured you are, certainly the more moral you are; but oftentimes in history this is not true. The more cultured these people were in Corinth, the more immoral they were. And somehow, the spirit of Corinth had entered into the church at Corinth. On the one hand, they were eloquent, clever, knowledgeable, gifted, talented. On the other hand, you observe that all these degradations, divisions, and quarrels mentioned earlier were in their midst. And hence, they were no different from the world. They should be different; as a matter of fact, they were saved to be different; but they were not any different because they were yet carnal.

The church ought to be different from the world. Is it? Oftentimes, the church is no different. It is not because of the weakness of God. Even His weakness is stronger than the strength of man. It is because God's people remain carnal, babes in Christ.

What is the solution to these problems? Paul knew the condition of the people in Corinth. He did not try to match eloquence with eloquence or logic with logic, even though he was well able to do that. He saw through them, and so he said, "When I came among you I was determined I would know nothing among you but Jesus Christ and Him crucified." Jesus

Christ is the solution to all your problems. If only you can see Him, then your problems will be solved. Or to put it another way: You have problems, but thank God, your problems will give you Jesus. Do not be afraid of problems, because the more you have, the better you are able to see the Lord Jesus. If you see the Lord Jesus through your problems, then the problems are solved and solved wonderfully.

The church at Corinth had the problem of division and party spirit. How could that problem be solved? Paul said, "Is Christ divided?" Is that not a simple solution? You are divided because you say, "I am of Paul, I am of Apollos, I am of Cephas." But is Christ divided? Who do you believe? In whose name were you baptized? Who do you follow? Do you follow Paul? Do you follow Apollos? Do you follow Cephas? Or do you follow Christ? Now, of course, you will say, "I believe in Christ. I am baptized in the name of Jesus Christ. I follow Christ." If you follow Christ, and I follow Christ, and we all follow Christ, is Christ divided? We are not divided. We are one. Thank God for that. The only reason you can be divided is because you are following man. No matter how spiritual these men are, you are using them.

Paul said, "Who is Paul? Who is Apollos? They are but God's servants. I plant, Apollos waters, but God gives the increase." We apostles are nothing. We are merely God's servants, God's instruments. If we are faithful, we will receive our reward, but it is God who gives the increase. Why do you think so much of us? Why be so small? You say, "Paul is mine." Yes, Paul is yours. You say, "Apollos is mine." Yes, Apollos is yours. You say, "Cephas is mine." Yes, Cephas is yours, but remember that you have not only Paul, you have Apollos and Cephas as well. All are yours. Do not just take Paul alone; take also Apollos and Cephas, because God has given all these servants to you. All are yours, but you are Christ's, and Christ is God's. If we only see Christ and no one else, then the party spirit is gone, the division is gone. We have one mind; we speak one word—Jesus. That is the solution. The solution is not trying to figure, argue or reason out things. The solution is a revelation of Jesus Christ.

Then there was the problem of that grievous sin of incest in their midst. And the church was so insensitive—yet, not only insensitive but even proud. Think of that! One among the Corinthian believers had committed a grievous sin, but the whole church looked upon that sin as though it were nothing, and they were proud of themselves as though they were so liberal and broadminded. There was no discipline; everything was loose. Yet they thought of it all as their being liberal and broadminded.

What is the solution? "Purge out the old leaven, that ye may be a new lump, according as ye are unleavened. For also our Passover, Christ, has been sacrificed; so that let us celebrate the feast, not with old leaven, nor with leaven of malice and wickedness, but with unleavened bread of sincerity and truth" (I Corinthians 5:7-8).

Let us remember Christ, our Passover. Let us remember how Christ offered himself spotless unto God. Let us remember how His blood was shed for the remission of our sins. Let us remember how His body was broken. We may eat the flesh of the Lamb that will give us strength to walk upon this earth pure and blameless. Let us remember Christ, our Passover. We are today celebrating the unleavened feast. In the Old Testament time, Passover was just one day, but immediately following Passover, the children of Israel had to keep the feast of unleavened bread for seven days. In their house, in their country, there should be no leaven found because they had to celebrate the feast with unleavened bread.

We who have had our Passover are today in the feast of unleavened bread. We should live upon this earth not with the old leaven of malice and wickedness but with the unleavened bread of sincerity and truth. If we are celebrating the feast of unleavened bread today, can we allow sin to exist in our midst?

Leaven in the Scripture speaks of something that will ferment, that will corrupt—either wicked conduct or evil doctrine. These should not exist in the church. We must purge ourselves from these things because we are in the feast of unleavened bread, celebrating what the Lord Jesus has done for us.

These Corinthian believers also had the problem of suing one another. Oh, what a shame! Paul said, "You are a brother; you should be willing to be defrauded." I wonder how many today are willing to be defrauded. You should not defraud others, but you should *be* willing to be defrauded. In the first place, if you have any problems in your midst, and if you are willing to be defrauded, then there *is* no problem! In the second place, if you are not willing to be defrauded and a brother defrauds you, is there not any wise brother in your midst who can help to settle your differences? Why do you go to the world, which you supposedly despise, to settle your account? Is that not a shame? You have been washed; you have been justified in the name of the Lord Jesus and by the Spirit of our God; you have been bought with a price. Therefore, now glorify God in your body. If only we see how much God has forgiven us in Christ Jesus, if only we see that this body belongs to Him and we are not our own, that He has bought us with a price, then we will not do anything to bring shame to His name. We would rather suffer and be defrauded, if necessary, than to have His name suffer because of us.

What about marriage problems? Very simply, Paul says, "As the Lord has divided to each, as God has called each, so let him walk" (I Corinthians 7:17a).

Whatever God has called you to, whatever He has given you, walk in it. If God gives you a family, thank God for it. Raise that family for the glory of God. If God does not give you a family and gives you the grace to remain single, then remain single. If the husband dies or the wife dies and you want to be remarried, that is fine, but marry those in the Lord. In other words, "Just as the Lord has given to each." It is not something forced, but everything is just as the Lord has divided to us and called us. How wonderful! That will solve all the marriage problems.

In chapters 8—10 you find this matter of social functions and activities, and the solution is the love of Christ. Knowledge puffs up, but love edifies. You can eat anything which is put on the table if you bless it. Thank God for it; it is given to you. But if you are eating and drinking, eat and drink and do all things to the glory of God. Paul said, "If I eat meat and a weak brother is offended, then I will not eat meat anymore. It is not that I cannot eat. I *can* eat, for I have the liberty, but for the brother's sake I will not eat. Do all things to the glory of God."

What about this matter of head covering? Is it such a burden for a sister to have a cover upon her head? Yet does it mean that only the sisters need to have a head covering and the brothers do not need to have their heads covered? No. Paul said in I Corinthians 11:3: "Christ is the head of every man, but woman's head is the man, and the Christ's head God."

If we could but see the divine order, then we would find it to be a privilege; it is not a burden. If we see Christ, He who is equal with God but who nonetheless submitted himself to God and had His head covered before Him, then it is our glory if we can have *our* heads covered before Christ. And if the sisters would bear the symbol as a reminder to the brothers that they need to be covered before God, is not that something beautiful?

How about the Lord's Table? It is the same thing. Paul said, "Do away with the love feast; it is not commanded." On that day with His disciples the Lord had only directed us to have the Lord's Supper. If we cannot have the feast in the proper way to help celebrate the Lord's Supper, then do away with it. The important thing is to remember the Lord. We are in communion with His blood; we are in communion with His body. Even though we are many, yet we are one loaf, one body.

How about spiritual gifts? If only we would see that spiritual gifts are the manifestation of the Holy Spirit. The Holy Spirit, according to His will, gives gifts to different members of the body of Christ for the building up of the body in love. Gifts are not for personal display.

What about resurrection? If Christ, being the first fruits, is resurrected, then, of course, we too will be resurrected. There is no problem even if you find it difficult to imagine how every atom of your body will be gathered together again and become your resurrected body. Some have observed as follows: "After you die and are buried, then probably you are corrupted and go back into the earth. Then some grass will grow up and the cow will eat the grass. Some of your body goes into that cow, which is then eaten by somebody else, and on it goes. So how can you be resurrected?"

Perhaps you find it is a problem, but there is no problem with God. As a matter of fact, scientifically, every seven years all the cells in the body undergo a complete change. Seven years ago you were a different person, so far as the body is concerned. There is no problem because in resurrection we shall be clothed with a spiritual body, not a physical one. It will be a spiritual body, a million times more beautiful and glorious. Today, we have this body of humiliation; but one day, we will be clothed in resurrection with a body of glory just like Christ's body in His resurrection. And thus, there is no problem.

What about giving? Let us remember that He who was rich became poor for us that in His poverty we may be enriched.

How about submission? If the Son has been obedient to the Father through the things which He has suffered, even unto death, and that the death of the cross, why can we not submit to one another and to those whom God has put before us? We are not submitting to man. Submit to *Him*. If we see Him, there is no problem.

What about love? If anyone does not love the Lord Jesus Christ, let him be Anathema Maranatha. *Anathema* means "cursed." *Maranatha* means "the Lord is coming." Oh, first love is so precious. Oh, that we may not lose our first love, that we may love Him with all our hearts. Let us not allow anything to come in and take away our love for Christ. Let our hearts be undivided towards Him. Let the love of Christ constrain us. If we want His love to fill us, let us think of how much He loves us and then we will learn to love one another. And thus there will be no problem, for the solution is Jesus. If only we have a revelation of the Lord Jesus Christ, then all these problems are solved and spiritually we grow.

What is the instrument, the means, which God uses to deliver us out of our flesh and get us into Christ? The cross. Therefore, Paul said, "I am determined to know nothing among you but Jesus Christ and Him crucified."

Do we see ourselves on the cross of the Lord Jesus? I think there is one person who should know this in a very deep, personal way, and that is Barabbas. Barabbas was a murderer. He was supposed to be crucified that day; but in God's sovereignty, someone was crucified in his stead—the Lord Jesus Christ. I wonder if Barabbas went off to Calvary's hill to see the Lord Jesus crucified there. If so, I wonder if he said to himself: "I should be there, but He died in my stead." I wonder if it affected his life so much that from then on he could not live again in his former murderous ways. He would have had to live as that Man lived.

Let us see that it is the cross. May we realize that on the cross we were crucified in Him and with Him. Therefore, no longer I live, it is Christ who lives in me. And if it is Christ who lives in me, I am delivered from carnality and delivered from all my problems. May the Lord help us.

Dear heavenly Father, we do praise and thank Thee for all our problems, knowing that these problems only drive us to Christ. Oh, how we praise and thank Thee that Christ is the solution to all our problems. We pray that when we are with problems that Thou wilt open our eyes to see Thy Son, our Lord Jesus. We ask that our problems will become our blessings. In the name of our Lord Jesus. Amen.

II CORINTHIANS

SEEING CHRIST IN SPIRITUALITY

II Corinthians 1:3-7—Blessed be the God and Father of our Lord Jesus Christ, the Father of compassions, and God of all encouragement; who encourages us in all our tribulation, that we may be able to encourage those who are in any tribulation whatever, through the encouragement with which we ourselves are encouraged of God. Because, even as the sufferings of the Christ abound towards us, so through the Christ does our encouragement also abound. But whether we are in tribulation, it is for your encouragement and salvation, wrought in the endurance of the same sufferings which we also suffer, (and our hope for you is sure;) or whether we are encouraged, it is for your encouragement and salvation: knowing that as ye are partakers of the sufferings, so also of the encouragement.

II Corinthians 13:11—For the rest, brethren, rejoice; be perfected; be encouraged; be of one mind; be at peace; and the God of love and peace shall be with you.

Let us pray:

Dear heavenly Father, we commit Thy word into Thy hand and ask Thee to bless it and break it, and distribute to us that we may be fed, we may be satisfied, that we may glorify Thy name. We commit this time into Thy hand and trust Thy Holy Spirit to do the work. In the name of our Lord Jesus. Amen.

The book of II Corinthians is very different from I Corinthians. In I Corinthians we find problems upon problems, but in II Corinthians we see glory upon glory. In I Corinthians we see carnality—saved, yes, but living according to the flesh. In II Corinthians we see spirituality—saved and living in the spirit. In I Corinthians we see the pitiful condition of the Corinthian church. In II Corinthians we see the glorious life of Paul, a servant of the Lord. What makes the difference between I Corinthians and II Corinthians is actually the working of the cross in lives. If we allow the cross to work in our lives, then we will be delivered from carnality and brought into spirituality.

The book of II Corinthians reveals to us Christ in spirituality. In other words, spirituality is Christ. If it is not Christ, in each and every aspect of our life, it is not spiritual. On the contrary, if it is you or me in each aspect, then it is bound to be something carnal; but if it is Christ in you or Christ in me, then that is spiritual. It is as simple as that.

As far as the historical background is concerned, Paul probably wrote this second letter to the Corinthians somewhere in Macedonia around 57 A.D. In Acts 20:1-6 you can find the occasion or background for this letter. It was during that period that Paul wrote this second letter to the Corinthians, and this was to be followed by a three-month stay in Corinth. He wrote this letter after he had heard good news from Corinth. When he wrote the first letter, he wrote it in tears. Now, through Titus, good news was brought to him that many in the church in Corinth had repented, and because of this he wrote this letter as one of encouragement.

In the first chapter he said, "Blessed be the God and Father of our Lord Jesus Christ, the Father of compassions, and God of all encouragement." In some versions, the word *comfort* is used instead of *encouragement*, but actually in the original it means "comfort, strengthening, encouraging." It is the complementary word for the name given to the Holy Spirit. Elsewhere in the New Testament the Holy Spirit is called *parakletos (comforter)*, and here in II Corinthians it is *paraklesis*. This latter word's multiple meaning is: "to comfort, encourage, console, strengthen, come alongside, help." This is the kind of letter II Corinthians really is.

Paul wrote this letter to encourage those who have repented—to strengthen them, to come alongside them, and to help them into maturity and spirituality. Therefore, at the beginning of this letter he mentioned: "Whether we are in sufferings, it is for your encouragement and salvation." In our encouragement or comfort "it is for your encouragement and salvation." Then at the end of the letter he concludes with, "For the rest, brethren, rejoice, be perfected [that is, be mature, grow up]; be encouraged [or strengthened]; be of one mind; be at peace; and the God of love and peace shall be with you" (II Corinthians 13:11).

This is a letter of encouragement. However, we know from this letter and from its background that even though the majority of the people in Corinth had repented, there were still some who continued in sin and refused to repent. There were still some who opposed the ministry of the apostle Paul. In the same letter he mentions that on this account he writes these things being absent, so that later, being present, he need not use severity according to the authority which the Lord gave him for building up and not for overthrowing (see II Corinthians 10). Paul wrote this letter to prepare those who refused to repent and opposed the authority that God had given him. In essence, this was a two-edged sword. On the one hand, it is for encouragement to those who repent, and on the other hand, it is for serving as a warning to those who refuse to repent.

This letter of Paul's is one that gives us a most intimate view of the apostle as a person. Of all his writings there are two letters which, in a sense, expose, disclose and reveal the man Paul as a person. One of those two letters is Philippians. There he opens his heart to the Philippian believers who love him so much. There is a mutual love between Paul and these believers, and so he has a heart-to-heart talk with them.

The other letter is II Corinthians. There is no other letter aside from the Philippian letter which reveals so much about Paul as a person, as a man. He exposes himself, as it were, without even the thinnest artificial veil. He lets us see himself as he is. That is the reason II Corinthians is so precious. There you discover all the different feelings of Paul are being revealed. Sometimes he is in anger; sometimes he is in anguish; at other times he is in fear; or he is hesitating; or he is bold; and sometimes he is full of love. Every kind of feeling is revealed in this letter. Through it we can see Paul the man; but gradually, we find Paul recedes and Christ comes to the fore. And thus we see Christ in Paul.

In this letter Paul mentions that the sentence of death was upon him. He gives up every hope of even living; and yet he says our hope is in Him who raised Christ from the dead.

In this letter we see that Paul changed his mind. He was thinking of going to Corinth to pay them a double visit, but when he was in Troas, he changed his mind. Instead of going to Corinth, he went to Macedonia, and people accused him of being a person who vacillates. Yes, he changed, but he declared that, "the Christ whom I preach is always 'yea' and always 'amen'—and He never changes." The apostle Paul reveals to us that he always has the dying of Jesus in him, yet the life of Jesus is also being manifested in him (see II Corinthians 4:10).

In this letter Paul mentions how much he has suffered, and yet out of all these sufferings, what consolation, what encouragement, what ministry has been produced! All in all, we can discern one thing, that when Paul is exposing himself, opening himself up to us—all his weaknesses; all his changeableness; all his failures, as it were, in people's eyes; all his pains and sufferings—we do not see Paul; we see Christ. And that is spirituality.

This second letter to the Corinthians can be roughly divided into three parts:

Chapters 1—7 Spiritual Ministry

Chapters 8—9	Spiritual Giving
Chapters 10—13	Spiritual Man

Spiritual Ministry

Paul said, "Having this ministry ..." (4:1). Of course, we do not all have the kind of ministry which Paul had. God had given him a special ministry, the ministry of an apostle. Not all are apostles; we have not all been given that special ministry. However, when Paul speaks about ministry, and even though he is speaking about *his* ministry, the principles he reveals apply to all ministries. Every believer has a ministry. Whether we fulfill it or not, that is the question. Nevertheless, every believer has a ministry because we are all priests unto God. Our ministry is called body ministry. We are members of the body, and every member has a ministry towards the body and towards the Head. Everyone has to minister one to another in the body for the building up of the body and the glorifying of the Head.

Do realize that you have a ministry to fulfill as a member of the body of Christ. You are not simply here sitting passively, receiving all the time, but you are also in the body to give. You are to receive what the Lord has through other brothers and sisters who minister to you, and at the same time you are to minister to your brothers and sisters. So, in principle, the ministry which we are all to be engaged in ought to be a spiritual ministry. If what we minister to other people is ourselves, it is not spiritual ministry; but if we minister Christ to other people, then it is. If we minister ourselves to people, it is a ministry of death; but if we minister Christ to people, it is one of life. It is very important that we understand what spiritual ministry really is so that when we minister it will be spiritual and not carnal.

In I Corinthians the members of the body ministered; but the more they ministered, the worse the body became. It is because they were not ministering Christ to the body; they were ministering themselves. They displayed themselves instead of displaying Christ. We need to understand what spiritual ministry truly is because we are all involved in it. Do not be fearful. In a parable which our Lord Jesus mentioned, there was a servant who was afraid whether he would be ministering spiritually or carnally, so he buried his talent. He thought it was the best thing for him to do so he would not make any mistakes. When his master came back, he told him he was a wicked and lazy servant. Even if he felt unable to do anything, he could at least have taken his talent to the bank to gain interest (see Matthew 25:27).

Let us not try to hide what the Lord has given us by burying it. Let us use it for the Lord, and in the process we will learn what is spiritual and what is carnal.

A Ministry of Encouragement

What is spiritual ministry? Spiritual ministry is a ministry of encouragement. We have already mentioned that encouragement means "comfort, strengthening, coming alongside to help." The Holy Spirit is the Comforter, the Strengthener, the Parakletos, the One who comes alongside and helps. And our ministry, if it is spiritual, should be of the same nature and have the same quality. However, in order to have such a ministry of encouragement, let us recognize that it does not arise just by knowledge; it has to come about by personal experience. In other words, we cannot comfort, strengthen, or encourage a person if all we have is nothing but words. Perhaps they are even the right words, but they are not the words of power.

Sometimes, we are like the three friends of Job. They came to visit him with good intention. They wanted to help, yet the more they tried to help the worse it became because they did not have such experience. All their words came from their studies or from tradition. As we read the book of Job we will find that what they said was right, but unfortunately, those words of theirs did not apply. Sometimes you may say the right words but to the wrong person, and therefore, that person is not comforted or encouraged.

Here we are told of the sufferings the apostle Paul had gone through. He said, "The sentence of death was upon me. I had given up all hope. It was a hopeless case." But when he was in that kind of situation, the Lord lifted him out of it, and he experienced the power of the resurrection of the Lord Jesus. Having such experience, he could comfort those who, too, were helpless and hopeless. He could say to the Corinthian believers that they were helpless and yet not hopeless. There is still hope but the hope was not to be found in them. The hope is in God. *He* is our hope. God is a God of all comfort and a Father of all compassion.

When we try to minister to one another, is it merely out of our studies, out of tradition, or out of our minds? We may have the best of intentions, but it will be of no avail. If God would use us to encourage our brothers and sisters, oftentimes, it will arise out of our personal experience. Probably, we will have to go through much in order to help others; but let us remember that God never allows us to go through anything just for ourselves. Whatever we have gone through in life and however we have learned Christ, it is for the body. It is for ministry in order that we may have something to offer, that we may have something to give to the church.

A Ministry of Love

Spiritual ministry is also a ministry of love. Paul said in II Corinthians 2:4: "For out of much tribulation and distress of heart I wrote to you, with many tears; not that ye may be grieved, but that ye may know the love which I have very abundantly towards you."

Paul's first letter seemed to be a very harsh letter, a very strong letter, but he said, "I wrote it out of much tribulation and distress of heart. Oh, I was agonizing even with tears; I wrote it with tears. It is not that I want to put you to grief, but it is because I love you so much." It was written out of love.

Let us all realize that we are not here simply trying to please everybody. It is relatively easy trying to please everyone, but sometimes it is difficult to hurt someone in love. Paul knew that his letter would hurt the Corinthian believers very deeply, but because he loved them so much he could not afford not to speak the truth in love. In a sense, you will see that it cost Paul even more than it cost them. If our ministry does not cost us anything, it is nothing. Ministry must come from our love, but it is not human love. Human love will try to please everyone, and in pleasing others, we please ourselves, too. Divine love, agape love, loves so much that we are able even to hurt, if necessary; but of course, we hurt ourselves first. It is a ministry of love. Oh, that God will fill us with His love so that we may love one another so much that we are able to speak the truth in love! It is not a matter of trying to hurt everyone; yet sometimes, if it is necessary, it has to be done. It may hurt us more than the one who will be hurt.

A Ministry of the Fragrance of Christ

Spiritual ministry is a ministry of the fragrance of Christ. Paul said in II Corinthians 2:14-15: "But thanks be to God, who always leads us in triumph in the Christ, and makes manifest the odour of his knowledge through us in every place. For we are a sweet odour of Christ to God, in the saved and in those that perish."

Fragrance is a most mysterious thing. It is seemingly intangible. You cannot see it, you cannot hear it, but it is here, nonetheless, and you smell it. You know it is present. Oftentimes, odor or fragrance goes further than sight and sound. You may not yet hear anything, you may not yet see anything, but you have already smelled it. And sometimes it has a more lasting effect upon you, too. Sound may come and go; sight may be seen and then lost; but odor you may carry with you for quite awhile.

In Jeremiah 48:11 the prophet speaks there about Moab: "Moab hath been at ease from his youth, and hath settled on his lees; he hath not been emptied from vessel to vessel, neither hath he gone into captivity: therefore his taste hath remained in him, and his scent is not changed."

When you make wine, you have to pour it from vessel to vessel so that all the sediments will sink down and the wine will be clear and pure. But Moab had never been emptied; he had never been dealt with. He had such a comfortable time. He was always settling on his lees. The result was that his taste had never changed; his scent had never changed; he had the same smell about him. What was that smell? It was the arrogance of Moab. Moab was proud and arrogant.

That is a description of the natural man. That, too, is the description of a carnal Christian. A carnal Christian is one who has not been dealt with. He remains the same. Even though he is saved, yet he has not been emptied from vessel to vessel; he has not been purified. And because the cross has never worked in his life, the result is that his taste remains the same. His scent is not changed. You can still smell the original odor. But thank God, Paul said that wherever we go, we are to carry the fragrance of Christ. Paul has been emptied from vessel to vessel. All the original taste and scent have gone and now it is the fragrance of Christ. To those who are saved it is life; to those who are perishing it is death. A spiritual ministry does not require words to speak or even deeds to do. A spiritual ministry is the very presence of that person who does the work and speaks the word. We who are the followers of Christ ought to have a special scent. Wherever we go people will smell the fragrance of Christ which comes from the experiential knowledge of

Christ. The more we know Him the more fragrant we are, and this is a ministry.

A Ministry of the Spirit

A spiritual ministry is a ministry of the Spirit. In this letter's chapter 3 Paul wrote: "We are writing the epistle of Christ." The church in Corinth—the Corinthian believers—is a letter, and it ought to be a letter of Christ. In other words, the Corinthian church is to be read, and when people read it, they ought to read Christ. They ought to see Christ because the Corinthian church is supposed to be a letter of Christ. Paul is the scribe, the ink he used is the Holy Spirit, and the letter he writes is Christ. By the power of the Holy Spirit he is writing Christ, alphabet letter by alphabet letter, upon the hearts of the Corinthian believers. And that is what we are to be—we are to be a letter of Christ.

That is what spiritual ministry is. We are writing upon human hearts, not on stones. We are not merely writing upon people's minds; we are writing upon their hearts. Yet how do we write? What ink do we use? It is to be the power of the Holy Spirit, and it is to be Christ that we write upon human hearts. We do not preach ourselves; we preach Jesus Christ the Lord. Such should be our ministry.

Therefore, in these first four chapters of II Corinthians Paul shows us what spiritual ministry is. It is a ministry of encouragement, a ministry of love, a ministry of the fragrance of Christ, and it is a ministry of the Spirit.

The Minister

In chapters 4 and 5 Paul shows us what kind of minister he is. The first four chapters show us the ministry, but chapters 4 and 5 reveal to us the minister. He said, "Having this ministry ..." Now what do we do? What kind of person should we be?

This is important, since ministry has much to do with the minister. If we are the wrong person, we will not have the right ministry. Even if the Lord may use us to build up, we will soon tear down everything we have built up and more. So the minister is very important—what kind of vessel he is.

A Pure Vessel

"Therefore, having this ministry, as we have had mercy shewn us, we faint not. But we have rejected the hidden things of shame, not walking in deceit, nor falsifying the word of God, but by manifestation of the truth commending ourselves to every conscience of men before God" (II Corinthians 4:1-2).

When we try to minister, remember, we are commending ourselves to every conscience of men before God. We are not merely ministers with words and deeds, we are not merely trying to serve brothers and sisters with the gifts which God has given us; it is much more than that. When we minister, we are actually commending ourselves to the consciences of our brothers and sisters. If in their consciences there is an accusation, or some ground for them to doubt, then our ministry is hindered; our ministry is broken. We need to commend ourselves. The vessel has to be pure. If there is any impurity there, anything hidden, it will affect the ministry. How we need to be pure before God! Oh, that the Spirit of God will search our hearts that He may purify us, that there will be no ulterior motive in us, that our whole motive will be towards Him! We need to commend ourselves to the conscience of all the brethren before God, and for this we need the blood of the Lord Jesus.

A Broken Vessel

The vessel must also be a broken vessel. We cannot keep ourselves intact. If we try to keep ourselves whole, that is, try to keep our soul-life whole, the radiance of the treasure in us will be hidden. We are vessels, earthen vessels, but we have a treasure in us, and the power of the radiance is of God and not of us. Yet, for the light of God to come forth, these vessels of ours must be broken and then the inner life of Christ may be manifested. That is the reason why Paul said, "In every way afflicted, but not straitened." We may be afflicted, but not crushed; we may see no apparent issue, but our way is not entirely shut up.

Oftentimes, we are brought to our wit's end but not to our life's end. "Persecuted but not abandoned. Knocked down but not knocked out. Bearing in our body the slaying of Jesus that the life of Jesus may be manifested in us and may be manifested in you." Such, then, is a broken vessel, and only in and through such a vessel can Christ be ministered. Otherwise, all that we minister is ourselves. People will touch our cleverness or our dynamic personality, but people cannot touch Christ.

A Constrained Vessel

A minister is a constrained vessel. In chapter 5 Paul declared this: "I am constrained with a love of Christ, knowing that one died for all, that all died, so that they who live no longer live for themselves, but for him who died and lives for them."

How we need to be constrained by the love of Christ, not constrained out of duty but out of love. When the love of Christ constrains us, then we are able to be that vessel which is fit for the master's use.

The Ministered

In chapters 6 and 7 we learn about the ministered. In the first four chapters we see the ministry, in chapters 4 and 5 the minister, and in 6 and 7 the ministered—those who are being ministered to. We learn here that those who are being ministered to have their responsibility as well.

"We also beseech that ye receive not the grace of God in vain" (II Corinthians 6:1). The grace of God has been ministered to you. Christ has been ministered to you. Do not receive the grace of God in vain. In other words, do not let the grace of God carelessly fall away from you; rather, let it work in your life, so that you too may be gracious.

"Be not diversely yoked with unbelievers" (II Corinthians 6:14). Be separated; do not be unequally yoked with the world. Come out from the world and be separated. And God said, "Then you shall be my sons and my daughters."

"Having therefore these promises, beloved, let us purify ourselves from every pollution of flesh and spirit, perfecting holiness in God's fear" (II Corinthians 7:1). Let us purify not only our body—our flesh, but even our spirit, being perfected in holiness in the fear of God. This is spiritual ministry.

Spiritual Giving

Chapters 8 and 9 speak of spiritual giving, and giving is a spiritual ministry. Let us not think giving, which is something physical or material, is not spiritual. As a matter of fact, oftentimes, we will find that the test of spirituality is in giving. We should give spiritually because giving is spiritual. To a carnal person it is getting, but to a spiritual person it is giving. Giving oftentimes reveals what kind of person we are. Today, we separate giving from so-called spiritual ministry as though it is not spiritual. However, according to the word of God, giving is as spiritual as any other ministry because it is according to the giving of God. God gives and He gives in a particular way. Christ gives. "He being rich ..." Who is as rich as Christ? And yet for our sakes He became poor that we might be enriched in Him. That is giving.

Giving is to be patterned after God's giving; giving is in the spirit of the giving of Christ. That is the reason why it is called "grace" in the Scriptures to be found in chapters 8 and 9.

Why is it grace? Because it is the grace of God that enables us to give. All that we have comes from Him. It is His grace that constrains us to give.

Giving is also called blessing because as we are blessed by God, we bless Him by giving. Do not think that giving is law. Today, people think of giving as law. Who can keep the law? But giving is grace. Paul said, "Look at the Macedonians. Because of the abundant grace of God upon them, out of their deep poverty, they gave abundantly beyond their measure. They did not just give material things but they gave themselves to God first and to us apostles so that they might have a part in the grace and fellowship that we are engaged with of helping the poor in Jerusalem." That is grace.

Let us give graciously, let us give as He gives. Let us give in a spiritual way and not in a legalistic way, as though we cannot get out of it. Let us give because God has been gracious to us. God has blessed us so much. We have to bless Him; we have to show grace that He may be glorified. Give until Christ is glorified. That is spiritual giving.

Spiritual Man

In chapters 10—13 Paul focuses upon the spiritual man. It is not only a ministry that is spiritual, not only a giving that is spiritual, but also the man himself is spiritual. Paul writes as follows: "A spiritual man is a man in Christ. I know a man in Christ. Fourteen years ago he was caught up to the third heaven; whether he was in the body or out of the body, I do not know. He was caught away to Paradise and heard things unutterable, and for that man I boast, but for myself I have nothing to boast of but my weaknesses."

Who is a spiritual man? He is a man in Christ. God has blessed us with every spiritual blessing in the heavenlies in Christ (see Ephesians 1:3). If we abide in Christ, we will find that every spiritual blessing is ours, yet not in ourselves but in

Christ. God has put us all in Christ, but we need to abide in Him. Positionally, by His grace, we are all in Christ, and we ought to be spiritual men and women. But conditionally, we may or may not abide in Him. If we abide in Him and make our home in Him, then we shall bear fruit to the glory of God.

Paul said, "I do not know whether that man was in the body or out of the body." We may think he is not telling the truth. Of course he is telling the truth. He knows the man in Christ, but when that man experienced the third heaven and Paradise, he did not know whether it was a case of being in the body or out of the body. He is trying to tell us: "Of that man in Christ I had much to boast, but of myself there is nothing to boast of except my weaknesses."

A spiritual man is one who does not speak about himself. A spiritual man is a man who is not even conscious of himself. A spiritual man forgets himself, and all he is conscious of is Christ.

In these few chapters there are a number of things concerning the spiritual man. He is a man powerful according to God. He is not a man fighting in the flesh but is one whose arm of warfare is powerful before God—divinely powerful.

The spiritual man is not a man of argument but of prayer. He is a man of prayer because he is powerful according to God, even to the extent of overthrowing all the strongholds of the enemy, all the thoughts and imaginations of the mind, carrying them into captivity and bringing them into obedience of Christ.

A spiritual man is one having authority, yet not the natural authority of position but the spiritual authority of love.

A spiritual man is one possessed of the holy zeal of God. For he says, as did Paul: "I am jealous as to you with a jealousy which is of God; for I have espoused you unto one man, to present you a chaste virgin to Christ" (II Corinthians 11:2). This is just as the Lord had said, "The zeal of thy house devours me" (John 2:17b).

A spiritual man is one who suffers for the sake of Christ.

Paul mentioned how much he had suffered—physically, mentally and spiritually. All the cares of all the churches are upon his heart. He said, "Who is stumbled, and I burn not?" (II Corinthians 11:29)

A spiritual man is someone with visions and revelations. The Lord has shown him His purpose.

A spiritual man is a man who knows the sufficient grace of God. He knows that God said, "My grace is sufficient for thee."

Such, then, is a spiritual man. In a word: *A spiritual man is a man in Christ; a spiritual man is Christ in that man.*

So, II Corinthians reveals to us Christ in spirituality. We all ought to be spiritual. Our ministry ought to be spiritual so that it will truly build up the body of Christ. Our giving ought to be spiritual so that God may be glorified. Our person ought to be spiritual so that Christ may be manifested. Yet what is spirituality? In sum, spirituality is a Person—Christ. Christ in you is spirituality.

May the Lord help us.

Dear heavenly Father, we do praise and thank Thee because Thou hast put Christ in us and put us in Christ. We praise and thank Thee that all the secret is there, all the power is there, all the glory is there. We only ask that Thou wilt open our eyes and our understanding and our heart so that we may see Christ as our spiritual ministry, our spiritual giving, and even our spiritual person, that we may see Him as our all. Oh, do reveal Christ to us in an increasing manner so that we may be transformed and conformed to His image, to the glory of God. In the name of our Lord Jesus. Amen.

GALATIANS

Seeing Christ through Errors

Galatians 1:6-17—I wonder that ye thus quickly change, from him that called you in Christ's grace, to a different gospel, which is not another one; but there are some that trouble you, and desire to pervert the glad tidings of the Christ. But if even we or an angel out of heaven announce as glad tidings to you anything besides what we have announced as glad tidings to you, let him be accursed. As we have said before, now also again I say, If any one announce to you as glad tidings anything besides what ye have received, let him be accursed. For do I now seek to satisfy men or God? or do I seek to please men? If I were yet pleasing men, I were not Christ's bondman. But I let you know, brethren, as to the glad tidings which were announced by me, that they are not according to man. For neither did I receive them from man, neither was I taught them, but by revelation of Jesus Christ. For ye have heard what was my conversation formerly in Judaism, that I excessively persecuted the assembly of God, and ravaged it; and advanced in Judaism beyond many my contemporaries in my nation, being exceedingly zealous of the doctrines of my fathers. But when God, who set me apart even from my mother's womb, and called me by his grace, was pleased to reveal his Son in me, that I may announce him as glad tidings among the nations, immediately I took not counsel with flesh and blood, nor went I up to Jerusalem to those who were apostles before me; but I went to Arabia, and again returned to Damascus.

Galatians 3:1-3—O senseless Galatians, who has bewitched you; to whom, as before your very eyes, Jesus Christ has been portrayed, crucified among you? This only

I wish to learn of you, Have ye received the Spirit on the principle of works of law, or of the report of faith? Are ye so senseless? having begun in Spirit, are ye going to be made perfect in flesh?

Galatians 6:11-18 — See how long a letter I have written to you with my own hand. (Some versions say, "What large letters I have written to you with my own hand.") As many as desire to have a fair appearance in the flesh, these compel you to be circumcised, only that they may not be persecuted because of the cross of Christ. For neither do they that are circumcised themselves keep the law; but they wish you to be circumcised, that they may boast in your flesh. But far be it from me to boast save in the cross of our Lord Jesus Christ, through whom the world is crucified to me, and I to the world. For in Christ Jesus neither is circumcision anything, nor uncircumcision; but new creation. And as many as shall walk by this rule, peace upon them and mercy, and upon the Israel of God. For the rest let no one trouble me, for I bear in my body the brands of the Lord Jesus. The grace of our Lord Jesus Christ be with your spirit, brethren. Amen.

Let us pray:

Dear heavenly Father, we do look to Thy Holy Spirit to illumine Thy word, to bring Thy word to our hearts that we may not only understand, but we may enter into Thy truth. We commit this time into Thy hands, and may Thy Son be glorified. In the name of our Lord Jesus. Amen.

We have mentioned many times that the Bible is the revelation of Jesus Christ. It is the will of God that in every book of the Bible, each of the sixty-six books, we would see Jesus. If we do not see Jesus in any book of the Bible, then we miss the very reason why God has given us His word. We shall see Jesus in His many aspects within many different settings.

Now we would like to enter into the letter to the Galatians.

We may say that this letter enables us to see Christ through error—doctrinal error. We know from Acts 13 and 14 that the Holy Spirit set apart Barnabas and Paul to do apostolic work. As they started their work they first visited some cities in Galatia—Antioch of Pisidia, Iconium, Lystra and Derbe. They preached the gospel of Jesus Christ in these places, and many came to the Lord. Churches were established. We can say these churches in Galatia were the first love of the apostle Paul because they were his first work. Again and again, he visited them. Almost every journey that he made afterward he passed through Galatia. But within ten years time, towards the end of his third apostolic journey, Paul had to write a letter to the believers in Galatia combating that basic doctrinal error which had come in among them.

Now what is that doctrinal error which Paul addresses in his letter to the Galatian believers? When we compare I Corinthians with the letter to the Galatians, we find the Corinthian believers had many problems, but mostly these were moral and practical issues. Even though they did have some doctrinal problems, it was not to be compared with all the problems they had morally and in their practical lives. But the Galatian believers had only one problem, not many like the Corinthians, and it was a problem of doctrine, a problem of truth. And because of this error, it affected their daily lives. With respect to the Corinthian believers, they did not want to go on with the Lord. They thought that to be saved was enough for them. They were content to be babes all their lives, to be taken care of and taking no responsibility of their own. So they remained in babyhood, in carnality. They did not grow into sons and daughters of God, and how it grieved the heart of God.

But with respect to the Galatian believers, it was almost the exact opposite. After they had believed in the Lord Jesus, they desired so much to grow into perfection that they began to be enticed into an error that promised them instant spirituality. Paul's reaction, or may we say God's reaction, as seen in Paul, was even stronger towards the Galatian believers than towards the Corinthian believers. Paul wrote a very severe letter to the churches in Galatia in which we can sense the very agony of his heart. When he wrote I Corinthians, he shed many tears; but I think probably when he wrote this letter to the Galatians, he really wept and cried over it. His heart was truly broken because there was a basic error in their midst which would destroy not only the work of Paul there but the very gospel of Jesus Christ.

Now what is the error which Paul had to combat in this letter to the Galatians? It is that of "another gospel." There are two different Greek words for "another." One is *allos*—"another of the same kind." And the other is *heteros*—"another of a different kind." This "another gospel" which Paul was talking about was not *allos* but *heteros*. It is not a gospel which comes along with the gospel of Jesus Christ. On the contrary, it is a gospel opposite to the gospel of Jesus Christ. It was being preached as a gospel but it was not a gospel; it was bad news, not good news. The only gospel that is really good news is the gospel of Jesus Christ. In other words, Jesus Christ is the gospel; He is the good news. If anything is preached aside from the Lord Jesus, that is not glad tidings; it is bad tidings because it will lead us into destruction.

This "another gospel" which Paul had to combat with such spirit was a mixture of law and grace. The gospel of Jesus Christ, though, is the gospel of grace. Nevertheless, some Judaizers had come to the churches in Galatia. Probably, these Judaizers were Jews, perhaps of the sect of the Pharisees, who had been converted to Christianity. They had accepted the Lord Jesus, yet they were still clinging to their Judaism.

Even in the very early days some Judaizers had come from Jerusalem to Antioch. And they had begun to tell the believers there, who were mostly Gentiles, that they needed to be circumcised and to keep the law of Moses; otherwise, they were not saved nor could they be perfected. Because of this, there was great discussion and contention there. Finally, the church in Antioch sent Paul and Barnabas and some others to Jerusalem to see the apostles and the elders there in order to settle this very basic question: "Must a Gentile, who believes in the Lord Jesus, be circumcised and keep the law?" Or to put it another way: "Must a Gentile become a Jew in order to be saved and be perfected?"

There was a lengthy discussion in Jerusalem, and thank God, the Holy Spirit and the apostles and elders there decided that the Gentiles did not need to be circumcised or to be Jews. They did not need to keep the law of Moses because nobody could. All they needed to do was abstain from eating blood, abstain from idolatry, and abstain from adultery. Actually, these were not the laws of Moses anyway but were universal laws which went all the way back to the time of Noah. After the flood, God made a covenant with Noah, his children, and all other living beings, and this Noahic covenant is still valid today.

With the decision made in Jerusalem, letters were written and passed on to the different churches in Asia. Yet, strange to say, even with such a decision, this problem was not solved. Even after the council in Jerusalem, some Judaizers went into Asia and Galatia, teaching the believers in Christ Jesus that they must be circumcised, that they must keep the laws of Moses and certain ordinances of the Old Testament law. They mixed up law with grace, though they did not reject Christ outright. They accepted Jesus Christ, but in essence they said He was not enough; He was not sufficient. After a person receives the Lord Jesus, he needs to be circumcised and keep the Mosaic laws and other ordinances in order to be perfected. They Judaized Christianity. They tried to put Christianity into a Judaistic religious mold instead of it being a living relationship with Christ and Christ being everything. They began to reconstruct Christianity into a system, a religion of law, rules, regulations, rituals and ceremonies. By doing that, it would very subtly destroy the very foundation of the gospel of Jesus Christ.

One thing we must never lose sight of, which is human nature. This "another gospel" actually appeals to our human instinct because we always like to *do* something. If everything is *given* to us we feel there is no glory for us; and, hence, our human nature always likes to do something so that we can get some glory out of it, even in this matter of salvation. Why is it that so few receive this gift of God? It is because it is free. If God had demanded something, then probably more would try to measure up, but salvation is free: God has done it all. We cannot do anything. God does not require us to do anything because He knows we cannot. It is freely, universally given to us. And strange to say, because of this, it is too good to be true, it is too free; and so, people do not want to receive it. That is human nature.

Even after people have believed in the Lord Jesus, that human instinct is still there. In other words, when we have tried everything but nothing works and we finally realize that we cannot save ourselves, then and only then do we humble ourselves and accept the free gift of God in Jesus Christ. But even after we have done that, we will still say, "Now let *us* complete it; let us *do* something about it." This is the ongoing human instinct; we always want to do something. So these Judaizers came to the Galatian believers and said, "Well, you believe in the Lord Jesus; that is fine. You need to believe in the Lord Jesus. But if you want to be perfect then you will need to be circumcised and keep the law of Moses. Only then will you be complete." And hence, these Galatian believers fell into that trap because their flesh—their human nature and instinct—loved it.

There is another issue here, and this, too, is a reflection of our human instinct. We like to see everything done quickly. It is our desire that even our success come instantaneously. Oh, if we could arrive immediately, how good that would be! So these Judaizers came into the midst of these Galatian believers and counseled them as follows: "You want to be mature? You want to be perfect? You want to be a success? You want to be spiritual? That is very easy. All you need to do is be circumcised and keep a few rules and regulations. Then you will achieve completeness." How these Galatian believers jumped at this! They said, "Well, that is good because it will make us instantaneously spiritual."

We want everything to be instant. Even when we come to spiritual things, we want to be instantaneously spiritual. So if anyone offers us a gospel—which is really not a gospel but a counterfeit—that will promise us to be spiritual immediately, I am afraid many will go for it just as did the Galatian believers. They were so impatient that they would not allow the Holy Spirit to work day after day in their lives to work Christ into them more and more that they might truly grow up into Him. They thought that was too tedious, too slow. They wanted something quick and immediate, so they accepted it. Of course, we know the result was that they set aside the grace of God. They fell away from His grace. The very foundation of the gospel was destroyed. Instead of glorifying Christ, they glorified self. Instead of receiving the grace of God, they tried to be perfected by the works of law. Instead of faith in Jesus Christ, they trusted in their flesh, and of course, the result was evident. Because of this basic error, their very daily living was adversely affected. The works of the flesh were apparent while the fruit of the Spirit was missing. This is "another gospel"—which is not a gospel—that the apostle Paul had to battle against.

Four centuries ago we had the Reformation. Martin Luther and those other reformers were faced with a situation similar to the one Paul faced in Galatia. Martin Luther and the reformers found themselves faced with a Judaized Christianity. What was Christianity four centuries ago? Christianity was no longer Christ. Christ was buried; the Bible was chained. At that time, people sought salvation, not by faith in Jesus Christ, but by good works. If they accumulated enough merits they would go to heaven; if not, they would go to purgatory.

Christianity at that time had devolved into a system, a religion. Christianity was a collection of rules and regulations, rituals and ceremonies. People tried to save themselves, and yet they said they believed in the Lord Jesus. Christianity was Judaized; it was no longer Christ. It was man doing everything, even trying to save his own soul. We call it "the Dark Ages." It was very dark; so dark that the truth of the gospel was unknown. Thank God, He raised up Martin Luther and those reformers. And Martin Luther said, "The letter to the Galatians is my letter. It is my Catherine [the name of his wife]. I am wedded to it."

Martin Luther used the letter to the Galatians as a sword with which to strike at Judaized Christianity in the sixteenth century. And by this sword, he dismantled that system of Judaized Christianity in his time. He showed people that justification is by faith, not by works of the flesh. He gave the people in Europe at that time an open Bible in order that they could return to the word of God instead of listening to the traditions of the fathers. That was four centuries ago.

We are nearing the end of the twentieth century and what are we faced with today? Are we in a better position than Paul? Are we in a better place than Martin Luther and the other reformers? As we look at Christianity, what do we see it as being today? Has not Christianity again been Judaized? Is it not a mixture of law and grace? It is true that Christ is not rejected completely. He has not been thrown out. People are still mentioning the name of Christ, but it is as though He is not sufficient, and that we need a law to help us. We may come in by Christ, but we have to be completed by Moses. We may start with the Spirit, but we will have to be perfected by the work of the flesh. Here once again we are confronted with a mixture of law and grace.

After you believe in the Lord Jesus, what is expected of

you? You are expected to keep certain rules and regulations. You are expected to do certain things. If you do them, that is all which is required; you are made perfect. Christianity today has become a religion, not a living relationship. It has become a system of things, instead of Christ as all. Today, people do not know what grace is because they are under the bondage of law. People do not know what faith is because they are all involved in works. People do not know the Holy Spirit because it is all the efforts of our own selves. Christianity today is Judaized. The very foundation of the gospel of Jesus Christ is at stake. Oh, how we need to go back to Paul's letter to the Galatians! There we shall find what the gospel of Jesus Christ truly is.

In combating this error, this "another gospel," Paul did not write his letter in a negative way. Oftentimes, when we try to combat an error, we tend to be very negative. We see all the errors, but where is the truth? But Paul, as he was moved by the Holy Spirit, wrote this letter in a very positive way. It is not only by contrast, it is also by presentation of what the gospel of Jesus Christ really is; and if we know the truth, the truth shall set us free.

The letter to the Galatians can very easily be divided into three parts of two chapters each. Of course, we know these chapter divisions are arbitrary, but it so happens that the letter to the Galatians can be divided into three distinct parts. The first two chapters deal with the authenticity or origin of Paul's gospel. Where did Paul receive the gospel? How did he receive it? The third and fourth chapters speak of the nature of Paul's gospel. What is it all about? And chapters 5 and 6 tell us the effect of Paul's gospel. When the gospel is preached, what will be the outcome? What will be the practical outworking of this gospel?

The Origin of the Gospel

"But I let you know, brethren, as to the glad tidings which were announced by me, that they are not according to man. For neither did I receive them from man, neither was I taught them, but by revelation of Jesus Christ" (Galatians 1:11-12).

Paul said that the gospel he preached was not of man, because he did not receive it from any man nor was he taught it by any man. The gospel he preached came by the revelation of Jesus Christ. Then he mentioned a little of his personal history. He said that he had been brought up in Judaism, which he had fully endorsed. He had been a Pharisee of the Pharisees, and more advanced than his contemporaries in Judaism. He had been so occupied with the traditions of the fathers—that is, with the teachings of the rabbis concerning the word of God—that he considered it his duty to combat and persecute Christians: Christ and His followers. According to the teachings of the fathers in Judaism, they considered Jesus an impostor whom they needed to get rid of. So Paul said he persecuted the church excessively with zeal. He would have nothing to do with Christ; he followed Moses. He went even to the Gentile cities to seize those believers and bring them to Jerusalem to be sentenced. But the Lord Jesus met him on the road to Damascus and challenged him: "Saul, Saul, why do you persecute me? You do not even know Me. Why are you persecuting Me? Do you not know that it is hard for you to kick against the goads? Do you not know that you are in My hands and that you are supposed to do My will? But you are kicking against Me."

And when it pleased God to reveal His Son to Paul and in Paul, it changed him completely. He received the glad tidings through revelation of Jesus Christ. No man taught him, but it was the Lord himself who revealed himself to him.

After he had seen the Lord as *the* glad tidings, *the* gospel, *the* salvation, *the* hope, *the* faith, *the* love, what did he do? Did he run to Jerusalem to meet with the apostles who were there before him, that he might be taught more about the gospel of Jesus Christ? No. It was not out of pride but out of his desire to know the gospel firsthand and not secondhand that he went to Arabia. Now Arabia, at that time, was a very vague term. It could have meant many places, but if we carefully read the letter to the Galatians, we get some hint, because it mentions Sinai.

After the Lord had revealed himself to Paul and he had been with the disciples for a few days, most likely, he traveled to the desert to Mount Sinai. Mount Sinai was the place where the law had been given, and it was also the place to where the prophet Elijah had gone after he fled for his life in order to reevaluate everything before God. That was where the law and the great prophet had been present, and that was the place to which most likely Paul had himself gone. He had gone away from man in order that he might be with God himself. There, I believe, he re-read the Old Testament—which he knew by heart—in the new light of Christ. He knew the Old Testament, which was the word of God of his day, but he had read and studied it before from the perspective of the traditions of the fathers, and what a mistake he had made! Now, though, he must re-read the word of God in the light of Christ. Oh, how Paul must have discovered Christ in every page of the Old Testament!

He then came back to Damascus and preached that Jesus is the Christ—the Messiah. He is the very One promised in the Old Testament. Three years after his conversion Paul went to Jerusalem in order to have some fellowship and not be independent. He met Peter and James and stayed with them for fifteen days; then he went back to his home community of Tarsus and spent some years in Syria and Cilicia where Tarsus was. It was not until fourteen years later that he went to Jerusalem with revelation. Even though, outwardly, it was because of the controversy with the Judaizers in Antioch that the church there sent Paul to Jerusalem, actually, we are told by Paul that he went there by revelation. God had revealed to him that he should go there for the truth of the gospel. He brought Titus with him. Titus was to serve as a test case because he was a Gentile and had not been circumcised.

If we read the second chapter of Galatians and if we know Greek, we will discover that Paul got all mixed up in his grammar: it was absurd; it was very bad. In reading about the controversy in Acts 15 we have the impression it was not that heated; on the other hand, a reading of Galatians 2 reveals how Paul's grammar appears to be greatly confused because he was so agitated. No doubt those at Jerusalem had tried to put pressure on Paul to circumcise Titus, but he wrote that he would not yield, "... not for even an hour, that the truth of the glad tidings might remain with you."

Thank God, in the midst of that great conflict, Paul had stood adamantly for the truth of the gospel. For him the gospel is grace, not grace plus law. The battle had been won, but the war went on, because these Judaizers followed Paul wherever he went thereafter for the rest of his life. They went to these churches in Galatia and almost succeeded in Judaizing the Christians there, attempting to make Jews of them instead of allowing them to remain Christians.

After the council in Jerusalem Peter made a visit to Galatia, and there he ate with the Galatian believers who were Gentiles. Now in those early days the believers used to come together and have their common meal together. They called it *agape*—a love feast. Everybody contributed to this time of eating together, which was a fellowship of love. And while Peter was there, he attended this agape feast and ate with the Gentile believers. But while Peter was still there, some people came from Jerusalem, from James; and when these Judaizers came, Peter got frightened. "What will James think of me? What will these who are zealous for the law think of me?" And we know Peter and are therefore not surprised at what he did. He separated himself from the Gentile believers and would not eat with them anymore as though they were unclean; and even Barnabas did the same thing. This became, at that moment, the test of the gospel of Jesus Christ: Is the gospel going to be Judaized or is it to be pure?

Because of the truth of the gospel, Paul, who was junior, withstood Peter publicly and said to his face: "We all know that even we as Jews have to believe in the Lord Jesus in order to be saved like the Gentiles. How can we force the Gentiles to be Jews? We ourselves cannot keep the law. How, then, can we put this burden upon these Gentiles? If we are doing that, we have fallen from grace." Thank God, the gospel of Jesus Christ passed the test because, in Christ, there is neither Jew nor Gentile, neither circumcision nor uncircumcision. The gospel which Paul preached is the gospel of Jesus Christ. He had received it by revelation, and this revelation has been tested and proven to be true, and this is the gospel that we believe.

The Nature of the Gospel

"O senseless Galatians, who has bewitched you; to whom, as before your very eyes, Jesus Christ has been portrayed, crucified among you?" (Galatians 3:1)

The gospel which Paul preached is: "Christ crucified." In I Corinthians he had declared: "I am determined to know nothing among you but Jesus Christ and Him crucified." That is the gospel, and "Christ crucified" has been "portrayed" before them. It has been set forth in their midst as a poster, presented as something which has stood before them—"Christ crucified." That is the gospel. Christ has done everything for us. There is nothing that has been left undone. All we need to do is believe in Him. It is grace, all of grace.

Salvation is God's promise. God promised Abraham and his seed the inheritance, the blessing. If it is a promise, then it is not to be received by works, nor can it be annulled by law. God's promise to Abraham is not abrogated nor annulled by the law of Moses which came in four hundred thirty years *later*. The promise is to be received. It is given in grace and is to be received by faith. If that be true, then why was the law given? The law was given as a means by which we would have the knowledge of our transgressions. Hence, the law is like a guardian that shall lead us to Christ.

Paul is trying to tell the Galatian believers that Christ crucified is the gospel; Christ crucified is sufficient for them. It is God's promise in grace. It is to be received by faith, and when you do that, you receive the Holy Spirit of promise. The Holy Spirit is given to you in order that you may be perfected and arrive at sonship. God has done it all. Why would you want to go back to the works of law? If you want to do that, then please bear in mind that if you violate one law, you violate the whole law. You will then be under the curse of law. In God's word it says, "Cast the maidservant and her child out. They have no part in God's inheritance" (see Genesis 21:10). It is only those who are born of promise who can receive the inheritance which God has promised. This is the gospel—Christ crucified. May we always keep that before us.

We see Christ crucified on the cross. Why was He crucified? He was crucified not only to bear in His own body our sins so that our sins may be forgiven, but also He was crucified that our old man—the "I"—would be crucified with Him. No longer live I; it is Christ who lives in me, and now I live in the flesh by faith. It is not my faith but the faith of the Son of God who loved me and gave himself for me (see Galatians 2:20). This is the gospel.

The Effect of the Gospel

"Christ has set us free in freedom; stand fast therefore, and be not held again in a yoke of bondage" (Galatians 5:1).

When you believe in the Lord Jesus, He sets you free. If you know the truth, the truth shall set you free. If the Son of Man, if the Son of God shall set you free, you are free indeed. Thank God, we are free in Christ Jesus. Stand fast in that freedom. Do not go back and put yourself under the bondage of law. It is such a temptation for us to go back, to put ourselves under the yoke of law, even in our own lives as Christians.

Let me ask each of you: After you believe in the Lord Jesus, do you always keep Him before you? Do you always see Christ crucified as the truth? Or is it the case that after you believe in the Lord Jesus and get saved, do you then begin to muse within yourself and say, "Now that I am saved I have to do something to complete myself; I have to do this, I have to do that, I have to please God, I have to exert my own strength in order to keep the law of God"? Are you now reverting to thinking that you will complete yourself? Or do you see that even though you are saved, for you to live is not you, but it is Christ who lives in you? Instead of you trying to live the Christian life and trying to please God, you acknowledge that there is no good in your flesh, you are dead in Christ, and you are alive to God through His life. You are learning to live by the life of Christ in you. Are you again in bondage, yoked to rules and regulations? Or are you now free in Christ Jesus? Let us stand fast in our freedom.

But freedom in Christ does not mean that you are now free to do anything you wish. To the contrary, freedom in Christ means that now you are free *not* to do what the flesh wants to do; you are free to do the will of God by His life. That is why Paul said, "For the flesh lusts against the Spirit, and the Spirit against the flesh ... that ye should not do those things which ye desire" (Galatians 5:17).

This is a tremendous verse, and it is quite different from Romans 7. Romans 7 tells us that you cannot do what you want to do and you do what you do not want to do. That is bondage. But here in verse 17 it says, "... and these things are opposed one to the other, that ye should not do those things which ye desire." Because the Holy Spirit is in you and you live by the Holy Spirit, you will not do what your flesh wants to do. You are able not to do what you do not want to do, and you are able to do what you want to do because now you walk by the Spirit of God.

Freedom in Christ does not mean that now we are free to live as we wish. It instead means that now we are free to live as God wants. Freedom in Christ does not mean that we are free to live in our flesh but rather we are free to live in the Spirit. And when we live in the Spirit, we are indeed free because the works of the flesh will be crucified and the fruit of the Spirit will be produced. That is the effect of the gospel of Jesus Christ.

Some people think because it is grace, all of grace, therefore, after you believe in the Lord Jesus, then it is a "free-for-all"—i.e., anything goes, observing no rules or restrictions. No. If you really know what grace is, it will produce in you the same character as Christ has. If you really know that grace is Christ living in you, you have to walk in the Spirit and not according to the flesh. That is grace.

Paul concludes by saying, "See how long a letter I have written to you with my own hand." When Paul wrote letters, he usually dictated them and somebody else wrote them down, probably because of his eyes. By this time he did not have very good eyesight. Some people have therefore thought that this phrase, "How long a letter I've written to you with my own hand" should say, "With what large letters I have written you with my own hand." He usually dictated, but this letter he probably wrote himself, and if he wrote it down himself, then for him it was indeed a long letter; and the individual letters for each word must have been very large because his eyesight was not too good.

Why did he physically write down the letter himself? It reveals how his heart was so agonized over the situation there in Galatia. Oh, he could envision that if this doctrinal error should continue, Christianity would become completely Judaized, and the gospel of Jesus Christ would eventually be known no longer. People will all fall from grace. He was so agonized over this possibility that he could not dictate, he had to write down this epistle himself. His letters were big, perhaps even ugly. His penmanship could not appear very attractive with such bad eyesight. Therefore, in a sense he was saying: "Do not look upon the outward appearance. If you want beautiful penmanship, I do not have it; but I do have the reality. I have Christ."

How do you have Christ? You will not be able to have Christ if you do not accept the cross. It is the cross which gives you Christ. Those Judaizers wanted to escape the persecution of the cross. Therefore, they wanted others, like themselves, to be circumcised—have something done on their physical bodies and then they would be all right. You do not need to allow the cross to work deep in your life to the setting aside of your flesh with its lusts and passions, so that Christ may live in you. Paul, however, said this: "I go for reality. I boast in the cross because that delivers me from the world, even from the religious world of Judaized Christianity. It gives me Christ." In doing that he bore in his body the marks of Jesus Christ. In his body were the wounds, the sufferings, the marks. But through these marks he proved to the world that the gospel he preached is powerful. It worked in his life.

The gospel you receive will make you the kind of person you are to be. If you receive "another gospel," that will make you another kind of Christian. It will make you another of a different kind, not of the same kind. But if you have received the gospel of Jesus Christ as Paul has preached, then it will make you the kind of Christian that God wants you to be. So may the grace of the Lord Jesus be with your spirit. Amen.

Shall we pray:

Dear heavenly Father, we pray that by the power of the Holy Spirit the truth of the gospel of Jesus Christ may be kept and may be a reality in our midst. Deliver us from being tempted and falling into the trap of another gospel of another kind. Oh, that we may not set aside Thy grace and fall from the grace of God, which is Jesus Christ. We pray that Thou wilt always put Christ crucified before us that we may walk in the way of the cross and find Christ as our all in all. We ask in the name of our Lord Jesus. Amen.

EPHESIANS

SEEING CHRIST IN THE CHURCH

Ephesians 1:9-10—Having made known to us the mystery of his will, according to his good pleasure which he purposed in himself for the administration of the fulness of times; to head up all things in the Christ, the things in the heavens and the things upon the earth. (In some versions you may find in verse 10: To sum up all things in the Christ.)

Ephesians 3:9-11—And to enlighten all with the knowledge of what is the administration of the mystery hidden throughout the ages in God, who has created all things, in order that now to the principalities and authorities in the heavenlies might be made known through the assembly the all-various wisdom of God, according to the purpose of the ages, which he purposed in Christ Jesus our Lord.

May we look to the Lord in prayer:

Dear heavenly Father, it is the desire of our hearts that we may see Thee face to face and we do praise and thank Thee because Thou hast made it possible for us through Christ Jesus; the veil has been rent. So we do come to Thee with unveiled face. We desire to see the glory of the Lord and be transformed according to His image by the Lord, the Spirit. We commit this time into Thy hands and trust Thy blessing. In the name of our Lord Jesus. Amen.

The Bible is the revelation of Jesus Christ, and the reason we study the Bible is that we may know Him. This is the only reason why God's word is given to us, and it is the only way that we can approach the word of God. Therefore, we desire to see the Lord Jesus in every book of the Bible. We began with Matthew and now we would like to see Christ in the letter to the Ephesians, or to put it another way, to see Christ through the church.

There is a similarity between the book of Acts and the letter to the Ephesians. In the book of Acts we see the risen Lord working and teaching in His corporate body, which is the church. In the letter to the Ephesians it is again the Lord Jesus as the Head of His church, but there is a difference. In the book of Acts it is the fact presented to us: Christ is seen in His body. But in the letter to the Ephesians it is the teaching: the teaching of Christ in the church. It is a wonderful thing that God always presents us with a fact first, and then He begins to tell us what it means.

In the book of Acts we are presented with the fact that the church is really Christ himself, working and teaching on earth just like when He was on earth during those years of His incarnation, in that body which He took upon himself. Likewise, in the book of Acts, we find that the risen Lord took upon himself another body, a corporate body, and in that corporate body He continued to do and to teach. This is the fact. In the letter to the Ephesians we find the interpretation, the teaching.

This letter to the Ephesians was written by Paul when he was in prison in Rome. Physically, he was restricted. He was unable to be active, to move around among God's people. But thank God, he was not bound in his spirit. On the contrary, we find his spirit soared to the third heaven, and there he saw the mystery of God. He tried to share that mystery of God with the believers in Ephesus and, of course, with us today.

The letter to the Ephesians reveals Christ to us as the Head of the church, His body. This is the mystery of God's will. In I Corinthians 2 Paul said, "I am determined to know nothing among you save Jesus Christ and Him crucified." But that does not mean that besides the fundamental, foundational teaching of Jesus Christ and Him crucified Paul knows nothing else. Because immediately following that statement he added this: "But among the perfect ..." Now the perfect here does not refer to sinless perfection. Nobody is sinlessly perfect except one—our Lord Jesus. He is indeed sinlessly perfect. But the word *perfect* in the New Testament means "grown up, mature." Paul said that among the mature people we talk about wisdom, a wisdom that is not known by the world nor by the rulers of the world. It is God's wisdom in mystery. It is a wisdom that has been hidden through the ages and it is for our glory. Now there is no contradiction here. "Jesus Christ and Him crucified" is the foundation, but the wisdom which Paul talks about, God's wisdom in mystery, builds upon that foundation. It is the same Christ.

Here, then, in the letter to the Ephesians Paul deals primarily with this matter of "God's wisdom in mystery." He leads us back to eternity past, through time, and also looks to eternity to come. In other words, Paul deals with this matter of the eternal purpose of God.

God has an eternal purpose. Why do we call it an eternal purpose? Because God purposed that purpose in eternity past. Before there was time, before there was creation, God had already purposed a purpose in himself according to the good pleasure of His will, and He has been working throughout time until He realizes that purpose in eternity to come. What He has purposed in eternity past must be and will be and shall be realized in eternity to come, because God cannot fail. But His work is in time, so He created time as a period or periods in which He can work out His eternal purpose. This is really what time is, and we are still in time now.

What is the purpose that God has purposed in himself in eternity past? To put it very simply: "To sum up all things in Christ," to gather up, to comprehend, to head up all things in Christ. God so loved His only begotten Son that He wanted to express His love to His Son. Love expresses itself by giving, and God loved His Son so much that He wanted to give Him everything. That is the reason why He created all things. He created the heavens and the earth and all the things in them for His beloved Son. The mountains, the oceans, the plains were created for His Son. The birds, the fish, the animals were created for His Son. Even the celestial angels and the terrestrial mankind were created for His Son. He created all things in His Son, by His Son, and for His Son, that His Son may inherit all things, and all things may be summed up in Him. That is the eternal purpose of God. And we know in eternity to come (and it *is* coming) that this will be the truth. All things will be summed up in Christ.

What is the meaning of summing up? This phrase *sum up, head up or gather up*, is used two times in the New Testament. It is used once in Ephesians 1 and also in Romans 13.

"For, Thou shalt not commit adultery, Thou shalt not kill, Thou shalt not steal, Thou shalt not lust; and if there be any other commandment, it is summed up in this word, namely, Thou shalt love thy neighbour as thyself. Love works no ill to its neighbour; love therefore is the whole law (or is the fulness of law)" (Romans 13:9-10).

There are many commandments, but whatever commandment it may be, all is summed up, gathered up in one word—love. Love is the totality of all commandments. Love gives meaning to all commandments, and it is the only way for the fulfillment of commandments; therefore, love sums up all commandments. Likewise, Christ sums up all things. Whatever thing it might be, including you and me, the angels, all created things—everything is summed up in Christ. He is the very meaning of all things; He gives meaning to all things. He gathers up all things into a harmony and unity, and He is the purpose of all things. And we know in eternity to come it will be a manifested reality. Thank God for that.

There is no problem in eternity past. When God purposes His purpose there is no argument, no opposition, no different opinion. And there will be no problem in eternity to come because everything which God has purposed shall be realized. There will be no more opposition, no more conflict. God will obtain what He wants for His Son.

However, there are many problems in *time*. After God purposed His purpose and began His creation, problems began to come in, first in the rebellion of the archangel, Lucifer. The archangel whom God had created rebelled against God and made himself a devil, an adversary of God; and because of that, the earth entered into chaos. As told of in the book of Genesis, when God recreated the earth by repairing it and making it habitable, He created man and put him in control of the planet earth. Man fell into sin, and the whole world was again plunged into *tohu* and *bohu*, which means "vanity" and "ruin." But thank God, He continued working. Through His beloved Son He redeemed and reconciled all things back to the fullness of God. Not only has Jesus redeemed us by His precious blood, but also His redemption actually has reached to the whole universe, and because of what He has accomplished on Calvary's cross, He has reconciled all things to His fullness.

God has also purposed in His Son that there will be a people, the church, who will be the bride of His beloved Son to share His glory as well as His responsibility, to share in His life, as well as in His work. This is part of the eternal purpose of God for His Son, and that is where you and I come in. It pleases God that as He gave all things to His Son, His Son would share all things, even His glory, with a redeemed people, the church. It is the good pleasure of God that after He finished the work of redemption through Christ on earth to accomplish His eternal purpose, He would have a people to carry that out in His Son and for His Son.

I always remember this illustration: One day a father was trying to move a table. It was a very heavy table but the father was strong, and he was able to lift it and move it all by himself. He had a little boy, and when the little boy saw that his father was going to carry the table, he wanted to help. The father agreed for his son to help. The son held on to one side of the table and the father took the other side and they started to move the table. Now actually, the son put more weight on the table than he carried. So the father not only carried the table but he carried the son as well. When they finished carrying the table together the son said, "We have done it."

This illustration is a picture of what God through Christ has done. The work has all been done by the Lord Jesus but it pleases Him to allow us to work together with Him. Actually, we put more weight on Him (if you don't, certainly I do), but He willingly takes up the extra weight and carries everything through so that the Father's purpose might be accomplished. Thank God for that!

The wonderful thing is that when God decides to put us in His eternal purpose concerning His Son, He does not want us to enter into it passively, mechanically, automatically, technically. He wants us to enter into His purpose in a living, spiritual, real, experiential way. Because of God's desire, the first thing He has to do is make known to us the mystery of His will.

Now, God's will is a mystery. Who knows the mind of God? Who knows what is going on in His heart? Who knows what He has determined in eternity past? Who knows what is behind all His workings in time? Who knows what His aims are? Nobody knows. It is a mystery. Not only is it unknown to the wise, but even the angels do not know. It is a mystery hidden in God. His will is a mystery, hidden in himself. Now, think of that: it pleases God to make known the mystery of His will to us. Yet who are we?

It touches my heart very deeply that God does not reveal the mystery of His will to the angels. As a matter of fact, the angels are to know His mystery through the church, the redeemed of the Lord (see Ephesians 3:10). We have sinned; we were dead in sins and transgressions; our minds were darkened; we were alienated from the life of God; we became His enemies; we hated Him; rebelled against Him, and kicked against Him. Yet, in His love and mercy, through the grace of Jesus Christ, He has not only saved us but He has made known to us redeemed sinners the mystery of His will. He does not treat us as slaves; He treats us as friends.

However, in order to make known to us the mystery of His will, God naturally has to first draw us to himself. He has to bring us to a living relationship with himself so that our knowledge of His will is not merely outward knowledge but a living, experiential knowledge of the mystery of His will. It is not a matter of mere teaching; it is a matter of a teaching based upon experience. If all we know is teaching, it is doctrine; but if teaching is based on experience, that is life. God wants us to know His will in life.

In the first chapter of Ephesians wherein Paul is trying to describe this mystery, it is beyond him. In order to make known to us the mystery of His will, God first blesses us with every spiritual blessing in the heavenlies in Christ Jesus. That is why He blesses us. What are these spiritual blessings with which He has blessed us in Christ Jesus? "According as He has chosen us in Him before the world's foundation." Before the foundation of the world God has chosen us in Christ Jesus. We have not chosen Him; He has chosen us, even before the world's foundation, long before we were born. He has chosen us in Christ Jesus, and marked each one of us out for sonship. He said that one day this one and that one whom He has chosen will become sons after the fashion of His only begotten Son. Wonderful! This one and that one may be holy and blameless before God in love. There is only one way to be holy and blameless before Him and that is in the way of love, because "love covers a multitude of sins."

Then Paul says this: "He has taken us into favor in the Beloved." God has favored us in the Beloved. Or, to put it another way, God says, "You are my favorite." He is very partial to you and me, but He is impartially partial because He is partial to everybody.

God has redeemed us through Christ's blood. What a cost He has paid for it. Christ had to shed His blood to redeem us according to the riches of God's grace.

God has given us an inheritance in heaven. Oh, that we may know the hope of our calling. We are called to be the body of Christ, and the hope of that body is that it will become the bride of Christ when it is fully grown, matured and perfected.

We are to know the glory of Christ's inheritance in the saints. Not only do we inherit Christ—and what an inheritance He is to us—but Christ is to inherit us. We will become a rich inheritance to Him.

We are also to know the surpassing greatness of God's power towards us who believe. Oh, the power that God works in us is nothing less than the power which has raised Jesus from the dead and has put Him at God's right hand over all things. This same power is now working in us.

God has done all these things in Christ to make us realize that it is only in Christ. It is in Christ we are chosen. It is because of Christ we can gain sonship. It is because of the blood of Christ we are redeemed. It is because of Christ we become co-heirs with Christ. Everything we experience in the grace of God is Christ. God is to make Christ as everything to us; He is to be all things in our lives. That is summing up all things in Christ.

In the second chapter of Ephesians we learn that this mystery of God's will also relates to us individually. When we were dead in sins and transgressions, God's love, mercy and grace came upon us so that we were not only raised from the dead, but were and are being seated together with Christ in the heavenlies. Corporately, all of us, being scattered, are now being made one new man in Christ Jesus. We are gathered together in Christ unto God. All these things are done to us, all these things we receive and experience, so that we may come to a real knowledge of the mystery of God's will. The mystery of His will is to be worked out in us first. We not only are to understand with our minds, but also it is to be worked out in our lives. Indeed, the church can say that all things are summed up in Christ. He is everything. He is the meaning of everything. He gives purpose to everything, and He is everything to us. That is the testimony of the church—to make known the mystery of God's will.

Do you know the mystery of God's will? Do you know that His will is that His Son may have the preeminence in all things? Do you know that God's will is to head up all things in Christ, to sum up all things in Him, so that Christ may be manifested in all things? Do you know that He is to be glorified in all things? Do you know this is the mystery of God's will? If we do not know, who then knows? If you were to ask the angels, the angels would say, "We do not know the mystery of God's will. We have seen many mighty acts of God, and we know He is working towards something, but what is it? Teach us." The church is not only to teach the world, but she is also to teach the mystery of God's will to the hidden world. This is what is meant in Ephesians 3:10: "In order that now to the principalities and authorities in the heavenlies might be made known through the assembly the all-various wisdom of God."

First, God makes known to us the mystery of His will in a living way. Then, through us, the church—the redeemed, God is to make known His manifold wisdom to the principalities and authorities in the heavenlies. These principalities and authorities in the heavenlies do not refer to kings and lords and nobles upon the earth. It is true, God is to make known the mystery of His will to the world through the church, otherwise the world would never know what that is; but additionally, it is to be made known through the church to the principalities and authorities. Most commentators agree that the principalities and authorities here refer to the good angels, if we can divide the angels into good and bad. The good angels are those who obey God and execute His will. The bad angels are those who rebel against God under that fallen archangel, Lucifer.

These principalities and authorities, which are the good angels, are more intelligent than we are in knowledge. But even though they are more intelligent than we are, they are not all-wise; they do not know everything. They indeed know more than we do, but they do not know everything. They need to be taught, and who is to teach them the wisdom of God? The church. When the angels observe what God is working in the redeemed, when they see the redeemed enter into the reality of Christ, then their eyes are opened to know the eternal purpose of God. We are to teach the angels the wisdom of God.

The reason most commentators believe these are good angels is because the bad angels are to know the authority and power of God. Only the good angels desire to know God's wisdom. The church is not only to teach the good angels the wisdom of God, but she is also to let the bad angels know the authority and power of God. (That is laid out in Ephesians 6.) After Christ accomplished all things on Calvary's cross, He gave His victory to the church to execute it and bring forth the purpose of God so that the bad angels may know God's power. We are to stand, to withstand and to continue to stand. This is the letter to the Ephesians.

If Christ is to be seen through the church, then you must first know what the church is. If you do not know what the church is, then how can you see Christ through the church? The letter to the Ephesians is a great letter on the teaching of what the church is. If you want to know what the church is, do not look around; you will never find it. If you want to know what the church is, do not even go into church history, because what you will find there is mostly official Christianity. If you want to know what the church really is, look into the letter to the Ephesians. There you will find the revelation concerning the church of God.

The Body of Christ

"The assembly, which is his body, the fulness of him who fills all in all" (Ephesians 1:23).

The church is the body of Christ who fills all in all. The church is the fullness of Christ. It is just like my body, which is the fullness of my head. All the wisdom, plans, purpose, authority, government: everything is in the head; but the head fills the body; so the body becomes the fullness of the head. That is what the church is—the body of Christ. All the wisdom, all the unsearchable riches of Christ, are all stored in that body and Christ says: This is My fullness.

This body of Christ is not only to store all the unsearchable riches of Christ, it is also to manifest His glory. The human body is always covered; the head is exposed. The church is not to speak of herself. The church is not to let the world see what she is: "Look, our steeple reaches to the heavens." That is the tower of Babel, not the church. The church is to reveal Christ the Head. When people enter the assembly of God's people, what they see is Christ. God is in your midst, and they bow down and worship Him. The church is the fullness of Christ; it is always to be covered, never to be exposed. Instead, what the church exposes is the Head—Christ. Let Christ be exalted and seen, and let us decrease and let Him increase. That is the church.

The church is the body of Christ. Through the church Christ can continue to do and to teach. There is much which needs to be done yet, and He is doing it in the church and through the church. There is much to be taught yet, and He teaches it through the church. The church has no teaching of her own. She teaches what Christ teaches. The church has no work of her own. She works only what Christ works. Do we see Christ in the church? If we only see the body and not the Head, it is an abomination. Let Christ be seen in the church. Unless He is seen in the church we fail. It is a misrepresentation, and the greatest sin in the whole world is the sin of misrepresentation.

Oh, may we represent Christ corporately in a living way.

THE ONE NEW MAN

The church is the one new man (see Ephesians 2:15). In Adam—the old man; in Christ—the new man. In Adam all die; in Christ all are made alive. In Adam we were all divided; in Christ we are one. There is neither Jew nor Gentile; neither circumcision nor uncircumcision; neither barbarian nor Scythian; neither bondman nor freeman, but Christ is everything to everyone. He is all and in all. That is the new man—the one new man. In the world you have the Jews, but in the church there is no Jew. In the world you have the Greek and the Gentile, but in the church there is no Gentile. In the world you have barbarians (many of them) and Scythians, who were worse because Scythians were more barbarous than even the barbarians. If you know history, you know that the Scythians were the most barbarous of all mankind at that time. So, actually, in God's eyes there is no civilized nation: you are either barbarian or Scythian. You are only civilized in Christ. All these natural distinctions and discriminations are found in the world, but there is no place in that one new man for them because we are all one in Christ Jesus.

When you look at a Christian brother or a sister, what do you see? Do you see a Chinese or do you see Christ? If you see a Chinese, it is unfortunate, not only for you, but also for me. In the church there is no Chinese, no American, no black or white or yellow or brown or red. In the church there is no Ph.D., no illiterate. In the church there is no master or servant. Yes, in the world there are such distinctions, but in the church there are none. As we gather around the Lord's Table, we are all brothers and sisters in Christ Jesus. We are one. Nothing can separate us from Christ; nothing can separate us from one another because the love of Christ is the bond that binds us together. The church is the one new man, and when people look at the unity of God's people they realize this is not possible naturally. This is supernatural. It is

Christ who unites us into one. That is to be our testimony.

Fellow Citizens of the Saints

What is the church? We are fellow citizens of the saints (see Ephesians 2:19). The church is the kingdom of God on earth. God has translated us out of the power of darkness and has transported us into the kingdom of the Son of God's love. We are now in God's kingdom; we are fellow citizens. Our citizenship is in heaven. We are strangers and sojourners upon this earth, and yet we have a citizenship. It is in heaven.

When you think of the kingdom of God in our midst, then you realize that as God's people we need to submit ourselves completely to the authority of our King—Christ. If we submit our lives to the rule of Christ our King, then in reality we express His kingdom. If we rebel against the authority of Christ in our own life, then how can we express the kingdom of God upon this earth? The world is full of rebellion, but are we any better? The church is the kingdom of God, but this kingdom is the kingdom of God's Son. In Matthew 17 we are told that Christ was transformed on a mountain and then the voice came: "This is My beloved Son, hear Him." That is the kingdom. To be in the kingdom of God our attitude should always be: "What do You say?" It is an attitude of obedience, of submission. And if we submit ourselves to God's Son in our lives, individually and collectively, the world will see Christ. His authority will be manifested through us. His will will be carried out through us.

The Household of God

The church is the household of God or the family of God (see Ephesians 2:19). We are not only a kingdom, we are also a family. Thank God, our family is a big one, and when we think of family, the first thing that comes to mind will probably be family resemblance. Oftentimes when we look at a person we think: "You must belong to that family." It is similar to what the Jewish people say: "Look at my nose, and you will know where I belong. The map of Jerusalem is on my face." There is a family resemblance. Being of the household of God, we are supposed to bear the resemblance of our heavenly Father. We are supposed to have a resemblance to our elder brother Jesus because God makes His only begotten Son the firstborn among many brethren. Christ has given His life to us and with that life we are to grow into an increasing likeness to God's Son. Are we growing into that likeness? What is our family resemblance? I think that is an important question to ask ourselves.

A Habitation of God in the Spirit

"In whom ye also are built together for a habitation of God in the Spirit" (Ephesians 2:22).

The church is the habitation of God in the Spirit. God dwells in the church by His Spirit. When we think of a habitation we may immediately recall the Lord saying: "I will build my church upon this rock and the gates of Hades shall not prevail against it." Christ is building us together as living stones upon himself as the foundation, and if we are being built together upon Christ, then the result is that God will take up His abode in our midst. "Where two or three are gathered together unto my name, there am I in the midst of them" (Matthew 18:20). That is the house of God.

Are we tearing one another apart or are we building up one another? Are we striving and struggling against one another; or are we edifying, exhorting, encouraging and comforting one another? Are we building with gold, silver and precious stones which is the life of God, the redemption of Christ and the work of the Holy Spirit? Or are we building with wood, stubble and hay which is building with human nature, human effort and all our own ideas? (see I Corinthians 3:10-15) What are we actually doing?

The church is the habitation of God and is to be inhabited by Him. It is not what you like, but what He likes. It is not with what you feel comfortable but with what He feels comfortable. It is not whether you are satisfied, but is He satisfied? That is the habitation of God, and whenever you go to someone's house, immediately you know the habits, the temperament, the likes and dislikes of the owner of that house. You see the arrangement of the furniture, you notice what is hanging on the walls, you behold the condition of the house; and immediately, you see the owner of the house because all these things are being manifested and they are a reflection of the owner. That is what the church is to be.

The Mystery of the Christ

The church is the mystery of the Christ (see Ephesians 3:4). God's mystery is Christ, but Christ's mystery is the church. If you want to know God you have to know Christ. The Lord said, "Have you known Me for so long and you still say, 'Show me the Father'?" Likewise, the mystery of Christ is the church. If you want to know Christ, look at the church. That is where you ought to recognize Christ. Unfortunately, today this is not true. But the church is the mystery of Christ. The church reveals Christ because the church is the Christ. In I Corinthians 12:12-13 we find mentioned one body and many members. Many members, yet one body, so also is the Christ. It is the body of Christ with many members, and even though there are many members, each member is not a body, but all these members taken together are one body. The Bible here says, "So also is the Christ." If we were writing I Corinthians chapter 12:12-13, we would say, "So also is the church." Yet the Holy Spirit says through Paul, "So also is the Christ," because the church is none other than Christ expressed corporately. It is Christ in you, Christ in me, Christ in everyone of us, together manifesting Christ. Remember: the church is not built with you and me; the church is built with the Christ in you and the Christ in me, and you and I have to experience the cross. The church is the mystery of the Christ.

The Bride of Christ

The church is also the bride of Christ (see Ephesians 5:23). When you think of the bride of Christ, you first think there must be a suitability. There must be a sameness, a counterpart, His like. You cannot put two who are unlike each other together into one. God said He would create a helpmate for Adam, his like. And that is what the church is—Christ's counterpart, His like. It is not only the church having His life; she is also to be purified and sanctified until the church becomes a glorious church without spot or wrinkle, just as He is. Then the church will be joined with Christ in one—the bride of Christ.

The Warrior of Christ

The church is additionally the warrior of Christ (see Ephesians 6). The church is to be used by God to fight the good fight of faith. It is to apply the victory of Christ over all things so that all things may be led into subjection to Christ. The church is to be used by God to defeat the enemy, the fallen angel who was created higher than man; and yet, God uses one lower than this fallen angel to defeat him. In Romans 8 it says that when the sons of God are manifested, then all things in the creation will be delivered from the bondage of corruption and from vanity, and they will be released into the liberty of the sons of God. All things will be subjected to Christ.

Let us realize that God first works in us that we may subject ourselves to Christ in all things. Then, through the church, all things will be brought into subjection to Christ in order that Christ may sum up all things, so that God's purpose shall be fulfilled. This is the letter to the Ephesians. May we see Christ.

Shall we pray:

Dear heavenly Father, show us Thy Son through Thy church. Do not allow us simply to have a mental knowledge of what Thy church is. But, Lord, Thou art working to bring us into the reality of the church so that Thy Son may be manifested and may be glorified. Oh, make this all real to Thy people on earth. We ask in Thy precious name. Amen.

PHILIPPIANS

Seeing Christ in Christian Experience

Philippians 1:21—For me to live is Christ.

Philippians 2:5-8—For let this mind be in you which was also in Christ Jesus; who, subsisting in the form of God, did not esteem it an object of rapine to be on an equality with God; but emptied himself, taking a bondman's form, taking his place in the likeness of men; and having been found in figure as a man, humbled himself, becoming obedient even unto death, and that the death of the cross.

Philippians 3:13-14—Brethren, I do not count to have got possession myself; but one thing—forgetting the things behind, and stretching out to the things before, I pursue, looking towards the goal, for the prize of the calling on high of God in Christ Jesus.

Philippians 4:13—I have strength for all things in him that gives me power. (Or to put it more correctly: I have strength for all things through Him who empowers me.)

Let us look to the Lord in prayer:

Dear heavenly Father, how we do praise and thank Thee for Thy precious Son, the unspeakable gift that Thou hast given to us; and we do treasure this gift very, very much. Our Father, we do ask that Thou wilt continue to open our eyes to see Thy Son. Make Him even more precious to us than ever before. Make us see that without Him, where would we be? Oh Lord God, we do pray that we may truly see Him as Thou hast seen Him. We ask in Thy precious name. Amen.

The letter to the Philippians gives us the very depth of Christian living. In Ephesians we find the height of teaching, and there can be nothing higher than that because we see the eternal purpose of God which is Christ Jesus. It is the will of God that His Son should have the first place in all things, that He is to sum up all things, that He is to be the All in All. There is no teaching higher than that. And then we find in the letter to the Philippians the very depths of living because it is said, "For me to live is Christ." Can we find a deeper life than that? These two epistles were written by one person, the apostle Paul, which shows us that teaching and living are inseparable. We need teaching, but teaching without living is merely theoretical. Living without proper teaching is undisciplined and limited. We thank God that side by side we have the letter to the Ephesians and the letter to the Philippians. We need both teaching and living.

In this letter to the Philippians we shall see Christ in our daily life or, to put it another way, we shall see Christ in Christian experience. Of all the letters written by the apostle Paul to the church, this is the most intimate letter written by him.

If you have read Acts 16, you know that Philippi was the first place in Europe where the gospel was preached. Before that time the gospel was preached in Jerusalem, in Judea, in Samaria and in Asia, that is, in Asia Minor. But, then, the Holy Spirit led the apostle Paul to cross the Aegean Sea into Europe, and the first place where the gospel of Jesus Christ was preached there was in Philippi. There God gathered a group of believers together unto the name of the Lord Jesus, and this church in Philippi had an intimate relationship with Paul. He loved this church very much, and the brothers and sisters there loved him very much. When Paul wrote this letter to the Philippians, it had been ten years since he had first stepped into Philippi. Throughout these ten years they had maintained a very intimate, loving relationship. Now, though, Paul was in prison in Rome where he was writing this letter to those whom he loved very dearly, and who loved him very dearly. So this is a love letter.

Even though there is very deep teaching of Christ in this letter (for instance in chapter 2), basically this letter is a fellowship, a sharing of love. Of all the letters written by the apostle there are two which reveal Paul the most. One is II Corinthians and the other is Philippians. In II Corinthians he is revealed to us as Paul the apostle, but here in the letter to the Philippians he is being revealed to us as Paul the man—the person. In II Corinthians it is spiritual authority that is in view, but here in Philippians it is love. So in this letter Paul reveals himself to the saints in Philippi, and unveils the very secret of his life as a Christian.

Life is made up of experiences. What we experience day after day makes up our life eventually. It is more than mere knowledge; it is experiential knowledge. The knowledge which the Bible speaks about is *epignosis*, which is full and experiential knowledge. The knowledge of Jesus Christ is not a theoretical, speculative kind of knowledge; it is full and it is experiential. It can be experienced. Therefore, knowing Christ is not simply knowing about Him. That does not make up our Christian life. Knowing Christ is to experience Him; experiencing Him makes up our Christian life. The Christian life is actually a life of experiencing Christ Jesus. The more we experience Christ, the deeper our Christian life becomes; and the less we experience Christ, the shallower our Christian life will be.

We know that when Paul wrote this letter to the Philippians he was in prison in Rome for the sake of the gospel. Even though he was allowed to stay in his own hired apartment, it was situated in the area where the imperial guards were stationed. We are told that when he was there as a prisoner in Rome, there was an imperial guard chained together with him around the clock. True, it was a long chain; nevertheless, he was chained to an imperial guard continuously twenty-four hours a day. There was never a time of privacy. He was always under the eyes of a Roman guard. When he received friends, visitors, brothers and sisters and talked about the Lord, a guard was always there. When he was resting in the night, a guard was there. There was absolutely no privacy.

Paul was waiting to be judged by the Roman Emperor, who at that time was Nero. He never knew when he would have the opportunity of a hearing, so he had to wait and wait until it pleased the Emperor to hear him. We know he was there for two years. Everything in Paul's life was suspended; nothing was definite. The outcome was uncertain, and Paul had to live that kind of life day after day, night after night.

Paul was a very active person but he was confined to his Rome apartment. He was unable to travel, he was unable to go out to meet with people. He lived a very confined, restricted life. And added to that, he said that it was known to all—to the imperial guard as well as everybody else—that he was not in prison because he had committed any crime but because of the gospel of Jesus Christ. This very fact stirred up some believers to preach the gospel out of love; yet there were also some who preached the gospel out of jealousy. We do not know exactly who these latter people were. Probably they were the Judaizers who had followed Paul all his life, or perhaps it was somebody else; but one thing we do definitely know: some people preached the gospel out of love and some preached the gospel out of jealousy and contention. These latter ones did not preach the gospel because of Christ; rather, they preached the gospel in order to add affliction to the apostle Paul (see Philippians 1:17).

If we were placed in that kind of circumstance, how would we react? Probably we would be overwhelmed by all these adverse circumstances; yet Paul was not overwhelmed. He overcame all his circumstances and wrote one of the most joyous writings in the entire Bible. In this letter to the

Philippians he repeatedly mentioned the word *rejoice*, and this word or its equivalent is repeated sixteen times in this short epistle. He was overflowing with joy, and he was able to share his joy with these Philippian believers.

Life is lived in many circumstances. We do not live in a vacuum but are surrounded by all kinds of circumstances. Some people say that we are the product of our circumstances; but are we? If we were to put it more accurately, we might say that we are the product of our reaction to our circumstances. How do we react to them? Circumstances change ever so often, just like the four seasons. Sometimes we have spring, sometimes we have summer, sometimes autumn, and sometimes winter. But we believe our circumstances are ordered by our God. He rules and overrules our circumstances. Yes, it is true, sometimes our circumstances are caused by the adversary, but even then, it is with the permission of our God.

The Lord Jesus said not to be afraid, for the very hairs of your head have been numbered by your heavenly Father. Every morning when you comb your hair some of it falls out. Most likely, you never count how many hairs fall out, you do not even know how many hairs you have in the first place. But the Lord Jesus said that the very hairs of your head have been numbered—not only counted, but numbered! Every hair on your head has a number, and in the morning when you comb your hair, number one thousand and three and number three thousand and four fall out. God knows exactly which number falls off your head. Such an occurrence is very minute and insignificant, not even worthy to be noticed by man; yet our heavenly Father notices everything. Now that is the care of our heavenly Father.

The Lord once said that a penny will buy two sparrows, but with two pennies you can get five sparrows because sparrows are so cheap. In other words, when you buy two pennies' worth, an odd sparrow will be thrown in free. In short, that odd sparrow is worth nothing, yet the Lord said that even the odd sparrow will not fall to the ground without the Father's knowledge. How much more worth you are than the sparrows! This is the loving care of our heavenly Father, and remember, it is this same heavenly Father who has ordered all our circumstances. Whether our circumstances are favorable or adverse, it is all under the control of our heavenly Father. He places us in our circumstances for a reason—to know Christ in and through our circumstances. He wants us to find out the secret of Christian living. Circumstances are opportunities to learn Christ.

It is very strange that when two persons can be found in the same circumstances, they may come out very differently from each other. For instance, let us look at Abraham and Lot: they left Ur of Chaldea together; they went to Canaan together; they went down to Egypt together; they returned to Canaan together. They were in the same circumstances all along the way, but the result was so different afterwards the one from the other.

Another example to be considered is David and Saul: they had gone through all the same kinds of circumstances, but Saul failed in prosperity whereas David succeeded in adversity. Do not think that good environment or good circumstances will always produce good life. Sometimes it may end up in is just the opposite way. It is not the circumstance—rather the secret lies in our reaction. It is the secret of the life within. If you have mastered this secret, then you can be in any circumstance and the result will be increase; the result will be a deeper experiencing of Christ Jesus.

Paul was confronted with a bad circumstance, but the Philippian believers were free. They were not chained, they were in far better circumstances than Paul; yet they were under the weather, so to speak, because there were some small problems in their midst. Basically, two leading sisters who loved the Lord had somehow developed a kind of rivalry which had cast a cloud over the whole assembly. As a result, the believers had lost their joy. They were under the circumstances, whereas Paul was above them. What is the secret?

The Secret of Overcoming

Paul opened his heart to these brothers and sisters whom he loved. He proceeded to tell them that in whatever circumstances they might be, there is a secret. If they know that secret, then circumstances do not matter. The thing that matters is to master that secret. And what is that secret? Paul simply said, "For me to live is Christ."

Paul does not say, "I am Christ." Some people today say, "I am Christ." No. People went to John the Baptist and asked, "Are you the Messiah? Are you the Christ?" And John the Baptist said, "Oh no, I am not the Christ. I am merely a voice in the wilderness."

Paul also does not say, "For me to live is for Christ." Now of course it is true, for us to live is to live for Christ. If we are not living for Christ, well, what are we living for? There is nothing else worth living for. But Paul does not say that here.

Paul likewise does not say, "For me to live, I hope, will be Christ." That would be an expectation, but Paul is making a statement of fact here: "For me to live *is* Christ." I am not Christ, but for me to live is Christ because it is not I, but Christ, who lives in me. The explanation to this verse is Galatians 2:20: "I am crucified with Christ, and no longer live, I, but Christ lives in me; but in that I now live in the flesh, I live by faith, the faith of the Son of God, who has loved me and given himself for me."

If you live by the strength or power of yourself, no matter who you are, you are no match for your circumstances. One day some particular circumstance will find you out. You may, for a time, live by your own strength, by your own cleverness, by your own wisdom and by your own will. You may even be able to weather your circumstances successfully for a time, but there will come a time in your life when you will realize that your circumstances are more than you can handle. Sooner or later you will find it out because no one is able to live a Christian life in and by himself in this world—not even Paul. There is only one way you can meet all kinds of circumstances, whether smooth or rough, good or bad, in prosperity or in adversity, hungry or full; there is only one way for you to live a Christian life and that is to recognize and accept this fact: "Not I but Christ." Paul said, "I am crucified with Christ. I know I cannot live a Christian life. I know I cannot handle all the circumstances of life in this world. I know that if I try to do it, sooner or later I will fall. Thank God, when Christ died on the cross, God put me in Him and crucified me with Him." Paul acknowledged that verdict.

Do you not know that God has already pronounced a verdict over you, and that that verdict was carried out two thousand years ago on Calvary's cross? The verdict is, that you must die because you are unable to live. You cannot be improved, reformed, changed. God says, "You are finished; I have finished you on Calvary; when Christ died, you died in Him and with Him." Do you accept that? Or do you think you are too good or too powerful to die? Do you think you can still live? If you do, then you will not accept that fact. But if you acknowledge that there is no good in you—that is, in your flesh—that there is no strength in you, that you cannot do it, that you cannot make it, it is beyond you, then it is the easiest and most natural thing for you to accept God's fact. You can declare as did Paul: "I am crucified with Christ, and no longer live I." And hence, who is now living? It is Christ who lives in me. That is the reason why Paul said: "For me to live is Christ. Yes, I am living in various and at times difficult circumstances but it is not I who live, it is Christ who now lives in me. He is living out His life through me, and no circumstance is too hard or difficult for Christ." That is resurrection life. It is life out of death and it always rises above and never descends below. "For me to live is Christ."

Have we discovered this secret? Christ is in us, the hope of glory. We who believe in the Lord Jesus have Christ in us. If we do not have Christ in us, then we are not Christ's. But thank God, when we believe in the Lord Jesus, Christ comes into us. He is in every believer, but let us always bear in mind that He is in us as life. He is in us to live for us. If we can only see this, then daily, when we open our eyes each morning, we can simply lift our hearts to the Lord and say, "Thank God, here is another day to live, here are circumstances through which I must live this day; but it is not I, it is Christ who lives." If we just stand on this fact day by day: "For me to live is Christ," then how different our life will be. There is nothing impossible with Him. Let us not look at circumstances; let us simply look at Christ. Let us not blame our circumstances; if we have Christ, our circumstances will serve us.

"But we do know that all things work together for good to those who love God, to those who are called according to purpose" (Romans 8:28).

A story was told about St. Augustine who was a brilliant young man. When he was in his early twenties, before he was saved, he became a professor of rhetoric, the highest seat of professorship at the university at that time. He lived a very dissipated life, committing many sins. But then, thank God, he was saved, and one day, when he was walking along the street, he heard a woman's voice behind him calling his name. But he walked on, and finally that woman caught up with him and faced him, saying, "Augustine, don't you know me?" Augustine said, "To whom are you talking? The one whom you knew is dead."

Now *that* is the secret: "For me to live is Christ." But sometimes you may think the following: "Yes, I do have the life of Christ in me. I know Christ lives in me, but why is it that I still live and He does not live? How can His life be released in me? Where is the blockage? Is there a key which can open the way for the life of Christ to come forth instead of myself?" Yes, there is, and that is the reason why Paul mentions this matter of the mind of Christ in the second chapter.

The Release of Life

"Let this mind be in you which was also in Christ Jesus" (Philippians 2:5). Life can be blocked or it can be released through the mind. It is just like the faucet in the home. The water tower may be full of water, but if the faucet is shut off, no water can come out. We have to open the faucet, and then the water will flow. This is the same thing with our Christian living. We have all the resources within us. Christ as our life is our resource, and this resource is unsearchably rich and abundant. It cannot be exhausted. It is there, but somehow it is shut off. All we need to do is open the faucet; and that is our mind.

Let me explain it this way: The letter to the Romans can roughly be divided into two parts. In chapters 1—11 you find the mercies of God. God has done so much for us in Christ Jesus. He has done everything for you in Him. If you want your sins to be forgiven, it is in Christ Jesus. If you want to overcome the power of sin, it is in Christ Jesus. If you want to live a holy life, it is in Christ Jesus. Everything is in Him. God has given Christ to you by His mercies. This Christ is in you, and all the spiritual blessings in the heavenlies are in Him and therefore in you.

On the other hand, Romans chapters 12—16 speak of practical living. After you have received all the mercies of God and stored them within you, then let these flow out to the glory of God. But at the point of transition (you thinking of all which God has done for you in Christ Jesus), you have Romans 12:1-2: "I beseech you therefore, brethren, by the compassions of God to present your bodies a living sacrifice, holy, acceptable to God, which is your reasonable service. And be not conformed to this world but be transformed by the renewing of your mind, that ye may prove what is the good and acceptable and perfect will of God."

You have the life of Christ in you. Now you need to open it up. How do you do that? By the renewing of your mind. You may have heard the Greek philosopher say, "I know I am because I think;" or, "I think, therefore I am." In other words, your thinking has much to do with what you are. What do you set your mind upon? What occupies your mind? What do you evaluate in your mind? What do you consider as important or unimportant? Your viewpoint, the way you look at things, all these have much to do with the way you live. You have the life in you. Now, how are you going to live? That has much to do with your mind.

Even though we are saved and have a new life in us, our mind is still old. Our mind still thinks in the way which the people in the world think. We still consider things in the world as important, precious, dear to us. We still hanker after these things. We still evaluate things in the same way we did before we were saved. No wonder we still follow the old way. Our minds need to be renewed, but how? God has done everything for us by giving us the life of His beloved Son, and in that life is all we need. But there is one thing God does not and will not do for us. It is something we have to do ourselves, and that is, to present our bodies a living sacrifice. Even though God has purchased us with a price—even by the blood of His beloved Son—and we belong to Him by right, God never forces anyone. He wants voluntary service. God says to us: "Look at what I have done for you. Look at what I have given you. I have given Christ to you; He is yours, but if you want to live by His life, there is one thing you have to do; you have to present your bodies a living sacrifice to Me."

What is a sacrifice? A sacrifice is something given to God for His consumption. Therefore, sacrifice is called food—God's food. Let God be satisfied with a sacrifice. So today, we who are the Lord's, are to become a living sacrifice. Every day we live, we are for His pleasure. We do not live here for our own pleasure, for our own enjoyment. We live here as a sacrifice to God. We live here for Him, for His pleasure, for His satisfaction, for His will, for His purpose. So this is something we have to voluntarily present to Him—even ourselves. The wonderful thing is, that when we present our bodies a living sacrifice to God, something happens to our mind. The Holy Spirit so renews it that we begin to see, value and look at things differently. What we treasured before becomes refuse to us, or contrary-wise, what we previously despised suddenly becomes very precious to us.

Let me use an illustration. Paul once said that before he knew the Lord he had boasted in his heritage (see Philippians 3). He was a Jew, born in the tribe of Benjamin that had never rebelled. He was circumcised on the eighth day according to law and brought up as a Pharisee who had kept the law continuously, and according to the righteousness of the law, he was blameless. He had considered these things most highly, and because of that, this was the way he had lived. He said, "I lived as a Pharisee." But after he came to the Lord and surrendered his life to Christ, what happened? He said this: "What I considered as gain, now I look at as loss. I consider all things as dross, worth nothing. I am willing to let everything go for the excellency of the knowledge of Jesus Christ." Now that is a renewed mind. You and I need a renewed mind but to have this renewed mind you have to do something—present your bodies as a living sacrifice. You have to give yourself to God. You have to give up your right over your life. You have to let Him manage your life; and if you do, the Holy Spirit will do the work of renewing your mind. Then you will find the faucet is open.

When your mind is renewed, what do you realize? You realize that in you, that is, in your flesh, there is no good. Therefore, it is but right for God to have you crucified with

Christ. You accept this and, with a renewed mind, you begin to understand that you should not continue to struggle; Christ lives in you. Christ lived a glorious life when He was on earth. Why not let Him live again in and through you? That will be the happiest thing for you to do; so, you let Him live, and life is released.

Running for the Goal

This life is not static at all. It is a life that continues to grow, and therefore Paul said, "I do not say I have attained. I do not say I have arrived. I am pressing on towards the goal that is before me for the prize of the calling on high of God in Christ Jesus. I want to possess what I am possessed of by God. This life is thrilling. This life is progressing all the time to know Him and the power of His resurrection, the fellowship of His sufferings, being made conformable to His death, so that I may arrive at the out-resurrection from among the dead." It is a continuous gaining of Christ, and as we experience Christ more and more, our Christian life deepens more and more.

Sometimes I like to use an illustration which I acknowledge is not a very good one, but you will forgive me for that. When I was a boy in Shanghai there used to be a race course for greyhounds there. I have never been there, but I was told that when they raced these greyhounds they could not let them loose without an object to pursue. So they employed an electric rabbit. When they released the electric rabbit, all the greyhounds would pursue it, trying to catch the rabbit. Of course, they ran very fast.

Sometimes I feel our Christian life is like that. We are running all the time, but we cannot run without an object, without a goal. So here we have Christ as our goal. He is not only the life within us, He is also the goal outside of us that we are running after. The strange thing is, however, that if we are never able to catch up with Him, we will be disappointed. So, from time to time He lets us catch up with Him, for a while; but after we do so, suddenly He proceeds to run ahead of us again, and thus we have to run again. That is the Christian life, and that is why Paul said, "I do not say that I have attained fully." Yes, he has attained much, but he says that Christ is still before him. He has to pursue after Him, forgetting the things which are behind. This is Christian living. It is a life lived *by* Christ and it is also a life pursuing *after* Christ—a glorious life. The Christian life is never dull. There is always something ahead of us because Christ is always ahead of us. That is Christ.

Twice in the New Testament we learn that Christ was passing by someone. He appeared as though He were going on and those whom He was passing had to call Him back. On one occasion the disciples were rowing a boat in a storm and Christ was walking on the water. But Jesus was not walking *towards* the boat, He was walking *past* the boat and they called Him back. The other time was when He was walking with those two disciples to Emmaus village; and when they came to Emmaus, Christ intended walking onwards; but they implored the Lord to stop: "Oh no, do please stay here; have supper with us." Now that is the way of the Christian life. We have to catch up with Christ at times, pause for a while, and then we have to catch up with Him again. Such is the Christian life.

Initiation into Christ-Living

Again I would inquire, How do we enter into that kind of Christian living? It is not natural. And because of that, we need to be initiated into it. Paul in essence has said: "I have been initiated into this kind of living. I know how to be full and I know how to be hungry; I know how to live in prosperity and I know how to live in adversity. I have been initiated into this kind of Christian life." He then added this: "I can do all things through Him who empowers me."

Do you want to be initiated into this kind of life? Do you

want to be initiated into the reality of Paul's declaration: "I can do all things through Him who empowers me"? Yet how? It is through experience and through circumstances. God will arrange your circumstances so that you may be initiated into Christ—into the all sufficiency of Christ.

I wonder if I am correct in saying that Paul was probably initiated into this Christian lifestyle on the occasion of what is recorded by him in II Corinthians 12. At that time Paul had a thorn in his flesh and we are told repeatedly that this was not a *tiny* thorn in his life but was an issue the size of a stake. Paul had a *stake* driven into his flesh. That was the circumstance. It had weakened him. It had put him to shame. Indeed, it was a drawback for him in preaching the gospel of Jesus Christ; and because of this, he prayed three times, "Oh God, remove this stake. You can do it. Change my circumstances so that I may be strong." But he received the answer: "My grace is sufficient for thee" (see II Corinthians 12:9a).

Instead of removing the stake or changing the circumstances, which God could verily do, God let His grace rise up so high that Paul was able to overcome the stake and its effects. It is similar to what our brother Watchman Nee once said: "Sometimes God can and does remove the rock so that the boat can sail through; but at other times He can raise the level of water high enough so the boat can sail through." Here with Paul we find God saying: "I will not remove the stake but I will raise the level of My grace; for My grace is sufficient for you." And thus Paul was initiated into the secret that "I can do all things through Him who empowers me."

Let us not despise or murmur against our circumstances. Let us not always pray and ask that God change our circumstances. Sometimes He does, but let us accept these circumstances as opportunities for us to experience Christ. If we can learn to experience Him in one circumstance, when the next one comes our way, then we shall be able to rise above the situation so that we come into knowing Christ in our daily life.

This, then, is the letter to the Philippians. Paul has shared the secret of Christian living with us and may we learn it.

Shall we pray:

Dear heavenly Father, we do worship Thee because Thou hast already put that secret of living in us—Christ as our life. We do pray that Thou wilt open our eyes to see it and renew our minds that Thy life may be released. We pray that we may, in our circumstances, be initiated into that secret: "I can do all things through Him who empowers me." May it be real to every brother and sister here in this place so that Thy name may be glorified. We ask in the name of our Lord Jesus. Amen.

COLOSSIANS

Seeing Christ as the Fullness of God

Colossians 1:9-13—For this reason we also, from the day we heard of your faith and love, do not cease praying and asking for you, to the end that ye may be filled with the full knowledge of his will, in all wisdom and spiritual understanding, so as to walk worthily of the Lord unto all well-pleasing, bearing fruit in every good work, and growing by the true knowledge of God; strengthened with all power according to the might of his glory unto all endurance and longsuffering with joy; giving thanks to the Father, who has made us fit for sharing the portion of the saints in light, who has delivered us from the authority of darkness, and translated us into the kingdom of the Son of his love.

Colossians 2:9-10—For in him (that is in Christ) dwells all the fulness of the Godhead bodily; and ye are complete in him.

Let us look to the Lord in prayer:

Dear heavenly Father, how we do praise and thank Thee for giving us such a high privilege of coming to Thy table to remember Thy beloved Son, and through Thy Son to come to Thy throne of grace to receive help and mercy and grace. Our Father, how we do praise and thank Thee that we are indeed in Thy presence. We thank Thee that the veil has been removed. We thank Thee that we can approach the throne of grace with boldness. Now our Father, we ask that Thou wilt reveal Thyself to us; reveal Thy Son to us through Thy word. We ask in Thy precious name. Amen.

In the letter to the Colossians the Holy Spirit intends to reveal to us Christ—the glory, the supremacy, the fullness, and the all-sufficiency of Christ—and because of Christ being such, therefore we find our completeness in Him.

There are two letters written by the apostle Paul which are considered to be twin letters—Ephesians and Colossians. Both were written from the Roman prison; both were written at about the same time; and both were sent by the same messenger, Tychicus. In the letter to the Ephesians we see the glorious vocation of the church as the body of Christ. In the letter to the Colossians we see the glory of Christ as the Head, and in Him the church, which is His body, finds its completeness. So these two letters reveal to us Christ and the church. As far as is known, the letter to the Colossians was written a little before the letter to the Ephesians. There are reasons for that, but we will not dwell on them. However, I think that this order of writing must be so because, logically speaking, we have to see the Head first before we can see the body. We must see Christ first before we can ever see the church, which is His body.

Perhaps a little background will help in our understanding of this letter. Colosse was a very small city, and probably today we would not even call it a city. It was just a little town situated in the Roman province of Asia located in what is Turkey today. Paul had never been to that town, but we know that he was in Ephesus for three years. During his stay in Ephesus the word of the Lord was heard by all those in Asia Minor, both Jews and Gentiles, and evidently some of the Colossians came to that great city for various reasons, perhaps for trade. Among the people who came to Ephesus and heard the word of God through the apostle Paul were Epaphras, Philemon, Apphia and others. These people went back to Colosse and there the church in Colosse began. Even though Paul had never been to Colosse, he was used by the Lord as a channel or instrument in the very founding of the church there.

While the apostle was in prison in Rome the church in

Colosse sent to Paul a messenger, Epaphras. He went to Rome to see Paul for two reasons. One was to convey to him the sympathetic greetings of the saints in Colosse, and the other was to report to him the trouble they had in Colosse. The problem the church in Colosse began to experience was later called the Colossian heresy. In order to correct that heresy, Paul wrote this letter to the Colossians. I do not think we need to know in detail what the Colossian heresy was, even though it is very interesting. Actually, when the great apostle Paul wrote this letter, he did not dwell on the heresy. To the contrary, he focused his attention on Christ. He took a positive approach by presenting Christ to them. If they could see Christ, if they could know Him, then that heresy would drop away automatically and very quickly.

Graham Scroggie once remarked: "A true Christology is the best answer to all heresy that ever has been or ever will be." In other words, a sight of Christ is the answer to all false teachings and false doctrines. If we only knew Christ as we should, then we would be delivered from all heresies and all false teachings. I do believe that this is what it ought to be.

Perhaps the question can be raised: "Why is it that the Colossian believers would fall into such heresy?" Probably there are two reasons. First, human beings are naturally curious. In human nature there is an intellectual urge. We want to know; we want an explanation for everything. We can see it very clearly from childhood onward. When a child is growing up he is always asking questions: "Why, why, why?" He wants to know the reason for everything. I do not know if that kind of natural urge is the result of eating from the tree of the knowledge of good and evil, but within human beings there is this natural desire to know, to be curious about things, to speculate, to be able to explain. With that kind of curiosity and intellectual urge, we would like to know what the origin of the universe is. We would like to know how this thing came to happen or how that other thing came to be. Instead of trusting in God with a childlike faith, we try to look around, speculate, imagine, explain everything around us. In doing so, we fall into the trap of the enemy.

Second, there is within us a desire for quick solutions and success. We are all naturally impatient. We like to see things fixed or resolved quickly, instantaneously, and successfully. I think this is the reason why Eve fell for the trick of the enemy because she wanted so much to be like God. Man was created according to the image of God, and therefore, naturally, there is within us a desire to be conformed to that image, and I think this is right. We are made according to that image; therefore, we have an inward desire to be conformed to that image. But the problem is, how are we to be conformed to the image according to which we were made? Are we to be conformed to the image by the way that God has prescribed for us, eating of the tree of life, receiving God's life in us, and letting that life grow in us, being transformed and conformed to His image? That, of course, will take time. Or are we to be conformed by searching out some instantaneous technique—whether that be through some mystic experience or by performing some external exercises? If so, we will see how the enemy will come in and offer something along that very line: "If you simply are initiated into this mystery, then you shall be complete," or, "If you just practice certain things—do this and do that, don't do this and don't do that; then you shall become perfect." Oh, how man so readily falls into that trap because he desires instantaneous success. I think probably these are the two reasons why the Colossian believers fell into the so-called Colossian heresy.

Colossian Heresy

Now let me speak a little about the Colossian heresy, because I know you are curious! As far as we know, the Colossian heresy was a combination of two things: one was heathen gnosticism and the other, Jewish ceremonialism. It was a very strange combination. In those days there were people called the Gnostics (derived from the Greek word *gnosis*, meaning "knowledge.") They considered themselves to be people "in the know," those who knew everything. They knew how the universe began, they knew how all of creation began to evolve, they even supposedly knew the hierarchy in the unseen world, and so on. And they claimed that if you were initiated into such knowledge, then you would know everything. It was an intellectual speculation, a kind of mystic approach; but simultaneously it was combined oddly enough, with Jewish ceremonialism—that is to say, with certain Jewish rituals and observances. And they believed that if anyone followed these two approaches to life, that that person would possess full knowledge—knowing everything—and would achieve fullness and perfection. In essence, that was the Colossian heresy.

Full Knowledge of God's Will

How then, would Paul resolve this kind of problem present in the Colossian assembly? I believe a clue can be found in his prayer for the Colossian believers recorded in Colossians 1:9: "For this reason we also, from the day we heard of your faith and love, do not cease praying and asking for you, to the end that ye may be filled with the full knowledge of his will."

The Gnostics always talked about having full knowledge; they continually spoke about wisdom; they talked endlessly about fullness. So here Paul turned the tables on them and said, "I am going to talk about fullness. I am going to talk about full knowledge. I am going to talk about how we can be filled and indicate with what we should be filled. And my prayer for you brethren is that you may be filled to the full—not just somewhat filled but filled completely, filled to the full." But with what? With full knowledge—even a full knowledge of God's will.

Let us ask ourselves: what are we filled with? Are we filled full with the knowledge of God's will? Do we know what God's will is? Do we know what is the full knowledge of His will? The full knowledge of God's will has reference not only to a mental apprehension of the complete, the perfect and the full knowledge of God's will but also to the experiential and living apprehension of His will. I do believe that it is of tremendous importance here that we be filled with this kind of knowledge. It does not matter if we do not have other knowledge, even though that other knowledge may be good. However, if we are lacking in the full knowledge of God's will, then something is basically wrong with us, and we shall be exposed to all kinds of deceptions and heresies. What we need today is to be filled with the full knowledge of God's will, to know what His will is—even the perfect will of God.

I would say again that we need to realize that this will of God is not merely a mental knowledge; it is also a knowledge which is living, that which we can experience, enter into, and be involved with. This in fact is the substance of Paul's prayer for the Colossian believers, and I do believe that this is the prayer which is likewise needed for us today: "... that ye may be filled with the full knowledge of God's will in all wisdom and understanding."

What is wisdom? There are different explanations, but if we look back into the Old Testament period we find that there was one particular man who asked God for wisdom. God gave him wisdom, and wisdom we are told, is having "a heart that hears." Wisdom is not primarily conceived in the mind. We always think of wisdom as something having to do with the mind, but true wisdom in a man is having a heart that hears the voice of God. *That* is wisdom.

Understanding on the other hand, is the conscious assimilation of knowledge into oneself. A person knows it and knows how to apply it to one's life. This full knowledge of God's will must be apprehended and applied in all wisdom and understanding. It is not merely something in our mind, it is also something which our heart hears. It is that which has been assimilated consciously and practically into our life. It is not speculative knowledge; it is a practical knowledge. Gnostic teaching is speculative; it does not affect one's life in any practical way. This full knowledge of God's will enables us "to walk worthily of the Lord unto all well-pleasing, bearing fruit in every good work, and growing by the true knowledge of God; strengthened with all power according to the might of his glory unto all endurance and longsuffering with joy; giving thanks to the Father" (Colossians 1:10-11).

Such knowledge affects our life, and this is the knowledge which we must have. I think the key to that can be found in the second passage which we read at the very beginning: "For in him [that is, in Christ] dwells all the fulness of the Godhead bodily; and ye are complete in him" (Colossians 2:9-10).

This is the full knowledge of God's will. What is God's will? His will is centered upon His Son. In His Son all the fullness of the Godhead dwells bodily. That is God's will.

What is the fullness of the Godhead? This fullness of the Godhead *dwells*. We know that the word *dwells* in John 15 is the same word translated as *abides*. And in the original language it simply means "make its home." All the fullness of the Godhead makes its home in Christ; it not just visits but stays, remains, abides, dwells, makes its home in Christ Jesus. This is our Lord Jesus. He is the fullness of God. Whatever you can think of concerning the Godhead, whatever area it may be—His love, His holiness, His justice, His righteousness, His virtue, His power—all the fullness of the Godhead makes its home in Christ Jesus. He is the fullness of God, and in this little letter Paul tried to explain a little of what he meant.

Image of the Invisible God

First of all, Paul said, "All the fulness of the Godhead dwells in Christ." How? Christ is the image of the invisible God. We know that God is spirit; therefore, He is invisible. No one can see God. But Christ the Son is the image of the invisible God. The image (Greek, *eikon*) here does not refer to outward form but to the inward quality. All the inward qualities in God are also in the Son, and He is the full representation and the full manifestation of God and His inward qualities. You may recall that the Lord Jesus once said, "No one has ever seen the Father, but the Son, who is in the bosom of the Father, He has declared Him" (see John 1:18). The disciples had been with the Lord for three years and during that last night together one of them still asked, "Now show us the Father and it suffices us." And the Lord Jesus replied: "Phillip, I have been with you for three years, and you are still asking this question. Do you not know that if you see Me you see the Father?" (see John 14:8-9)

Who is the Lord Jesus? He is the image of the invisible God. Today all we know of God is through knowing Christ Jesus, because Christ Jesus the Son has declared the Father. He has manifested the Father. In the former days God spoke in many ways to our fathers and in many parts through the prophets, but in these last days He has spoken to us in the Son (see Hebrews 1:1-2). Only the Son is the full representation of the Father, and only through Him is the Father fully manifested—nothing more and nothing less. He is the image of the invisible God, and it is according to that image that man was created, and it is to that image that one day we will be conformed by the grace of God.

Firstborn of All Creation

All the fullness of the Godhead dwells in Him bodily (see Colossians 2:9) because He is the firstborn of all creation (Colossians 1:15). This word *firstborn* does not refer to what we ordinarily think about firstborn. This word in the Scriptures has two uses: one is the common use and the other is the special use. Suppose in a family you are the firstborn and after you there are others who are born who are your brothers and sisters. That is the common usage of the word. But in the Scriptures there is a special usage of it and it does not refer to that kind of order. It refers to the notion of having "priority to" and "sovereignty over." If you are the firstborn in this more special sense, then you are prior to everything that follows. You are not *within* the order; you are *before* that order. You are prior to, and you have sovereignty over everything that comes afterwards. That is the meaning here of the firstborn.

So the firstborn of all creation simply means that our Lord Jesus is prior to all creation. I think it is itself explained here because the Scripture reads: "He is before all" (Colossians 1:17). He is not created; He is the Creator. He is before all. He is considered as the firstborn of all creation because all things were created in Him, by Him, and for Him. Unfortunately, in Colossians 1:16, the translators changed the word *in* because they could not understand it. They translated it to say, "Because *by* him were created all things ..." We find this again in the same verse: "All things have been created by Him and for Him." But in the original it is a different word. It says all things were created *in* Him because He is the designer. He designs all things. All things take their character from Him. And, then, we read that all things were created *by* Him: He is the builder, the engineer; He makes all things. And lastly, all things were created *for* Him: He is the owner, the heir of all things. Here we find the fullness of the Godhead in Christ Jesus. He is the Creator of all things—all things were created in Him, designed by Him, and took their character from Him. All things were created through Him—He made them. And all things were created for Him—He is the owner and the heir of all things. That is our Lord Jesus.

Head over the Church

"And He is the Head of the body, the assembly; who is the beginning, firstborn from among the dead" (Colossians 1:18).

Christ is not only the Creator of the universe, of all creation; He is also the beginning, the Head, the foundation of the new creation, which is the church. The church is a new creation, and this new creation begins with Him. He is the Head, and out of Him comes the church. On the cross when the soldier thrust that spear into His side, water and blood came out, and the apostle John said with emphasis, "I saw it, I witnessed it, I say this is true" (see John 19:34-35). Why was John so emphatic? Through the death of our Lord Jesus, and out of His broken heart, came forth blood for the remission of our sins, and water (life) that we may live. Out of the travail of His soul the church, the new creation was born, and it was on the basis of resurrection. It is not the old creation. It is a new creation, therefore it is on resurrection ground. He is the Head of the body, which is the church.

Reconciler of All Things

He is the reconciler of all things (see Colossians 1:20). After God had created all things man fell, and because man sinned, the whole earth entered into corruption and vanity (see Romans 8). The whole of creation entered into the bondage of corruption and vanity, not because all things in creation were willing to, but because they were compelled to through the fall of man. When our Lord Jesus, who is the fullness of God, came into this world and died on the cross, He reconciled not only mankind, but all things. He brought them all back into harmony. All things had disintegrated, had fallen into chaos, had lost their purpose; but the Lord Jesus restores everything back into harmony, into meaning, into purpose, and into His fullness. This is our Lord Jesus. This is the full knowledge of God's will. In Him all the fullness of the Godhead dwells bodily.

Do we see Christ as being as large as the Bible reveals Him to us, or do we see Him merely as a little Christ? Thank God, we do see Him as our Savior. To us that is as large as the universe; however, so far as God is concerned, that is but a tiny speck, because in God's will Christ His Son is everything. All the knowledge is in Him, all the wisdom is in Him; indeed, everything is in Him.

If we look with the creation in view—Christ is the firstborn. If we look with the new creation in view—Christ is the beginning. If we look from the viewpoint of reconciliation—it is through Christ. And if we look at God—Christ is the very image of the invisible God.

The full knowledge of God's will is simply this: to God, Christ His Son is all and in all. If this is so, why should we ever go outside of Christ in search of an explanation for all things or in search of a solution to any problem?

Complete in Him

There is not only the glory of Christ as the fullness of God, but the Scripture declares this: "In Him ye are complete" (Colossians 2:10). This word is spoken to us believers. All the fullness of the Godhead dwells in Christ, and the Bible further says that we are complete in Him. If this is what Christ is and we are complete in Him, then why should we seek for anything else? It is absurd! Before the apostle Paul knew the excellency of the knowledge of Jesus Christ, he had pursued after other knowledge, he had boasted in other things, he had considered his achievements in things other than Christ. But one day when he saw the excellency of the knowledge of Jesus Christ, he came to the following conclusion: "I count all things but dross, I count everything as loss for the excellency of the knowledge of Jesus Christ. To know Him, that is my one desire" (see Philippians 3).

In European church history there was a man named Count Nicolaus von Zinzendorf. He was saved when he was between four and six years old. He belonged to the nobility, and while a little boy growing up in the castle, he loved the Lord very much. He used to sit at the window and write on a paper, "Jesus loves you," and throw it out of the window hoping that someone down below would pick it up. Throughout his life he loved the Lord Jesus very much. He said, "I have only one passion. I have but one passion, Jesus Christ."

If we really are filled with the full knowledge of God's will, if we truly see who Jesus is and what He is, I wonder how it can possibly be that we can have more than one passion in life! Should that not just fill us with that one longing, one desire to know Him? Paul said, "To know him and the power of his resurrection" (Philippians 3:10). "In Him ye are complete."

Union

When we believe in the Lord Jesus, are we aware that something tremendous has happened? We often dwell upon the fact that when we believe in the Lord Jesus our sins are forgiven. Thank God for that; that is true. When we believe in the Lord Jesus we receive a new life; that is also true. But how? Why is your sin forgiven when you believe in the Lord Jesus? He died two thousand years ago and you committed your sin only in this century. Why is it that when you believe in the Lord Jesus all your sins are forgiven? Why is it that when you believe in the Lord Jesus you receive a new life? He poured out His life two thousand years ago. Why, then, is it that you receive that new life today? How does it happen? Something tremendous, indeed, happens! When you believe in the Lord Jesus, a union takes place: "By God you have been put in Christ, whom God made unto us wisdom, righteousness, sanctification, and redemption" (see I Corinthians 1:30). When you receive the Lord Jesus, not only does the Lord Jesus come into you, but also God puts you into the Lord Jesus; a union occurs: you are in Christ and Christ is in you, and because of this, your sins are forgiven and a new life is received.

Let me illustrate it this way: God delivered the children of

Israel out of Egypt, but His purpose was not to deliver them out of Egypt and then leave them in the wilderness to die. God's purpose was to lead them into the promised land, the land flowing with milk and honey. God gave the promised land of Canaan to the children of Israel as their inheritance. What kind of land was it?

> "For Jehovah thy God bringeth thee into a good land, a land of waterbrooks, of springs, and of deep waters, that gush forth in the valleys and hills; a land of wheat, and barley, and vines, and fig trees, and pomegranates; a land of olive trees and honey; a land wherein thou shalt eat bread without scarceness, where thou shalt lack nothing; a land whose stones are iron, and out of whose mountains thou wilt dig copper. And thou shalt eat and be filled, and shalt bless Jehovah thy God for the good land which he hath given thee" (Deuteronomy 8:7-10).

The land which God gave to the children of Israel as their inheritance was a good land. It was a land filled with every good thing, and when they were there they would eat and be filled and bless the Lord. When they entered the land this is what they found:

> "And it shall be, when Jehovah thy God bringeth thee into the land which he swore unto thy fathers, to Abraham, to Isaac, and to Jacob, to give thee: great and good cities which thou buildedst not, and houses full of everything good which thou filledst not, and wells digged which thou diggedst not, vineyards and oliveyards which thou plantedst not, and thou shalt have eaten and shalt be full" (Deuteronomy 6:10-11).

When they entered the land they found that the cities were already built. They did not even need to build them. They found that the houses were not only built but filled with good things. The fields were already planted, and the wells were already dug. They just entered in, enjoyed, and were full. Now that is the picture which can be painted when we read: "Ye are complete in Christ." When we believe in the Lord Jesus, God puts us into Christ. Christ has become our land flowing with milk and honey. He is the great and good land. Christ is our inheritance, and in Him everything is ready. All the spiritual blessings in the heavenlies in Christ Jesus are available to us. It is all ours. We are complete in Him. We do not need to dig a well; all we need to do is draw out of it. Everything is ready and available in Christ. He has done everything for us. Everything He has done is for our sakes. He simply says, "Just come in and enjoy Me." "Ye are complete in Him."

Forgiveness of Sins

"In whom we have redemption, the forgiveness of sins" (Colossians 1:14). "... having forgiven us all the offenses" (Colossians 2:13).

We have sinned terribly. We have offended God greatly, but thank God, in Christ Jesus, our sins are all forgiven.

"... though your sins be as scarlet they shall be as white as snow ..." (Isaiah 1:18).

All our sins are washed away. All the offenses are forgiven, and not only forgiven but forgotten. God does not remember your offense to Him anymore. Think of that! He has redeemed us out of the curse of the law so that we do not need to die anymore, and it is all in Christ. Because we are united with Him, therefore our sins are forgiven, our offenses are forgotten, and we are redeemed from the curse of the law. Yet that is just the beginning.

Circumcision

"In whom also ye have been circumcised with circumcision not done by hand, in the putting off of the body of the flesh, in the circumcision of the Christ" (Colossians 2:11).

When we believe in the Lord Jesus, not only are our sins forgiven and our offenses forgotten; not only are we redeemed from the curse of the law; but also we have been circumcised, yet not with hands. It is not a physical thing but is a circumcision of the heart. It is the circumcision of Christ. When we believe in the Lord Jesus He gives us a new heart, a heart that is tender and soft, a heart that hears, a heart that loves Him. Our heart has been circumcised.

Christ has delivered us out of the bondage of the flesh because when He died, you and I died in Him. We are now a new creation. The Scriptures tell us that when we were baptized, we were buried with Christ and have also been raised with him through faith in the working of God who raised Him from among the dead (see Colossians 2:12).

Christ not only has died for us and we died with Him and in Him, but also He was buried. The old things have passed away, and when we rise up out of the baptismal waters, we declare that from now on it is Christ who lives in us. Is that not wonderful?

Let us realize that it is no longer we who live. Sometimes we find ourselves very bothersome. It is as Paul said, "Oh, who can deliver me from this wretched body—this body of death?" (see Romans 7:24) According to tradition, we are told that in the Roman world, when the authorities wanted to punish a murderer, they would bind the corpse of the murdered person with the murderer face to face, hands to hands, feet to feet, mouth to mouth, until gradually the poison of the corrupted corpse penetrated that living man's flesh and so he died from it. That is what Paul meant when he cried out: "Who can deliver me from this wretched body—this body of death?" Is it not so that sometimes we feel this wretched "I"? Why is it that the "I" still comes forth? Oh, that it be buried, that it be put to death! Well, it was already dead, it was already buried; but we dug it back up. If we truly believe through the faith of Jesus Christ that when Christ was buried we were buried with Him and that when He was raised from the dead we were raised with Him from the dead in newness of life, then it is done.

Debts Paid

"Having effaced the handwriting in ordinances which stood out against us, which was contrary to us, he has taken it also out of the way, having nailed it to the cross" (Colossians 2:14).

What does this passage mean? In the olden days when people wanted to borrow from you, they would give you a paper, an I.O.U. (I owe you). With that I.O.U. paper you could demand repayment of the debt. But whether the debtor paid it or not, the I.O.U. paper was yours, and you nailed it. That handwriting, with the signature there—the I.O.U.—was nailed to the cross. When you publicly nailed that paper up, it signified that the debt was fully paid.

That is what Christ did for us. We each and all of us have signed an I.O.U. God has said to us, "These are My laws." And we have said in response, "All which you have commanded, we will do." For have we not, like the children of Israel, said again and again, "We will do all which God has commanded"? We each, as it were, had signed a handwritten I.O.U. But we were not able to fulfill our I.O.U. obligation. We each of us therefore owed God our own handwriting or certificate of debt. But when Christ died on the cross He paid all the debt, the handwriting having been nailed by God to the cross. What grace! What mercy!

Deliverance

"He has delivered us from the authority of darkness, and translated us into the kingdom of the Son of his love" (Colossians 1:13).

We are no longer under the authority of darkness. The

enemy tries to keep people in darkness, and he has authority to do that because people belong to him. But we are the Lord's; and hence, the enemy no longer has any authority over us to keep us in darkness. God has already translated us out from the authority of darkness and has transported us into the kingdom, power and authority of the Son of God's love. So all we need to obey is the Son of God's love.

Defeat of the Enemy

What happened to the enemy? "Having spoiled principalities and authorities, he made a show of them publicly, leading them in triumph by it" (Colossians 2:15).

When Christ died on the cross He disarmed and spoiled (or stripped naked, as it were) all principalities and authorities, even all the powers of wickedness and all the spiritual powers of darkness. He has spoiled Satan and all his hosts, and made a public show of them by means of the cross. He has completely routed and defeated the enemy; and because He has defeated him, there is no reason why we should be defeated today. We can claim the victory of Christ over the enemy and all his works.

These, then, are but a few examples to demonstrate how we are complete in Him. There is nothing we need, whether to know or to live, that we cannot find in Christ Jesus. "All the fulness of the Godhead dwells in Him bodily and ye are complete in Him." *Complete* here means "made full in Him." If this is the case, then what should be our attitude in life?

Our Walk

"As therefore ye have received the Christ, Jesus the Lord, walk in Him, rooted and built up in Him, and assured in the faith, even as ye have been taught, abounding in it with thanksgiving" (Colossians 2:6-7).

If this is so, then what are we to do? How are we to conduct ourselves? We are to walk in Christ, we are to be rooted in Him, to be built up in Him, abounding in it with thanksgiving. Let us not—as the Colossian believers were doing—look outside of Christ. Let us find everything in Him, and if we do, we shall be delivered from all heresies; for instance, from Jewish ceremonialism—meat, drink, feast, new moons, Sabbaths. These things during the Old Testament times had indeed been instituted by God, but they were meant as shadows or symbols, preparing for the reality to come. When Christ, who is the reality, fulfillment and substance of these shadows, has come, then these shadows ought to disappear. There is no need for these external exercises any longer because we now have the inward reality, even the Christ. And if this be the case, then what is the need indeed of such strictures as "do not touch, do not taste;" and additionally, what is the need for all these mystical gnostic inquiries and speculations? We do not need that because, as Paul has written here, we have been delivered from the elements of this world. Our life is now hidden with Christ in God. Let us therefore think and inquire after the things in heaven, for we have become a heavenly people. We shall be delivered from all these earthly things. Such is the will of God.

True Ministry

Finally, when we come to the ministry of the apostle Paul, here is a description, in his own words, of what his ministry truly is: "I rejoice in sufferings for you, and I fill up that which is behind of the tribulations of Christ in my flesh, for [the sake of] his body, which is the assembly; of which I became minister" (Col. 1:24-25).

To what end, though, is Paul willing to suffer for the church? Let us listen carefully to what he had to say: "Whom we announce, admonishing every man, and teaching every man, in all wisdom, to the end that we may present every man perfect in Christ" (Col. 1:28).

True Christian ministry has only this goal, this one end, which is to present every man perfect in *Christ*, and not in anything else. If we try to be perfected in anything else we are unperfected. If we want to be perfect, it has to be in Christ, and this was the ministry of the apostle Paul. He admonished, he taught, he agonized, he toiled, he prayed: all and only for this one purpose, that he might present the believers perfect in Christ. This was also the ministry of Epaphras, because Paul mentioned him and his ministry in his prayer: "Epaphras, who is one of you, the bondman of Jesus Christ, salutes you, always combating earnestly for you in prayers, to the end that ye may stand perfect and complete in all the will of God" (Colossians 4:12).

What is the will of God? It can be summed up in this one statement of Paul's: "All the fulness of the Godhead dwells in Christ, and ye are complete in Him." As we approach this little letter to the Colossians, may we be filled with the full knowledge of God's will. Oh, that we may see Christ, the fullness of God, and be made partakers of that fullness.

Shall we pray:

Dear heavenly Father, we do look to Thee for the spirit of wisdom and revelation to the full knowledge of God. We pray that Thou wilt open our understanding, that we may see Christ as the fullness of the Godhead, and that we are complete in Him. We pray that as we see Him our faith would rise within us to claim Him as our all and in all. We pray that we may not in any way be distracted and drawn away by anything outside of Christ, that we may walk in Him, rooted and built up in Him, and be thankful all the time. In the name of our Lord Jesus. Amen.

I THESSALONIANS

SEEING CHRIST IN HIS PAROUSIA

I Thessalonians 1:10—And to await his Son from the heavens, whom he raised from among the dead, Jesus, our deliverer from the coming wrath.

I Thessalonians 2:19—For what is our hope, or joy, or crown of boasting? are not ye also before our Lord Jesus at his coming?

I Thessalonians 3:12,13—But you, may the Lord make to exceed and abound in love toward one another, and toward all, even as we also towards you, in order to the confirming of your hearts unblamable in holiness before our God and Father at the coming of our Lord Jesus with all his saints.

I Thessalonians 4:15-18—For this we say to you in the word of the Lord, that we, the living, who remain to the coming of the Lord, are in no way to anticipate those who have fallen asleep; for the Lord himself, with an assembling shout, with archangel's voice and with trump of God, shall descend from heaven; and the dead in Christ shall rise first; then we, the living who remain, shall be caught up together with them in the clouds, to meet the Lord in the air; and thus we shall be always with the Lord. So encourage one another with these words.

I Thessalonians 5:23, 24—Now the God of peace himself sanctify you wholly: and your whole spirit, and soul, and body be preserved blameless at the coming of our Lord Jesus Christ. He is faithful who calls you, who will also perform it.

Let us pray:

Dear heavenly Father, how we do praise and thank Thee that we can call Thee "Abba, Father." It is all because of Thy beloved Son, who gave His life for us. Now our Father, with hearts of worship, adoration, and love, we continue in Thy presence. We pray that Thy Holy Spirit will reveal Thy word to us that through Thy word, we may indeed see Thy beloved Son, who is all and in all to Thee and to us. In the name of our Lord Jesus. Amen.

We believe that the whole Bible reveals Christ Jesus to us, and the first letter to the Thessalonians is no exception. We may entitle this book "Seeing Christ in His Parousia." The word *parousia* is the term which is translated in this letter to the Thessalonians as *coming.* The word *coming* in Greek is *parousia*, which means "presence."

This first letter to the Thessalonians is the first extant letter written by the apostle Paul to the churches of his day. You may remember that at the time of Acts 16, Paul and his companions were traveling in the Roman province of Asia. The Spirit of God did not allow them to go to the north or to the south, so they went straight to the west until they arrived at Troas, a seaport. They could not go any farther because of the Aegean Sea, and it was during this time that in the night the apostle saw the vision of a Macedonian calling him to come over to help them. The next morning Paul and his companions decided it was from the Lord, and so they crossed the Aegean Sea into Europe. That was the first time the gospel of Jesus Christ had gone into Europe. And the first European city where Paul and his companions stayed for a time was at Philippi. They suffered greatly there, and Paul and Silas were thrown into prison because of the preaching of the gospel. However, through the travail of the apostles a church was raised up in Europe, which was the first church there. Paul and Silas were not allowed to stay in Philippi, but most likely they left the beloved physician Luke behind to help that young church in Philippi, and what a help he gave to that church!

Paul, Silas, and Timothy continued on until they came to the next city in Macedonia, Thessalonica. Now Thessalonica had been founded in 325 B.C. by Cassander, and he named it after his wife who was a sister of Alexander the Great. Today, of course, we know it is Salonika. At that time Thessalonica was the capital of Macedonia. Unlike Philippi there was a synagogue in that city because a number of Jews resided there. Paul and his companions went into the synagogue and for three Sabbaths reasoned with those who worshiped there. He presented to them the Lord Jesus: according to the Scriptures, Paul explained, He had to suffer; then He was raised from the dead, and this was Jesus, the Messiah. And because of his reasoning there in the synagogue we know that a number of people came to the Lord, among them quite a number of Greeks and some women. The Jews became jealous, and stirred up the whole city against Paul and his companions. These Jews came to Jason's house where Paul was residing, and when they could not find Paul there, they took Jason and some of the others and brought them to the officials at that time. That very night the brethren in Thessalonica sent Paul away secretly. He went on to Athens, and there he waited for Silas and Timothy to join him. After Silas and Timothy joined him in Athens, Paul proceeded to Corinth. But before he went to Corinth he sent Timothy back to Thessalonica.

The church in Thessalonica was born through much affliction and tribulation, and after Paul had left them that young church continued to suffer persecution, yet not from the Jews but from the Greeks—the Gentiles. It was similar to the churches in Judea in the way they suffered from the hands of their countrymen the Jews. Paul was deeply concerned about the suffering of this young church in Thessalonica at the hands of their Gentile countrymen. From this letter of I Thessalonians we learn that more than once Paul had attempted to return to Thessalonica, but he was prohibited from going back, and because of his deep concern for that young church he sent Timothy. Since Timothy was a younger man, perhaps he was not noticed as much by those hostile to the gospel; therefore, he was able to go back to visit that young church in tribulation. And while Paul was yet in Corinth, Timothy returned to him with a good report, telling him how that young church was standing fast in the Lord, but also that they had some problems. So Paul wrote this first letter to the Thessalonians. Evidently Paul wrote it from Corinth, for it was not too long after his departure from Thessalonica since in this first Thessalonian letter of his he had written how bereaved he was concerning them for a little while—"for a little moment."

As was noted earlier, this was the first extant letter we have of Paul writing to any church. In this letter he tried to comfort them; he tried to encourage them in the Lord. As we have already mentioned, this young church in Thessalonica had been founded in affliction and tribulation, but it had such a good foundation because it possessed all the essential qualities of life: both individual and corporate. There are three essential qualities of the Christian life which are of paramount importance, whether one considers this subject in relation to the individual Christian or in relation to a church—faith, love and hope. This young church had all three of these essential facets of the Christian life. They had the "work of faith" in having turned from idols to God; they had the "labor of love" in serving the true and living God; and they had the "endurance of hope" because they were awaiting God's Son from heaven whom God had raised from the dead—"Jesus, our deliverer from the coming wrath." This young church was very solidly founded, and even while they continued in tribulation and affliction, they grew in their faith, in their love, and even in their hope. It was a very beautiful picture of a young church.

Of course, they also had some problems; and here the apostle Paul felt led to write this first letter in an attempt to comfort and encourage them in the Lord. Now the question may be asked: How are you going to comfort and encourage a young church in the midst of tribulation? What will be the best way to do this? Here Paul shows us that the best way to encourage a church under persecution is to remind them—to underline, emphasize and reinforce to them—about the coming of the Lord Jesus, "the parousia of Christ."

In the history of the early church during the second and third centuries when the church repeatedly underwent persecution from the Roman Empire, the Christians would greet one another with the simple watchword or greeting of *maranatha*. And we know that *maranatha* means, "the Lord cometh, the Lord is coming." What can comfort Christian people's hearts in tribulation or under persecution more than the fact that the Lord is coming? This was not only true in the second and the third centuries, it has likewise been true throughout the centuries wherever Christians have been under persecution. Whether it be in Europe, in Asia, in Africa, or wherever it may be, and at whatever time it may be, when Christians are under persecution, the one thing which strengthens them more than anything else is to be reminded of the fact that the Lord is coming soon.

I want to read to you a hymn written by our beloved Watchman Nee. This hymn was written after the Communists had conquered and occupied all of China, and in a way it expressed the feeling of the Chinese believers under persecution at that time. It is a lengthy hymn, with seven long verses; nevertheless, I would like to read it to you in its entirety. He wrote it in Chinese; then it was translated into English. The Chinese is much better, but I am afraid if I read the Chinese you would not understand, so I must read it in English. This is the way our brother wrote, and I believe he composed it to represent the sentiment of the believers at that time.

Since Long Ago at Bethany

Since long ago at Bethany we parted,
Within my heart there is a ceaseless void:
How can I take my harp down from the willows?
How can my songs without Thee be enjoyed?
And when at night I'm keeping lonely vigil,
Grown dumb alike to sorrow and to cheer,
Then I recall the promise of Thy coming,
But sigh: O Lord, why, why dost Thou not yet appear?

Thy manger wakes the thought: I too am homeless;
Thy cross strips earthly pleasures from my soul;
Thy coming bids me seek a better country,
For Thou Thyself art now my final goal.
Since Thou art gone, my joy has lost its flavor;
My song the sweetness I would fain convey.
Since Thou art gone, the sense of void o'erwhelms me.
Oh, how I long that Thou wilt come and not delay.

Though even now I know Thy loving presence,
Yet in my heart there's still a sense of lack.
Enlightening and tenderest sustaining
Can no more satisfy: I want Thee back.
Despite Thy peace within, I still feel lonely;
Despite Thy joy, there still remains a sigh;
When I feel most content, the silent yearning
To see Thee face to face becomes an uttered cry.

What exile cannot but desire his homeland
And long his people once again to greet?
What soul on alien soil forgets his kindred?
What parted lovers never yearn to meet?
O Lord, how can these earthly loves and pleasures
With all the joy of Thy return compare?
Then, if I cannot here behold Thy countenance,
What can I do but sigh till Thou, my Lord, appear?

Could'st Thou, O Lord, forget Thy word of promise
Soon to return and take me unto Thee?
Yet day by day and year by year I've waited,
And still I wait, and no return I see!
Remember, Lord, the years I have been waiting
While Thy dear footsteps linger far away.
How long? How long? Oh! must I wait still longer
Till Thou shalt come again in glorious array?

From generation unto generation
Thy saints have come and gone, but have not seen
Thy glorious promise passed into fulfillment.
How long, how very long the time has been!
Why cannot we, dear Lord, discern Thy footsteps?
Why are the heavens still so closely sealed?
Oh, must our waiting be prolonged still further
Before Thou in Thy matchless splendor art revealed?

Lord, I recall the many years I've waited
For Thy return—yet, Lord, not I alone.
But Thy dear saints, throughout many generations—
Beseeching Thee to come back for Thine own.
To countless tears and countless fervent pleadings,
By Thine appearing haste to make reply.
Oh, may Thou come, the echo of the ages.
Come, come and answer now this mighty corp'rate cry!

Throughout the centuries this has always been the case. In a sense, the desire, the longing, for the coming of the Lord is a sure sign of first love. Paul said that we are as chaste virgins betrothed to one man, the Lord Jesus Christ (see II Corinthians 11:2). And as a virgin engaged to that perfect man, Christ Jesus, what can be more expressive, more telling, of that virgin love towards Christ than the longing for His return?

Today, the Lord Jesus is absent from us. But, of course, spiritually He is still with us. Before His departure He had said, "I will never leave you nor forsake you." He is with us in the

Holy Spirit, who dwells in us; yet, in another sense, we would say that our Lord Jesus today is absent. He left us two thousand years ago; He is now in heaven. If we are in our first love, we, as His church, as that chaste virgin, will long that we may see Him soon and see Him face to face. That is the sure sign of first love. Whenever we think the Lord delays, that He will not come back, it actually reveals that our love has grown cold. Our Lord Jesus noted this in one of His parables: It is the wicked servant who says that the lord delays, that the lord will not come back. And therefore, he began to live a life that was careless, riotous, full of drinking, and the beating of his fellow servants; yet, unexpectedly, the lord returned (see Matthew 24:48-51).

So throughout the centuries, in the heart of all believers while in their first love for the Lord Jesus, there is this longing and desire, a yearning for the Lord's return. It is not wrong for Christians to wait for the Lord's return in their lifetime, in every generation, in every century, because it is the sure sign of first love. Especially true is it that when believers are in tribulation or under persecution and that longing, yearning and desire increases, it is the coming again of the Lord which becomes a great comfort and encouragement to believers. So when Paul wrote this first letter to the church in Thessalonica he mentioned the coming of the Lord to them in every chapter.

Blessed Hope

"Await his Son from the heavens, whom he raised from among the dead, Jesus, our deliverer from the coming wrath" (I Thessalonians 1:10).

When these Thessalonians turned away from idols unto God, we can say this is the past, but in the present they serve the true and living God. In other words, it is not only that we turn away from idols to God, but now we serve the true and living God. This is what we ought to do; this is that with which we ought to be occupied. We are here to serve the true and living God. While we are serving Him, of course, there will be difficulties, there will be opposition, there will be tribulation, there will be problems; yet we are able to persevere because we have a blessed hope. We wait for the Son of God to return from heaven, and when He shall return from heaven He will deliver us from the coming wrath. It has been said that our Lord Jesus once offered himself to bear our sins, but when He appears the second time, He will appear for the purpose of complete salvation to those who look for Him without sin (see Hebrews 9:28). One day the wrath of God will come upon this earth, but before that terrible event, our Lord Jesus will return and deliver us from that coming wrath. He will come the second time without the issue of sin in view because our sins have already been forgiven; it will be for full salvation this time. And that is our blessed hope.

Gift of Love

In the second chapter Paul said: "For what is our hope, or joy, or crown of boasting? are not ye also before our Lord Jesus at his coming? for ye are our glory and joy" (vv. 19-20).

Paul was like a father to these Thessalonian believers, and at the same time he was like a nursing mother to them. He not only preached the gospel to them, he also told them he willingly gave himself to them. What was the reward for his labor? He did not look for his reward here and now. Instead, he looked for it at the coming of the Lord Jesus. He was looking forward to that day when he would appear before the presence of the Lord; and, while appearing in the Lord's presence, he would be able to present these Thessalonian believers to the Lord as his gift of love. In short, these Thessalonian believers would be his hope, joy and crown for boasting.

If you love the Lord, surely you would like to present to Him something as a way to show your love. Surely you would like to know what it is that He wants more than anything else. Our Lord Jesus desires, more than anything else, to have people—to have people who are redeemed and who have been perfected by His grace. And if this is what the Lord desires more than anything else, then this is what we should present to Him as our expression of love. No cost is too great for the apostle Paul if only he can present these people as his love gift to Christ, and I do believe that no cost is too great for any one of us if we like Paul, can present to the Lord people perfect and complete in Christ. That will be our joy, our hope and our boasting.

Holiness

In the third chapter of his epistle Paul encouraged the Thessalonian believers in the following way: "But you, may the Lord make to exceed and abound in love toward one another, and toward all ... to the confirming of your hearts unblamable in holiness before our God and Father at the coming of our Lord Jesus with all his saints" (vv. 12-13).

Paul now turns to the Thessalonian believers themselves. One day, at the coming of the Lord Jesus, we shall all be gathered together in His presence. That is the time when we shall stand in His presence with hearts which are unblamable in holiness before God. Paul said we will all stand before the judgment seat of Christ and be judged according to our works. Now do bear in mind that the judgment seat of Christ is different from the judgment of the great white throne. Do not be fearful. The judgment before the great white throne, as is described in Revelation 20, is the final judgment. It is the judgment of all the dead throughout the ages, and it is a judgment according to the works that everyone did during his lifetime. Everything will be judged before the great white throne.

A throne here speaks of judicial judgment. It is a great white throne; for it means that this judgment is of such purity. Who can stand before such a judgment? It is a judgment of life and death, of eternal life or eternal death. The Bible declares that according to God's appointment, everyone will die, and after death there shall be judgment (see Hebrews 9:27). That is the judgment being referred to, that of the great white throne. It is the judgment which shall pronounce either eternal life or eternal death. But those who have believed in the Lord Jesus will never stand before that great white throne because the Lord Jesus has taken that judgment upon himself on Calvary's cross. While He was on the cross He bore our sins in His body, and there He was judged in our stead. He tasted death for every man, and therefore, because He has taken that judgment for us, there is no more judgment and no more condemnation to those who are in Christ Jesus. Thank God for that!

However, that does not mean we will not be judged. We will still be judged, but not as a created being before the Creator. We will be judged as children in the family of God, and it is called the judgment seat of Christ. It is not a "throne" but a "seat," and the word *seat* in Greek is "bema."

In the Eastern tradition there are big families, the clans. In a clan there is the head of the family who is perhaps a grandfather or great-grandfather. Once in awhile there will be a family gathering and the whole family will be called into a big room. On one side of the room there will be a lifted place called a *bema*, and the head of the family will sit on that *bema*. The rest of the family will stand before him, and there he will judge them. Some members of the family may have done something to bring glory to the name of the family, and there they will be recommended and rewarded. But some of them may have done something to bring disgrace to the family, and these members will be reproached and even disciplined. None but the family members can attend such a meeting.

And hence, one day at the coming of the Lord Jesus we shall all stand before the judgment seat of Christ. He is our Elder Brother (see Hebrews 2:11-12), the Head of the family, and we will all stand before Him, and we shall be judged according to what we have done on this earth. Remember, this judgment is not for determining the matter of going to heaven or not; it is not for determining eternal life or eternal death because we each have received the life of the family Head, even that of Christ. Rather, this judgment is for the purpose of determining whether we, as members of the family, have glorified the name of the family or whether we have put the family name to shame. There we each will be judged to be worthy of reward or whether all our labors of hay, stubble, and wood are to be burned though we ourselves shall be saved, yet barely so (see I Corinthians 3).

When we shall gather with the Lord in His presence, will it not be good if we can present ourselves before Him as "unblamable in holiness"? Unblamable in holiness simply means wholly separated for God, and by that is meant in our hearts; in other words, in our hearts we are completely separated unto God. The Scriptures never teach sinless perfection. There is but one man who is sinless and perfect; and that is the Lord Jesus. What is being mentioned here is not sinless perfection; rather, it is a perfect heart which is in view. You may recall that David had a perfect heart before God. Now certainly David was not perfect, but thank God, he had a perfect heart, and that is what God is looking for in us. Do we have a perfect heart towards God? Or is our heart towards Him divided? Do we really love Him with all our hearts, even though we sometimes fall, sometimes falter, sometimes stumble? In our hearts, are we wholly for Him? Have we given our hearts to Him? That is what God in Christ is looking for. When Christ shall judge our works, it shall be according to the heart, because God is not like man who looks at outward appearance. By His grace, when we shall stand before Christ with a heart unblamable in holiness, what a joy that will be.

Resurrection

In chapter 4 of Paul's letter we read that these Thessalonian believers had a problem. After Paul left them, some of the new believers died. The Thessalonians were eagerly looking forward to the coming of the Lord and a problem arose because they did not understand the truth surrounding resurrection. They thought that those who died had missed the opportunity of being participants when the Lord returned, or that when the Lord would come they would be secondary to those who were living at the coming of the Lord. Therefore, they were troubled. Paul tried to comfort their hearts with the truth, and so he wrote: "For this we say to you in the word of the Lord ..." (v. 15). Nowhere can we find "the word of the Lord" about this matter in the Gospels. Such was not recorded there. How, then, could Paul say, "in the word of the Lord"? Well, either he had received a direct revelation about this matter from the Lord (which he sometimes did about other matters), or there might have been an oral tradition to this effect going around among the disciples—the truth about this aspect of resurrection was not recorded as coming from the Lord himself but it was understood. It can be either of these. There is a truth about this very matter, and the matter is, that at the coming of the Lord, those who have fallen asleep in Christ will rise up first. In other words, there will be a resurrection, and those who, at the time of Christ's coming, are alive will then be caught up with the resurrected dead in Christ to the clouds to meet the Lord in the air, and thus shall we always be with the Lord (vv. 16-17). To put it another way, those who could not delay their death until the Lord comes and will have meanwhile fallen asleep (that is, they had died), shall be resurrected, and those who are alive and remain at the time of Jesus' return will be caught up together with these resurrected saints to the clouds to meet the Lord in the air. And thus this problem among these Thessalonian believers is solved. Therefore, Paul exhorted them to comfort one another with this word.

Preserved Blameless

"Now the God of peace himself sanctify you wholly: and your whole spirit, and soul, and body be preserved blameless at the coming of our Lord Jesus Christ. He is faithful who calls you, who will also perform it" (I Thessalonians 5:23, 24).

What is the will of God for us? The will of God for us is that we may be preserved—spirit and soul and body—blameless at the coming of our Lord Jesus. The Lord Jesus is coming again, and when He does so, we shall find ourselves being preserved blameless—spirit, soul and body. Not only is our spirit blameless, but even our soul and even our body are preserved blameless. Our spirit is preserved blameless in the sense that the Holy Spirit fills our spirit and our spirit is one with the Holy Spirit: we do not grieve Him, we do not despise Him, we do not quench Him, but rather, we are filled with the Holy Spirit and ruled by the Holy Spirit. Our soul is preserved blameless in the sense that we love the Lord with all our heart and with all our soul and with all our intelligence. Even our body is preserved blameless as we make it a living sacrifice here on earth to do His will.

Now this is the will of God for us. It is true that we cannot preserve ourselves blameless, but He is able. "The God of peace himself sanctify you wholly." He is able to preserve us. Our Lord Jesus is not only able to save us, He is able to save us to the uttermost. Our Savior is our Keeper. He has given His life to us. He has given His Holy Spirit to us; and by the grace of God He is able to keep us until that day. Said Paul elsewhere: "I know whom I have believed, and am persuaded that he is able to keep for that day the deposit I have entrusted to him" (II Timothy 1:12).

On our part we need to commit ourselves to Christ for

keeping. That is the preservation of the saints. The preservation of the saints is not that we keep ourselves or preserve ourselves; it is that we commit to Him, who is our Preserver and our Keeper. So God, who calls us, is faithful. He will perform it. What a comfort that is!

The Coming of the Lord

Finally I would like to share with you something on this matter of the *parousia* of Christ, the coming of the Lord. The word coming in Thessalonians is the word *parousia.* We know that in Greek there are several words which have been translated into "coming," but this word *parousia* is used especially in I and II Thessalonians. As a matter of fact, this word is used twenty-four times in the New Testament—seven times in relation to man, seventeen times in relation to Christ.

In this word *parousia, para* means "with" or "together," ousia means "to be," or "being." *Parousia* simply means "presence." It includes in its meaning the idea of arrival, and consequently, that involves a presence. The word *parousia*—or *presence*, as those who know the Greek tell us, speaks of the concept of a period, which covers a series of events and not just one event. This is important for our understanding of the second coming of the Lord Jesus, because today we find there is much confusion among God's people about the second coming. Probably the questions you are always asked are, "When will the Lord be coming? Must more prophecies be fulfilled before the Lord can come, or can the Lord Jesus come at any time?" I think these are very practical questions. If there are more prophecies to be fulfilled before the Lord can come, then we need to look at those prophecies and not focus ourselves on the coming of the Lord. Why? Because He could not come if these prophecies have not yet been fulfilled. However, if the Lord can come at any time, even before some prophecies are fulfilled, then we need to watch for Him and not for the fulfilling of prophetic events.

What are we watching for? I am afraid most Christians today are watching for events to happen as fulfillment of prophecy. Now I do believe in prophecy. I do believe all these prophecies will be fulfilled; but the Lord says, "Watch for Me." We are to watch for Him, not for events, because nobody knows when the Lord is coming. The Lord himself said, "Nobody knows the hour; nobody knows the date; nobody knows the season; only the Father knows." So do not try to know. In reading church history we learn that people have tried to figure out when the Lord will come, and they have been proven wrong every time. Then, also, I hear people say, "Well, isn't it the seventh dispensation? The last dispensation is a thousand years. And today we are towards the end of six thousand years, therefore ..." There may be an element of truth to this, but let us not try to figure it all out. Nobody knows when He is coming. But there is one thing He did say which can be helpful: "When you see these things happening, you know I am near" (see Matthew 24:33). That we *can* know—what will be the general atmosphere for His coming.

Do we know that the general atmosphere for His coming is here with us already? If we carefully read Matthew 24, we see that Jesus said that we will hear of wars and rumors of wars, famines, pestilences, earthquakes, and all these things, but that this is just the beginning of birth pangs; the end is not yet come. In other words, when we observe wars and rumors of wars, famines, pestilences, earthquakes, and all these turmoils in the world, we realize that the world is going through various birth pangs in anticipation of giving birth to something. When a woman is in travail, we know that birth is near. Now it may turn out to be a false alarm; yet even if it should be a false alarm, the birth event is not too far away, and when the time of birth comes nearer, the pangs shall be shorter and more intensified. From the moment our Lord Jesus spoke about this on the Mount of Olives and up to our time—about two thousand years—these events of which He spoke have been happening and happening, intensifying and intensifying, broadening and shortening—birth pangs. There is more and more labor. What is labor for? A woman with child labors not in vain but for the birth of that child. The woman mentioned in Revelation chapter 12 was in labor, and we are told that a manchild is to be born. The world has labored long enough; most certainly, therefore, the birth is coming soon.

The Lord Jesus is recorded in Matthew 24 as saying: "As the days of Noah, so shall be the days of the coming of the Son of man." The word *coming* here is *parousia.* Can we at all doubt that the general atmosphere today is as the days of Noah? It has become more and more like the days back in Noah's time: the moral situation, the corruption, the blood-shedding, the wickedness, even the imagination of the mind is continually wicked. Is not the situation ripe for the coming of the Lord?

The Lord also said: "When you see a fig tree bud, begin to leaf, then you know that the summer is near. When you see these things you know that the Son of man is near, even at the doors." We know the fig tree in Scripture represents the Jewish nation. For two thousand years they were a people without a nation, without a land, without a government. God preserved them through persecution of every description for two thousand years, and suddenly in 1948 the nation of Israel was established—budding, leafing, therefore a sign that Jesus is at the doors.

In Luke 21 the Lord Jesus is quoted as declaring: "Jerusalem shall be trodden under the feet of the Gentiles until the times of the Gentiles shall be fulfilled." If our interpretation is correct, then in 1967 during the Six Days War, Jerusalem passed out of the hands of the Gentiles into the Jewish hands for the first time. May it therefore be that the times of the Gentiles have been fulfilled?

Let us look about everywhere: at the political and

international situation, at the economic situation, at the moral situation, and at the situation of Christianity. We cannot help but believe that the general atmosphere of the *parousia* of Christ is with us. It is true there are still many prophecies to be fulfilled, but if parousia means a period of time that covers a series of events instead of only one event, then all the prophecies which precede the beginning of *parousia* have been fulfilled already.

I do not have time here today to go into details, even though I love the coming of the Lord. But just to put it very simply, one day—it may be today, it may be tomorrow, it may be ten years from now—a group, a number of people in the world will suddenly disappear.

For did not the Lord Jesus prophesy the following: "Two people are in bed: one is taken, one is left. Two women are grinding meal in the morning; one is taken, one is left. Two men are out working in the field at noontime; one is taken, one is left" (see Matthew 24:40-41).

Why the difference here with respect to the time of day for these events? Because the earth is round. In some places it is night, in other places it is morning, and in some other places it is noontime. Simultaneously on the earth, some among God's people will be taken. This word taken is the same word which is used in Acts chapter 1 which describes the Lord being taken up to heaven. Who are these who are to be taken? Outwardly, there is no difference among them. Two shall be in bed, so do not be afraid to go to bed tonight for going to sleep, because if you will be taken, you will be taken. And do not leave your job. Continue to work, because you will be taken at your work. Outwardly everything is still going on as usual, but the Lord knows the inward heart condition of the believer. Those whose hearts are wholly for Him, who are prepared and ready, who are waiting for Him, who have been overcoming: these shall be taken. Such will be the beginning of *parousia*. The sign of the beginning of *parousia* is the rapture of the overcomers. They will be as the manchild, raptured to the throne where Christ is, to escort Him from the throne to the air. What a privilege that is!

Then there will be war in the air. The archangel Michael and other angels will fight against Satan and his angels because the air is the headquarters of the power of darkness. There will be no more place for Satan. Satan and his followers will be cast down from the air to the earth. The air is cleared for the Lord to be escorted by the overcoming company from the throne to the air. And what can you expect when Satan is thrown upon this earth? The trio of evil will then be upon this earth together—Satan, the false prophet, and the antichrist. So what can you expect but the Great Tribulation?

Many believers who are not ready will be readied during the Great Tribulation. Let us imagine for a moment a harvest. If you have a field of wheat, usually there will be a patch of wheat that ripens first because it receives more sunshine. It dries first, and its kernels of grain will loosen first. Therefore, the firstfruits will be cut first, and according to the Jewish law, the law of Moses, the firstfruits, a sheaf, will be presented in the temple to God. It is always the best of the crop, but it also guarantees the coming of the entire harvest. These firstfruits are the overcomers. The rest have to receive more sunshine, more scorching to be dried, and to be loosened up. Then finally, we learn from Revelation 14 that the man with the golden crown in the clouds did cast down the golden sickle and harvested the harvest up to the cloud, and that is I Thessalonians chapter 4: "Those who are asleep in Christ Jesus will be raised from the dead and those who live and remain ..." In other words, some who live do not remain on earth anymore; they have already gone, they have already been taken up. But those who live and remain will be caught up together, yet not to the throne but to the air, to meet the Lord in the air; and that is where the judgment seat of Christ is set to take place.

After the judgment seat of Christ is over, the Lord will then come from the air to the earth with His army. There will be a large battle, the battle of Armageddon. People today are talking about the battle of Armageddon, but it is not a battle between nation and nation; it is a battle between Christ and the antichrist. That is the end of *parousia.* The sign of the beginning of *parousia* is: *"He comes like a thief"* (see Matthew 24:43-44). The sign of the end of *parousia* is, *"He shall come like lightning"* that shines from the east to the west, and every eye shall see it (see Matthew 24:27). When our Lord Jesus was taken up and the disciples were looking up to heaven, two men in white appeared and said: "Men of Galilee, why are you looking up? Because this Jesus who has been taken up, in like manner shall he come" (see Acts 1:11). In other words, the way of His return will be the way of His departure. He departed from us in two stages: from the Mount of Olives to the cloud—visible; from the cloud to the throne—invisible. And His return presence is to occur in just the reverse order: from the throne to the cloud—invisible; from the cloud to the Mount of Olives—visible. The whole period is called *parousia*, the arrival and presence of the Lord.

If we love the Lord Jesus, we love His presence. Today it is as we have read in that hymn written by our brother, for even though we *do* enjoy His presence spiritually today, yet somehow there is still a longing in our hearts to see Him face to face, and when we shall see Him we shall be like Him. Come, Lord Jesus, come!

Dear heavenly Father, do hear the cry of Thy church throughout the ages. Do answer our prayers. Oh, hasten, hasten Thy coming. Strengthen us while we are yet waiting. Preserve us pure unto thyself that when we shall see Thee, we shall not be put to shame, but we shall be glorified in Thee as Thou art glorified in us. Increase in us the yearning, the desire, for Thy coming. Keep us from being rooted in this earth so that before Thy return we may live the remainder of our time as though our hearts were already there with Thee. In the name of our Lord Jesus. Amen.

II THESSALONIANS

SEEING CHRIST IN THE DAY OF THE LORD

II Thessalonians 2:1-17—Now we beg you, brethren, by the coming of our Lord Jesus Christ and our gathering together to him, that ye be not soon shaken in mind, nor troubled, neither by spirit, nor by word, nor by letter, as if it were by us, as that the day of the Lord is present. (Now probably in the King James Version you find it is said, "The day of Christ had come," but most manuscripts read Lord, not Christ ... "The day of the Lord is present.") Let not any one deceive you in any manner, because it [the day of the Lord] will not be unless the apostasy have first come, and the man of sin have been revealed, the son of perdition; who opposes and exalts himself on high against all called God, or object of veneration; so that he himself sits down in the temple of God, shewing himself that he is God. Do ye not remember that, being yet with you, I said these things to you? And now ye know that which restrains, that he should be revealed in his own time. For the mystery of lawlessness already works; only there is he who restrains now until he be gone, and then the lawless one shall be revealed, whom the Lord Jesus shall consume with the breath of his mouth, and shall annul by the appearing of his coming; whose coming is according to the working of Satan in all power and signs and wonders of falsehood, and in all deceit of unrighteousness to them that perish, because they have not received the love of the truth that they might be saved. And for this reason God sends to them a working of error, that they should believe what is false, that all might be judged who have not believed the truth, but have found pleasure in unrighteousness. But we ought to give thanks to God always for you, brethren beloved of the Lord, that God has chosen you from the beginning to salvation in sanctification of the Spirit and belief of the truth: whereto he has called you by our glad tidings, to the obtaining of the glory of our Lord Jesus Christ. So then brethren, stand firm, and hold fast the instructions which ye have been taught, whether by word or by our letter. But our Lord Jesus Christ himself, and our God and Father, who has loved us, and given us eternal consolation and good hope by grace, encourage your hearts, and establish you in every good work and word.

Shall we pray:

Dear heavenly Father, our hearts do rejoice knowing that we are in Thy presence, and in Thy presence there is light, there is revelation, there is life. So our Father, we just come to receive light, revelation, and life from Thee. We ask that the breaking of Thy word may bring forth light and love into our hearts. We commit this time into Thy hand. In the name of our Lord Jesus. Amen.

The two letters of the apostle Paul to the Thessalonians are the first letters written by the apostle. He wrote these shortly after God had used him to bring forth the church in Thessalonica. We know that the church there was born through the travail of Paul's soul, and after the church was founded it had to go through continuous persecution. It was a young church in suffering and Paul wrote the first letter to the church in Thessalonica when he was in Corinth in order to encourage these young believers who were in tribulation. And we know that the best encouragement which can ever be given to anyone or to any church in any generation so that they may stand and continue on is the blessed hope of the coming of the Lord. That is the reason why the apostle Paul mentions again and again in I Thessalonians this matter of the coming of the Lord, because that event is a great hope, and it is the best encouragement believers can ever receive.

We mentioned before that the coming of the Lord or the *parousia* of the Lord means "presence." The word coming in Greek is *parousia*. Para means "with" and *ousia* means "being." It speaks of an arrival moment as well as the subsequent time afterwards. So the *parousia* or the coming of the Lord actually signifies a period of time and is composed of a number of events.

Briefly speaking, the parousia of the Lord covers two stages. At the time of Acts 1:11 the disciples were on the Mount of Olives, and they witnessed our Lord Jesus being taken up until He was received in a cloud. As they continued to gaze upward upon this scene, two men in white appeared to them and said in so many words the following: "Men of Galilee, why are you looking up? This Jesus who has been taken up from you into heaven shall come back in like manner, that is, in the manner in which He has been taken up from you."

Accordingly, when Jesus was taken up from His disciples, it was in two stages: the first being from the Mount of Olives up to the cloud—something visible, and the second stage, from the cloud up farther to heaven's throne—something invisible. And the word of the two men to the disciples was that He shall come back in like manner. His departing absence from them proceeded in two stages and His returning presence will likewise occur in two stages, but the order shall be reversed. In His coming back, that is, in His parousia, the first stage will be from the throne to the air—something invisible, and the second will be from the cloud in the air to the Mount of Olives, which will be something visible. If we can remember these two stages, then probably we will not be confused.

The problem with the Christians in Thessalonica concerning this matter of parousia had been created by their concern for those who had believed in the Lord Jesus but had died (see I Thessalonians 4). As they thought on the return coming of the Lord, which is the blessed hope for all believers, it troubled them because they probably thought that those who had gone to sleep (that is, who had died) in the Lord had missed the coming back of the Lord. They perhaps thought that they had missed the greatest blessing of being taken up, of being raptured. So in the first letter to the Thessalonians Paul had tried to tell them that in the return coming of the Lord there will be a rapture, yes, but that the rapture will involve not only the living but also those who had fallen asleep in Christ Jesus. They will be raised from the dead, and they will be caught up to the air with the living, and thus they shall all be with the Lord. Paul had tried to comfort these people with these words.

Yet, not long after the first letter had been written and sent, fresh news came from Thessalonica, and because of this new information which Paul received, he felt constrained to write another letter—that is, the second letter to the Thessalonians. Actually, these two epistles were written within a very short time of each other, perhaps only a matter of months.

Now in this second letter to the Thessalonians Paul attempts to help them regarding the second stage of parousia or, to put it another way, in the first letter to the Thessalonians he dealt with the first stage of parousia: the coming of the Lord from the throne to the air. We know that today our Lord Jesus is seated at the right hand of the Father, but one day He is coming back to earth, and His return coming has to begin with the throne. In reading the word of God and in fitting the whole Bible together, we are able to learn that one day, suddenly, something will happen upon this earth, and thank God, we are aware that this something can happen any day. One day, throughout the entire world, some believers shall disappear, that is to say, they will have been taken. In Matthew 24 we are told that two shall be asleep: one is taken and one is left; two people shall be grinding the meal in the morning: one is taken, one is left; two shall be working in the field at noontime: one is taken, the other is left. And we also know that the number *two* in each of these instances represents the living believers at the time of the coming of the Lord.

Let all of us be aware that we believers in Christ have a great opportunity here. At the coming of the Lord those Christians who are prepared, those who have watched and prayed, those who have been willing to take up the cross and follow the Lord, those who have been loosened from the grip of this world and are ready—all these are the overcomers of the church. They constitute the manchild mentioned in Revelation 12 and will accordingly be taken first. For do let us carefully note there that it states that as soon as the man-child is born, he is taken up to the throne, there to prepare the way for the Lord to come back from the throne to the clouds in the air. The man-child is a collective term insomuch as it states there that *they* have overcome the accuser by the blood of the Lamb, by the word of their testimony, and they have not loved their soul-life even unto death (see Revelation 12:11).

After these overcomers are taken up to the throne, there will be war in the air. Michael and other angels will fight with Satan and his angelic followers, and there will be no more place for Satan in the air, which heretofore has been his headquarters. Satan shall be cast down with his followers upon the earth, and thus the air is cleared for the Lord to descend from the throne to the air. During this period on earth there will be the Great Tribulation, because the trio of evil will be together on earth—Satan, the false prophet, and the antichrist. But thank God, during the Great Tribulation the harvest will be readied.

The firstfruits, represented by the overcomers, have already been taken, but what about the harvest? The rest of the believers will have been made ready and at the sound of the last trumpet, which is the seventh trumpet, those who are dead in Christ will be raised from the dead and those who are living and remain upon the earth will then be caught up together with the resurrected saints into the air to meet the Lord there. There is to be found there the judgment seat of Christ. All those who are of the family of God will be gathered around the Lord, and they shall be judged as a family. Their works will be judged, and those who have worked with gold, silver and precious stones will be rewarded. And as for those who have worked with wood, stubble and hay, their works shall be destroyed, but they themselves shall be barely saved (see I Corinthians 3:12-14). This is the first stage of *parousia* which we find mentioned and discussed in I Thessalonians, but it seems that Paul left off the second stage—the coming from the air to the earth. Actually he mentions it there, but it is especially dealt with in II Thessalonians.

I Thessalonians deals with the first stage of parousia, which is especially related to the church. It is the coming of the Lord for His saints, and the rapture is included in that period. On the other hand, II Thessalonians deals especially with the second stage of parousia, and it is mainly related to the world. It has been variously described in the following terms: the appearing of His coming, the epiphany of His parousia, the apocalypse of His parousia, the revelation, the outshining of His presence. In sum, it is the coming of the Lord with His saints, and it is mainly connected with this matter of judgment. Please bear this in mind as we proceed further on in our discussion.

The church in Thessalonica now had a new problem, and we do not know for sure how this new problem had arisen. However, in his second letter to these believers Paul wrote the following: "If anyone should come to you, any spirit, any word, or any letter as if by us, saying that the day of the Lord is present, do not be shaken and do not be deceived." Probably during that short period between Paul's two epistles someone had prophesied, saying to the believers there that the day of the Lord was already here. Perhaps someone had passed a word around stating that the day of the Lord was already present, or perhaps someone had falsified a letter, as though making it appear that it had been written by the apostle Paul and which told them that the day of the Lord was now here. When the believers heard these things they were deeply troubled. In I Thessalonians we learn that their original problem had been a concern for those who had died in the Lord, but this new problem of theirs was concerned with the living. If the day of the Lord is already present, then it is most terrible, because the day of the Lord is the day of wrath, the day of judgment and the day of vengeance; and they were now in it!

Perhaps we need to provide some clarification here. In the first letter to the Thessalonians Paul did mention the parouisa's second stage that involves in particular the day of the Lord, the day of His judgment:

"For ye know perfectly well yourselves, that the day of the Lord so comes as a thief by night. When they say, Peace and safety, then sudden destruction comes upon them, as travail upon her that is with child; and they shall in no wise escape" (I Thessalonians 5:2-3).

Somehow the enemy had attempted to insert some falsehood into the truth concerning the day of the Lord. As we can easily discern from this passage, Paul did indeed mention the day of the Lord in his first Thessalonian letter. For he wrote: "The day of the Lord shall come as a thief by night." It shall come suddenly, unexpectedly. Paul wrote, "When they may say, Peace and safety"—as though everything appears peaceful and safe—suddenly destruction occurs. The day of the Lord is destruction, and "sudden destruction comes upon them as travail upon her that is with child, and they shall in no wise escape." Apparently someone had therefore begun to say in their midst that the day of the Lord is now here. For, this person went on to say, "Are you not in trouble? Are you not being persecuted? Are you not in sufferings? Well, then, this must be the day of the Lord; you Thessalonian believers are already in it." "Now if this be the case," these Thessalonians said among themselves, "then what is our hope? We have none!" Actually, when Paul wrote I Thessalonians, he had tried to comfort the believers at Thessalonica with the hope of the coming of the Lord. For in chapter 4 he had written: "The Lord is coming soon, and when He comes the dead in Christ shall be raised, and those who live and remain shall be transformed, and we will all be caught up to meet the Lord in the air. Use these words to comfort one another; it is for comfort."

But as we noted a moment ago, in chapter 5 and verse 3 Paul went on to mention the day of the Lord: "When they may say, Peace and safety, then sudden destruction comes upon them, as travail upon her that is with child; and they shall in no wise escape." Now please note that in chapter 4 he employs the pronoun "we," referring to himself and the Thessalonian believers. In this same chapter 5 he also said: "Concerning the time and the seasons, brethren, ye have no need that ye should be written to, for ye know perfectly well yourselves ..." Again, we see that Paul is writing and referring to the Thessalonian believers themselves: "ye." (You plural). Yet in verse 3 he had said, "When they may say ..." In other words, once Paul had dealt with the believers about the first stage of parousia as a comfort and hope, he then turns briefly to the second stage of parousia, declaring: "There will be the day of the Lord coming which is a day of destruction; but this is not for you, this is for *they*." And who are the *they* here? The they are the people of the world. The world will say, "Peace and safety," and then destruction will suddenly come upon *them*, and *they* shall not escape. But so far as you Thessalonian believers are concerned, Paul went on immediately to say this:

"But ye, brethren, are not in darkness, that the day [of the Lord] shall overtake you as a thief: for all ye are sons of light and sons of day; we are not of night nor of darkness. So then do not let us sleep as the rest do, but let us watch and be sober" (vv 4-6).

So these words about *the day of the Lord* are concerned with the world, not the church. As far as the church is concerned, they are the sons of day and sons of light, and the day of the Lord will not come upon them as a thief. But somehow these Thessalonian believers did not understand. They mixed up the whole thing. They began to think that the day of the Lord was already here and, accordingly, they thought they had no hope—they had missed the opportunity to be raptured—they were in the day of judgment! So Paul in his second letter tried again to correct their misconception, their misunderstanding, and so, as we shall shortly see, he told them: "No, the day of the Lord will not come unless two things happen first—the apostasy, and the revelation of the man of sin, the son of perdition."

Perhaps I should explain somewhat more here because I think there is probably still some confusion. Some people have thought the Thessalonian believers were troubled because they expected the coming of the Lord too soon, and because the coming of the Lord had been anticipated to occur so soon, they began to think they were already in the day of judgment and had therefore missed the opportunity of the rapture. But this was actually not the problem for them since in I Thessalonians the apostle Paul had used the coming of the Lord as a means of giving hope and consolation to these believers. In other words, they were being taught by Paul to expect the Lord to come. "Awaiting the Son of God whom God has raised from the dead for deliverance from the wrath to come" (1:10).

Hence, the fact of the return coming of the Lord for these believers served as a great hope and a great consolation. As believers we must expect Him to come, and as soon as possible, because it will be a joyous day. It is to be a day when we shall see Him face to face. It is a day of great expectation, of great anticipation. It will be a day when we shall see Him and be rewarded. So it is a day to be looked forward to. The problem among these Thessalonian believers was not that they expected the Lord to come too soon, and that therefore Paul was trying to tell them that the Lord would not be coming that soon because certain things would have to happen first before He comes. No, that was not the case at all. Rather, the problem was that they had mixed up the two stages of parousia; or, to phrase it another way, they had mixed up the two days.

In the Bible we find mentioned both "the day of Christ"

and "the day of the Lord." Now these are two different terms. Unfortunately, the translators of the King James Version of the Bible had translated the day of the Lord as the day of Christ. People seem to mix up these two days. But if you read Scripture very carefully, especially the New Testament, you will discover that "the day of Christ" and "the day of the Lord" are two different days. "The day of Christ" is connected with the first stage of parousia which is for the church, for the believers. "The day of the Lord," however, is connected with the second part of parousia, and it is related to the world involving judgment. For the sake of clarity let us look into this matter more deeply.

The Day of Christ

"Having confidence of this very thing, that he who has begun in you a good work will complete it unto Jesus Christ's day [or, the day of Jesus Christ]" (Philippians 1:6).

That good work which God has begun in you and me He will complete unto the day of Jesus Christ.

"That ye may judge of and approve the things that are more excellent, in order that ye may be pure and without offence for Christ's day, being complete as regards the fruit of righteousness, which is by Jesus Christ, to God's glory and praise" (Philippians 1:10).

In other words, if, by the grace of God, we can discern the things which differ, we may be pure and without offense for the day of Christ. When the day of Christ comes we shall be pure and without offense.

"Holding forth the word of life, so as to be a boast for me in Christ's day, that I have not run in vain nor laboured in vain" (Philippians 2:16). He said to the believers that they were holding forth the word of life as light to this world, and in doing so they will be a boast for Paul in the day of Christ. In other words, Paul shall boast of them in the day of Christ.

"... Who shall also confirm you to the end, unimpeachable in the day of our Lord Jesus Christ" (I Corinthians 1:8). That is the prayer of Paul for the Corinthian believers, that they shall be confirmed to the end, unimpeachable in the day of Jesus Christ.

"To deliver him, I say, being such, to Satan for destruction of the flesh, that the spirit may be saved in the day of the Lord Jesus" (I Corinthians 5:5). Even in this matter of discipline, it is for the sake of that day—the day of Christ.

"Even as also ye have recognised us in part, that we are your boast, even as ye are ours in the day of the Lord Jesus" (II Corinthians 1:14). In the day of the Lord Jesus Paul may boast of these believers, even as the believers shall boast of Paul.

So we find that the day of Christ—the day of the Lord Jesus, the day of Jesus Christ—is connected with, and has a relationship to, the church. One day, when the day of Christ comes, we shall all appear before Him. We shall see Him, and our works shall be rewarded. It is the day that we, as believers, are looking forward to.

What exactly are we looking forward to? We are looking forward to that day when we shall see Him face to face. It will be a day of great joy. We love Him even though we have not seen Him, but one day we shall see Him face to face, and what a tremendous joy it shall be! It is a day when we shall all gather together in His presence. It is a day in which we shall appear before Him pure and without blame, unimpeachable. It is a day when our work shall be rewarded. It shall be a glorious day.

Now, of course, if today you are working with wood, hay and stubble, if you live in the flesh, according to the flesh, if you do not follow the Lord, if you are like the wicked servant, burying your talent, if you are like the foolish virgins who do not prepare extra oil in their vessels, but fill their vessels with many things of the world, then, naturally, when that day comes and you appear before the judgment seat of Christ, there shall be something to be ashamed of. On the other hand, if you love the Lord, if you follow the Lord, if you are filled with the Holy Spirit, if you faithfully serve with whatever God has given you, then it is truly a day to look forward to. The day of Christ is for the church and every day we should live in the light of that day, knowing that one day we shall see Him. Therefore, we want to please Him in all things. The apostle Paul lived every day in the light of the day of Christ. He labored, suffered, toiled, and travailed because of that day when he shall be rewarded. Now this is our blessed hope, the day of Christ.

The Day of the Lord

There is another day, however, which is called *the day of the Lord.* Yet the day of the Lord is not an *original* New Testament expression. It is first to be found in the Old Testament, and was later carried over into the New. In the New Testament we find it in I Thessalonians 5:2-3: "The day of the Lord so comes as a thief by night … then sudden destruction comes upon them."

And likewise in II Thessalonians 2:2: "That ye be not soon shaken in mind, nor troubled, neither by spirit, nor by word, nor by letter, as if it were by us, as that the day of the Lord is present."

But the expression, the day of the Lord, when found in the Old Testament, is used by the prophets.

For instance, the day of the Lord can be found in Isaiah 2:12; 13:6, 9; 34:8—that day refers to the last day of Babylon, and to the judgment of the nations.

In Jeremiah 46:8-10, 27—Judgment is meted out upon Egypt; and Israel shall return.

Lamentations 2:22—This speaks of the day of the Lord's anger upon Judah.

Ezekiel 13:5; 30:3—Judgment upon Israel and upon Egypt is brought into view here.

Joel 1:15; 2:1; 3:14—This expression is used in these passages in relation to the judgments of drought, the

Chaldean invasion, the valley of decision, and the judgment of the nations.

Amos 5:18—The day of the Lord shall come as the day of darkness.

Obadiah 15—This speaks of judgment upon Edom and the nations in the last days.

Zephaniah 1:7, 8, 18; 2:3—The judgment of Judah is pronounced, as well as there is the exhortation to seek the Lord.

Zechariah 14:1—The Lord shall come and fight against the nations and deliver Israel.

Malachi 4:5—Elijah shall come before the day of the Lord in order to strengthen the people of Israel to return the heart of the father to the children and the children to the father.

In the Old Testament the day of the Lord is described in terms of it being a day of judgment, of wrath, of vengeance, of woe. God sent this day to the nation of Israel because of its sins. God likewise sent that day to Egypt, to Edom and to Babylon because of their sins, and in the last days God will send this day upon the whole world—it being the judgment of the nations over the controversy of Zion. The day of the Lord is the day of judgment, darkness and terror, and one day this day will come upon the world. God will judge the entire world.

The Thessalonian believers were troubled. They were deceived by spirit, by word, by false letter conveying the false notion that the day of the Lord was now present, that the judgment had already come. Of course, that troubled them, because where now was their hope? They had missed everything. But Paul says, "No, the day of the Lord will not come unless certain things come first."

Let me point out another matter here: today is the day of mercy; today is the day of grace. And in the day of mercy a strange thing happens—the believers suffer; they do well and suffer for it. The Thessalonian believers believed in the Lord Jesus. They had faith and they had love. Their faith increased, their love abounded, but their suffering was not lessened.

The persecution continued. It is as though the world is able to persecute the believers and nothing happens to the world. Is that not a strange thing? Where is the righteous judgment of God? Why is it that the righteous suffer and the wicked prosper? (see Psalm 73)

The apostle Paul gives a very strange explanation. In I Thessalonians Paul mentioned that these Thessalonian believers possessed three basic cardinal qualities—faith, hope and love—"the work of faith, the labor of love, and endurance of hope." But in II Thessalonians he mentioned only two: "Your faith increases, your love abounds," but he mentioned nothing about hope. That is because they are troubled. They are under the illusion that they have lost all hope.

"So that we ourselves make our boast in you in the assemblies of God for your endurance and faith in all your persecutions and tribulations, which ye are sustaining; a manifest token of the righteous judgment of God" (II Thessalonians 1:4-5).

Notice: "You are sustaining persecution." Paul then adds this startling thought: the fact that you are suffering persecution is a manifest token of the righteous judgment of God. Is that not strange? Now read on:

"To the end that ye should be counted worthy of the kingdom of God, for the sake of which ye also suffer; if at least it is a righteous thing with God to render tribulation to those that trouble you, and to you that are troubled repose with us, at the revelation of the Lord Jesus from heaven, with the angels of his power, in flaming fire taking vengeance on those who know not God, and those who do not obey the glad tidings of our Lord Jesus Christ" (II Thessalonians 1:6-8).

We are living in the day of mercy, and in the day of mercy it seems as though God allows the righteous to suffer, allows the troubler to trouble the righteous. Paul said, "This is a manifest token of the righteous judgment of God." How can we explain that? The explanation is as follows: God uses these sufferings to perfect us. It is with a view of the glory into which we are to enter. It is with the view of the kingdom of God, so that we may be counted worthy of His kingdom. Our Lord Jesus Himself suffered first and then He entered into glory. Therefore, we too must suffer in order that we may be matured, perfected, counted worthy of the glory which we are to obtain. In other words, God is using our enemies to perfect us. This is the righteous judgment of God.

Will the righteous God allow such a thing to continue forever? No. The day will come when He shall judge the troubler who troubles us, and we shall find rest in Him. That is the day of the Lord, the revelation of the Lord Jesus, the apocalypse, the unveiling of the Lord Jesus. One day the Lord Jesus shall come from the air to the earth, and He will come with myriads of angels. He shall come with His heavenly hosts, and with the overcomers of the church. He will come down upon this earth and there will be the last war, the war of Armageddon. It is the war of Christ and His army against Satan and his followers, and Christ shall destroy the enemy with the breath of His mouth. Satan shall be bound and cast into the bottomless pit. The false prophet and the antichrist will be cast into the lake of fire, and those who follow the beast will be killed. Judgment will come upon this earth, and Christ shall reign upon this earth for a thousand years. Do not think that the world will go by without being judged. God is just waiting. One day judgment shall come upon this world, and every evil shall be destroyed. Righteousness shall rule upon the earth. Christ shall reign forever, and those who are with Christ shall reign with Him. Such is the day of the Lord.

Apostasy

But before this day comes, two things must happen. One is

the apostasy, and the other is the appearing—the revealing—of the man of sin. Now remember, this all has something to do with the second stage of parousia, not with the first stage. So this is not something which we believers look forward to. We look forward to Christ, not to antichrist; rather, this is something which the world has to bear.

First, there will be the apostasy. The word *apostasy* means "falling away, departure, withdrawal from." It has reference to the falling away or the departure from faith. Our Lord Jesus said, "In the last days shall He find faith upon the earth?" We sense that the spirit of lawlessness is already upon the earth. Indeed, I think there is no question about it. The spirit of lawlessness is already present, and, in fact, one ought not be surprised by a general falling away. Not only the world will go further and further away from truth and law and order, but even among God's people, there will be a falling away. It becomes a general phenomenon—marked by an almost universal falling away. People do not believe the truth. They instead believe the untruth, they believe liars. There is little if any standard, there are no more absolutes; everything appears to be following error. Now when this happens, it prepares the way for the unveiling of the man of sin.

The Man of Sin

The man of sin, the antichrist, is the embodiment of sin just as Christ is the embodiment of righteousness. He is the righteous One; but the man of sin is precisely the opposite. He is the man of perdition, just as Christ is the Man of eternal life, the Father of eternity. Christ is the Lamb, but this man is a beast. One day the antichrist will appear upon this earth, and he will set himself up as God. He will destroy all religions. He wants people to worship him as God. He will perform false miracles, and so forth. But the Lord shall appear and destroy him with the breath of His mouth.

He Who Restrains

However, Paul said this has not happened yet. The spirit of lawlessness is already here, but the lawless one himself has not appeared yet because there is that which restrains. Only when he that restrains is removed will the lawless one appear. Who is that who restrains? In Christianity there are so many different interpretations, but I am not going to give you all of them because it would take too long. I will simply share with you what seems to satisfy me most. If it does not satisfy you, then do search it out for yourself.

I feel that he who restrains refers to the manchild in Revelation 12. The church on earth is the light of the world, the salt of the earth. That is what the church ought to be. In Matthew 5 the Lord Jesus is quoted as saying: "You are the salt of the world; you are the light of the world." We are to shine so that darkness will not prevail. When light comes, darkness retreats. We are the salt of the world because if the salt is there, corruption cannot continue; it cannot spread. When the Lord says, "You are the salt of the world; you are the light of the world," to whom is He speaking? He speaks to the disciples, to those who follow Him.

"Blessed are the poor in spirit for theirs is the kingdom of the heavens ... Blessed are the pure in heart for they shall see God ... Blessed are those who are persecuted for righteousness sake, for theirs is the kingdom of the heavens ... Ye are the salt of the earth …; ye are the light of the world" (see Matthew 5).

That is what the church ought to be. The church ought to be that vessel which is separated, sanctified and Christ-filled. Therefore, it is a testimony to the world. It is a restraining power towards the evil corruptions of the world. That is what the church ought to be, but unfortunately, the church today is so mixed up with the world that one can hardly distinguish which is the church and which is the world. Therefore, there is no collective corporate testimony, no light; there is no restraining power, no salt. But thank God, in the church there are those who are still faithful to the Lord. They are still the salt and the light of the world. These are the overcomers in the church. They overcome the enemy by the blood of the Lamb. It is not that they are perfect, but they trust in the blood of the Lamb and live by the word of their testimony. Their testimony is real. Jesus is their Lord, the Lord of their life, and they do not love their soul-life. They are willing to lay down their soul-life for the sake of the kingdom of God.

Do we not realize that the spirit of lawlessness is already in the world? Yet it could be worse, much worse. Indeed, it will become much worse when the lawless one shall appear, but today he is still under restraint. Who today restrains him? The overcomers of the church restrain him. I think it is evident. Suppose a believer, who lives a very close life with the Lord, enters upon a group of people who are using bad language, are mocking, and uttering all kinds of gross things. What happens? Suddenly, there is silence. That is the restraining power, and Christians ought to have that power. If we lose or have already lost our restraining power, then may God have mercy upon us because we are not separated. But if we are separated, there will be that restraining power there. The world most likely does not appreciate separated believers because they neither know nor realize what these believers have done for them. But one day, God will take them away, and when they are raptured, then the lawless one shall appear and all woe shall come upon the world. We are told in the book of Revelation that when the church shall be gathered together in the air, then the seven vials, the wrath of God, will be poured out upon this earth. That is judgment. God is righteous. He is righteous in allowing us to suffer today. He is righteous in judging the world and the evil which makes us suffer.

Paul said, "Knowing these things, lift up your heart, encourage yourself. Be firm, do good. Follow the Lord because you know that nothing is in vain, for the Lord will remember everything" (see II Thessalonians 2:15-17). We do thank the Lord that He is righteous. He is righteous in allowing us to suffer today for His name's sake, to complete us, to make us worthy of His kingdom. Being righteous, one day He shall come back as the King of kings and the Lord of lords, and all His enemies shall be destroyed, and His kingdom shall know no end. Praise God!

Shall we pray:

Dear heavenly Father, we do bow and worship Thee because Thou art righteous. Thou art righteous in saving us and allowing us to suffer for Thy kingdom's sake because Thou dost desire that we shall inherit the glory of Christ Jesus. Thou hast called us to that glory, and Thou art making us worthy of it by Thy grace. Oh, we worship Thee because Thou art righteous. One day Thou wilt send Thy King to this earth and all His enemies shall be put under His feet, and His kingdom shall know no end. Oh, our Father, we do ask Thee to stir our hearts that we may not be discouraged but be encouraged to press on unto that goal to win Christ, knowing that He is our eternal prize. We ask in the name of our Lord Jesus. Amen.

I TIMOTHY

Seeing Christ in Church Order

I Timothy 3:14-16—These things I write to thee, hoping to come to thee more quickly; but if I delay, in order that thou mayest know how one ought to conduct oneself in God's house, which is the assembly of the living God, the pillar and base of the truth. And confessedly the mystery of piety is great. God has been manifested in flesh, has been justified in the Spirit, has appeared to angels, has been preached among the nations, has been believed on in the world, has been received up in glory.

Let us pray:

Dear heavenly Father, as we continue in Thy presence we do look to Thee to open Thy word to us that through Thy word we may see Thy beloved Son, our Lord Jesus Christ; and seeing Him, be transformed according to His image to the praise of Thy glory. We do commit this time into Thy hand and trust Thy Holy Spirit to reveal Thy Son in us. In the name of our Lord Jesus. Amen.

We have mentioned many times that the Bible is the revelation of Jesus Christ. Every book in the Bible speaks of the Lord Jesus, and it is the will of God that as we approach His word we may get a glimpse, a revelation, a seeing in our spirit of our Lord Jesus. This is true in every book of the Bible. We do look to the Lord that in this first letter to Timothy we may see Christ.

I and II Timothy and Titus form a special group in the New Testament. They are the last letters written by the apostle Paul.

These letters were written to individuals, unlike his other letters, which were written to the various churches. These individuals, Timothy and Titus, were entrusted with the work of God upon this earth, so these are personal letters which Paul writes to them. But they are very different from that one personal letter Paul wrote to Philemon. When he wrote that letter, it was really personal because it was concerned with a personal matter. On the other hand, even though the letters to Timothy and Titus were written to individuals, they dealt with this matter of the church. Paul wrote to these two young brothers, who were engaged in God's work, exhorting them, instructing them, helping them to set the house of God in order. For this reason, these epistles are often called Paul's pastoral letters.

Paul was used as an instrument by God to write a number of letters, a number of books, in the New Testament. All his writings can be divided up into four groups according to the approximate time he wrote them. In the first group there are I and II Thessalonians, most likely written around the years 52-53 A.D. The second group consists of I and II Corinthians, Galatians and Romans, written probably in the years 57-58 A.D. In the third group we have what we call Paul's prison letters—Ephesians, Colossians, Philemon, Philippians—written probably in the years 62-63 A.D. Finally, in the last group we have I and II Timothy and Titus. They were written probably in the years 67-68 A.D.

One brother has put it very beautifully. He has observed that the first group of letters was written as though in the *morning* of Paul's ministry; therefore, we see the brightness of hope in these letters. In the second group of letters, we come to the *noontime* of Paul's work, and in them there is the conflict with error. The third group reveals Paul in the *afternoon* of his work—he has entered upon the calm of reflection. Finally, in the last group, we witness the *evening* of Paul's work, for there he calls attention to duty. I think these observations made by this brother regarding Paul's letters are very beautiful.

Before we look into this first letter to Timothy, we need to reconstruct a little bit with regard to its timing. We know that Paul was put into prison in Rome for two years, but during those two years, he was able to live in his own rented apartment and receive all those who came to visit him. He was given a comparative measure of freedom. Luke's narration of events in his book of Acts came to an end at this point in Paul's life. (Of course, we now know that the kind of activities recorded in the book of Acts has actually never ended.)

Most likely, the apostle Paul was released from what we believe to have been his first Roman imprisonment, because when he wrote the letter to the Philippians he mentioned that he did not know what to do. On the one hand, it was his desire to depart from this world to be with the Lord (and there is nothing better than that). On the other hand, Paul was torn by the thought that his presence with the believers could be of great help to them. So, finally, he came to the conclusion that God wished him to remain in life a little longer. Therefore, in that letter to the Philippians, which he wrote from prison, he said he hoped to send Timothy to them very soon to let them know the condition he was in. In other words, Paul was actually expecting to be released. The same thing is true of the letter he wrote to Philemon. For he even told Philemon to prepare a place for him that after he was released he might visit them. So we do believe that Paul was released after two years of imprisonment. And upon his release he probably sent Timothy immediately to Philippi, to tell the brethren there that he was released and would visit them.

Paul began his journey back to Asia Minor, and most likely he passed through the island of Crete at this time. Nowhere in the book of Acts do we find it stated that he stayed in Crete; he simply passed through the island hurriedly. Evidently there were believers there, and when he passed through Crete and saw the situation there, he did not have time to stay longer. So Paul left Titus on the island whereas he himself went on to Asia

Minor. Most likely he came to Ephesus, and then he went on to Colosse to be with Philemon briefly, after which he came back to Ephesus. Paul found that the situation in Ephesus needed care but he did not have the time to handle it himself; so he left Timothy behind in Ephesus and moved on to Macedonia, Corinth, and to other places. Paul was hoping to return to Ephesus very soon, but somehow, he was delayed. Therefore, he wrote the first letter to Timothy from Macedonia telling Timothy that if he was delayed, then Timothy would know by means of this letter "how one ought to conduct oneself in the house of God."

Most likely, during that same period Paul wrote a letter to Titus asking Titus to meet him in Nicopolis where he intended to winter. Probably he did go to Nicopolis where he is believed to have spent the winter. (Now it is necessary for us to employ these words of uncertainty here because we do not have any definite record, but this is something that we can conclude by putting things together which have been derived from various sources.) There at Nicopolis he met Titus and together they went to Spain. We may recall that in the letter to the Romans he had mentioned that he hoped to visit Spain one day. When he came back from Spain he revisited Asia Minor. In the second letter to Timothy Paul mentioned a tearful departure between him and Timothy which probably occurred at the time when he revisited Ephesus. Then, separating himself from Timothy, Paul went on to Troas. From Troas or some other place he was rearrested and brought back to Rome.

We do not know for sure where he was rearrested, whether it was at Troas, in Corinth or somewhere else. We do not know because the situation had greatly changed. He was probably released in 63 A.D. because we know from history that there occurred the burning of the city of Rome in 64 A.D. Nero gave orders to burn the city, and while Rome was burning he was playing a harp in celebration of it. We do not know fully why he did it. Perhaps he was thinking of rebuilding

Rome or for other reasons, but because of the burning of Rome, the people became so angry that there developed an atmosphere of revolt. In order to appease the people, Nero attempted to create a scapegoat, and the Christians were a ready target. So he declared that the Christians had burned the city, and because of this, all hatred began to be poured out upon Christians. We know that this was the beginning of the great persecution of Christians in Rome, and because of this, Paul became a marked man.

Evidently Paul was arrested, but it was not to be like before. He was arrested as a criminal of Rome because anyone who was a Christian was now declared to be a criminal. Paul was taken back to Rome to be tried, but this time his personal situation was not as comfortable as before: this time he was treated as a real prisoner of Rome; he was probably put in a dungeon where he awaited his trial. We know, of course, that Paul was finally beheaded. Indeed, he could not be crucified because he was a Roman citizen, so he was beheaded. Yet before he was martyred, Paul wrote his last epistle, which was the second letter to Timothy.

All the above historical background is probably a fairly accurate reconstruction of what happened. So we know from this that the first letter to Timothy was written after Paul had been released from the first imprisonment, and that it was written from Macedonia instructing Timothy on how a believer is to behave in the house of God.

The Church in Ephesus

Another thing which needs to be presented as background before going further into this letter is some of the history of the church in Ephesus. From Acts 19 we learn that during the third missionary trip of the apostle Paul he went to Ephesus, and there God began to raise up a church, a testimony. A glorious thing happened in the city of Ephesus. Many came to the Lord, and those who did so were quite absolute in their obedience to God. Ephesus was a large city, full of people engaged in magic and such other occult things. At one point these converts brought forth all the magic books they had and publicly burned them. They followed the Lord in a very absolute way, and the Lord truly blessed that church. Paul was in the city of Ephesus for three years. And during that time the whole Roman province of Asia heard the gospel of Jesus Christ. The church in Ephesus had had a glorious beginning indeed.

Then Paul left to go to Jerusalem, feeling constrained in his spirit that he must arrive there before Pentecost. And while on this journey the apostle purposely avoided the city of Ephesus on his way to Jerusalem because he well knew that if he went into the city to be with the brethren there, he probably would be unable to get away from them. So by prearrangement he called the elders of the church in Ephesus to meet him at Miletus. Acts 20 tells how he shared with the elders there. Paul told them that for three years, day and night, and with tears, he had instructed them, not only publicly but also privately. During these years he had not withheld anything from them but was able to share with them the whole counsel of God. Paul also shared with these Ephesian elders how he had worked to maintain a living during those same years so as to be an example to them. In this same sharing at Miletus Paul also committed them to the grace of God and told them that he might not see their faces anymore. He warned them, saying, that after he left there would be grievous wolves coming into their midst, and that even among the believers themselves at Ephesus there would be people who would rise up teaching perverted things to lead people away from Christ to themselves. These were Paul's final parting words to the Ephesian elders, and then he traveled on to Jerusalem where he was first arrested.

Paul spent two years in prison in Caesarea and then was sent to Rome to be tried by Nero, the current Caesar. It was while he was in prison there that he wrote a letter to the church in Ephesus—the Ephesian letter. In the Ephesian letter one can discern that the brethren in Ephesus loved the Lord very much. The Lord through Paul had opened their understanding so greatly that they were able to receive the mystery of God, to understand it, and even to apprehend it. The letter to the Ephesians touches the height of Christian teaching, and Paul was able to share with them in this way.

Then Paul was released after his first Roman imprisonment and went to Ephesus again, but things had changed there. It was only perhaps five years since he had written his letter to the Ephesians. He found the situation was different: the elders had all passed away, and new elders had to be appointed; moreover, during this intervening period of years the things he had warned them about before had actually happened—grievous wolves had begun to come into their midst trying to devour them, and even among themselves were people who had commenced talking about perverted things in order to lead people away from Christ to themselves. That was the changed situation—the church was in disorder, and order had to be restored in the church there.

However, Paul felt an urge in his heart to visit many other places and hence he was not able to stay at Ephesus longer; so he left Timothy in Ephesus to be used of God to set the church in order. Paul went to Macedonia, but he was still concerned about the situation in Ephesus. Accordingly, he wrote this first letter to Timothy in order that he might know how to set the house of God in order there. Very likely Timothy was successful in doing that because in Revelation 2 we learn of the perfect order in the church in Ephesus. Bear in mind that by the time of Revelation another generation had passed on and thus this was a new generation being spoken about in Revelation, and there was now no problem with order. In fact, the Ephesian believers had continued on with their works, with their labor, and they had discernment. They seemed to have everything, but something was missing. The outward order was restored but the inward quality was lost. These people continued on orderly, and yet inwardly they had lost their first love, and because of this, the risen Lord opposed them. He said, "I oppose you, I am against you. Even though you have perfect order, I am against you because you have lost your first love. Repent, and do the work you had been doing at the beginning" (see Revelation 2:2-5). This is about all one can fault the church in Ephesus about. We must now come back to this first letter of Paul's to Timothy.

Church Order

In this first letter to Timothy we would like to see Christ in church order. What is church order? What is order? We often think of order as something external. When we think of church order we think of different things which need to be set right, but mostly, we think that church order is a matter of organization. If we are able to organize things as they should be, then the house of God will be in order. Well, we can do that; nevertheless, so far as God is concerned, the church would still be in disarray because order, in the Scriptures, is not simply a matter of outward appearance. Order, in the Scriptures, is the outgrowth of an inward life. For example, let us look at our body. This body of ours is in perfect order, because when there is disorder we are sick. Yet this order is not organized from outside; this order is the out growth of the life within. The same thing is true with the church. The order of the church is not something which people can organize. Oftentimes, when people are intending to organize a church, they will choose some elders and some deacons. And thus they believe they now have a New Testament church because there is perfect order therein. But they do not. For in such a circumstance everything will collapse within a few months, or, if it is better organized, within a year, because this is not the truth.

Church order actually is the corporate expression of Christ. It is the life of Christ among God's people, and this life is developed or manifested or expressed in perfect divine order. Church order is not merely something outward. It is true, order does touch upon the outward appearance, but it actually has its origin in Christ. Therefore, in church order we have to see Christ. If we do not see Him, then whatever order we may institute is a counterfeit and not real; it has no value before God. But when there is a real order which comes from the growth of the life of Christ among God's people, there is nothing more beautiful, nothing more edifying, nothing more healthy than that. That is what this book, the first letter to Timothy, is all about.

This letter has six chapters. Of course, we know these chapters are arbitrary because when the Bible books were written, there were no chapter or verse divisions. Each book was one piece of writing. However, for the sake of convenience, this Pauline letter to Timothy has been divided into six chapters; and interestingly enough, these six chapters seem to tell us six things about church order. So we will take them up one by one.

God's House

"But if I delay, in order that thou mayest know how one ought to conduct oneself in God's house, which is the assembly of the living God, the pillar and base of the truth" (I Timothy 3:15).

What is the church? The church is God's house. You will remember that our Lord Jesus said, "*I* will build my church upon *this* rock and the gates of hades shall not prevail against it" (see Matthew 16:18). That is the church. "I will build my church upon this rock." The Lord is the builder. He is building this church, this house, upon himself. He is the Rock, and because of this, all the gates of hades shall be opened to assault the church. But thank God, the gates of hades shall not prevail against it because it is Christ who builds. This house that Christ builds is God's house; it is the habitation of God in the Spirit. God dwells in this house.

The church is not a physical building. The church is not something built by man. The church is built by Christ himself. "I will build My church." If He is not building it, no matter how much we labor, we labor in vain. It is true that in the building of the church, we are called to labor with Him, but when we are laboring with Him, actually, He is laboring in us and through us. Unless the church is built by Christ it is not God's house, and God can never dwell in it because He is never at peace with it.

Called-Out Ones

What is the church? It is the assembly of the living God. The word *church* in Greek is *ekklesia,* and means the "called-out ones" gathered together unto the name of the Lord Jesus. "For where two or three are gathered together unto my name, there am I in the midst of them" (Matthew 18:20).

That is the church. We, who are redeemed of the Lord, are the called-out ones. We are not only saved from eternal death but we are called out. We may recall that God saved the children of Israel from death by the Pascal lamb, but they had to come out of Egypt—they were separated from the world of the Egyptians because they were called out. They could not celebrate the Passover in Egypt and remain there. No, they were called out from there. So the church is the called-out ones. We are called out of the world from every nation, every people, every tongue, every tribe. God has called out a people unto himself, and we are gathered together as an assembly of believers unto the living God. God is living; therefore, that assembly is a living entity. We are assembled before the living God as a living assembly, and this church is "the pillar and the base of the truth."

What is a pillar? A pillar in Scripture always stands for testimony, because a pillar is something one sets up to be seen by everybody. Something is inscribed on the pillar or the pillar is something in and of itself. When it is set up it stands forth to represent and speak for something. In short, it is a testimony to something. That is a pillar.

What is a base or a foundation? A base is a reservoir; it is that which receives everything. Everything is based there, and out of the base everything comes forth. "The church of the living God is the pillar and the base of the truth." What is the truth? Our Lord Jesus said, "I am the way, and the truth, and the life. No one comes to the Father unless by me" (John 14:6).

The Lord Jesus is the truth. Of course, there are many aspects to truth. We find truth all through the Bible, but all these aspects of truth are summed up in a Person, our Lord Jesus. The Lord said, "I am the truth."

What is the church? "The church is the pillar and the base of the truth." The church does not have a truth in or of itself. This is very important to recognize and to acknowledge. The church does not have a truth or a dogma of its own, as though the church speaks of herself. No. When the church speaks, she speaks of Christ. Christ is the truth. Therefore, because the church is the base of the truth, Christ has deposited himself in the church. The church is a reservoir that receives Christ in all His fullness. If we cannot find Christ in the church, where can we find Him? If we cannot find the truth in the church, where can we find it? Christ has committed himself to the church in totality, in fullness. The church is thus the base or keeper of the truth of God. The church is also the pillar of the truth, to bear witness to the truth. The church is to uplift Christ in order that everybody may see Him. The church does not stand forth so that people may see the church. No. The church stands forth in order that everybody may see Christ.

SOUND TEACHING

As we consider church order in chapter 1, we may think that the first thing concerning order to be established should be the appointment of elders, but that appears in chapter 3. The first thing in instituting church order is having sound teaching. In other words, the church must teach Christ. In the church we are to hear no other teaching but Christ. Unfortunately, in the church in Ephesus, which had had such a glorious beginning, we learn that during the ensuing period of some five years something had happened to this church. There were some in the church who began to teach other doctrines, and there were some people who began to speak and teach about fables, myths and endless genealogies. We do not know for sure what these were, but probably, they were Gnostic notions and Jewish observances.

Toward the latter part of the first century Gnostic teaching and doctrines began to bud. It was not until the beginning of the second century that it really blossomed, but in the first century, Gnosticism had already begun to spring up. Gnosticism has to do with people saying they are "in the know." "You people do not know, but we know the secret to all things; we know the mystery." They said they knew the origin of the universe, they knew all the mystical notions which had begun to pop up, all kinds of philosophical speculations. We also know that in Judaism, as it had gradually developed, people began to take seriously genealogies, fables and myths, and things like that. So all these teachings and Jewish things began to be spread in the church in Ephesus instead of Christ being taught.

Sound teaching is the teaching of Christ. It is not only teaching about Christ but it is *Christ* that is being taught. When He is being taught, you will obtain the end result of love. Paul said to Timothy: "Enjoin some not to teach other doctrines, nor to turn their minds to fables and interminable genealogies, which bring questionings rather than further God's dispensation, which is in faith" (I Timothy 1:3b-4).

In the church at Ephesus, people were talking about the law. Believers were being told to keep the law of Moses. Now the law of Moses has its use, and Paul says the law has its application, but it is to be applied to the lawless and to the wicked ones. Christians are to live above the law—yet not without the law. We are to live beyond what law requires because we live under grace which is a higher level of life than under law.

Then there were people talking about speculative, imaginative, philosophical things. It may make people feel good that they are clever, wise and intelligent, but Paul says that when you are teaching these things, what is the result? Look at the fruit and you will know the tree. The result—the fruit—is questionings, doubtings, strife, and all these things.

Isn't it true even today in Christianity that if we all preach Christ and nothing but Christ, there will be no questionings, no strife, no divisions? But too often in Christianity today we are talking about things other than Christ; therefore, we find all the confusion, the division, and the strivings among God's people. If we teach Christ, the end result will be to "serve the dispensation of God which is in faith." The end of what is enjoined is love, and the love in view is not human love but agape, divine love. If Christ is being taught and people receive Him, the result is that they will have a pure heart; they will have a good conscience. Their conscience is being washed by the blood, and they will have unfeigned faith in Christ Jesus as their Savior and their Lord. And the ultimate result is a love towards God which is pure and a love towards one another. By observing the teaching we shall know what the end result will be. To set the house in order we need sound teaching. Christ is the only teaching. If we learn Christ, our life shall be transformed and we shall be conformed to the image of Christ, who is love.

Paul illustrates this with his own experience. In the first chapter of I Timothy he said, "Look at me. I was an arrogant, self-righteous, violent person, a persecutor of believers, thinking I was serving God. But God in His great mercy gave me an encounter with Christ. I saw the righteous One, and I heard Him."

Because of that encounter, he was completely transformed, and he became an apostle of the gospel of Jesus Christ. That is sound teaching. If we want to set the house of God in order, we have to have sound teaching, which is Christ. Let us teach nothing but Christ. You might say that that will be monotonous. Never!

"In him (Christ) dwells all the fulness of the Godhead bodily; and ye are complete in him" (Colossians 2:9-10a). We can never exhaust the teaching of Christ. He is inexhaustible—for in Him are the unsearchable riches. If only we know Him, if only we experience Him, we will be changed, transformed, and conformed to His image just like Paul. That is sound teaching.

Assembling Together

What is the church? The church is the assembly of the living God. The very word *assembly* tells us that we need to assemble. You cannot be a Christian and shut yourself in a closet. There is no such Christian according to the word of God. We are not to be individual believers only. It is true, we are saved individually. No one can be saved for the other person. Everybody is saved personally and individually. We each must have a personal faith in Christ Jesus, but after we are saved, we assemble together to be the body of Christ, the assembly of the living God. The Bible says that the saints are not to forsake the assembling together, knowing that the day is near (see Hebrews 10:25). We know the coming of the Lord is near; therefore, we should assemble as much as possible.

We should come and assemble together.

Do we assemble together to have a good time, to have a social time together? Well, if you want to have a social time, seek it in society itself, but if you go to the assembly of God's people, you are assembled to worship God. God is looking for worshipers, true worshipers, those who worship Him in spirit and in truth. God is tired of those who worship Him in body or in soul only, those who only worship Him in a physical way or worship Him in an artistic way.

We gather together to remember the Lord at His table—what love, what kindness, what mercy, what grace, what redemption, what deliverance, how much He is to us! We come together to remember Christ and to praise Him. We are a holy priesthood, and we need to come together and serve as a priesthood. The priests in the old days did not serve separately, with one serving here, one serving there, or one serving according to his wish. No. However many there were, the priests served as a priesthood, and they served in the temple together under the direction of the high priest. Of course, our Lord Jesus is the High Priest. He is represented on earth by the Holy Spirit in the church. And we, as a holy priesthood, need to gather together as a temple of God and serve Him together, offering spiritual sacrifices, praises, worship, prayer and songs. We offer spiritual sacrifices, we offer Christ back to God to His satisfaction. This is what the church is. Therefore, the church must have so-called public worship. In other words, the church has to gather. If we do not gather, we do not have the church in practice. So we have to come together. We come together to worship, we come together to sing praises to the Lord, we come together to remember Him at His table, we come together to pray. Of course, we need to pray individually, that is true; nevertheless, as the church we have to come together and pray, and we come together to be taught. We come together to fellowship and to minister to one another, and so on.

PRAYER

The second chapter of I Timothy is concerned with this matter of assembling together, this matter of public worship. Two things are especially mentioned there and the first is prayer. The principles of prayer which are mentioned here are not primarily related to personal prayer. This does not mean that because they are not related to personal prayer, therefore, when we are in private prayer we do not need to notice these things. These principles apply, but the emphasis is on corporate prayer. The church has a ministry. It is true, each one of us has a ministry, and we each need to discover that. It needs to be developed so that the church may be edified; but the church, as a corporate vessel, has a particular ministry. The ministry of the church is corporate prayer.

"I exhort therefore, first of all, that supplications, prayers, intercessions, thanksgivings be made for all men" (I Timothy 2:1).

This is concerning the church as a corporate prayer vessel. The church has a responsibility. The church has a ministry to fulfill and that ministry is to pray for all men—not just for our dear ones. We are to pray for all men because it is the will of God that all men might be saved and come to the knowledge of Jesus Christ. That is the heart desire of God our Father. Therefore, when the church comes together to pray, we need to pray for all men, for all kings, and for all those who are in authority. It is not only that they may come to know the Lord, which is primary, but because God has placed them in authority. Even though we are strangers and pilgrims on earth, we are living on earth and we are living under their authority. So we need to pray for them that they may truly fulfill what God has appointed them to be, that they may truly be His servants, that they may carry out the righteousness of God instead of being perverted. We have a responsibility to pray for them.

Another reason to pray for those in authority is in order that we may live a quiet, tranquil life, that we may live godly before God and before man. It is very difficult for believers living under authority which is evil to live a tranquil life. We may be persecuted, thrown into jail, consigned to labor camps. We may be questioned, tested, and tempted. It is difficult to live a godly life. Therefore, we need to pray for all those in authority so that we may live a godly life to the glory of God. Let us not be so presumptuous and foolish as to think that if only we live under some kind of *wicked* authority how much greater God may be glorified in us. Let us not be that foolish. If God places you in that situation, His grace will be sufficient for you, but to think that you can do it—you never will. The norm is that we should pray for all those in authority in order that we may live a quiet and tranquil and godly life. This is the corporate prayer of the church.

Regarding the prayer of the church there are further instructions. "I will therefore that the men pray in every place" (I Timothy 2:8a).

The "every place" here means public assemblies of the church. Whenever we come together we should pray with pious hands, without wrath or reasoning. When we come together to pray, we need to intercede, to supplicate, to pray. But let us remember that if our prayer is to be effective, then we who pray must be right before God. In other words, the prayer of the righteous is powerful. It is not that we are righteous in and of ourselves but that He has made us righteous; and if He has made us righteous, let us be righteous.

It says that the men are to pray without wrath or reasoning. It is a great temptation for men, especially, to burst into wrath against their brothers and sisters, against people. It is also the great temptation of men to doubt, to reason. Men always like to reason, and it is against God we like to reason, doubting Him. So when we pray, let us be sure there is no wrath and no reasoning, that we are at peace with our brothers and sisters, with the generality of men, that we are submissive to our heavenly Father, whatever His will may be. In that kind of spiritual condition, then we are able to pray.

"In like manner women ..." I like the word "in like manner," because it shows that the women are to pray, too. In some places people say only the men are to pray in the public meetings and that the women should not pray; they should be silent. I often say that if the women should be silent, then they should not sing. But the Bible never forbids the women to pray. Indeed, it says, "In like manner women ..." Women are to pray, too, in public; but how? The temptation with man is wrath and reasoning; the temptation of women is outward adornment instead of inward beauty. So Scripture says to let the women pray, but when they pray, let them be dressed and adorned with modesty and discretion. I think it is very wonderful here because the word "adorn" in the original is cosmos, which has reference to the world as a system. Let the women adorn with an other-worldly spirit—not like the people in the world trying to follow its fashion, but to be other-worldly and marked by a spirit of fear of the Lord. Now it does not mean that women should dress shabbily. I read somewhere about what is proper. I do not know whether this is right or not, but I will mention it. The proper way for women to dress is neither to be the first in fashion nor the last out of fashion, but to dress moderately. I leave it with you.

Teaching

It also mentions here about this matter of teaching, and by teaching here it has reference to public teaching in church gatherings. "Let a woman learn in quietness in all subjection; but I do not suffer a woman to teach" (I Timothy 2:12a).

The word *teach* actually means that they not be teachers nor exercise authority over men. In the church gatherings there is a divine order; the man represents Christ, the woman represents the church, and both need to represent correctly. It is for this reason that in this matter of teaching there is such a divine order.

Church Government

The third chapter is on church government. As God's people come together there is bound to be government, administration. In church government there are two offices—the elderhood and the deaconhood. God will raise up among His people some who are to assume the functions of the elders. Their functions are to supervise, oversee, and to shepherd the flock. Then there will be deacons or deaconesses who will be raised up to take care of the daily administrative things, routine things—serving the tables, visiting the sick, all these physical things that need to be taken care of, and so on.

As we look into the qualifications given here for the elders and deacons, it is strange that the emphasis is not on ability. We would think that to be elders—to govern—you need to have ability. Therefore, if you are a chief executive in General Motors, no doubt you can be an elder in the church. But no; it is not a matter of ability. Very little on ability is mentioned here. Almost everything mentioned is concerned with moral character. But again, it is not only moral character, because if it is merely that in view here, then an unbeliever might have some of the qualifications. What is required of the elders, those who lead, is *spirituality*; and the same is true for deacons. That is the reason why in the early church, when they selected the seven persons to serve the tables, they had to be full of the Holy Spirit (see Acts 6:3). Even in this aspect of church order, it is Christ. It is Christ being manifested. It is Christ being expressed in and through men and women; and because of this, they can serve the body of Christ.

Ministry of the Word

Chapter 4 focuses on ministry in the house of God. By ministry here is meant the ministry of God's word. There is not only the government side, there is also the ministry of the word side, the teaching side. God gives to the church some apostles, some prophets, some shepherds and teachers, and some evangelists in order to perfect the saints (see Ephesians 4). God gives these people to the church but they are for the body universal; yet, in the local assembly, there will be prophets and teachers.

You may remember from Acts 13 that in the church in Antioch, there were five prophets and teachers, and they were local prophets and teachers. They were there taking care of the ministry of God's word for the church there. They were not the elders but were those who ministered the word of God to the church there. Paul used Timothy as an example, saying, "Timothy, in order that you may minister the word rightly, you have to take care of yourself spiritually." In other words, it is not simply a matter of teaching people. He who teaches has to be one who is deeply taught by God. It is not just the word spoken, it is the man who speaks the word. Therefore, Paul says this to Timothy: "Exercise godliness because it is profitable not only for the present age but for the age to come." We need to be disciplined. We need to be exercised by the Holy Spirit. We need to be developed in order that we may be like God, so that in love, in word, in deed, in conduct, in our relationships—in everything, we may truly let Christ be seen; and also that when we speak, it is Christ who is imparted to other people. So Paul said, "Take heed to yourself and to your teaching—to your ministry."

Discipline

In chapter 5 we find discipline. Discipline is very important in the church. If there is no discipline, there is no church. We cannot call it a church if there is no discipline present, because everything is in disorder, everything will be according to his or her own thought and opinion and desire. Therefore, there ought to be church discipline. Yet discipline must be exercised with caution and love.

Good Confession

Chapter 6 deals with a good confession of the church. The church, being a testimony, has to maintain a good confession before the world. The Lord Jesus made the good confession before Pilate; therefore, we need to do the same before the world. Our confession is: Jesus is our all; we trust Him; we have committed our lives to Him; He is the One in whom we trust; He is the One whom we serve. This is our confession. Paul is saying, especially to those who are rich in earthly things, not to trust in earthly riches, the uncertainty of riches, but trust in God. We tell the world that we trust in God; we trust in Christ; He is everything to us. This is a good confession, a very good testimony.

This first letter to Timothy is a letter dealing with church order; and church order, if it is real, has to be Christ—His expression, His manifestation, His pouring out. Otherwise, it is merely an organization. It is not real; and it has no spiritual value.

Shall we pray:

Dear heavenly Father, we do praise and thank Thee knowing that Thou art building Thine own house. We have the confidence that Thou wilt build it until it becomes a glorious church without spot or wrinkle or any of such sort, but holy and without blame. Oh, our Father, we do praise and thank Thee that Thou art establishing Thy church upon this earth, and that Thou dost reveal to us that the order is not just something outward; it has to come from within. Oh, that we may know Christ, and by knowing Him we may have that order in the church to the praise of Thy glory and the building up of Thy people. So we now commit Thy word back into Thy hand and pray that if it is usable, use it for Thy glory. In the name of our Lord Jesus. Amen.

II TIMOTHY

Seeing Christ in Church Crisis

II Timothy 2:1-6—Thou therefore, my child, be strong in the grace which is in Christ Jesus. And the things thou hast heard of me in the presence of many witnesses, these entrust to faithful men, such as shall be competent to instruct others also. Take thy share in suffering as a good soldier of Jesus Christ. No one going as a soldier entangles himself with the affairs of life, that he may please him who has enlisted him as a soldier. And if also any one contend in the games, he is not crowned unless he contend lawfully. The husbandman must labour before partaking of the fruits.

II Timothy 2:20-22—But in a great house there are not only gold and silver vessels, but also wooden and earthen; and some to honour, and some to dishonour. If therefore one shall have purified himself from these, in separating himself from them, he shall be a vessel to honour, sanctified, serviceable to the Master, prepared for every good work. But youthful lusts flee, and pursue righteousness, faith, love, peace, with those that call upon the Lord out of a pure heart.

II Timothy 4:6-8—For I am already being poured out, and the time of my release is come. I have combated the good combat, I have finished the race, I have kept the faith. Henceforth the crown of righteousness is laid up for me, which the Lord, the righteous Judge, will render to me in that day; but not only to me, but also to all who love his appearing.

Let us pray:

Dear heavenly Father, we have read Thy word, and now we look to Thy Holy Spirit to quicken Thy word to our hearts that these may not just be words, but we may hear Thy voice. We commit this time into Thy hands and pray that through the working of the Holy Spirit Thy purpose for this time may be fully realized to the praise of Thy glory. In the name of our Lord Jesus. Amen.

This second letter to Timothy is the last extant letter we have that was written by the apostle Paul. We can thus call this Paul's last will and testament. We mentioned before that after Paul was released from his first Roman imprisonment he was able to fulfill his desire to visit his friends, God's people in various places—in Ephesus, in Colosse, in Philippi and, we believe, even visiting Spain as he had wished. But the times began to change. We know from history that in the year 64 A.D. Nero, the Caesar, burned the city of Rome. We do not know for what reason. Probably he was mad, or perhaps he wanted to rebuild the city of Rome; but a third of the city was razed to the ground. We are told that while the city was burning he was there playing the harp, gleefully enjoying the scene. Because of this the people in Rome fell into a spirit of rebellion. Therefore, Nero tried to find a scapegoat on which to put the blame, and he found an easy one—the Christians. Because of this, Christians were greatly persecuted everywhere. To be a Christian was now a crime, and because of the change in situation we know that the apostle Paul was rearrested and brought to Rome to be judged. It was very different this time from the first time he became a prisoner. For even though he was a prisoner the first time, he was allowed to live in his own hired apartment. He was given the freedom to receive all who visited him, and he was finally acquitted.

This time, however, it was very, very different. He was taken as a prisoner of Rome, a criminal in the sight of the Empire. Therefore, he was put into the dungeon. Probably he was put into a terrible place called "The Sepulchre," where many died—eaten up by rats. The situation was so tense that all the people in the province of Asia deserted the apostle Paul out of fear for their own lives, and therefore not wishing to be associated with Paul the "criminal." During his first defense, for example, nobody was willing to be his character witness because it was too dangerous. All were simply thinking of themselves, and so, Paul was left there alone, deserted even by those among whom he had labored so long and had given so much.

Paul lay in the dungeon, deserted by all; and we must not forget that he was a human being. Some of us think that Paul was a superman, but he was not. As a human being, no doubt he felt deeply the desertion of his friends and of those whom he loved. Inwardly, he must have suffered intensely. That is the reason why any token of sympathy and loyalty and love was greatly appreciated by him. He remembered what Onesiphorus had done for him when he was in prison, which he mentioned in this last letter (see II Timothy 1:16-18). This man, who was from Asia, came to Rome and inquired about Paul. Finally, he found Paul in the dungeon, and he was able to see him. It was a danger to Onesiphorus, and we do not know whether he was also killed because of that. But Paul appreciated the slightest token of sympathy and loyalty. Being human, how could a man bear all these things and stand? In this last letter, which was his last will and testament, he testified, and this was his secret: "I know whom I have believed and I am fully persuaded that he is able to keep for that day the deposit I have entrusted to him" (II Timothy 1:12).

It was not because of what Paul was in himself; it was not because he had such an iron will; it was because he knew whom he had believed. He knew the Lord. It was his knowledge of the Lord Jesus, a living knowledge of the Lord Jesus that kept him through all these trials. He had the confidence that what he had entrusted to the Lord, He would keep until that day. That day is the day of Christ, when he shall appear before Christ and there be rewarded: as a "good and faithful servant."

Paul wrote this letter to Timothy. We know that Timothy was

a relatively young man, even though at that time he was around thirty-eight to forty years old. But he was still a young man in comparison with the aged Paul, and Paul considered him as a son in faith. Now Timothy was by nature a timid person with a shy disposition, and we know that he was very weak physically. He had stomach trouble. He was a person who did not like to stand at the front. He liked to live under the shadow of somebody else. He lived under the shadow of the great apostle Paul, and he was contented. But now his friend, his father in faith, was taken prisoner, and he was soon to lose him. He was pushed to the forefront and given the responsibility of carrying on the testimony of Jesus after Paul departed. It was a tremendous responsibility and in a most unfavorable situation. Would Timothy falter? Humanly speaking, he would. Would he try to hide himself and shun the responsibility? Probably, he would. It is for this reason that the apostle Paul wrote this last letter to him, knowing what Timothy was, trying to encourage him and rekindle the gifts that were in him. Timothy needed such encouragement. Paul said, "Be strong; do not be weak. Be strong in the grace that is in Christ Jesus." That is the secret. So far as Timothy was concerned he could not meet the situation; it was beyond him. But there is always sufficient grace, and it is only by the grace of Jesus Christ that he would be able to carry on.

Consider the situation of the church at that time, not only at Ephesus, but the church of God throughout the world. The Roman Empire was the greatest empire in the world. It had tremendous power and it was the announced will of that empire to crush, to annihilate, to wipe out Christianity. It had the ability to do that; it had the will to do that; and it was doing it. Would the church be able to exist, to continue on? Or would it be completely wiped out? No doubt such thoughts must have gone through the mind of Paul, the mind of Timothy, and many others. The church was in crisis. Would the testimony of Jesus be maintained, carried on, and even strengthened? Or would the testimony of Jesus be wiped out in the world? Does God have any direction to give to His people at such moments? This is the reason why this letter to Timothy was written: (1) to give a last testimony to his faith in Jesus Christ, (2) to encourage the timid Timothy to take over the torch of the testimony of Jesus, and (3) to show the church how to behave in the time of adversity in crisis.

We believe this letter is most relevant and important to us today. This is not to say that this is the only book in the Bible relevant to us today. No. Every book in the Bible is relevant and important to us today, because they are all written for our admonition. But this letter, in a very special way, is very near to our heart because we are living in the last days, even as Paul had mentioned in this letter. Not only that, the church today, is in a very critical time. We are in a crisis. The world is pressuring the church of God to compromise, to yield, to capitulate and, unfortunately, the world seems to be very successful in such attempts. Within the church, the people of God are divided, scattered. Heresies are rampant. Moral corruption is everywhere. As a consequence, we may frequently wonder: where is the testimony of Jesus? Will God be able to maintain His testimony on earth in such an hour? Does God give us any direction as to how we should act or react, how we should behave when we are in such a situation? We believe this last letter of the apostle Paul provides answers to these questions. We need to take this letter to heart and find God's direction for us as to how we can stand and how we should behave when the church is in crisis. It is our hope that through this letter we may see Christ in church crisis.

A Great House

In the first letter to Timothy the apostle had written: "The church is God's house, the assembly of the living God, the pillar and base of the truth" (see I Timothy 3:15). But in the second letter he wrote this: "The church is a great house in which there are vessels of honor and vessels to dishonor, vessels of gold and silver, and vessels of wood and earth" (see II Timothy

2:20). Why this difference? When Paul wrote the first letter to Timothy the church was still in its normal state. Normally speaking, the church is the house of God, where God dwells. The church is the assembly of the living God and composed of those living souls assembled together unto the living God. The church is also the pillar for maintaining the testimony of the truth. And it is also the base, reservoir and keeper of the truth. That is what the church is to be in its normal state; but a change had come. The church was no longer called God's house; it was now called a great house. Outwardly, it seemed to be great because at that time the gospel had been preached throughout the known world, but in actuality it had become a great house with vessels to honor and vessels to dishonor. In other words, it had now become a great mixture within. What, then, should we Christians do when we are in such an abnormal situation? We believe this is what we will learn from this second letter of Paul's to Timothy.

The Promise of Life

When Paul wrote I Timothy, he had declared: "Paul, apostle [that is, a sent-out-one or one commissioned] of Jesus Christ according to the command of God our Saviour and of Christ Jesus our hope" (1:1). But later in II Timothy he wrote, "Paul, apostle of Jesus Christ by God's will, according to the promise of life, the life which is in Christ Jesus" (1:1). This is really eye-opening because in the first letter he had written: "According to the command of God our Saviour ...," but here he says, "According to the promise of life which is in Christ Jesus ..." When it is in a normal time, God's command is sufficient—God issues the word and that is it. In abnormal times, however, the emphasis is shifted from command to life because, unless life is supplied, that command can never be carried out. So at the very outset the apostle Paul is in essence saying here: "Now is a time within which we must emphasize life." For the recovery of God's testimony on earth in the difficult times or for the maintenance of the testimony of Jesus in the last days, the secret lies in life.

"But has been made manifest now by the appearing of our Saviour Jesus Christ, who has annulled death, and brought to light life and incorruptibility by the glad tidings" (II Timothy 1:10).

What are the glad tidings? What is the good news? What is the nature of the gospel? The nature of the gospel is to bring to light life and incorruptibility. What Christ has done on this earth, what He has accomplished on the cross is to annul death and to bring to light life and immortality. This is what the gospel is. When death has set in, the only way to counter it is by life—the resurrection life of our Lord Jesus. When death has come upon this earth, when death has come upon a person, when—spiritually speaking—death has come upon the church, how are we going to fight against the intrusion of death? There is only one way—the way of life. The life that we received from the Lord Jesus, the life that is released in the gospel of Jesus Christ is none other than resurrection life. It is the life that has gone down into death, swallowing and defeating death, and coming out of death victoriously. If only we trust in, and depend upon, this life, then we will obtain the spirit of power, love and a sound mind. If we ignore this life and try to meet death with any other resources, we will find that there is nothing else equal to death. But thank God, life overcomes death, and the life which we have received in Christ through the gospel is that life which overcomes death. Accordingly, if we simply follow life, we will be delivered from all confusion and deception. If we cultivate life, we will be able to rise above everything and carry on the testimony of Jesus. In short, life is the secret.

We discover this especially when we study the writings of the apostle John. We often say that John was the apostle of recovery. Peter as a fisherman had cast the spiritual net and drew many into the church. Paul was a tentmaker; he began to build up those who had been drawn into the church of God. But when the church had suffered and there came to be in it many holes and cracks, John—who when called by Jesus to be His disciple was seen mending his fishing nets—came in to mend the deteriorating condition of the church. Hence, the ministry of John can be described as the ministry of recovery. His writings are the last books of the New Testament. His Gospel was written as the last of the four New Testament Gospels; his epistles were the last ones written; and, of course, John's book of the Revelation forms the last book of the entire Bible. John always comes at the very last because his ministry is the ministry of recovery—how to recover the testimony of Jesus when it has suffered damage. The whole emphasis in the writings of the apostle John is an emphasis on life. "In him was life, and the life was the light of men" (John 1:4).

In the first epistle of John he said: "We share with you the word of life" (see I John 1:1). And in the book of Revelation you will read how "life swallowed up death." In John's description of the New Jerusalem mentioned in Revelation, life is to be seen everywhere: the river of life and the tree of life are all over the city. Everything speaks of life.

We are living in a very critical time—critical not only in relation to our personal Christian life but critical also in relation to our corporate life as the church of God. We find death everywhere. Death is attempting to make its way into the church to corrupt it and destroy it. How are we going to battle against such spiritual death that is coming into the church and coming into our lives? Life is the secret. Let us seek life, even the eternal life of Christ. Let us think of the life which God has given us. Trust that life; depend upon that life; follow that life; cultivate that life; develop that life; let that life increase in us. For when life increases, death decreases—such is the promise of life.

We do believe that in these days our emphasis should be on life. This is not the time to emphasize command: "Do this and do not do that," because that will not work. It is the time when we should emphasize the glorious and powerful life of our Lord Jesus. Know this life that is in us, and if we know this life, we shall overcome. This is not the time that we merely emphasize knowledge, even though knowledge is good; but knowledge alone cannot fight and win against death. The solution: *life is the secret.* The reason why Paul was able to stand, to withstand, and to stand yet again is because he knew life: "For me to live is Christ. It is not I, it is Christ." If it had been Paul himself who had stood and withstood, there is no doubt at all that he—like every other human being—would have had to capitulate in the face of death's onslaught; however, it was Christ who lived in him. He knew Christ as his life. How we also need to know Christ as our life. He is not only the Savior who saves us, He is even also our very life. And this very life is to be known, to be experienced, to be increased in us. For this is the only way we can stand, the only way we can maintain the testimony of Jesus in these difficult times.

Pursue

"Pursue righteousness, faith, love, peace, with those that call upon the Lord out of a pure heart" (II Timothy 2:22).

When situations become difficult, our natural reaction is to withdraw; we choose not to pursue, not to advance, but to withdraw, in order that we might be able to preserve ourselves. But the apostle Paul wrote that this was not the time to withdraw but the time to pursue.

We have already mentioned that the church is now a great house, and in the great house there are vessels to honor and vessels to dishonor, that there are gold and silver vessels and also wooden and earthen vessels. The vessels of honor are gold and silver. Gold represents the nature of God. Whenever the nature of God is represented in the Bible or His glory is manifested herein, gold is used. On the other hand, silver in Scripture represents the redemption of Jesus Christ because back then a person needed silver shekels as redemption money. Hence, vessels to honor is a reference to such people.

All of us are vessels in the great house that the church today has become. Vessels, we know, are for the purpose of the house owner, and of course, the house owner in view here is God himself. We are His vessels, and He desires to use us for His purpose. Some vessels are vessels to honor; and thus they are to be used for an honorable purpose, if such are vessels of gold and of silver. In other words, if we live by the life of God, we have His life in us and this life has a divine nature. If we live by that divine nature which is in us and if we live by the redemptive work of Christ Jesus which is accomplished by His grace, then we will become vessels to honor. But if we do not, we will be vessels of wood and earth.

Wood, in the Scriptures, always represents human nature. We are human, like wood—corruptible; and earth—we are made of dust. If we are the Lord's, we are in the house; and yet, if we continue to live by our natural life, by our earthen life, if we continue to walk in the flesh in the human way, we will become vessels of wood and earth—and therefore vessels to dishonor. It does not mean that God has predestinated some believers to be vessels to honor and other believers to be vessels to dishonor. No, if you read this passage carefully, you will find that, actually, whether you are a vessel to honor or a vessel to dishonor depends on how you respond. In other words, if you are not content to be a vessel to dishonor; on the contrary, if you are willing to purify yourself, are willing to let the Holy Spirit discipline you, are willing to cooperate with God, and are willing to deny yourself, take up your cross and follow the Lord, then you shall purify yourself of the wooden and the earthen in you, and thus you shall become what is of gold and of silver. You shall become vessels fit for the Master's use—sanctified and honorable.

In a house you have many vessels, but I would think that usually you have more vessels of wood and earth than vessels of gold and silver. Gold and silver vessels are probably very rare, so there are just a few, but you have many earthen and wooden vessels in the house. And spiritually speaking, this is also true. At the time when Paul wrote this letter, the church in general had fallen. All who were in Asia Province had fallen away and had deserted Paul. Think of that—how much labor Paul had undertaken for the Lord in Asia; how he had wept much, shedding tears day and night; how he had given his life to those saints there. He had not withheld anything from them but had communicated to them the whole counsel of God. He poured himself out upon those people in the Province of Asia, but all in Asia had deserted him. Nevertheless, this did not mean that there were none in Asia who remained faithful to God and loyal to Him. The house of Onesiphorus was an example. He was a man who had despised the danger to himself. While in Rome he had searched out Paul's whereabouts—imprisoned in a dungeon—and his very presence comforted Paul greatly. Then there were Priscilla, Aquila, Timothy, and a number of other people, but they were in the minority.

We like to be popular, do we not; we desire to go with the crowd, flow with the crowd. We do not want to be in the minority. But those in the minority may very well be those who are vessels to honor, vessels of gold and silver. This will always be the case. It was true in the time of Paul; and it is true today. What should we do? Should we compromise? Should we go along with the crowd? Or are we willing to purify ourselves and "pursue righteousness, faith, love, peace, with those that call upon the Lord out of a pure heart"?

"The Lord knows those that are His; and, Let every one who names the name of the Lord withdraw from iniquity" (II Timothy 2:19).

The Lord does not look at outward appearance; He looks upon the heart. He is looking for those who have a pure heart. A pure heart is different from a good heart. Some people may have a good heart, but a pure one is a heart that is single towards God. "Blessed the pure in heart, for they shall see God" (Matthew 5:8). The pure heart is a heart that sees God; indeed, that sees God only. It has not a double vision; rather, it is like a dove's eye. A dove can see only one thing at a time. When things and situations begin to be difficult, it is very easy for us to have double vision, but the Lord is looking for a pure heart. Wherever we can find people with pure hearts, pursue with them, be with them, so that together we may seek for righteousness, faith, love and peace.

Pure Conscience

When things begin to be difficult, when the church falls into disarray, what do you do? How can you withstand the current and maintain the testimony of Jesus? *Go back to the source of things.* It is very interesting to see that in this last letter, his last will and testament, as it were, Paul went back to the source and root of all things in his life when writing this to Timothy: "I am thankful to God whom I serve from my forefathers with pure conscience" (II Timothy 1:3).

Before discussing the root and source of things in his life, let it first be noted that Paul always tried to maintain a pure conscience, a good conscience. That was his testimony. If you read the book of Acts, again and again you will find Paul saying: "Before God and man I try to keep a good conscience, a conscience void of offense." Conscience is very important, especially for a Christian. Or may I put it this way: Conscience is the last link between God and fallen man. After man had fallen, the last link with God was his conscience. Somehow, your conscience will tell you that there is a God. Somehow, your conscience will tell you what you do is wrong. Why is it wrong if there be no objective standard? Somehow, your conscience will tell you that if you do wrong you will suffer for it. There will be wages; there will be a penalty attached to it. For this reason, whenever the gospel is preached, people are pricked in their hearts; that is to say, they are pricked in their conscience. It is through the conscience that the gospel of Jesus Christ is able to enter into people's lives. Conscience is the last link between man and God.

However, a fallen man's conscience is undependable. Nobody in a fallen state can legitimately say, "I live by my good conscience;" for what is the condition of his conscience? It is seared. A fallen person cannot live by his conscience because it has become hardened; an unbeliever's conscience is totally undependable. But for us who believe in God and Christ, our conscience is very important because the blood of Jesus Christ has cleansed it. All the accusations, all the evil things in the conscience, have been washed and cleansed by the precious blood of our Lord Jesus. We can now stand before God with a clean conscience, and such we need to maintain continually. Any believer who begins to neglect his conscience will eventually find his faith shipwrecked.

We shall now look at Paul's roots. Paul said at the very last, "I have served God from my forefathers with a pure conscience." Paul's forefathers had served God with a pure conscience. This apostle had acknowledged: "I am a Pharisee of the Pharisees." He had come from a devout Pharisee family. We usually look upon the Pharisees of old as hypocrites and they were; but there were true Pharisees, too. Evidently, Paul's forefathers had been true Pharisees like Paul. According to the knowledge they had, according to the tradition they followed, they had served God with a pure conscience in accordance with all which they knew. They had served God according to the light they had in their conscience. Of course, that is not perfect, but thank God, on the road to Damascus Paul the Pharisee received the revelation of Jesus Christ and now his conscience was able to live under a perfect light. Christ Jesus became his conscience, and thereafter he always tried to serve God with a pure conscience, with a good conscience. He could say, "I was not disobedient to the heavenly vision" (Acts 26:19). He had always obeyed the heavenly vision. He served God with a pure conscience, and that had its roots in his forefathers. The latter had served God with a good conscience under lesser light, but now, with more light, Paul served God with a pure conscience in a better way. And such was the root in Paul's faith.

The same thing was true with Timothy. Paul wrote: "Timothy, the unfeigned faith, the sincere faith that was in your grandmother Lois, and in your mother Eunice, I believe is in you, too" (see II Timothy 1:5). We do not know how Lois and Eunice came to the Lord. There have been different theories offered. Some think that probably Lois and Eunice were two widows—mother and daughter from Lystra—who were among the original disciples who were saved on the day of Pentecost back in Jerusalem. Others have surmised that probably, when Paul and Barnabas had first visited Lystra, these two women had come to the Lord because they were devout Jews. They were looking for the hope of Israel. So when they heard the gospel that Jesus is the fulfillment of the hope of Messiah, they had believed in the Lord Jesus. However, it really does not matter much. In grandmother Lois and mother Eunice there was that sincere faith, and this faith was also in Timothy—how very precious!

Doubtless, Paul had been the instrument that brought Timothy to the Lord, since Paul called him "my son in the faith." But, evidently, these two women had great influence upon this young man. He was brought up under the nurture, admonition and discipline of these two women. In one sense, that was marvelous, but in another sense, we can understand why Timothy was somewhat feminine. Nevertheless, Timothy could trace his faith—the root thereof—to both his grandmother and mother. Yet more than that, Paul said this:

"Remember from whom you have received and what you have received." Timothy was brought up spiritually under Paul, and Paul must have spent a great amount of time with him, trying to build him up in the Lord. He said in this letter: "Timothy, you remember my teaching, my conduct, my life, my persecution, my suffering, my purpose, and everything about me. You know all of it. You know the source of it. Therefore, abide in them, and if you will abide in them, you will not be distracted or deceived" (see II Timothy 3:10-12). There is a root source there.

Yet in addition to all that, Paul also had this to say: "Timothy, from your youth up you have known the sacred letters. The Holy Scriptures are God-breathed for our correction, for our instruction, for our teaching; in order that the man of God may be fully equipped to do every work of God" (see II Timothy 3:15-17). Timothy knew the Scriptures.

When things and situations begin to change, when heresies commence to spread, when doubts begin to arise, it is a time when we must go back to the source, and the source is the word of God. If we know God's word by heart, we will not be deceived. If we know from whom we have received and what we have received and abide therein, we will not be distracted. If we know the faith of our fathers, we shall be able to continue on.

Faithful Men

"Entrust to faithful men, such as shall be competent to instruct others also" (II Timothy 2:2).

It is extremely interesting to note that in I Timothy Paul had mentioned elders and deacons—the order in the church. In II Timothy, however, he did not mention elders or deacons at all; he only mentioned faithful men. When the church is in its normal state, it is the house of the living God; therefore, there is a divine order established in the church with elders supervising and deacons serving. But when the church is in an abnormal state, then you will discern that God is no longer looking for outward order; God is looking for inward quality. Office is of no importance anymore; the reality is all which God is looking for. It is not a matter of setting up elders and deacons; it is a matter of who is faithful. And those who are faithful are to be entrusted with the deposit which God has deposited in the church.

In a sense, Paul here represents the first generation and Timothy represents the second. The first generation is passing. Paul will soon be dead. So the testimony of Jesus is being handed over to Timothy—who represents the succeeding generation—to carry on for that generation. How is it to be carried on? "Entrust to faithful men those who are able to instruct others." When God used Paul to write his seven letters to the churches, the church was in a normal situation. For instance, in Philippians he had written: "Bishops or elders, deacons, brothers ..." But in a second set of seven letters to the churches—those cited by John in Revelation chapters 2 and 3—these things are no longer mentioned: "Write to the angel, to the messenger of the church in Asia, that is in Ephesus," and so on. Who are these messengers? They are not those who have official positions but those who are faithful to the testimony of Jesus. They are those who overcome: "He that overcomes." When the church is in crisis, what God emphasizes is no longer the outward organization: He is not trying to reorganize. What He emphasizes instead is the inward reality. He is looking for faithfulness. It is those who are faithful who will carry on the testimony of Jesus. It is not only Timothy who must carry on, but he must find others who are faithful and who can go on together with him because it is much more than what one person can do. And this we believe is what God desires for us today.

The Call to Suffer

"Take thy share in suffering as a good soldier of Jesus Christ" (II Timothy 2:3). The call of the gospel is not only that we are called to life and incorruptibility and to glory, but it is also a call to suffer. We must not forget that our Lord Jesus suffered and then He entered into His glory. Therefore, all those who want to live a godly life on earth must suffer. Let us not think suffering is something strange. Suffering is normal; it is a part of our calling. We are called to suffer, not for our sins, but to suffer for Christ's name, to suffer as a Christian. Let us not be ashamed to suffer. Paul said in essence, "Do not be ashamed of my sufferings. Do not be ashamed of my bonds, because I am in bonds for Christ's sake. Share my suffering with me."

If we have the mind to suffer, if we know we are called to suffer, then, when sufferings come, we will not be overwhelmed. We know it is a part of our calling, and it is through suffering that God is able to perfect and mature us and to prepare us for glory. "If we suffer with Him we shall also reign with Him" (see II Timothy 2:12) Are we willing to suffer for Christ's sake?

Paul's Last Will and Testament

Finally, Paul wrote as his last will and testament: "I have fought the good fight, I have run the course, I have kept the faith" (see II Timothy 4:6-7). We know, of course, that it was not because of himself but because of Him whom he believed. But Paul could also write: "I can testify that I have fought the good fight, I have kept the faith, I have run the course, and now there is a crown of righteousness waiting for me." He went on to say, "No, it is not only for me but also for all who love His appearing, all who love the apocalypse, the epiphany of our Lord Jesus, the coming of our Lord Jesus." The Lord is coming soon. The time will not be long. Paul said, "God will keep me. He will keep me for His heavenly kingdom." Even though

Paul had to lose his life, he knew he was being kept for that heavenly kingdom.

Do we know whom we believe? Are we fully persuaded that He is able to keep what we have committed to Him until that day? (see II Timothy 1:12). If we do, then there is nothing to fear. Instead of retreating, let us advance. The cause of God has to go forward until His purpose is fully realized. May the Lord help us.

Shall we pray:

Dear heavenly Father, we have heard the last will and testament of Thy servant Paul. May we be encouraged by Thy grace. May we also bear such testimony that we know whom we have believed and we are fully persuaded that Thou art able to keep that which we have committed to Thee until that day. To Thee be the glory. In the name of our Lord Jesus. Amen.

TITUS

Seeing Christ in Church Discipline

Titus 2:1-15—But do thou speak the things that become sound teaching; that the elder men be sober, grave, discreet, sound in faith, in love, in patience, that the elder women in like manner be in deportment as becoming those who have to say to sacred things, not slanderers, not enslaved to much wine, teachers of what is right; that they may admonish the young women to be attached to their husbands, to be attached to their children, discreet, chaste, diligent in home work, good, subject to their own husbands, that the word of God may not be evil spoken of. The younger men in like manner exhort to be discreet: in all things affording thyself as a pattern of good works; in teaching uncorruptedness, gravity, a sound word, not to be condemned; that he who is opposed may be ashamed, having no evil thing to say about us: bondmen to be subject to their own masters, to make themselves acceptable in everything; not gainsaying; not robbing their masters, but shewing all good fidelity, that they may adorn the teaching which is of our Saviour God in all things. For the grace of God which carries with it salvation for all men has appeared, teaching us that, having denied impiety and worldly lusts, we should live soberly, and justly and piously in the present course of things, awaiting the blessed hope and appearing of the glory of our great God and Saviour Jesus Christ; who gave himself for us, that he might redeem us from all lawlessness, and purify to himself a peculiar people, zealous for good works. These things speak, and exhort, and rebuke with all authority. Let no one despise thee.

Shall we pray:

Dear heavenly Father, we do thank Thee for the precious

blood of our Lord Jesus and for the new and living way which He has opened for us through His body. And we do praise and thank Thee that knowing He is our High Priest, interceding for us at Thy right hand, we dare to approach the throne of grace looking for mercy and for grace. We ask Thee, oh Lord, that as we are in Thy presence, Thou wilt shine upon us, give us the spirit of wisdom and revelation so that we may truly know Thee. We pray that Christ will reveal himself, not only to us, but in us, in order that Christ may be formed in us and that Christ may be expressed through us. And to Him be all the glory. In the name of our Lord Jesus. Amen.

We mentioned before that the letters of I and II Timothy and Titus form a particular group of New Testament writings because these three letters are all written to individuals—I and II Timothy to Timothy and Titus to Titus. However, even though they are written to individuals, they nonetheless deal with church matters. In I Timothy we see Christ in church order; in II Timothy we see Christ in church crisis; and now in this letter to Titus we shall see Christ in church discipline.

Before we go into this letter, probably a little bit of background will be helpful. Who was Titus? It is very interesting to learn that the name Titus is never mentioned in the book of Acts. Paul has two young associates in the work of God—Timothy and Titus. We find the name of Timothy many times in the book of Acts, but the name of Titus is never there. Even though his name is never mentioned in the book of Acts, we know he is there because we find him in some of the other writings of the apostle Paul; for instance, II Corinthians, Galatians, and this letter to Titus.

Titus was probably a native of Syrian Antioch. Unlike Timothy, he was a Gentile by birth. Timothy was half Jew and half Gentile because Timothy's father was a Greek, but his mother was a Jewess. Titus came to know the Lord Jesus through the apostle Paul as had Timothy, and that is the reason why Paul sometimes called Timothy and Titus his sons in the faith. Both of them served the Lord with Paul and under Paul.

We learn from the account in Acts 15 of the council in Jerusalem that Paul had taken Titus with him to Jerusalem, yet not for the purpose of participating in the discussion, but of using him as a test case to determine whether a Gentile believer must be circumcised. As it turned out, Titus was never circumcised because the truth of the gospel prevailed.

We do not see Titus with the apostle Paul in his second missionary journey. During his third journey, however, Paul sent Titus from Ephesus to Corinth to find out and report back to Paul what happened after he had sent his letter to the Corinthians. He came back and met Paul in Macedonia and gave him a good report that comforted Paul very much. Then Titus was again sent back to Corinth to complete the work which Paul had started there.

Most likely, Titus was somewhat older than Timothy. Both of them had been with Paul as the apostle's companions, but it seems that the relationship between Paul and Timothy was more intimate than his relationship with Titus. These two young men were very different, not only in their background, but also in their temperament and in their gifts. Timothy was brought up by his grandmother Lois and his mother Eunice, both of whom were devout women. They had trained Timothy when he was a boy in the Jewish ways, in Judaism. Timothy knew the sacred letters from his boyhood, but Titus did not have that kind of background because he came from a totally Gentile family. By nature, Timothy was timid and shy, but Titus seemed to be made of a stronger and sterner disposition. Timothy was a born follower; he liked to live under the shadow of someone else. He had to be stirred up to push himself to the front because that was not his temperament. But Titus seemed to be different; he was born with a leadership capacity, and hence he had no trouble taking the initiative. He had something of Paul's aggressive character.

Paul sent Timothy to Ephesus, but he sent Titus to Corinth and later on to Crete. It is interesting to see that Paul knew the limits, the gifts and the ministry of his young associates. Corinth and Crete were both very difficult places, but it seems that Titus was a good troubleshooter. He was a careful person, was discerning and disciplined, had affection, but was strong and patient, and was greatly used of the Lord in this area.

After Paul was released from the first Roman imprisonment, he began to travel and visited some old places, such as the province of Asia and Philippi, after which he probably went off to Spain with Titus. Early on after his release and while on his way to Ephesus in Asia Minor, Paul passed through the island of Crete, a large island in the eastern Mediterranean Sea. We have no record that Paul had ever visited that island before and had engaged in the Lord's work there. It seems as though this was now the first time he really visited that island. However, when he passed through Crete he discovered some Christians and churches were there. We do not know how these Christians happened to be on that island or how these churches began, but most likely these Christians were the original believers, meaning that these were some of the many people who had been gathered together in Jerusalem on the day of Pentecost and had heard Peter's gospel message.

In honor of the day of Pentecost Jewish people had come to Jerusalem from all over the world to attend this feast, including some people from Crete (see Acts 2:11). Evidently, these Cretans had heard the message given by the apostle Peter and the eleven other apostles. They were converted, saved and baptized, and had then returned to their native island. And probably thereafter, through their preaching, other people there got saved and churches were thus established on the island; not just one, but the Bible speaks of "churches." In other words, in different localities on the island there had come into being assemblies of God's people. So when Paul visited the island of Crete, he found Christians already there, and churches already established.

From history we know that the Cretans did not have a very good reputation. Even their own prophet, Epimenides, had once said, "The Cretans are liars, evil wild beasts, lazy gluttons" (Titus 1:12). The Cretans evidently did not have a very good name because they were natural liars. Even in English, there is a word, *cretanizing*, which is synonymous with "lying." There is also a saying: "Play the Cretan with a Cretan," which means "out-tricking a trickster." So the Cretans did not have a very good name. They were not only liars, they were also like evil wild beasts. Moreover, many of them were bandits, and they were lazy gluttons. They loved to enjoy the pleasures of this world so as to satisfy their lusts.

Strangely, every race or nation seems to have some special national or racial traits. The Cretans had these kinds of traits which were not very commendable; but the wonderful thing is that even with Cretans, God is able to save them. The salvation of our Lord Jesus is so wonderful that it can save anybody, even a Cretan. And now there were Christians and churches on that island. Such is the glory of the gospel of Jesus Christ. There is no sinner too impossible for God to save. The salvation of our Lord Jesus reaches the chief of sinners; therefore, there is hope for everybody. Thank God for that!

Even though these Cretan believers naturally possessed such bad dispositions, habits, customs, environment and behaviors, the Lord is able to save them to the uttermost after they are saved. He is able to transform them completely; but transformation takes time. So when Paul visited the Cretan churches he found that everything was in disorder. They were the Lord's, but their understanding of the finished work of Christ on the cross was insufficient. They did not know the daily working of the Holy Spirit in their lives, sanctifying them, transforming them. They lacked that kind of experience. They probably did not even know that on the cross of Jesus Christ our old man was crucified, and certainly their old man was not very commendable. It seems they were still living most of their lives according to their old Adamic life; and hence, all the old habits and old dispositions were evident among these believers in the Cretan churches to the great disgrace of God.

Paul did not have a long time to stay there because he had burdens elsewhere, and he had to travel and see many other places. So he left Titus behind on the island of Crete and traveled on. From Macedonia he sent a letter to Titus, saying, "I left you behind to set right the things that remain unordered" (see Titus 1:5). Therefore, even though this letter is written to an individual, it is centered upon this matter of personal and church discipline because the Cretans were an undisciplined people, not only by nature but continued to be so even after they had become believers. They were undisciplined in their personal lives and undisciplined in their church life; therefore, this letter of Titus is a letter on church discipline. And accordingly, from this letter we shall see Christ in church discipline.

Saving the Mind

Discipline is a necessity of life, even in the natural realm. When human life came upon this earth, it needed to grow and develop, to mature into manhood and womanhood. But how can a life develop properly? It needs discipline, because if there is no discipline, it will be wild; the growth will not be right. So even in the natural realm, discipline is a necessity. If there is no discipline, that child will never grow into proper manhood or womanhood. Character is developed through discipline, and if this be true in the natural life, it must also be true in the spiritual life. Spiritually, we have received a new life, but this new life in us can only grow and develop through discipline. And interestingly, the word discipline in Greek means "saving the mind."

Even though we have received the life of Christ in us, the Adamic life that we received from Adam needs to be dealt with by the cross. If the self-life—that is, the Adamic life or the flesh in us—is not put away through the cross of the Lord Jesus, then it will suppress the new life, the life of Christ, in us. It is by the setting aside of the flesh that the life of Christ in us is given the opportunity to grow and develop, and to be expressed. However, this can only be done through discipline. It is through discipline that Christian character is established and built up, and this is what God is looking for in us—that we be conformed to the image of His beloved Son, the Lord Jesus Christ. And the "image" here does not refer to the outward appearance; it refers to the inward character. So today, the Holy Spirit is building up Christ-character in the believers, but in the process of this building up of Christ-character, discipline is the means; indeed, it is the absolute necessity.

Unfortunately, when we hear the word discipline, we draw back. We think that discipline is a hard word. We do not like to hear the word *discipline.* We instead like to hear the word freedom. But do we not realize that discipline is actually a sweet word? It is not negative at all. Sometimes, negative means have to be applied, that is true, but discipline itself is very positive. It is "saving the mind." In other words, it is to save, develop and complete a person, to mature a person. Without discipline all these are impossible.

Forms of Discipline

In this book of Titus many forms of discipline are mentioned by the apostle. For example, Paul wrote: "These things speak and exhort and rebuke with all authority" (Titus 2:15).

Speak: To speak is a form of discipline, because the latter is not only corrective, it is also instructive and educational. It is not only to correct what is wrong, it is also to instruct what is right.

Exhort: To exhort is to encourage on the one hand and to warn on the other; to encourage what is on the right track in one's life and to warn if a person is going in the wrong direction.

Rebuke: To rebuke is another form of discipline. Sometimes rebuke has to be applied with all vigor and authority.

Teach: In Titus 2:12 it reads, "Teaching us," and the root word *teach* there in the original carries with it the thought of "discipline." Teaching is a form of disciplining—"put to mind, remind people, shut their mouth up;" or, in the original, "have their mouth gagged."

Admonish: Paul also declared this: "After a first and second admonition have done with" (Titus 3:10)—that is to say, do not keep company with anymore. That, too, is discipline.

So discipline can come in many different forms, but let us constantly bear in mind that discipline is not negative at all.

Discipline, in Scripture, is based upon love. There can be no discipline without love. Let us not try to exercise discipline if there is no love behind it. God loves us; therefore, He chastens us, He disciplines us. He loves us because we are His children; and because of His love, God disciplines us as His children. It is because of love that we need to be disciplined. It is because of love that sometimes we may be used as instruments in God's hands for exercising discipline, but it must all be based on love. There is nothing legalistic about it. Discipline is in the power of the Holy Spirit. Unless it is done in the power of the Holy Spirit, it will not be effectual.

In this letter to Titus we can see at least three areas of discipline: (1) in the church, (2) in personal and family life, and (3) in social life.

Discipline in the Church

The church is not a democracy; it is not Laodicea where

the opinions of the people rule. The church is a theocracy—God rules over His own. Christ is the Head of the church; and hence, the government is upon His shoulders, and He is the authority of the church.

The Cretan believers seemed to be very democratic. Everyone could do or say what he or she wanted to do or say. There was absolutely no order. But the church is not a democracy; it is not the opinion of the people; it is not where things are settled by "a majority rule." The church is a theocracy. God rules in the church—He rules through the Son over His house. *Christ is the Head,* and because of this, there needs to be order in the church. The church is not to be a place of chaos. There is order in the church, but church order is not a matter of organization; it is a matter of the outgrowth of life. There must be order, but this order is not done through organizing. This order comes from the growing up of life. Life expresses itself in order. Therefore, Christ, as the Head of the church, and to maintain order in the church, appoints some to responsible positions—for example, the eldership.

Eldership

Although the churches in Crete had existed for a long time (if, as is thought, these whom Paul met here were the original believers), it seems they never had elders appointed. They maintained a kind of democratic society, and hence, there was no order, no authority—all was chaotic. Paul told Titus that elders had to be chosen and appointed in order that the church may have its order. But who are the persons to be chosen as elders to assume responsibility in the church? The apostle mentioned a number of qualifications—fifteen or sixteen of them—but this was not an exhaustive list. In other words, even if a person is able to fit in with every qualification in this list, it does not mean that such a person is automatically fit to be an elder because this was simply a *suggestive* list, not an exhaustive one. For when one reads this list with the one in I Timothy, one finds that there are variations between the two. Paul was merely illustrating the kind of elders who need to be chosen.

Qualifications for Elders

As you read this list of qualifications, you discover how different such a list is from the qualifications a company would look for in a potential candidate to be chosen as one of its executives. When a company's governing board is wanting to choose an executive for its corporation, the board will look for people with ability. But in selecting elders for the church, ability in this list is very, very minor; it is a minimal qualification to be considered. Out of all the qualities mentioned here in Titus, probably only two have to do with ability. One is to "rule his house well." He has a family, and his children are not wild, but are well-behaved. That probably speaks of some ability. He also needs to have some ability to refute those who teach false teachings. All other characteristics in Paul's list here are what the world would consider having to do with morality but what we would deem to be spirituality. Morality, as such, is what is developed by the old man. It is the improvement, cultivation, refinement, reformation and pretense of the old man. But spirituality is that which is developed through the spiritual life in a person. It is your intimate, experiential knowledge of the Lord that is developed into spirituality. And hence, we may say that spirituality actually means the development of Christian character.

Who are those elders chosen to represent the government of the Head in the body? It is not people with ability, but people with spirituality, which is Christian character developed through discipline. How can a person rule, supervise, oversee, shepherd, lead, and govern the church and assembly of the living

God unless he himself is a disciplined person? The necessary quality of an elder is a person who has been disciplined by the Lord, a person who knows in experience what discipline is. When Christian character has been developed in a person through discipline, that qualifies him to oversee, shepherd and lead the flock of God.

Responsibility of the Elders

The elders of the church shepherd the flock of God. In reading Psalm 23 we see that a shepherd has two instruments in his hand—a staff and a rod. The staff is necessary to lead; the rod is required to discipline. Those in church leadership—especially in eldership—have a responsibility over the spiritual affairs of the flock. They must lead God's people and sometimes they must exercise discipline over God's people. Unless we ourselves are disciplined, how can we exercise discipline over other people? In this matter of church government God is looking for disciplined people so that *His* discipline may be exercised by them.

The churches in Crete had a deep problem: "For there are many and disorderly vain speakers and deceivers of people's minds, specially those of the circumcision, who must have their mouths stopped, who subvert whole houses, teaching things which ought not to be taught for the sake of base gain" (Titus 1:10-11).

In I Timothy Paul mentioned to Timothy that in Ephesus there were some—not many, but some—who were teaching other things that should not be taught. But in Crete "there are many and disorderly and vain speakers and deceivers of people's minds." Think of that! The ministry of the word of God is very important to the church. When God's people assemble together, they hear the word of God. Therefore, there should be people who minister God's word in order to build up the faith of His people. But throughout church history there has been the tendency for the churches to go to one of two extremes: one is all-persons ministry and the other is one-person ministry. In some places everybody can minister the word of God. For example, in Crete everybody was permitted to do that: "many and disorderly." Everybody could make vain speeches and bring in all kinds of notions by which to deceive people in order to make gain for themselves because the churches there were wide open; everybody could talk. That is democracy; but if that were what the church is, then it would be necessary for God to have given the gifts of speaking and teaching to every member in the body of Christ. The reality is, however, that He gives to some but not to all. Let those minister God's word who are called and gifted and trained and developed—not everyone.

Then there are churches that go to the other extreme and have one-person ministry. In the whole assembly, there is only one man who is always teaching and preaching, and nobody else. Such is not to be! It is to be neither all-persons ministry nor one-person ministry; it is the ministry of those teachers and prophets whom God has called and gifted. Then the church will truly be edified. But in order to set this matter right, those in responsibility—the eldership—must attend to this matter.

The Shepherd

What does a shepherd do? A shepherd always goes before the flock in search of the right pasture for the sheep and to keep the sheep away from those pastures which have poisonous grasses and herbs. There is a certain season, a certain time, a certain growth, a certain kind of grass for the sheep to feed on, and such is the responsibility of the shepherd to search this out. Spiritually speaking that is part of the responsibility of the eldership, the leadership, in the church. They are to see to it that the people of God are well fed with sound teaching, solid teaching, the teaching of Christ; because only the teaching of

Christ can build up God's people. *He is our food.* Sometimes, church leaders must exercise authority to gag the mouths of those who try to make vain speeches and even try to deceive people with notions that are unsound. We may think that that is being somewhat harsh; but let us remember that it is all because of love—the love for God's people. God so loves His people that He does not want them to be fed with poisonous food. He desires His people to be well fed with the finest of the wheat, which is Christ himself. This is part of the work of the eldership. Therefore, it requires those in the eldership to be highly disciplined themselves. They need to set an example and be a model to all the others.

Fellowship

Of course, church discipline also involves this matter of fellowship because the church is the assembling of God's people. The church, in action, is a fellowship—God's people coming together to fellowship. Fellowship means to share together, to have things in common, to share with one another the Christ we know so that we may enrich one another. Whoever Christ receives, we receive. (This can be found in Romans 15:7.) The church, as a fellowship, has to receive everyone whom Christ receives because we believers are all given His life. Everyone who believes in the Lord Jesus has His life in him or in her. Therefore, we are exhorted, even commanded, to assemble together to encourage, to exhort and admonish one another, and build one another up in love through the life we share.

But let us remember that fellowship is a fellowship of light. There is no fellowship between light and darkness. The fellowship of the church is one of life; it is also a fellowship of light. "If we walk in the light as he is in the light, we have fellowship with one another and the blood of Jesus Christ, His Son cleanses us from all sin" (I John 1:7).

Therefore, when sin, disobedience, rebellion, the flesh, the world, or anything else not of God comes in, then all these things, which represent darkness, will affect our fellowship. I think this is quite obvious, and because of this, discipline is needed for fellowship.

Application of Church Discipline

Unfortunately, even God's people do not like discipline. Not only do they not like it in their personal lives, they do not like it in the church—perhaps *especially* in the church. Some want the church to be a free-for-all; they wish to do whatever they like because that is love. Is it true that discipline and love are contradictory? On the contrary, discipline is because of love. The church is God's house; it is the kingdom of the Son of God's love. There is love in the church; therefore, discipline should be most evident in the church. As a matter of fact, if there is no discipline, there is no church. But how is church discipline to be applied? Unfortunately, throughout the ages in Christianity, discipline has been abused. It has become a legalistic thing, a judicial thing. But discipline, in nature, is not judicial; it is based on love.

In the New Testament we can find at least three levels of discipline. One we could call the discipline of brotherly relationship (see Matthew 18:15-17). The next is the discipline of fatherly relationship (see Galatians 6:1). And the third is the discipline of the Son over His house, which is church discipline (see I Corinthians 5). Let us be reminded that this last one mentioned is to be the one of last resort to be employed. In other words, after everything else has been exhausted, then those in church responsibility must resort to the last level, which is the discipline of the church, because not every situation among the believers requiring discipline must be resolved at the church level. If we have been disciplined within the context of the other relationships, then there is no need for the church to exercise discipline because it has already been accomplished.

Discipline in Brotherly Relationships

In Matthew 18 is to be found the matter of discipline in brotherly relationships. We have all these brothers and sisters, and because we are not perfect, once in awhile one will sin against the other. And if that happens, what should be done? Do we bring it to the church and ask the church to judge this matter? That will be judicial. No, if a brother should sin against you, do not broadcast it among the brethren and do not bring it to the church right away. For if the latter action is taken, the church will become a permanent court. If a brother should sin against you, first, on the basis of love, you forgive him; but that is not enough. Even if you forgive him, he is in darkness; you have to restore him. Discipline is for restoration, never for punishment. Therefore, it is your responsibility in love that after you have forgiven him, you should go to him and speak to him the truth in love. You do not do this to vindicate yourself. Perhaps somebody wrongs me, and so I go to him because I want to set him right; I want to vindicate myself. No! If you go that way, you and the other person will grow far apart. But if you go in love and say, "Brother, you may not know it, but you have done such a thing to me, and it is wrong. It is not right before the Lord." You try to bring light to that brother in darkness because if he is in darkness, then his fellowship with the Lord and his fellowship with you is being affected. If a brother sins against you and this sin is never dealt with, there is always a kind of shadow between you and that brother. Your fellowship is affected. Therefore, it is your loving responsibility to go and say, "Brother, I want to have full fellowship with you, but this matter stands in the way; it has to be cleared. You have done the wrong thing; you have to come back to the Lord." If he listens to you, you have gained your brother.

But if this brother does not listen to you, what do you do? Your responsibility is not finished yet because love goes a second mile. You find one or two other brethren, and these should not be just any one or two brothers or sisters, but those who are respected by both parties involved, so as to serve as witnesses, because by the mouth of two or three witnesses everything is settled. It is not that you want to show that you are right; it is because you want your brother to be recovered, to be restored. And if that brother is humble, he should humble himself at that point. If he does not, then you go to the church, and the church, represented by the leadership, will deal with this brother and say, "Now brother, we see that you are still in darkness. You have to repent, because your fellowship is affected."

If he does not listen to the church, what happens? "Excommunicate him!" No! This is what Christianity has done wrongly in the past. People have used this verse to incorrectly excommunicate people; but if we read the relevant verse carefully, this is what it says: "If he does not listen to the church let him be *to thee* as one of the nations and a tax gatherer [emphasis added]" (see Matthew 18:17).

If he does not listen to the church, too many people today believe that in a situation like this the church should excommunicate him, but the Lord has said here to let him be "to thee"—that is to say, only "to you yourself." You are henceforth to look upon him as one of the nations and a tax collector. Only *your* personal fellowship with him is affected. He is still in the church because that sin of his is not serious enough to affect the entire assembly. It is serious enough to affect your personal relationship with that offending brother; therefore, the discipline has to be exercised by you personally. From that day onward you look upon that brother as an unbeliever, as a tax collector. But how does one look upon an unbeliever and a tax collector? Does one despise him? No, you must still love him. That is discipline on a brotherly basis, and if more of such kind of discipline were exercised in the church, the church herself would not need to exercise discipline because things will have been settled properly beforehand. But today, discipline in the church has become so judicial in character, and it is wrong.

Discipline in Fatherly Relationships

God, as our heavenly Father, disciplines us in order to make us His sons and daughters. Among God's people there are those who are more spiritual than others. They have known the Lord in a deeper way. They have a larger measure of Christ in their lives. They have gone through more things. They have been disciplined by the Lord more, and because of that, they are more experienced. "Brethren, if even a man be taken in some fault, ye who are spiritual restore such a one in a spirit of meekness, considering thyself lest thou also be tempted" (Galatians 6:1).

Those who are more spiritual in the church have a kind of fatherly care over the other brothers and sisters who are less spiritual, less mature. When you see someone in some fault who does not see it himself because he does not have that experience, then you try to restore him in the spirit of meekness because you do not want to see him, as it were, go down the drain. You love him, you are as a father in the Lord to him. Do not go to him in a spirit of rebuke and blame him: "You have done such a thing; therefore, you are damned!" No, you restore him in a spirit of meekness. "The Lord has dealt with me in this matter, therefore my eyes are open. I can see what this thing in your life will lead you to. So I exhort you; I beg you; I plead with you with tears that you repent and come back." Most likely, you will restore that brother. But when you are doing so, you must be careful. Do not think that you are better than he, because you yourself may be tempted, and may fall, too. Such is the discipline on a fatherly basis.

Church Discipline

If none of these lower-level approaches works and the issue seems to be a matter which will corrupt the whole church, then the church has to exercise discipline. The church is like a loaf of unleavened bread. In I Corinthians 5 Paul said the following: "Do you not know a little leaven will leaven the whole bread?" Sometimes there are evils in the church—either corrupt conduct or false teaching; and if these things are allowed to stay there, they will begin to leaven the whole loaf. Such a thing can cause the whole church to implode, and in such a case the church has to exercise discipline. But when the church is required to exercise discipline, let us not forget that it is always to be done in love. One brother has said, "The very thought that it may be necessary for one brother to discipline another brother whom the Lord loves is a terrifying thought." Who are we that any of us can judge another one whom the Lord loves? Do we not know ourselves? Do we not know our own weakness? How dare we do such a thing? Yet, the thought of love overcomes this, not because I am better than you, but because I love you for God's sake. Therefore, I am willing to pay the cost, sometimes even to be misunderstood, but I want to "save your mind."

Discipline is never to be divorced from love. When the church exercises discipline, she has to do it in love. In I Corinthians 5 the brother mentioned there had committed a sin that even the world rarely knew—the act of incest; and so Paul was compelled to write: "This is a leaven. If you allow it to remain in the church, it will break up the church. It will leaven the whole church. It will destroy the testimony of the church." So what did Paul do? He tried to arouse the conscience of the whole church. Before the church could exercise discipline, the whole church had to repent. In other words, the entire church had to identify herself with that brother in sin and repent before the Lord. It is only when the conscience of the whole church is stirred—"Oh, we have sinned against God"—that then discipline can be applied to purge the loaf of that corrupting leaven. Cast out that man. But in casting out that man it is with tears and sorrow of heart. To cast out a brother or sister from fellowship is a serious matter. How dare we do such a thing unless it is done in love? The reason why that man had to be cast out was to put him to shame in order that he might be restored. He is cast out in order that the loaf not be leavened—that is, to keep the purity of the testimony of Jesus. But it is not done in a self-righteous sense; it is done in deep humility. He is cast out so that nobody will keep company with him; he is cast out in order to make him ashamed and that he will desire to repent and be restored. The result was that we learn from II Corinthians that this man was ultimately restored and recovered.

The limit of discipline is the church. Once a person is cast out, he or she is no longer under church discipline since we can only judge those who are inside, not those who are outside. Even though fellowship is not extended, it does not mean that we can hate that offending person. We can look upon that person as an unbeliever, but we still love an unbeliever. We want to see an unbeliever saved and come to the Lord. Let us admonish that person as an unbeliever but let us not hate him or her as an enemy. That is the discipline of the church.

Discipline in Personal and Family Life

The church is the assembly of the believers. Therefore, if we as individual believers are disciplined, then the church does not need to exercise discipline. Unfortunately, if we as individuals are undisciplined, then the church will have many disciplinary problems. Hence, fundamentally, discipline has to begin with each individual.

Now let us notice that the word *sober* or *discreet* appears again and again in the second chapter of Titus that deals with personal and family relationships. The word actually means "self-control," and self-control is one of the fruits of the Spirit of God. In Galatians 5 we are told that the fruit of the Spirit is love, joy, and so on, and that the last one listed is self-control. Let us not think self-control here means that a person controls himself. Self-control means putting oneself under the control of the Holy Spirit. Again and again in Titus the apostle mentions this: Teach the older men to be sober—or, self-controlled; the older women are to be self-controlled; the younger women are likewise to be self-controlled; the younger men are also to be self-controlled.

The younger men and women need self-control. You who are younger need to put yourselves under the discipline of the Holy Spirit. In your daily life, let the Holy Spirit speak to you. Let the Holy Spirit train you. Let Him take away things in your life which God is not pleased with. Let Him build within you whatever will satisfy God's heart—the life of Christ in you. In your daily life, if you follow the Holy Spirit and are under His discipline, you will be self-controlled.

Younger men and women need self-control, but that does not mean older men and older women do not need self-control; they need it, too. As a matter of fact, when you are young, you still have some will power, and for policy sake you can control yourself. What do I mean? Suppose you are in a store selling things and a very difficult customer comes in and looks at all kinds of merchandise and then leaves without buying anything; you will try to control yourself. But that is for the sake of policy. You definitely have your will power to do this. We can all exercise some kind of self-control for policy sake, but that is not real. The only real self-control is through the Holy Spirit. No discipline is effective without the power of the Holy Spirit. But when you get older, your will power becomes weaker. Therefore, the older men and women need self-control, too. If you had never been disciplined when you were young, later, when you grow old, you will discover that it is very, very difficult. However, even if you are disciplined when you are young, you will still need discipline when you grow older. Everybody needs discipline. It is not only your children who need it; you, too, need discipline.

Discipline is not only necessary in your personal life, it is also needful in your family life because there is a relationship involved. Relationships with one another need to be under discipline. Children, obey your parents in the Lord. Parents, do not offend your children to the extent that they lose their will and desire to be good. Husbands, love your wives. Wives, submit yourselves to your husbands. Older women, those who are disciplined, can teach the younger women to be disciplined: to do their housework, to love their husbands, love their children, submit to their husband, and so forth. These family relationships need to be under discipline.

Social Discipline

We still live in this world even though we are strangers and sojourners. We have a testimony to bear before this world and, therefore, we need to submit and be subject to those authorities whom God has placed over us. All these things are not mere teaching or mere rules and regulations. No. As we read this letter, we shall find that everything is connected with the mercy of God, the salvation of our Lord Jesus, and the power of the Holy Spirit. God has saved us from all these undisciplined things, and by His grace we have become a peculiar people to God, even His possession. Therefore, with such mercy and grace upon us, He is able to discipline us, to bring us to that point where we will be perfected—that is, matured—and be transformed and conformed to the image of God's beloved

Son. *That is the ultimate.*

Now, therefore, I hope we will correct our concept regarding discipline, that we shall have a right concept concerning it, and that we will not shun it. On the contrary, let us welcome discipline, because it is for our maturity and our perfection.

Shall we pray:

Dear heavenly Father, we need Thy Holy Spirit to impress upon our hearts and to interpret what we have just shared so that we may come to a right understanding, and that we may be brought to a willingness to submit ourselves to Thee, to Thy discipline. Oh, our Father, we pray that we may not be a wild people, but we may be a peculiar people, a people disciplined unto the Lord. We ask in Thy precious name. Amen.

PHILEMON

Seeing Christ in Amazing Love

Philemon 1-25—Paul, prisoner of Christ Jesus, and Timotheus the brother, to Philemon the beloved and our fellow-workman, and to the sister Apphia and to Archippus our fellow-soldier, and to the assembly which is in thine house. Grace to you and peace from God our Father, and the Lord Jesus Christ. I thank my God, always making mention of thee at my prayers, hearing of thy love and the faith which thou hast towards the Lord Jesus, and towards all the saints, in such sort that thy participation in the faith should become operative in the acknowledgement of every good thing which is in us towards Christ Jesus. For we have great thankfulness and encouragement through thy love, because the bowels of the saints are refreshed by thee, brother.

Wherefore having much boldness in Christ to enjoin thee what is fitting, for love's sake I rather exhort, being such a one as Paul the aged, and now also prisoner of Jesus Christ. I exhort thee for my child, whom I have begotten in my bonds, Onesimus, once unserviceable to thee, but now serviceable to thee and to me: whom I have sent back to thee: but do thou receive him, that is, my bowels: whom I was desirous of keeping with myself, that for thee he might minister to me in the bonds of the glad tidings; but I have wished to do nothing without thy mind, that thy good might not be as of necessity but of willingness: for perhaps for this reason he has been separated from thee for a time, that thou mightest possess him fully for ever; not any longer as a bondman, but above a bondman, a beloved brother, specially to me, and how much rather to thee, both in the flesh and in the Lord? If therefore thou holdest me to be a partner with thee, receive him as me; but if he have wronged thee anything or owe anything to thee, put this to my account. I Paul have written it with mine own hand; I will repay it: that I say not to thee that thou owest even thine own self also to me. Yea, brother, I would have profit of thee in the Lord: refresh my bowels in Christ. Being confident of thine obedience, I have written to thee, knowing that thou wilt do even more than I say. But withal prepare me also a lodging; for I hope that I shall be granted to you through your prayers. Epaphras salutes thee, my fellow-prisoner in Christ Jesus; Mark, Aristarchus, Demas, Luke, my fellow-workmen. The grace of our Lord Jesus Christ be with your spirit.

Shall we pray:

Dear heavenly Father, we do praise and thank Thee for the boldness which Thou hast given to us through the blood of our Lord Jesus through the new and living way which He has opened for us in His body. And knowing that He is our great High Priest, living forever interceding for us, our Father, we thank Thee that we have this access to Thy throne of grace, and we come with holy boldness and with deep humility. How we do praise and thank Thee for all that Thou hast done for us. Our Father, we do desire to give ourselves to Thee. We do desire that as Thou hast satisfied us, that in a small way we may be Thy satisfaction. We commit this time into Thy hands, and pray that by Thy Holy Spirit Thou wilt breathe Thy life into us. We pray that Thy word may truly be life and spirit to us, to the praise of Thy glory. In the name of our Lord Jesus. Amen.

The letter to Philemon is unique. It is the shortest letter written by the apostle Paul that we find in the Holy Scriptures. It is different from all the other letters which he has written because most of them were written to the churches in different places. Some of them he wrote also to individuals; for instance, he wrote to Timothy and to Titus, and we call these pastoral letters. Even though they were written to individuals, they deal with church matters. But this letter to Philemon, written to an individual, does not deal with church affairs, nor does it deal with doctrines. It deals with a domestic affair, and yet we find it is in the Holy Bible. Its value is beyond what we would usually expect.

I would like to quote two or three persons relative to their estimate of this little letter to Philemon. One is Martin Luther: "This epistle showeth a right, noble, lovely example of Christian love. Here we see how Saint Paul lays himself out for poor Onesimus and with all his means pleaded his cause with his master and so setteth himself as if he were Onesimus and had himself done wrong to Philemon. Even as Christ did for us with God, the Father, thus also doth Saint Paul for Onesimus with Philemon ... We are all Onesimus, to my thinking."

John Calvin said this about the letter and its author: "Though he dealeth [with] a subject which otherwise was low and mean, yet after his manner he is borne up aloft to God. With such modest entreaty doth he humble himself on behalf of the lowest of men that scarce anywhere else is the gentleness of his spirit portrayed more truly to life."

And Bishop Lightfoot had this to say: "This epistle to Philemon stands unrivaled."

The letter to Philemon can be considered at three levels. One can look at it as a personal letter involving an historical fact. One can also view it as probably the only letter which deals with social problems in a unique way. And lastly one can consider it from the spiritual viewpoint, which speaks of Christ in His amazing love.

Paul's Personal Viewpoint

The letter to Philemon was written by the apostle Paul while he was in prison in Rome. He would write several letters at this time—the letter to the Ephesians, the letter to the Colossians, and this letter to Philemon. The latter one was sent to Colosse together with the letter to the Colossians, but the Colossian letter was addressed to the church, whereas this letter was addressed to one individual.

There was one particular slave in Colosse who had defrauded his master. His name was Onesimus. We do not know exactly what happened; but probably, he had stolen from his master and had then fled to Rome. Although it was a long way off, Rome was a large metropolitan city and was thus the ideal place to get lost in. So he fled to Rome thinking that from now on he would be free from his master and do whatever he wished. We do not know how, but somehow he had an encounter with the apostle Paul who was a prisoner at that time in Rome. Bear in mind that during this first imprisonment of Paul's, he could live in his rented apartment and receive everyone who came to see him.

Somehow, Onesimus went to see Paul. He may have known the apostle in the past when the latter was in Ephesus for over three years. His master, Philemon, must have visited Ephesus, and while he was there he was brought to the Lord through the apostle Paul. Onesimus, probably being a very trusted slave, had met Paul before. So while he was in Rome as a fugitive his conscience might have begun to bother him. Perhaps he had spent all his money or was in trouble and so he tried to find Paul, thinking he might obtain some help from him. Some people have speculated that Epaphras, who was a servant of the Lord in Colosse, was visiting Paul in Rome and had met Onesimus on the street and brought him to Paul. However it came about, Onesimus, a runaway slave, thief and fugitive, came into contact with the apostle Paul and was brought to the Lord. He was soundly saved and had stayed in Rome to serve Paul. As a slave he was used to serving his master, but now he served Paul out of love. Paul even mentioned him favorably in his letter to the Colossians: "Onesimus, beloved and faithful brother ..." (see 4:9). He was faithful in serving Paul.

When Paul was in prison he was in need of someone to serve him and to assist him. Evidently, Paul had found Onesimus' service quite beneficial, but the apostle felt it was not right for him to keep Onesimus with him any longer. He felt that even though God had forgiven Onesimus of all his sins, restitution had to be made; restoration had to be undertaken; reconciliation with his master had to be made. Paul knew that if he asked Philemon about keeping Onesimus in Rome to serve him, he would agree to it; yet he did not wish to do anything without the willingness of Philemon. Finally, he decided to send Onesimus back to Colosse to his master.

In this letter Paul mentions that Philemon was a very wonderful person. His love towards the Lord and his love towards all the saints was well known. He was a brother full of love, full of compassion, hospitable towards everybody. The very name, *Philemon*, means "friendship." He had a beautiful family. His wife, Apphia, which is a term of endearment, was one with him in this whole expression of love and hospitality. They also had a wonderful son, Archippus, who was even serving the Lord there. This was a beautiful family and the church in Colosse, being a small church, actually met in their house. Onesimus must have heard the gospel many, many times while serving under such a kind master, and it is strange that he had not been converted earlier. His heart was hard. He had even defrauded such a good master and had fled away; but God, in His marvelous providence, eventually brought this slave into the house of God. So Paul decided to send Onesimus back to Colosse.

Slavery

According to the Roman custom at that time in the ancient world, people had slaves. When the Romans conquered the world, those who were conquered became slaves, and oftentimes, in a large family, there were numerous slaves doing all kinds of works. In the eyes of the Roman law, these slaves had no rights whatsoever. They were the property of the master, just as would be a cow or a horse; and the laws concerning the slaves were very strict. A master could whip a slave or even kill him because he was his property, especially if the slave should run away and be caught again. Sometimes he would be killed; at other times he would be branded. That was the slave system in the ancient world; and hence, to send a slave back to his master was a dangerous thing.

Return of Onesimus to Philemon

If Onesimus should go back to his master Philemon, whom he had defrauded, Philemon would have every right to punish him and even to kill him. But Paul felt that restitution had to be made, so he sent Onesimus back to Philemon. He used the opportunity, when Tychicus was to carry the letters to the Ephesians and to the Colossians, to send Onesimus back with him to prepare the way for the slave's return. Not only that, but he wrote, as it were, a kind of cover letter to Philemon. Although this letter is a very short one, it is written with such a spirit of love, humility, tact and gentleness that when Philemon received the letter he could not help but do what he was begged to do. Paul did not command him to do what he should do even though Philemon was a son of Paul's in the faith. He owed his very life to Paul. Nevertheless, Paul wrote: "I am not going to command you what to do, but I am going to plead with you for my son born in my bonds. If Onesimus has wronged you (and he indeed had), put it to my account. I, Paul, will repay it." And he signed the letter. "I am sending him back to you—yet not as a slave, but more than a slave—a beloved brother of yours. Receive him as you would receive me."

Paul used this letter to open the way for Onesimus to return. We do not know exactly what happened afterwards, but I am sure that when Philemon received the letter he did even more than Paul had asked him to do. He not only received Onesimus as a beloved brother in Christ, probably he set him free, emancipated him. He no longer treated him as a slave but as a beloved brother in the Lord and found Onesimus of great profit.

We have looked at this letter from a personal or historical viewpoint, and it is a wonderful letter. But if we look a little deeper into it, we shall find this letter deals, in a sense, with a social problem which we do not find mentioned very much in other parts of the New Testament. Slavery was a social institution at that time. We know that it was not of God because God created man from one family. So far as the human race is concerned, we are all of one family; we are all brothers and sisters. There should not be any such unequal status; but because of the sin of this world, gradually, the institution of slavery came into existence, and it was found everywhere throughout the world in ancient times.

Paul's Approach to Social Evil

Now how would Christianity deal with such a problem? When one considers social evils, slavery is at the lowest in the scale of all human institutions which are evil. How would the gospel of Jesus Christ deal with this matter? In this little letter the apostle Paul does not attack this slavery problem directly. He does not attempt to tell Philemon that it is wrong for him to have slaves. He does not even encourage Onesimus that he should rise up and revolt against such a social evil. It is an institution which was deeply rooted in the society of that day, and if anything were done in such a direct way it could create hatred. It would mean bloodshed. There would be revolution, tearing society into pieces. That is not the spirit of the gospel. So Paul approached this whole social evil from a higher level.

Down through history people have usually viewed slaves as the meanest and lowest element of humanity. Perhaps there is some justification for it because slaves were so ill-treated that, knowing they had no rights, they were against everybody. A kind of mentality was developed, according to which they tried to steal and do anything for themselves because nobody would take care of them. Gradually, slaves became the meanest and lowest of human beings.

This slave Onesimus was no exception. For even though he had been under such a kind master, he rebelled against him and defrauded him. Then he ran away. What can one do with a person like that? God has a wonderful way. He saves that person. Onesimus was saved and, of course, he became a brother in the Lord. He received a new life; he was transformed. Even though he was still a slave and a fugitive outwardly, inwardly, he was a new creation. With this new life in him Onesimus began to serve Paul. He was supposed to have served Philemon, but he had not served him well. He was under no obligation to serve Paul; yet he served the apostle out of a pure heart, for a tremendous change had come into his life. From the human standpoint he was still a slave, a fugitive, and a thief; but in God's sight he was now a beloved brother in Christ Jesus.

In time Paul sent Onesimus back to Philemon. Philemon was a brother in the Lord, and he was Paul's fellow workman. He served God together with Paul, although he was not a fellow worker in the sense of his having traveled with Paul and of having preached the gospel with him. Nevertheless, whoever is engaged in the furtherance of the gospel of Jesus Christ in the kingdom of God is considered to be a fellow workman. Philemon may also have been a businessman. Probably he was a man of means, since he had a house which was large enough for church meetings, and was able to be hospitable to many people. He gladdened the hearts of many saints. Now in that sense he worked together with Paul, and Paul considered him to be a beloved brother and a fellow workman.

Now the social system at that time was such that most all people who were Roman citizens had slaves; and hence Philemon, not surprisingly, had a number of slaves in his household. And at the time Onesimus was sent back to Philemon, the latter was already himself a brother in the Lord and perhaps even a responsible brother or elder in the church there. Likewise, Onesimus, though a returning fugitive slave, was also a brother in the Lord. What, therefore, do you do? As one reads this letter one discovers that there is not a single word from Paul to Philemon suggesting that he *free* Onesimus. One does not find Paul saying: "I am sending Onesimus back to you, Philemon; please emancipate him." Not so. Nevertheless, though he never pronounces it, the word *emancipation* is not far from the thought—even from the lips—of Paul. He simply wrote: "Please receive Onesimus as you would receive me, because he is a part of me. He is my very heart. Receive him not as a slave, but as a brother in the Lord."

How would Philemon receive Paul? Had Paul come instead of Onesimus, Philemon would, of course, have provided hospitality for Paul. He would have prepared lodging for the apostle of the Lord and would have graciously served him. He would have received Paul as a most honorable guest, as a beloved brother in the Lord, even as a father in Christ. Knowing all this, Paul wrote: "Receive Onesimus as you would receive me."

What could Philemon do? One possibility is that Philemon could look at Onesimus and say, "Well, you did me so much wrong, but because Paul said to put it to his account, I will let it go. But you are still my slave and I expect you to serve me very faithfully as a slave from now on." Yet under the circumstances, could Philemon do that? For even though outwardly Onesimus was in fact still a slave, inwardly, he was now a brother in Christ. How, therefore, will Philemon treat him? Doubtless, Philemon will not only forgive all his wrongs, he will also receive him as a dear brother in the Lord. Indeed, he will do even more than emancipate that slave; he will receive that Christian brother into his very heart. And such is the way the Scriptures solve social evils.

This letter was sent together with a letter to the Colossians, and if a person carefully reads the latter letter he will find a very strange thing. In that letter Paul included a section on the relationship between slaves and masters. He well realized that there existed such an evil human institution. Of all the relationships in human society, this was one which was far apart from the gospel. Even so, Paul wrote the following in his letter: "Bondmen, obey in all things your masters according to flesh; not with eye-services as men-pleasers, but in simplicity of heart, fearing the Lord. Whatsoever ye do, labour at it heartily, as doing it to the Lord, and not to men; knowing that of the Lord ye shall receive the recompense of the inheritance; ye serve the Lord Christ. For he that does a wrong shall receive the wrong that he has done, and there is no respect of persons" (Colossians 3:22-25).

Instead of attacking slavery directly as an evil institution, Paul lifted the slave-master relationship up before the presence of God and transformed it. He said, "Slaves, obey your masters in all things. Even though you are slaves do bear in mind that you are actually serving the Lord. Accordingly, while serving your master, do not think of the physical relationship, but transcend and transform it, even sublimate it by lifting the relationship up to the realm of the fear of the Lord: as you serve your master treat it as though you are serving the Lord himself, and you will be rewarded."

Paul said the same thing to the masters. "Give to bondmen [slaves] what is just and fair, knowing that ye also have a Master in the heavens" (Colossians 4:1). Here we observe that Paul likewise elevated the master-slave relationship upwards into the presence of God by declaring that though you are master, do not ever forget that you yourselves have a Master over you: you yourselves are slaves—even slaves before God; and because of that fact, you all should treat your slaves fairly.

In the first century when the gospel was being widely preached, numerous slaves became Christians. Probably more slaves than freemen became Christians because there were more slaves in the world. Yet when these many slaves came to the Lord there was the possibility of a great problem being created because Christianity was in direct conflict with the institution of slavery which was evil. How was this matter to be addressed and solved?

"Hast thou been called being a bondman, let it not concern thee" (I Corinthians 7:21). Here Paul advised that when you are saved into the kingdom of God and you are a slave, "Let it not concern thee." Do not be troubled by it as though this is everything; yet, if you are able to be freed, use it. The freedom gained is good. "For the bondman that is called in the Lord is the Lord's freeman" (I Corinthians 7:22).

Why is it that in being a slave you are not to be concerned? Because even though you are a slave, you are a freeman in the Lord. The Lord has set you free. Outwardly, you are still bound; inwardly, however, you are free. Your bondage outwardly is temporary, but your freedom in the Lord is eternal. When you weigh these two things, why should you be bothered or concerned? You have something far better. In like manner also, the freeman who has been called is nonetheless Christ's bondman. If you are a freeman, do not forget that you are a slave to the Lord; you are bound under Christ. You are to serve Christ as a slave: a love-slave. Actually, there is no difference. If you are free, you are a slave; and if you are a slave, you are free. There is no difference, for you have been bought with a price; therefore, do not be a bondman of man. If it is possible and freedom is open to you, have it. You will be in a better position (see I Corinthians 7).

The word of God seems to take up a social problem and, instead of attacking it directly which could result in the creation of hatred and bloodshed, it encourages the regulation of a relationship within, sublimating it, and bringing it before the presence of God so that it can truly transcend what it inherently is. In other words, it is already different. The Scriptures also give us some broad principles: "In Christ there is neither slave nor freeman, but Christ is all and in all" (see Colossians 3:11). When the slave and the master come together before the communion table of the Lord, they sit side by side remembering the Lord as brothers and sisters together in Christ. And given that reality, the whole human institution of slavery is gone. It is impossible to keep that slavery system. Such is the way this whole matter of social evil can be solved, and in this letter we find a practical application of it. When Philemon received Onesimus, their relationship had changed, and we can even believe that they were no longer master and slave but were beloved brothers in Christ Jesus.

The Lord Jesus' Approach to Social Problems

When the Lord Jesus was on earth, He lived under the rule of the Roman Empire, and in a sense, the Jewish people never recognized the Roman rule. Among them were people called Zealots who attempted to use violence to overthrow the yoke of Roman authority over the Jewish people. When Christ was on earth, the expectation of the Jews was that if He were indeed the Messiah, then He would throw off the yoke of the Empire and make Israel the head of the nations. But Christ did not do that; He submitted himself to the Roman authority. He denounced the evil climate among the Jews of His generation. He denounced the hypocrisy of the scribes and the Pharisees. He cleansed the temple of the money-changers and the traffic which they had created therein. But while our Lord Jesus was on earth, He did not change the social system of His time. Instead, He preached the gospel of love. He made people into new creations, and that is the way He transformed lives and social relationships, bringing about the kingdom of God.

Is the Lord not concerned with social problems? Of course He is. He fed the hundreds and thousands; He healed the sick; He loved the children; He pitied the people; but His approach was not the external worldly way. His approach was an inward heavenly one. He brings life to the people. He is building His kingdom, a kingdom that is based on love. In His first coming He came as a Lamb, slain for the sins of the world. It is the spiritual path, the divine life, the inward reality that is the foundation of everything. If we try to solve problems outwardly and the inward situation remains, then the problems are not solved. So the Lord Jesus came offering a new life, a new nature, a heavenly way. He came as a Lamb slain for the sins of the world so that we may become a new creation: old things have passed away, all things have become new and all things are of God. But we know the Lord Jesus will come again. When He comes again, however, He will come as the Lion of Judah. That is the time when He will deal with all these political and social problems directly. He will judge the world. In His first coming, He came to save the world. In His second coming, He will come to judge it and make all things right.

Therefore, what should be our attitude towards social and political institutions and problems? Liberation theology, for example, is not Christianity; it is another form of humanism. God's way is higher than man's way. God's way is dealing with the inward life, and when that life is transformed, then everything around us is changed. That is the way social problems are to be solved and resolved. Do we not think that this is a much better way? Do we not think that this is a more permanent way? Do we not think this is according to the principle of Christ, which is the principle of love? So let us read this quite short letter to Philemon very carefully. Let us meditate on it before the Lord and see if in this little letter we are given some glimpse of God's way in dealing with social and political problems.

God's Amazing Love in Christ Jesus

However, this is not what I want to share with you now. We have to look at this letter from an even higher standpoint because this letter not only shows us the personal side and the social aspect, but it also reveals Christ in His amazing love. This letter is but a small representation of what God has done to and for us in Christ Jesus. The value of this letter is similar to the value to be found in the book of Ruth in the Old Testament. It unveils to us a much greater picture of God's love towards us in Christ Jesus. Of course, when one seeks to make such spiritual application, one cannot fit in every detail; nevertheless, in broad outline, we shall uncover a beautiful picture of God's love towards us in Christ Jesus.

In a very, very small, incomplete and imperfect way, Philemon himself represents God. He is a wealthy man and has many slaves. Philemon is a good man—kind and hospitable. Does this not in a small way show us our God? Our God is rich; He owns the universe; He owns everything. We are created by Him, and by right of His creation we are His slaves. But man forgets his position. He forgets that he is created for God's pleasure. The slave Onesimus was supposed to please Philemon, to be profitable to Philemon; this we know very well because the very name *Onesimus* means "profitable;" yet he became so unprofitable. Is that not what we were? As created beings of God we are supposed to be for His pleasure. We are supposed to serve Him well. We are supposed to be profitable to Him. But we think that we human beings are here merely to profit ourselves—to rob God and profit ourselves. That is what man throughout history has been doing. Like Onesimus with Philemon, we have all robbed God and fled away from His presence.

Do we think God is an angry God? The great American evangelist, D.L. Moody, in his early days, preached the gospel as though God were angry, chasing after sinners to punish them. But a dear brother in England, Henry Moorehouse, came to his church in Chicago. Moody did not think much about this young man. What could he preach? But since Moody was to be away, he told his deacons to give the young man a brief opportunity and see how he did. When Moody came back after a week he asked his wife what happened. "Ah," she said, "everybody is bringing a Bible to the church."

"And what did he preach?"

"Oh," she said, "for seven days he preached nothing but John 3:16: 'God so loved the world.'"

After Moody heard Henry Moorehouse for himself, his

whole concept and approach about the gospel was changed. From then on he never preached God as an angry ogre chasing after sinners. Thereafter, Moody always preached God as a loving Father waiting for and running after the prodigals.

Our God is not an angry God. He has every right to be angry with us, but He is not angry; He loves us. Let us not think that Jehovah in the Old Testament is an angry God but that in the New Testament He is a loving God. No. God is the same yesterday, today, and forever. When He revealed himself to Moses on the Mount, what did He say? "Jehovah, Jehovah God merciful and gracious, slow to anger, and abundant in goodness and truth, keeping mercy unto thousands, forgiving iniquity and transgression and sin, but by no means clearing the guilty" (Exodus 34:6-7a).

Our God is a righteous God and yet He is love. But we have wronged Him. We ran away from Him. We are the meanest of all God's creation. We are worse than a dog, even a flea; yet, God in His abundant mercy saved us. How?

Paul was in prison, and in his suffering he begets Onesimus. But Christ, who is God, emptied himself. He took up the form of a man, even the form of a slave, serving God's purpose. He humbled himself and gave himself up to be crucified on the cross. In His bonds He begets us. By His blood He saves us. He sends us back to God, no longer as fugitives. Instead, He sends us back to God as members of the family, as though He were saying to His Father, "Receive them as Thou wouldst receive Me." And thank God, He receives us in this manner.

Paul said to Philemon, "Onesimus may have departed from you for a time so that later you may possess him fully forever." And is it not true with us today? It is as though the Son were saying to the Father, "You may have lost them for a time, but now You can possess them fully forever." The Lord says about us who were not profitable to God earlier that we are now to be profitable to the Father. When we come back to God, will we not be so constrained by His amazing love that we shall most willingly give ourselves fully to Him to serve Him, to be possessed by Him forever, and to be profitable to Him? Once we were unprofitable servants, but now we shall be profitable to the Father. And this is what this short letter to Philemon reveals to us. Oh, that we may see Christ—how Christ was willing to be in bonds, willing to die on Calvary's cross, just to bring us back to God the Father.

Shall we pray:

Dear heavenly Father, we do praise and thank Thee for this letter to Philemon. We do see the great amazing love of God in Christ Jesus towards us. We all acknowledge that we are as Onesimus, unprofitable and unworthy. Yet, we do praise and thank Thee that Thou, in Thy great love, hast pursued us, hast found us on Calvary's cross and hast brought us back to the family of God. Oh, our Father, it is the great desire of our hearts that from now on we will not look to Thee as though Thou art a hard master, but Lord we want to be Thy love-slaves, to be profitable and to serve Thee throughout our lives because Thou art worthy. Thou hast won our hearts. Oh, our heavenly Father, we do pray that because of what Thou hast done to us and in us, that we may do the same to others. We do believe that Thou hast taken us out of the authority of darkness, full of evil, and Thou hast translated us into the kingdom of the Son of Thy love. Father, we pray that we may always live in that kingdom. We ask in the name of our Lord Jesus. Amen.

HEBREWS

Seeing Christ as Our Apostle and High Priest

Hebrews 3:1—Wherefore, holy brethren, partakers of the heavenly calling, consider the Apostle and High Priest of our confession, Jesus.

Let us pray:

Dear heavenly Father, as we continue in Thy presence we do pray Thou wilt remove any veil that may be upon our hearts, that we may see Jesus, the Apostle and High Priest of our confession. We ask Thee to grant us the spirit of wisdom and revelation unto the full knowledge of God. We pray, that as we see Him, we may be transformed, that glory may be unto Him. We commit this time into Thy hands and trust Thy Holy Spirit to make Thy word life and spirit to us. We ask in the name of our Lord Jesus. Amen.

This letter to the Hebrews is unique among the books of the Bible. Probably you will say that I usually introduce every book in the Bible in this way. That is very true, because every book in the Bible is unique, and Hebrews is no exception.

We know this letter must have been written before the destruction of Jerusalem and its temple (which occurred in 70 A.D.). It conveys within its pages a very vital message—yet, not only to the Hebrew believers in those earlier days, but also to us who live at the end of the last days. We do not know for sure who the human instrument of this letter was. Quite probably it was Apollos, because he fits all the circumstantial evidence available. He was a Hellenistic Jew, schooled at Alexandria, mighty in the Scriptures, and familiar with the thought and teaching of the apostle Paul. But through the centuries there have been many other suggestions—nearly everyone we can find prominently mentioned in the New Testament.

We do not know for sure whether this letter was addressed to the Hebrew believers in Jerusalem or to the Hebrew believers in Rome, but we do know it was addressed to them at a most critical time. These Hebrew believers were once under the bondage of the law, but now they were free in Christ Jesus. However, even though they were free in Christ Jesus, they were still attached to Judaism. It was a very critical moment, a transitional time.

At the time this letter was written, sometime before 70 A.D., an important change had come upon the world. At the beginning of Christianity, it was considered by the world to be a sect of Judaism, but by the particular time of this letter this attitude had changed. To be a Christian was now considered a crime in the Roman Empire, but Judaism was still recognized as a legal religion in the empire. So Hebrew believers were under great pressure at that time to return to Judaism in order that they could be protected and secured. At this same time, however, the Spirit of God was moving ahead. God was going to do a tremendous thing by destroying Jerusalem, the center of Judaism, and even the temple, the very center of it all. God had concluded that it was high time for these Hebrew believers to be completely freed from Judaism in order that they might enter into the fullness of Christ. And hence, a conflict had arisen. Outwardly, circumstantially, pressure was being brought to bear to bring these Hebrew believers back into the fold of Judaism; and on the other hand, the Spirit of God was moving to take away Judaism so that these Hebrew believers might enter into the fullness of the gospel. Accordingly, with all of that in view this letter was written for the purpose of setting the Hebrew believers free from any bondage to Judaism and thus encouraging them to enter into the fullness of Christ.

We need to realize that in one sense, we today are likewise

at a very critical juncture in our lives. We know that our Lord is coming back soon. We know that He is looking forward to having a bride who is His counterpart. He desires to see in His bride every character which belongs to Him, so that He may be united with His bride and that His bride may be united with Him into one. This is the time that we know that all outward appearance shall sooner or later be shaken. And that only what is reality shall remain.

At the very beginning of God's relationship with the Israelites, when He first revealed himself to the Jewish people, the faith of the Jews was a living faith. But unfortunately, this living faith gradually became a religious system. It became an "ism"—Judaism. Historically speaking, Judaism had had its beginning at the time of the Babylonian captivity. It was during that time that the scribes and the Pharisees had somehow reduced the living oracle of God to a religious system called Judaism. When God first gave divine revelation to the Israelite fathers, these revelations were given as a means to prepare the way for the coming of Christ, their Messiah. But when these divine revelations were reduced to a religious system, instead of preparing the people for the coming of Christ, these religious leaders had begun to provide a substitute for Christ on the one hand and oppose Him on the other. That is the reason why, when Christ appeared to them, they rejected Him.

Are we not in the same situation today? The faith of Christian believers, at its beginning, was a living faith, but through the centuries that living faith has been gradually reduced to a religious system called Christianity. Instead of introducing us to Christ, Christianity as a system began to provide substitutes for Christ, and in doing that it actually opposed Christ, taking Him away from us. May I illustrate this by using baptism as an example of this development. Baptism is a living testimony in which we testify that we have been identified with Christ in His death, burial and resurrection. By going down into the water we testify in faith to the greatness of the finished work of the Lord Jesus—in His death He has included us, in His burial He has put us away, and in His resurrection He lives in us. It is a tremendous testimony. Through the centuries Christianity did indeed practice baptism, but gradually, it developed into a ritual, a form. Then there was developed the teaching of baptismal regeneration which declared that once a person is baptized he is regenerated, he is safe, he can go to heaven. Many people in Christianity thus rest their salvation on water baptism instead of on the blood of Christ. It has become a deception and it takes Christ away from us. But today, as we approach the soon coming of the Lord, all these things as a system—as an "ism," as external appearances—will be shaken off. They will not avail anything. Only what is real, only what is of Christ himself, will bring us into glory.

We therefore believe that this letter to the Hebrews is very important for us today. Just as this letter in those earlier days had delivered the Hebrew believers from the bondage of Judaism into the liberty of the fullness of Christ, so we believe that this same letter is able to deliver us today from Christianity as a religion and bring us into the liberty of the fullness of Christ.

We know this letter is one of exhortation, because at the end of it the writer tells us that he is writing this letter to exhort his readers. It is a letter of only thirteen chapters written to exhort the believers. The word exhortation in the Greek carries within it at least two meanings. On the one hand, an exhortation is to encourage us to press on. On the other hand, an exhortation is to warn us lest we fall back. Hence, the whole purpose of this letter is to warn us not to fall back into that from which we have been delivered but to encourage us to press on to perfection. *Perfection* simply means "full-grown," "a growing into the measure of the stature of the fulness of Christ" (see Ephesians 4:13b).

What is the message of this letter? I believe the verse which we read at the beginning gives us the message. "Holy brethren, partakers of the heavenly calling, consider the Apostle and High Priest of our confession, Jesus." Here we have a brief description of a confession. I was told once that there is a difference between confession and profession—"pro" and "con." Profession of faith is to be made among friends, but a confession of faith is to be made before the world which is in enmity with God: "Christ Jesus who witnessed before Pontius Pilate the good confession" (I Timothy 6:13). So for us, it is not a profession; it must be a confession. We have a confession to make, and actually, our confession is our faith. What is our faith? Here we read: "Consider the Apostle and High Priest of our confession, Jesus."

The letter to the Hebrews can be divided into two parts. The first is found in chapters 1:1-10:18, and that gives us the vision. Chapters 10:19-13:25 gives us the vocation. On the one hand, we need to see what our confession is; what is the faith; what is the truth. Then, having seen it, it should become our living, our practice, our way of life, our testimony in the world.

The vision in the book of Hebrews is two-fold. In chapters 1-4 it is the vision of Jesus our Apostle. In chapters 5-10 it is the vision of Jesus as our High Priest. We need to ask God to give us this vision of the Lord Jesus because it is so vital; it is life and death to us. If we are to be delivered from a religious system such as Christianity, if we are going to be able to enter into the fullness of Christ and press on to perfection, such a vision is absolutely vital. We must have this vision. If we lack it, we do not know how to live as a Christian and we cannot live as a Christian.

Christ Our Apostle

First of all, we need to see Christ as our Apostle. The word *apostle* means "one sent forth." He is one who is sent forth with a mission, with a work to do. Probably, we will connect this word apostle with the twelve apostles, whom our Lord Jesus chose to be with Him to be trained by Him and then to be sent forth with a work. But, actually, the Lord Jesus was the very first Apostle in the New Testament order. He is the One who was sent forth by God the Father with a special mission.

At the beginning of this letter, in the first two chapters, we find the credentials of the Apostle of God, Jesus. When anyone is sent out as an envoy, as an ambassador, or as an apostle, he must have certain credentials. And here at the letter's beginning, we find that the credentials of Christ our Apostle are presented.

Credentials of an Apostle

In the Old Testament time, God sent forth many prophets. In a sense, these prophets who were sent forth by God were apostles; they were sent-out-ones with a message and with a mission. Accordingly in these olden days, God spoke to the fathers in many ways and in many forms by means of these prophets; but in these last days since then God speaks to us in the Person of His Son. Even though in the past God had sent many "spokesmen" to His people in order to reveal His mind to them and to give a message to them, all who were sent forth were men. They were holy men of God, moved by the power of the Spirit to speak, but they were still only human beings—imperfect, limited, full of weaknesses. God could only speak through them in parts, in bits and in fragments; but in these last days God has sent forth His only begotten Son as His Apostle. This Apostle, our Apostle, is none other than the Son of God, and His seven-fold glory is being presented before us here in this letter to the Hebrews:

He is the heir of all things.
He is the full representation and manifestation of God.
He is the Creator of the world.
He is the Upholder of all things.
He is the Purifying Fire of our sins.
He is seated at the right hand of the Most High.
He is so much better than the angels.

These are the credentials of our Apostle, Jesus as the Son of God.

In the second chapter are the credentials of our Apostle, Jesus, the Son of Man. This Son of God has become the Son of Man. He is the Man of God's mind. When God created man according to His image, Jesus is the man He had in mind. He was made a little inferior to the angels and tasted death for every one. Jesus was crowned with glory and honor, and by His death He destroyed the devil who had the power of death (see Hebrews 2:9, 14). He is waiting to have all things subjected under His feet, and He is the One who is to bring many sons into glory (see Hebrews 2:8, 10). These are His credentials as the Son of Man. Just think of it! This Son of God and Son of Man is our Apostle! He is the Apostle whom God has sent into the world to us. What an Apostle He is!

Christ is the Full Representation of God

What is the Apostle of our confession to do? First of all, an apostle is to represent the one who sends him, and there is no one who can represent God better than the Son. All the prophets who had been sent prior to Him could represent God only in a very limited way; but when the Son was sent into the world He represented God fully.

"No one has ever seen God at any time; the only-begotten Son, who is in the bosom of the Father, he hath declared Him" (John 1:18).

That is the reason why, when the Lord Jesus was having that last supper with His own, Philip said, "Show us the Father and it suffices us." And the Lord Jesus turned around and sadly said to this disciple: "Philip, you have been with me for so long and yet you are still asking that question. Do you not know that if you see Me you see the Father?" (see John 14:8-10).

While the Lord Jesus was on earth as the Apostle of God, He fully represented the Father to us. If we want to know what God is like, let us look at Jesus: "The Word became flesh and tabernacled among men, full of grace and truth" (see John 1:14). God is love and we see this divine love in the grace of Jesus Christ. God is light and we receive this light through the truth in Jesus Christ. In Him we see God fully, or to put it another way, we cannot know God better than what we can know in Christ Jesus: "All the fulness of the Godhead dwells in Him bodily" (see Colossians 2:9). He is the full representation of God the Father. If we want to know God, we must know Christ. We cannot know God apart from Him, because there is nothing more. Everything is in Him. He is the full representation and the exact image of the invisible God. How we do thank God that He is so gracious and merciful to us, that He who is invisible is now made visible through Jesus His Apostle. He who is unknowable is now made known to us in the Person of the Son, the Lord Jesus. In sum, knowing Jesus is knowing God.

Christ Speaks for God

An apostle is to speak for the one who sends him. We will recall the Lord Jesus saying, "I cannot say anything by Myself. I say it because I heard My Father say it" (see John 8). Whenever the Lord Jesus opened His mouth He was not saying His own words but was speaking the word of God. He speaks for God. In the days of the Old Testament the prophets spoke for God, but their speaking was in parts and fragments. But when the Son speaks for God, it is the full revelation of God; it is the final word, the complete word. There is nothing more to say; Christ has spoken it all.

Christ Does the Will of God

An apostle is to do a job, accomplish a mission. And the mission which the Lord Jesus was sent out for was to do the will of the Father. He said, "Sacrifice, burnt offerings, and oblations:

God, You do not want these things but You have prepared Me a body. Lo, I come to do Thy will and Thy law is the delight of my heart" (see Psalm 40:6-8). The whole life of the Lord Jesus on earth was not living to do His own will. His whole life was to do the will of the Father, to finish the work which the Father had committed to Him to do. This work is the work of redemption. He came to die. On the cross He said, "It is finished." The work is done. Mission accomplished. Thank God for that!

Christ is Our Forerunner

As an apostle Christ is the One who will open a new and living way for us that will lead us behind the veil to the very presence of God. He is to be our forerunner, and we know He has already gone behind the veil into the very presence of the Father. Yet He is not there merely for himself; He is to lead us there. As the Apostle of God He opens the way; He goes before us as our forerunner, and He leads us into the very presence of God.

Moses and Joshua

Now these are the works of an apostle, and Christ is our Apostle. In the book of Hebrews He is typified by two men: Moses and Joshua. These two men were sent by God to the children of Israel as their leaders. Moses was used by God to lead the people out of Egypt, and Joshua was used by God to lead the people into Canaan. Yet how much better is the Lord Jesus than even Moses and Joshua, because Moses was but a servant, faithful in God's house; but Christ is the Son who builds the house and rules over the house. Joshua led the people into Canaan, but he did not give them everlasting rest. The Lord Jesus gives us a Sabbath rest that we may rest from our works as God has rested from His work.

Hearing Christ, Our Apostle

Knowing Christ as our Apostle is vital to our confession. If we do not know Christ as our Apostle, then we do not know Christ at all. Our attitude towards Christ our Apostle should first of all be that we need to hear Him. The writer to the Hebrews said, "For this reason we should give heed more abundantly to the things we have heard" (Hebrews 2:1). Christ is sent by God to speak to us. Let us therefore hear Him. Let us not harden our hearts as the children of Israel had done. They would not listen, and because of that, even though they came out of Egypt, they failed to enter into the promised land. Oh, how we need to hear Christ—the great salvation first spoken to us by Him and also by the prophets and the apostles. We need to hear. Oh, that the Lord Jesus would give us a tender heart, a hearing heart, in order that we may hear what He has to say. It is not only hearing what we would like to hear, or hearing only a small fraction of what He has to say, but it is hearing all which He has said to us. Let us listen to the Lord because, actually, to hear Him is life.

Believing Christ, Our Apostle

Then, we not only need to hear Christ, we need also to believe Him. The children of Israel had heard, but they did not mix in faith with what they heard. They heard with their outward ear, but their heart being hardened, they would not believe it. God said, "Go over and possess the land." They said, "No, that is a terrible land. It devours the inhabitants." They did not believe; therefore, their carcasses fell in the wilderness. When we hear what our Apostle says, let us believe it. This does not apply only to our initial salvation. That is to say, when we hear that He is our Savior and has borne our sins on Calvary's cross, we believe it. Thank God for *that*; yet we are also to hear all which our Apostle has to say to us who have believed. He is saying that there is a rest prepared for us, that there is a Canaan land for us, that there is a land flowing with milk and honey. He is saying to us that there are unsearchable riches of Christ to be received and experienced, that there is a kingdom prepared for us, an inheritance for us to inherit. Let us therefore go in and hear what He says to us.

Following Christ, Our Apostle

We need to follow. The children of Israel refused to follow Moses many times. They wanted to retreat back to Egypt and choose their own leaders. They refused to follow Joshua and Caleb. These two had said, "Let us go in." But the Israelites had said, "No, we cannot go in."

Let us always remember our Apostle, Jesus. He is the One whom we are to follow. No matter how difficult it may appear to be, no matter how strong our enemies are, if He says to come and follow Him, let us follow. Even though it means the way of the cross, let us nonetheless follow, because we know the way of the cross leads to glory, to the throne. Let us remember that the Lord Jesus is our Apostle. All our salvation is in Him. He has done everything for us, and all which is left for us to do is to hear Him, believe Him and follow Him. In doing that we will not be bound by a religious system but will be set free and we will be pressing on towards perfection, towards Christ. We need to see Christ, our Apostle.

Christ, Our High Priest

Next, though, we learn that the book of Hebrews spends more time on this matter of Christ as our High Priest. I can understand why, because I have the same problem. It seems to be easier to know Christ as our Apostle, but to know Christ as our High Priest seems to be a little vague. To know Him as our Apostle is the foundation, but to know Him as High Priest is for the building up. An apostle is one sent out to us by God; a high priest is one chosen from among men to lead us towards God. Christ, as an Apostle, represents God on earth to us, but as the High Priest, He represents us before God in heaven. As our Apostle, Christ brings God to us; as our High Priest, He brings us to God. This dual ministry must go hand in hand. We cannot have the one without the other.

We thank God that the Lord Jesus is our Apostle, and I do believe we know somewhat more about this aspect; but do we know much about the Lord Jesus as our High Priest? When He accomplished the work of redemption on Calvary's cross, He was buried for three days and then He was raised from the dead. He appeared to the disciples for forty days and then He was taken up—He ascended up to be seated at the right hand of God the Father. When our Lord Jesus ascended up to heaven, something happened there: He was anointed by God. On the day of Pentecost, the apostle Peter and the eleven testified together that this Jesus who was crucified God had exalted on high and had anointed as the Lord, the Christ. And that this is the reason for what the people that day had seen and had heard being poured out. The Holy Spirit had come down.

If we read Psalm 110 we shall learn that after the Lord had ascended up on high, He was anointed by God as the High Priest according to the order of Melchisedek. The picture is found in yet another Psalm which says this: "Like the oil poured upon Aaron's head, flowing down upon the beard over his body even to the skirt of his garment" (see Psalm 133). In the Old Testament period, when the Jews anointed the high priest, they did not simply sprinkle a few drops of oil upon him. We are told that when they anointed the high priest they poured an abundance of oil upon his head and it flowed down his face and all over his body. We know, of course, that the oil here represents the Holy Spirit. Therefore, when the Lord Jesus ascended, He received from the Father the Holy Spirit and poured the Holy Spirit down upon this earth. At that moment, He was anointed as our High

Priest according to the order of Melchisedek.

On the one hand, the work of the Lord Jesus, as God's Apostle, has been finished. His apostolic mission was accomplished. And because of this, we know that Jesus is now seated at the right hand of God. A person does not sit down until the job is done. Because His work as an Apostle was now finished, therefore He sits down. But let us not think that the Lord Jesus only sits there dozing, doing nothing. No; one phase of His ministry is finished, but another phase of it has begun. When He ascended to heaven and was seated at the right hand of the Father, He was anointed as the High Priest of our confession. Accordingly, the Lord Jesus is very busily engaged in heaven: indeed, "He ever liveth making intercession for those who approach God through Him that He may save us to the uttermost" (see Hebrews 7:25). If the Lord Jesus were not a High Priest today, we would not be able to be blessed with any blessing in the heavenlies in Christ Jesus. We would not be able to be a Christian, much less be able to live a Christian life. We are unable. It is impossible. It is all because today the Lord Jesus is our High Priest.

The Credential of Christ as High Priest

What is Christ's credential as our High Priest? He is our High Priest according to the order of Melchisedek. Now Melchisedek is mentioned in the Bible only three times; and so far as his history is concerned, he is only mentioned once within a few verses included in Genesis 14. There we learn that Abraham overcame the four kings, rescued his nephew Lot, and returned to the King's Valley. It is within this context that Melchisedek, which means "king of righteousness," is mentioned. He was the king of Salem, that is to say, the king of peace; and there in the King's Valley he came forward to meet Abraham with bread and wine. Melchisedek blessed Abraham in the name of the Most High, because at that time he was the high priest of the Most High God, and Abraham gave him one tenth of all which he had. As far as history goes, that is all that we have in Scripture concerning Melchisedek.

The land of Canaan at that time was occupied by seven wicked tribes which actually represented the evil forces of darkness. Yet, in this land there was a place called Salem (that is, Jerusalem), and Melchisedek, the king of Jerusalem, was the king of righteousness in the midst of all this wickedness and idolatry. He was the high priest of the Most High God. Is that not wonderful? God still had His testimony even in that place; and Melchisedek came forward to bless Abraham, and without any doubt, the superior blessed the inferior. In other words, he was greater than Abraham.

The second mentioning of Melchisedek in Scripture is found in Psalm 110. A thousand years have passed, and there the Psalmist, through inspiration, said that one day the Messiah would be anointed as King. "God said to My Lord, 'Sit at My right hand until I make Your enemies Your footstool.'" Then He added: "You are being anointed as the High Priest according to the order of Melchisedek."

Still another thousand years would pass. In the book of Hebrews Melchisedek is mentioned yet again. The writer of Hebrews wrote this: "This Melchisedek has no beginning, no end, no genealogy—all just like the Son of God." Now let us not think that Melchisedek was a fictitious person. He was a real person who had lived during the time of Abraham. And, of course, he did have a beginning and an end, but the Holy Spirit withholds such information about his beginning and his end because He wants to use him as a type of Christ the High Priest. By not including details concerning Melchisedek's beginning and end, he can appear as though he was without beginning and end so that he can represent Christ the High Priest.

The Lord Jesus is a high priest according to the priestly order of Melchisedek; and what is the order of Melchisedek? In what way is this order different from the Levitical order of priesthood? There is a great difference. The Levitical priesthood chooses men as priests, but the Melchisedek order has the Son of God as the High Priest. The Levitical order chooses weak and mortal men as priests, but the Melchisedek order chooses the immortal Son of God as Priest. In the Levitical order the priests die, therefore the priesthood changes often; but in the Melchisedek order the priesthood never changes because Christ lives forever. He is a priest according to His indissoluble life. He lives forever. In the Levitical order the priests are weak themselves; therefore, they can sympathize with the weak. In the Melchisedek order, Christ came into this world to be a man, to be tempted in all things yet without sin, so that He can sympathize with us. However, He not only sympathizes with us, He is constituted according to the power of an indissoluble life; therefore, Christ can save us to the uttermost.

Let me inquire, do we know the Lord Jesus as our High Priest? Consciously or unconsciously, knowingly or unknowingly, we are where we are today because of Christ's High Priestly ministry. But how much better it can be if we realize how much more He is able to save us—if we only know. That is why we need to know Him as our High Priest. I believe we know Christ as our Apostle to a certain degree but, unfortunately, the reason why Christians are so weak today is because we do not know Him as our High Priest.

The Work of a High Priest

Sacrifice

What did the earthly high priest do? First of all, he was to offer sacrifices. Once a year, the Jewish high priest would take the blood of goat and bull and enter behind the veil before the mercy seat of God. There, he would sprinkle the blood to make atonement for the sins of the entire nation. The Lord Jesus is our High Priest. If the blood of goats and bulls and heifers' ashes can purify the defiled, how much better, how far superior, is the Lord Jesus, who offered His body spotless unto God by the eternal Spirit. Once and forever He has completed our eternal redemption. He has perfected the sanctified ones once and for all by offering himself as *the* sacrifice to God. The Lord Jesus, in ascending up to heaven, brought His blood, as it were, (let us not however, think of it physically, because it is not) and laid it before the Father, and that blood speaks mercifully for us forever. Abel's blood spoke for vengeance, but the blood of the Lord Jesus speaks for mercy. The Lord Jesus as our High Priest has presented the sacrifice to God—even himself—so that our redemption is an eternal one. It is eternally available and full of power.

We know our sins are forgiven because He is our High Priest. He has presented His blood before the Father and this is once and for all. Before we were saved we came, we repented, we believed in the blood of the Lord Jesus, and we accepted Him as our Savior; and because of this, the blood speaks for us and the Father forgives us. Our sin is all gone. But is it not true in our daily life that sometimes through our weakness or carelessness, we still fall, we still sin? And if we do, what will happen?

I am reminded of one reason why in Christianity there is baptism by sprinkling. If we read church history we shall learn that in the early days all baptism was by immersion. But later on a strange kind of theory—I would not call it theology—developed which posited the notion that all our sins would be washed away at our baptism, but that the sin which we might commit *after* baptism would be very difficult to be dealt with. So people postponed their baptism as long as they could, and on their deathbed they wanted to be baptized. Obviously, they could no longer be immersed then, so they would receive baptism by sprinkling. They failed to see the eternal efficacy of the sacrifice of the blood of our Lord Jesus once and for all in perpetuity and in perfection.

"If we [who are believers] confess our sins, he (God) is

faithful and righteous to forgive us our sins and cleanse us from all unrighteousness" (I John 1:9).

Since God is righteous and we confess our sins, that is very good. He does not need to torture us to bring us to make confession; for then we would be condemned. But He has once accepted His beloved Son as the sin offering. He has once crushed Him on the cross. The price is paid; the penalty has been executed. God being righteous, He cannot execute us again; for that would make Him unrighteous. God is faithful in the sense that the blood of Christ has sealed a new covenant between himself and us, and thus God has to be faithful to His covenant. Therefore, if we confess our sins, God is righteous and faithful to forgive our sins and to cleanse us from all our unrighteousness. That is the ministry of the Lord Jesus as our High Priest. That is why I say that if it is not because of His ministry as our High Priest, how could we live a Christian life? We would be under guilt all our days. We would be under accusation throughout our life. We could not live; but thank God, He is our High Priest.

Intercession

The work of a high priest is to intercede. The Jewish high priest of old went into the holiest place not only to offer the sacrifice, but also to pray for the nations. When he came out from the holiest of all, he could bless the people. What is the Lord Jesus doing today? He sits at the right hand of the Father interceding for us. He prays for us. The Lord Jesus takes up your cause and my cause and presents it before the Father on the basis of what He, the Lord Jesus has done for us. He is a surety and the mediator of the New Covenant. It is as though He is saying to the Father: "Father, look, this child of Yours has sinned; but I have shed My blood. I am the guarantor of the New Covenant, and according to the New Covenant, You will forgive their sins, and not only forgive them but forget their sins. Father, do it." And the Father does it. It is as though He is presenting our weakness to the Father and says, "Father, Your children are weak. They do not know Your will, but remember, according to the New Covenant, they should know You in themselves. May they know You in themselves." And He also says, "Father, I am the mediator of the New Covenant; I am going to channel the goodness, the blessing, of the New Covenant to these Your children that they may live by My resurrection life, that they may overcome." There the Lord Jesus as High Priest intercedes for us.

When the Lord Jesus was on earth, one illustration of this High Priestly ministry of His was related to Peter. The Lord said that He would be crucified and die, and on the third day He would be raised from the dead and all of the disciples would be scattered like sheep when the Shepherd was taken captive. Peter loved the Lord, but when he heard this, he said, "Oh, no, if others will flee, I will not. I will go with You even to death." But the Lord Jesus said, "Peter, Satan has asked to sift you as in a sieve, but I have *prayed* for you" (see Matthew 26:31-35; Luke 22:31-32).

Is this not wonderful? Satan cannot do anything to a child of God without asking for God's permission. And strangely, God does sometimes permit and, of course, for a very good reason. Peter did not know himself. He was self-confident; he thought too good of himself. So God used Satan to sift him so that the chaff would be blown off and he would be purified; but this is a dangerous process. Satan asked, and our Lord asked too. "I prayed for you; I interceded for you with the Father that your faith would not be lost but would be refined, and that you would be able to help your brethren." That is an illustration of the High Priestly ministry of the Lord Jesus.

The Lord Jesus is interceding for us before the Father. We do not really know ourselves, but He knows us. He knows everything, and it is by His intercession that we are being kept. What a powerful intercession that is! Without it, where would we be? We would be sifted out; but thank God, with Christ's intercession at work, and even though we are being sifted, the chaff is being blown away and the grain of wheat is being refined.

Presenting Gifts to God

A high priest not only presents sacrifices, he also presents gifts to God. There is a difference between gifts and sacrifice. First of all, the Lord Jesus presented himself as a gift to God. Oh, how He pleases the Father! He is the burnt offering. Actually, the burnt offering is more in the sense of a gift because the burnt offering is a voluntary and whole offering. It represents a life wholly devoted, and that is a pleasure to God. And because Christ is our High Priest, He presents us to God.

Romans 12 declares: "Present your bodies a living sacrifice." How can we present our bodies a living sacrifice unless it is presented in Christ? Today, we can present our bodies a living sacrifice, and the Father is pleased. Today, we can pray and He will mingle incense with our prayer, so that our prayer will be acceptable. Let us not think that *our* prayer is so powerful. Our prayer is so weak, it is almost nothing, but the Lord Jesus as High Priest adds His incense to our prayer; that is to say, He adds His merits to our prayer, He adds His prayer to our prayer; and that makes our prayer powerful. He enables us to praise and worship God. He enables us to serve God. All these are the Lord's presenting of us as gifts to God. It is all through Christ. Without Him our service will not be accepted; without Him our praise and worship will not be accepted; without Him our prayers will not be heard; without Him our devotion will not be accepted. Everything that is in the area of gift is accepted because He—Jesus our High Priest—has presented them to the Father.

Experiencing Christ as Our High Priest

How do we really experience the Lord Jesus as our High Priest? Our problem is that the Lord is in heaven and we are on earth. We know He is praying and interceding for us. We know He is functioning as our High Priest, but how do we experience it? How do we enter into that intimate, experiential knowledge of Christ as our High Priest? I believe that the key is as follows. Before the Lord Jesus went to heaven He said this to His disciples: "I go, but I will send another Comforter to you." The Lord himself is the Comforter, the Strengthener, the Guardian; and yet He said, "I go, but I will send another Comforter"—that is, another of the same kind. The Holy Spirit will come and dwell in us. He will never leave us nor forsake us. The Holy Spirit in us does not represent us; He represents Christ. Let us not make a mistake here. The Holy Spirit in us never represents you and me; He represents Christ. Christ in heaven represents us before the Father, and the Holy Spirit in us represents Christ. This is where the ministry of Christ our High Priest comes into play. As Christ intercedes, the Holy Spirit works in us: the Holy Spirit convicts, the Holy Spirit convinces, the Holy Spirit teaches, the Holy Spirit guides, the Holy Spirit leads, the Holy Spirit constrains, the Holy Spirit restrains, the Holy Spirit empowers, the Holy Spirit enables. All these workings of the Holy Spirit in our lives are according to the ministry of the Lord Jesus as our High Priest. If we truly know *this*, then the Lord as our High Priest shall be very real in our lives every moment of every day.

If we do not know the Holy Spirit, how can we live a Christian life? If we do not know the Holy Spirit, how can we know Christ as our High Priest? The Holy Spirit in us is to glorify Christ. He is to transform us and conform us to the image of Christ, and the work of the Holy Spirit is based upon the work of Christ. So let us ever be mindful that our experience of Christ as our High Priest lies in the working of the Holy Spirit. That is why when Paul was in Ephesus he asked the twelve disciples of John the Baptist: "When you believed, did you receive the Holy Spirit?" In other words, if we do not have the Holy Spirit, how can we be Christians? It is impossible. Everyone who believes in the Lord Jesus has the Holy Spirit dwelling in him or her, and the Holy Spirit is there representing Christ as our High Priest. It is as though the Lord in heaven is praying, "I see in this child that there is something not right; he needs to be convicted." And hence the Holy Spirit convicts. Or the Lord Jesus prays and says, "I see this child is in darkness; he needs light." And as the Lord prays, the Holy Spirit brings light to us. This is why we say that without the Lord as our High Priest we simply cannot live. He as our High Priest is ever living, never dying, always making intercession for us that He may save to the uttermost those who approach God through Him. Thank God for that!

So this entire letter's purpose is to enable us to see Christ as our Apostle and as our High Priest. And in seeing Him as such, let us approach the throne of grace with full assurance of faith; let us hold fast the confession of our hope to the end; and let us encourage one another, provoking one another to love and good works.

Shall we pray:

Dear heavenly Father, do open our eyes to see Jesus the Apostle and High Priest of our confession so that we may approach Thy throne of grace with full assurance of faith, that we may hold on to our confession, and that we will be able to encourage one another to love. We ask it in the name of our Lord Jesus. Amen.

JAMES

Seeing Christ in Living Faith

James 2:14-26—What is the profit, my brethren, if any one say he have faith, but have not works? can faith save him? Now if a brother or a sister is naked and destitute of daily food, and one from amongst you say to them, Go in peace, be warmed and filled; but give not to them the needful things for the body, what is the profit? So also faith, if it have not works, is dead by itself. But some one will say, Thou hast faith and I have works. Shew me thy faith without works, and I from my works will shew thee my faith. Thou believest that God is one. Thou doest well. The demons even believe, and tremble. But wilt thou know, O vain man, that faith without works is dead? Was not Abraham our father justified by works when he had offered Isaac his son upon the altar? Thou seest that faith wrought with his works, and that by works faith was perfected. And the scripture was fulfilled which says, Abraham believed God, and it was reckoned to him as righteousness, and he was called Friend of God. Ye see that a man is justified on the principle of works, and not on the principle of faith only. But was not in like manner also Rahab the harlot justified on the principle of works, when she had received the messengers and put them forth by another way? For as the body without a spirit is dead, so also faith without works is dead.

Let us pray:

Dear heavenly Father, as we continue in Thy presence we ask that the light of Thy countenance wilt shine upon us, upon our hearts, that our hearts may be opened and filled with understanding, and may come to know Thy mind. We do pray that Thou wilt breathe upon Thy word again and make it living and operative in our lives. We commit this time into Thy hands. In the name of our Lord Jesus. Amen.

JAMES THE JUST

I have to say that this letter of James is unique. It may very well be the first, the earliest, New Testament writing. Who is this James, the writer of this letter? It cannot be James, the son of Zebedee, the brother of John, because he was martyred by King Herod around the year 44 A.D. This cannot be James, the son of Alphaeus, one of the twelve apostles, because that James was a rather obscure person. So we believe this James is the brother of the Lord. In the book of Acts chapter 12, we are told that when Peter was released from prison by the angel, he went to the home of the mother of John and before he left he said, "Go and tell James and the other brethren." This James is the brother of the Lord.

We are told that James, the brother of the Lord in the flesh, was a very devout person. Tradition even says that he was a Nazarite. He was a very godly, Jewish person who was zealous in keeping the law of Moses. He lived a very righteous life. Therefore, they called him James the Just. But it is very strange that when the Lord Jesus was living, this brother of His just could not believe in Him as the Messiah, the Christ. Somehow he was so bound by the law, by the tradition of the fathers, that even though he must have been deeply impressed by what he saw and heard from his brother, he being in such close proximity to Him, nevertheless, James just could not believe in the Lord Jesus as the Messiah. He tried to keep the law as much as possible and, outwardly, he seemed to be such a righteous person. Actually, he was admired. However, I do not doubt that deep down within his heart there must have been a sense of emptiness, a sense of unfulfillment. As he looked upon his brother, I can imagine how much he longed that he might have what his brother had—that liberty, that glorious liberty—which he could see in the life of Jesus. But somehow James could not break through the barrier. He was bound. It is very possible that it was not until the death of the Lord Jesus, which must have made a deep impression upon James, that he began to believe in the Lord.

When the Lord Jesus was crucified on the cross, there was a centurion present, the Roman officer who watched the whole scene. When this centurion saw the Lord Jesus die on the cross He said, "This is the Son of God" (see Mark 15:39). His death was so unique, so majestic, so glorious that it moved the heart of a Roman centurion to say, "This is the Son of God." If this happened to the Roman centurion, I believe it must have happened to James the Just. After the resurrection of the Lord Jesus, He appeared to James alone (see I Corinthians 15:7). We do not know what the risen Lord said to His brother James but somehow this appearing of the Lord to James sealed his faith. Very soon this James became one of the three pillars in the church in Jerusalem—Peter, John and this James. Again, in the book of Acts, chapter 15, we learn that in the council in Jerusalem he was the person who gave the last word, and when Paul visited Jerusalem for his last time, it was James who seemed to be the leading brother in the church in Jerusalem.

Even the Jewish historian, Josephus, wrote in his history about James' death. He said the following: "There was a person called James the Just, a brother of Jesus, who is called Christ. In the interval between the death of Festus and the succession of the Governor Albinus, the high priest, Annas the Younger, seized upon James and some others. He accused them of violating the law of Moses and sentenced them to be stoned; and this James was stoned to death. However, this James was respected, not only by the Christians at that time, but by the Jews in general, so the Jewish people, the Pharisees, rose up in indignation. They accused the high priest before

King Agrippa and had this high priest deposed.

Hence, we can see here what a unique person this man James was.

Twelve Tribes in Dispersion

We are told that James wrote this letter to the Twelve Tribes in the Dispersion. These tribes here refer to the Twelve Tribes of Israel, and the Dispersion is a reference to the Jewish people who through the years had been scattered throughout the whole world and who lived outside of Palestine, the Jewish homeland. James was not written to the Twelve Tribes in dispersion in general; rather, it was written to those Jews scattered among the Dispersion throughout the world who had believed in the Lord Jesus.

Probably, this conversion to Christ of Jews among the Dispersion had begun on the day of Pentecost when many devout Jews had come from all over the world to Jerusalem to worship God. It was there that they heard the message of the Lord Jesus Christ, and many came to the Lord. Among the three thousand saved who had gathered in Jerusalem at that time there must have been many who had come from the Dispersion. And because of the persecution which occurred later on, they had returned to where they had come from, taking the gospel with them to all those various places; and many others throughout the Dispersion came to the Lord through their preaching. And hence, scattered among the Dispersion all over the world were now to be found Jewish people who had come to know the Lord Jesus Christ, and it was therefore to these people that James in his epistle addressed himself.

Now this was a most proper thing for James to do since he himself was a Jew, was zealous in the law, and who had come to know the Lord in a very real way. In a sense, James was the leading brother in the church in Jerusalem; therefore, it would be natural for such a person to write a letter to those Jewish believers scattered throughout the world. In the sovereignty of God, James was used as a special vessel during the transitional period from Judaism to Christianity, from law to grace.

Even though this letter was written by James to those believers among the Twelve Tribes in the Dispersion, we believe this letter is for us, too. Not physically but spiritually speaking, we may say we are the Twelve Tribes in dispersion; this is because all those who believe in God—who believe in the Lord Jesus as the believing Abraham—are the children of Abraham. Abraham had two seeds—or, to phrase it another way, one seed of two kinds—because God had said that his seed shall be as the stars in the heavens and as the sand on the seashore. The Jewish people, the Twelve Tribes of Israel, are as the sand on the seashore: the physical people of Abraham. But we who believe in the Lord Jesus are the spiritual people of Abraham who shall be as the stars in the heavens. That is why Paul once said, "You [who believe in Christ] are the true Israel" (Galatians 6:16). Even so, today we are in dispersion; we are scattered all over the world and are not in our homeland yet. So in a sense, we can say that this letter is addressed to us, and we can learn much from it.

A Wrong Concept of this Letter

Sometimes people can be easily influenced and perhaps influenced in the wrong way. Martin Luther once said concerning this epistle of James: "This letter, compared with the epistles of Paul and other writings in the New Testament, is a straw epistle, for it is lacking in evangelical truth." And because of what Luther said, people harbored the mistaken notion in their minds that this is a letter of no worth. Martin Luther loved the letter to the Galatians so much that once he said: "Galatians is my letter, my Katherine, my wife; I am wedded to it," and he used it as a powerful sword in the reformation of Christianity; but when he looked at the letter of James, he just could not understand. He said of this epistle: "It is a letter of straw. I cannot fight with this letter." Why? Martin Luther had emphasized so much on the Biblical truth of justification by faith that he thought this letter of James taught the law of God in contradiction to God's grace.

I hope we would know better. We know that there is absolutely no contradiction between Paul and James. On the contrary, the writings of Paul and the writing of James are complementary. It is true that Paul emphasizes justification by faith in Romans and again in the letter to the Galatians, because this is the gospel of Jesus Christ. It is true that when we read this letter of James, it seems as though its author emphasizes justification by works; but we must remember what faith is. Faith is not only believing, faith is also working. In faith there is the aspect of believing, yet there is another aspect to it which is that of working. We must believe, that is quite true; nevertheless, if that belief is real it has got to be put to work.

Paul was dealing with the Gentiles and he wanted them to see that a person is not justified by the works of law. At that time there were some legalistic Jewish persons going around telling people it was fine to believe in the Lord Jesus Christ, but they had to be circumcised and had to keep the law of Moses in order to be saved. Paul said, "No one can be saved by works; no one can be saved by keeping the law of Moses, simply because no one is capable of doing so. We are saved by grace through faith, by our believing in the finished work of Christ. We are justified by faith." And he is right.

However, we must remember that James had to deal with another kind of person. He was not dealing primarily with the Gentiles; he was dealing with the Jews who had tried to keep the law and had failed. Now they had come to see the grace of God in Christ Jesus and they were saved. He tried to tell them that now that they had believed in the Lord Jesus they were to prove their faith by works, so that their faith might be proven and perfected. So, in reality, there is no contradiction. We must first believe, but after we have believed, our faith then needs to be perfected and proven by works.

To put it another way, Paul's emphasis is on our standing position before God. We are justified before God not by works, but by faith. James's emphasis, however, is different; he is trying to show us how we can be justified before the world. In order to be justified before man we have to prove our faith by works. So what Paul begins, James concludes, and there is absolutely no contradiction.

Background of this Letter

If we want to really know this letter of James, we probably need to know somewhat more about the background. We have already said that this James was once a very devout Jew, zealous in keeping the law. What happened when he came to know the Lord Jesus? Outwardly, there does not seem to be any great change, because prior to his conversion, James was a good man. Hence, after he believed in the Lord Jesus, there did not seem to be much change so far as the outward appearance was concerned. Is it not true that if you were a so-called good man or woman, if you were not a raw sinner before you believed in the Lord Jesus, that after you believe in the Lord Jesus, the world will not see too much change in your life? But if you were a downright sinner and then got saved—oh, you changed a great deal in the sight of man.

So, here was this man James who previously had been a just man and who, after he believed in the Lord Jesus, was still just. There did not seem to have been much change outwardly; even so, we must realize that there was a tremendous transformation going on within him. In other words, even though in outward conduct James was not much changed, in the inward reality there was a tremendous transformation. He was freed, delivered, liberated from the bondage of the letter of the law. Earlier, he had been bound by the letter of the law, having tried but failed to keep every letter in the law. He had been a slave to the law of Moses but now he was completely freed from that bondage. James had now entered into the liberty of the sons of God. Because of the life of Christ in him, he lived ever afterwards in liberty; he lived thereafter according to the law of the spirit of life, he continually proved his faith by the works he did.

So we must see that there occurred a great difference in James. Outwardly, there did not seem to be much difference in him before and after his coming to Christ; but inwardly, there was a great difference. This was because the source was different. In the past he had tried to keep the letter of the law by himself, and outwardly, he seemed to have succeeded. They had called him the Just, but James knew better. After he came to know the Lord Jesus, the source of his just life was no longer from himself but from a living faith in the Son of God. It was therefore no longer James who was living, it was henceforth Christ who lived in him. And because Christ now lived in him, therefore he lived a just and righteous life. What a tremendous difference, indeed, all because the source was different.

From Bondage to Freedom

Now let us consider the people to whom James wrote his letter. Probably, these Jewish converts to Christ had in the past been most zealous for the law. If you were a devout Jew, then you must be zealous for the law; but they all knew they could not keep the law. They all felt that emptiness and dissatisfaction in their hearts. Accordingly, when they heard the gospel of Jesus Christ, they entered into tremendous liberty. They were delivered from the bondage of the law into the marvelous grace of God. What a transformation that must have been for them! But now they had a real temptation: "Now that we are free from the law, we can throw the law out the window. We today can live in freedom and liberty. Hallelujah!" And the result was that they began to live a careless life, that brought reproach to the name of the Lord. These Jewish believers thought they were freed: "It is grace; no more law; it is all grace."

Do we not have the same temptation confronting us? We can go to extremes, especially those among us who are new believers or those who have first tasted liberty in Christ—those who have first savored the good taste of grace. Let us suppose that you are living under the law. You try to keep the law, you attempt to do the right thing, you try to save yourself by good works, but you are under bondage and are under a heavy burden all the time. One day, however, you hear the gospel of Jesus Christ, and you at last realize that salvation is not by works because your works are considered as filthy rags in God's sight. You have finally seen that they cannot save you nor can they please God. So you are delivered from dead works; you today have a living faith in Jesus Christ, and you begin to worship God. What a great liberation you now enjoy! But do you realize that you have the same temptation because you are free? So you are free to do whatever you want to do, and thus you go to the other extreme. Hence, James has written this letter to address this very problem.

Corresponding to the Wisdom Books

When you read the letter of James do you have a feeling that this letter seems to correspond to some book in the Old Testament? Its contents has the appearance of one of the wisdom books. It seems to correspond in form or style at least with those wisdom books in the Old Testament of Proverbs and Ecclesiastes. That is the reason why it is very difficult to analyze the book of James because its contents are seemingly all proverbs. But there is a great difference between James and those two Old Testament wisdom writings. Even though, outwardly, James looks like a collection of proverbs and other wise sayings, we know that, inwardly, this letter comes from a different source; it comes from above.

Corresponding to the Sermon on the Mount

Another feature you will notice about this book of James is the similarity between it and the sayings and observations which comprise Jesus' so-called Sermon on the Mount recorded in Matthew 5, 6 and 7. James, being a brother of the Lord Jesus, grew up together with Him. They must have been very close, and after James came to the Lord, the words of Jesus seemed to have filled his heart and mind. So that it turns out that much in this letter of James corresponds very, very much to the Sermon on the Mount of the Lord Jesus.

What is the Sermon on the Mount? What does one make of the Sermon on the Mount? Some people believe that the Sermon on the Mount is actually the record of the Lord Jesus giving us a new set of laws which are even higher than the law of Moses. In fact, they do indeed look higher; yet, if that be the case, then who can keep such law? If the Jewish people could not keep the law of Moses, how, then, can Christians keep the law of the Sermon on the Mount? For unless our righteousness is higher than that of the Pharisees and the scribes, we cannot enter the kingdom of God. Indeed, who can? Nobody can.

The Royal Law of Love

To be most accurate, the Sermon on the Mount is not the Lord Jesus trying to give us a new set of laws; the Sermon on the Mount is the Lord Jesus describing a kind of life which the sons of the kingdom live. How will the sons of the kingdom of the heavens live? They will live the kind of life this Sermon on the Mount describes, since this is the way Jesus lived while on earth, and He now lives in you and lives in me. That is the Sermon on the Mount. Strictly speaking, it is not law, it is still grace. But if anyone wishes to call it law, then we may say it is the royal law of love or the law of liberty—the law of the Spirit of life in Christ Jesus (see Romans 8:2). It is the life of Christ in those who are discipled to Him, those people who let the light of Christ live in and through them. That is the way they will live, and that is the Sermon on the Mount.

The same thing is true with the letter of James. It is not giving us more laws, more regulations, more rules for us as Christians to keep. The letter of James is simply describing to us the kind of life we should live as believers and what good works should be exhibited before the world so that our faith may be proven and perfected.

Now it is most true that we are not saved by works because our works are as filthy rags in the sight of God, and not only our works but our so-called righteousnesses (see Isaiah 64:6). We think we are doing the right thing, the good thing, the best thing. We boast of these things, but when we present the best of our works before God, they are as filthy rags, and they cannot cover our nakedness before Him. They are filthy and they cannot stand before God. They are not only as filthy rags, but the Bible further says that all the works which we try to justify ourselves with are dead works. They are dead because they are done by dead people. Our spirit is dead, and hence, works done by dead people are dead works. They do not give us any life before God; therefore, we have to be delivered from our dead works. We must not only see that our works are no good, we also have to be delivered from our dead works. We have to be delivered from depending upon these dead works; otherwise, we will never come to the Lord Jesus. Unbelievers must give up their dead works; and then, they must receive the grace of our Lord Jesus. We are justified by grace through faith, and this is not of ourselves, it is the gift of God.

After Faith—Good Works

Now after we have been justified by faith, then what? Is it that because we are justified by faith and not by works that therefore God will never require any works from us? Can it be that because we are saved by grace we therefore do not need to live a lawful, ethical, moral life? Does it mean that because we are justified by faith and saved by grace that henceforth we can simply be free to do anything we like? That we will go to heaven no matter what we do or what happens afterwards, and that's it! Unfortunately, there is such a misunderstanding among God's people, and this misunderstanding actually began, strange to say, with the Reformation. Before the Reformation all people thought they had to be justified by works; yet, they could not. But with the coming of the Reformation, works were totally cast aside, and faith came in. "We are justified by faith;" no more works; that's it! Even to this day, many believers are still laboring under a kind of mist. We know we are not saved by works; but, does it mean that after we are saved, God does not require of us good works? Yes, the apostle Paul indeed said in Ephesians 2:8: "Ye are saved by grace, through faith," but then in verse 10 he added this: "For we are his workmanship, having been created in Christ Jesus for good works, which God has before prepared that we should walk in them." It is true you are saved by grace through faith, but after you are saved, God recreates you as a new creation for the purpose of doing good works, the works which He has before prepared for you to do.

I hope we will be very careful here in our understanding. Before we are justified by faith, our works are deemed to be of no value because they cannot justify us before God; they cannot save us; they cannot bring us to heaven; they cannot remit our sins. But after we are justified by faith, we are the Lord's; we are children of God; we are sons of the kingdom of the heavens; we have the life of Christ in us. And this life which has been given to us is able to please God and can enable us to do His will. Therefore, let us do it.

The Crown of Life

Perhaps someone will say and ask the following: "Why

should I do good works? I am saved; so I will go to heaven, after all. If I try to do good works, I will have to suffer, I will have to pay some cost. Why not just obtain the best of both worlds? I believe in the Lord Jesus and shall go to heaven. Then I can enjoy the world while I am living because, after all, when I die, I will go to heaven just as I am." Very clever; and it seems to be very logical. If we are justified by faith, if we go to heaven saved by grace, then why work? Naturally, we are all lazy people. It is true, we are justified by faith through grace; heaven is a gift of God; eternal life is His gift. But we forget that after the end of this age but before eternity comes, there will be another age on the earth of a thousand years. It is called the kingdom. God shall establish His kingdom upon this earth wherein Christ shall reign over this earth for a thousand years, and this is offered as a reward to the children of God who are justified by faith. Heaven is a gift but kingdom is a reward. Gift is freely given to those who believe. Reward, on the other hand, is only for those who work for it and earn it. A thousand years is a thousand years. Today we may live a hundred years, but compared with a thousand years it is only one tenth. No matter what honor and glory and pleasure of the world we may receive today, it cannot be compared with the reward on earth and in heaven: the crown of life, the crown of righteousness, the crown of glory, reigning with Christ.

This is what James in chapter 1 verse 12 is writing about. He said, "You who believe in the Lord Jesus, do you think because you are delivered from the law, you can live an immoral, unlawful, unethical life? That because you are saved, you are free to do whatever you please?" No. He also said: "You have a new life in you; therefore, you have to live a higher life. You have to live a spiritual life; you have to live a life that will glorify God; you have to prove that your faith is living and is real; and that by your good works you must do the will of God so that He may be glorified. If you do that, one day He will reward you with a crown of life." This is the message which James addressed to the new believers in his day, and I do believe that in our day this is the kind of message which we need to hear.

Thank God for the Reformation because it cleared up the issue of the justification by faith; but on the other hand, ever since the Reformation, Christianity has unfortunately been under a mist. After we have been justified by faith, then what? What does God require of us? What is this life given to us for? Is there any way we can glorify God on earth? and should we? must we? All this we can find answered in the letter of James.

After saying this much, I hope we are at least clear on this point, because I think it is very important. As a matter of fact, there are certain books in the New Testament which have been called catholic epistles: those of James, Peter, John and Jude. They are called catholic epistles because they are not addressed to just one local church but they are addressed to many more people in the church. They were written by these apostles for reading by the general Christian public. In these so-called catholic letters their authors all addressed this matter of the salvation of the soul and the kingdom. There is a kingdom before you and me and we are called to that kingdom; therefore, let us live like sons of the kingdom. If we live today like a kingdom son, then one day we will reign as a king in the kingdom of God. That is the message in these catholic epistles.

Temptation

Now that we have laid the groundwork, let us select some of the illustrations from James's epistle. James is a letter which very directly applies the principle of faith to our practical daily living: Christ in the faith that works. How does this faith which we confess work in our daily life? First of all, we see it realized in this matter of temptation. Temptation is something which we confront every day. It is true that God never tempts a person, nor can He be tempted. If we are tempted, it is by the evil one. There is a great difference between temptation and tests; God tests us but He never tempts us. Tests come from God; temptations come from the enemy. The purpose of temptation is to draw out the lusts of the flesh within us that we may sin, whereas the purpose of testing is to bring out what God has already deposited in us so that it may be purified and strengthened. Hence, there is a great difference between testing and temptation. God never tempts any person; He tests us. The enemy, the evil one, tempts us and tries to draw out the lusts of the flesh within us; and when he succeeds, we sin.

God has not promised that we will not be tempted, but God does promise that His grace is sufficient for us. Let us not think that we who believe in the Lord Jesus will not be tempted. Even the Lord Jesus, when He was a man on earth, was tempted in all things but without sin in order that He may be a sympathetic, merciful High Priest for us, to succor us and to give us grace for seasonable help. Temptation is inevitable. We will be tempted. The enemy will use the world to tempt us; the enemy will use pleasure to tempt us; he will use all kinds of things or events or people to tempt us; but that does not mean that we have to yield to temptation. If we yield to it, then we sin; but if we are tempted and endure the temptation, we will be strengthened and perfected.

"Blessed is the man who endures temptation" (James 1:12). What does that word *endure* mean? It means that if temptation comes to you in a strength of ten pounds, then you endure eleven pounds. Or if a temptation comes for ten days, you are able to endure it through eleven days. You overcome it; you do not yield to it. And if you endure temptation, the result is character. Christ's character will be built up within you, and you will be perfected and completed. Accordingly, temptation can either weaken you or strengthen you. If you try to meet temptation on your own you will be weakened, but if you meet temptation in Christ—that is to say, by His life and through His grace—then you can endure and you will receive the crown of life. Your spiritual life will increase. That is temptation.

Do you profess faith in Christ Jesus? If you profess faith in Him, then why is it that when temptation comes to you, you try to meet it on your own as though you are a person without faith? If your faith is real, then you meet temptation in Christ with Christ; and when you meet temptation with Christ, temptation will cease. This is the faith which works; this is living faith.

I must here tell the story of a little girl who believed in the Lord Jesus. She was so joyful in the Lord that one day a man tried to tempt her by saying: "Well, little girl, you believe in the Lord; and are you happy in the Lord?"

"Yes, I am happy in the Lord."

"All right," he said, "suppose Satan comes to your door and knocks. He wants to come in. You are just a little girl, what do you do?"

"Oh," the little girl said, "when Satan knocks at the door and wants to come in, I turn to the Lord and say, 'Lord, will You please open the door?' The Lord opens the door and when Satan sees the Lord, he says, 'Excuse me, I knocked at the wrong door.'"

That is the faith which works. This is living faith. How do you live? Do you live by faith? If you live by faith, then you have to prove it by works, so that you will not yield to temptation but will endure it.

Pure Religion

The only place this phrase *pure religion* is found in the Bible is here in James. We have a very negative feeling about the word religion, and no doubt James had the same feeling. The word *religion* in Greek really has reference to "the external aspects of religion—the ceremonies, the rituals;" it refers to all the things which are considered to be a part of religion: a creed, the outward form of piety, a listening to something religious—

but when you go out you forget all about it. When you hear the word *religion* it is like going before a mirror: you see your face in a mirror, but when you leave, you forget everything you have seen. That is religion. But James tried to compare religion with pure religion, which is something different. Pure religion is a living faith which works. You look at the mirror; you fix your gaze upon Christ; you abide in Him; you are being transformed by Him; He begins to live His life out in your life. It is not just a matter of hearing but doing the word. You live by the law of love. That is pure religion.

The Tongue

James says, "The tongue is the smallest member of the body, and yet it can do great disaster; and who does not know it?" Man can tame everything in the world. If a person goes to the circus in a town (I have never been to one), he will find that men can tame anything. They can tame a lion, they can tame an elephant, they can do anything like that. My, it is something tremendous! But James says, "Who can tame one's tongue? If anyone can control his tongue then he is perfect." As a matter of fact, if we read the context carefully, we will notice that James begins his discussion on this matter of the tongue by warning those who would be teachers: "Do not be many teachers" (see James 3:1). We would all like to be teachers, and, of course, teachers use the tongue a lot. So James says, "Do not be many teachers because you cannot control your tongue."

The one thing about which the rich man suffered most in Hades had to do with his tongue. He called to Abraham, saying: "Send Lazarus to come and merely put a little water on my tongue." His tongue suffered the most because formerly as a rich man he could say anything he wanted to and nobody had dared to say otherwise. That is the privilege of the rich. Therefore, this one had sinned a lot with his tongue.

What about our tongues? If we cannot control our tongues,

our godliness is false. One of the biggest problems in the world is the tongue, and one of the biggest problems in the church is likewise the tongue. A tongue can hurt more than a sword. But, thank God, there is a way of victory over our tongues. *We* cannot control our tongues, but He can. God is able to set a watch over our mouths so that whatever comes from our tongue may glorify Him. It will not be springs of bitter and sweet water at the same time (see James 3:11). Practical Christian living is to glorify God with our tongues; and that is faith. Without faith it cannot be done. It is only by believing and trusting in Him that He is able to control our tongues.

Wisdom

We need wisdom, and James says there are two kinds. There is the wisdom from beneath and the wisdom from above. The wisdom from beneath is full of jealousy, envying, party spirit, and divisions.

"But the wisdom from above is pure, then peaceful, gentle, yielding, full of mercy and good fruits, unquestioning, unfeigned" (James 3:17). He emphasizes especially the "meekness of wisdom" (James 3:13). I like that phrase, "meekness of wisdom." If you are worldly-wise, that kind of wisdom will become the pride of wisdom. But if you have the wisdom from above, it will be the meekness of wisdom in you, because if you are truly wise, you know you are but a fool: you dare not depend upon yourself but you will depend upon the Lord all the time. You dare not judge your brothers and sisters because you know you have a Judge who will judge you one day. Even if you intend to go to another place to do business or whatever, you dare not say, "I will go to the other place tomorrow; I will be there for one year, make good profit, and then return." On the contrary, if you have *real* wisdom, you will cultivate the quality of meekness. And thus you will sincerely say, "If the Lord wills, then I may go here, I may go there, or I may do certain things." You dare not depend upon yourself, but if you are truly wise, you will depend upon the Lord completely. That is the meekness of wisdom.

Provision for our Circumstances

James says in his letter: If you live in this world, you will find yourself in all kinds of circumstances. Sometimes you are happy, sometimes you are sorrowing, and sometimes you are sick. That is the way life is on this earth, so do not be surprised. But when you are in these various circumstances of life, how do you react? James wrote: "Does anyone among you suffer evil? Let him pray." If at times you find that everything is wrong, what do you do? Do you murmur? That will not help you. Instead, you should pray.

"Is any happy?" If you are very happy, what do you do? You should sing songs, thanking and praising the Lord, because happiness comes from Him. A person can far more easily fall spiritually in the midst of a happy, smooth, prosperous and favorable circumstance than a person who is in an adverse, hard and difficult circumstance. This is because when you are happy you become loose and careless. So pray and sing songs.

If we are sick, then we need to call the elders of the church, confess to one another, pray for one another, and the prayer of faith will raise us up. There is provision for any circumstance because it is Christ who lives in us; and if He lives in us, it is bound to work out. Faith without works is dead, yet the work in view here is not the work of the flesh; rather, it is the work of faith, and it is by such works that our faith is perfected.

Salvation of the Soul

"My brethren, if any one among you err from the truth, and one bring him back, let him know that he that brings back a sinner from the error of his way shall save a soul from death and shall cover a multitude of sins" (James 5:19-20).

This is addressed to believers. The one who errs from the truth is a believer. He may think that because it is all by grace he can do anything he likes, so he errs from the truth. The sinner here refers to the believer who falls into sin. If you bring such a one back from the error of his way, you shall save his soul from death and cover a multitude of sins. This is concerning the salvation of the soul. Today I shall not speak to you on that subject. God willing, in our discussion of I Peter we shall go into that matter.

Shall we pray:

Dear heavenly Father, we ask Thee that by Thy Holy Spirit thou wilt speak to our hearts, clarify and correct any misunderstanding, error, or wrong concept we may have. We pray that we may see we are not only justified by faith before Thee, but that we also need to be justified by works before the world. Lord, we pray that, as we have been recreated to do, thou wilt enable us to do Thy good will to the praise of Thy glory. We commit ourselves to Thee for the Spirit to work in us until Thy work is completed. In the name of our Lord Jesus. Amen.

I PETER

Seeing Christ as the Shepherd of our Souls

I Peter 1:3-12—Blessed be the God and Father of our Lord Jesus Christ, who, according to his great mercy, has begotten us again to a living hope through the resurrection of Jesus Christ from among the dead, to an incorruptible and undefiled and unfading inheritance, reserved in the heavens for you, who are kept guarded by the power of God through faith for salvation ready to be revealed in the last time. Wherein ye exult, for a little while at present, if needed, put to grief by various trials, that the proving of your faith, much more precious than of gold which perishes, though it be proved by fire, be found to praise and glory and honour in the revelation of Jesus Christ: whom, having not seen, ye love; on whom though not now looking, but believing, ye exult with joy unspeakable and filled with the glory, receiving the end of your faith, the salvation of your souls. Concerning which salvation prophets, who have prophesied of the grace towards you, sought out and searched out; searching what, or what manner of time, the Spirit of Christ which was in them pointed out, testifying before of the sufferings which belonged to Christ, and the glories after these. To whom it was revealed, that not to themselves but to you they ministered those things, which have now been announced to you by those who have declared to you the glad tidings by the Holy Spirit, sent from heaven, which angels desire to look into.

I Peter 5:10-11—But the God of all grace who has called you to his eternal glory in Christ Jesus, when ye have suffered for a little while, himself shall make perfect, stablish, strengthen, ground: to him be the glory and the might for the ages of the ages. Amen.

Shall we pray:

Dear heavenly Father, we do thank Thee for giving us the privilege of gathering together to remember Thy Beloved Son who died for us, who shed His blood for us, and gave His life to us. Our Father, we do appreciate what Thou hast done in giving, not sparing even Thy only begotten Son for us. And now Father, we gather again to thank and praise Thee for Thy word. We thank Thee for giving us Thy word and we do look to Thee to bless Thy word. Make it life and spirit to us that through the written word we truly may be partakers of the living Word. Father, we do commit this time into Thy hands. We acknowledge that without the revelation of the Holy Spirit we may touch the letter, but we will miss the spirit. So we just look to Thy Holy Spirit to reveal Thy Son in us through Thy word. We ask it in the name of our Lord Jesus. Amen.

The great reformer, Martin Luther, designates this first epistle of Peter as one of the most noble of all the writings in the New Testament because it exhibits such a wealth of thought: a dignity, a humility and love, a fervor, a believing hope, and a readiness for the coming of the Lord Jesus. It fits in very much with the individuality of the apostle Peter. I believe we know Peter better than any of the other disciples because he is such an open person. He exposes himself all the time. Even though he was disciplined more than any other of the twelve, we do thank God that He has committed so very much to this Peter.

Even though we know this man quite well, I wonder how much we know of his letters? Most likely Peter wrote I and II Peter in his later years, around 64 to 68 A.D. The last mentioning of him in the book of Acts is in chapter 15. In that council in Jerusalem we heard Peter, but after that nothing is mentioned of him. We know through Galatians that after the great council in Jerusalem, Peter went to Antioch where he had an encounter with the apostle Paul. Apart from these, we do not find any record of the years afterward involving Peter until we have these two epistles. However, we know that he was a very active person, and thus he must have been preaching, visiting, and traveling, busily occupied with the affairs of His Master and Lord.

When Peter wrote this letter, he mentioned that he was writing it from Babylon. Now I do not see why some commentators have spiritualized Babylon here as Rome. At the beginning of this letter Peter addressed it to the sojourners in the Dispersion of Pontus, Galatia, Cappadocia, Asia, and Bithynia. *Now if these* five places are real places, then there is no reason why we should think that Peter did not write this letter from Babylon itself. I personally believe that because Peter traveled a great deal, he in fact wrote this letter from Babylon. He wrote it as fulfilling his ministry. You will recall that the Lord Jesus said to Peter: "And thou, when once thou hast been restored, confirm thy brethren" (Luke 22:32).

Again the Lord said to Peter, "Feed my lambs; shepherd my sheep; feed my sheep" (see John 21). So Peter is fulfilling that which Christ had committed to him. In writing these letters, he was simply trying to strengthen, confirm, feed and shepherd the flock of God.

Peter wrote this letter to the sojourners among the Dispersion. This word *Dispersion*, as mentioned earlier, is a very special term. It has been used to describe those Jews who ended up scattered throughout the world outside of Palestine. Peter, being an apostle to the circumcision, no doubt had great concern for the Jews, yet God did use him also to open the door of the gospel to the Gentiles; and as we know, the church is composed not only of Jews but also of Gentiles. Now when he wrote this letter, it was not really addressed to the Jews in the Dispersion in general but to those Jews in the Dispersion who were believers. They were strangers and sojourners in this world. And the letter's readers also included the Gentiles, because in it we find such phrases as: "Once you were not [a] people, but now you are His people; once you did not enjoy His mercy, but now you have His mercy" (see I Peter 2:10). We know these words can only be applied to the Gentiles; therefore, we believe this letter, even though it is mainly directed towards the Jewish believers among the Dispersion, includes all believers—those who are elected by the foreknowledge of God and sanctified by the Holy Spirit unto the obedience and sprinkling of the blood of the Lord Jesus (see I Peter 1:2).

We know that we have been elected according to the foreknowledge of God, and this is a wonderful thing. It is something which we cannot explain. It is beyond us, but we do thank God that we have been chosen and elected according to His foreknowledge. God knew us even before we were born. He knew us even before the foundation of the world. He has chosen us according to His foreknowledge, we are sanctified by the Holy Spirit, and we have been set apart for God by the Holy Spirit unto the sprinkling of the blood of Jesus Christ. His blood has been sprinkled upon our wicked conscience, purifying it unto the obedience of Jesus Christ. We are not only to be sprinkled by the blood, we are also to obey our Lord Jesus Christ (see again I Peter 1:2). We are people who are strangers and sojourners in the world. So we believe that this letter is not only to those in the first century, it can likewise apply to us, too.

If we want to understand this letter, we should reconstruct the historical condition of the Christians in the years 63 and 64 A.D. Paul was probably released from the Roman prison around 64 A.D. The great persecution which occurred in the time of Nero had not quite yet come, but it was approaching. During that period, after the release of Paul but before the great persecution under Nero, the Christians were actually being assaulted, attacked and persecuted by both Jews and Gentiles everywhere. It would appear as though such pressure upon the believers not only did not decrease, it actually increased. They were constantly under harassment and persecution with no letting up. How, then, would you help these Christians in such a situation? What would you say to them? How are you going to encourage them?

Peter said he was writing to exhort them and to testify to them—exhort by word and testify through experience. He was not only exhorting, encouraging and warning them by words, he was also bearing witness with his personal experience that what he had said was true. He was trying to tell them that this is the true grace of Jesus Christ in which they stand; that they were not to think it strange, or be discouraged, or believe that something was wrong with them because the pressure was increasing and not letting up. Peter wrote: No, you are all right; you are on the right track. In fact, this is what the brotherhood should expect. This is following in the footsteps of the Lord Jesus Christ, and all this was happening according to God's plan and all because of one reason: God loves you so much that He wants to purify, complete and perfect you so that you may inherit the glorious inheritance which He has prepared for you. This is what Peter was trying to say to them in this letter.

If this was the case in their day, do we think this letter has relevance to us today? We are living at the end times, and we do feel that the pressure upon us is increasing. God's people everywhere are experiencing trials of many kinds, and sometimes they may begin to wonder if there is something wrong with them. Does God have a word for us today? God does have a word for us today and the word is, "the salvation of the soul." What does He expect us to see? God wants us to see Christ as the Shepherd and Overseer of our souls.

Griffith Thomas, a great Bible teacher, has divided this letter into three sections, and I think that his division provides us with the simplest analysis of this letter. He has divided the whole letter into three parts by means of one word—beloved. We will find this word twice in this letter: once in chapter 2:11 and another time in chapter 4:12. He called the first part, from chapter 1:1 to chapter 2:10, privilege. He called the second part, from chapter 2:11 to chapter 4:11, duty. And he called the third part, from chapter 4:12 to the end, trials. I will follow this division, but I would like to change the words. I would like to call the first part—the call, the second part—the commitment, and the third part —the consummation.

The Call

Peter begins this letter with privilege or, to word it differently, the call. God has called us with a calling, but actually, this calling is a tremendous privilege which God has offered to us.

"Blessed be the God and Father of our Lord Jesus Christ, who, according to his great mercy, has begotten us again to a living hope through the resurrection of Jesus Christ from among the dead" (I Peter 1:3).

God, in His great mercy, has begotten us through the resurrection of the Lord Jesus. To be begotten of God is a tremendous mercy because mercy is something given undeserved. We are the undeserved people; and yet, God is willing to show mercy to us, not only giving us something, but even begetting us. We are born from above. God has washed us from all our sins and has given His very life to us. We are begotten into the family of God; we have His life in us; we are His children.

This new birth is a tremendous experience. Before that, we were dead in sins and transgressions; now, we are alive unto God. Before that, we were enemies of God; now, we are in the family of God. Before that, we were condemned; now, we are forgiven. Before that, we were under guilt; now, we are freed. Before that, we had no life; now, there is life in us, bringing into being a relationship with God. This new-birth experience is a tremendous mercy of God for those who have experienced it, and we cannot cease thanking God for that great mercy. But do we realize that to be begotten of God is just the beginning of God's mercy? To be saved, to be born again, is but the beginning of the grace of God that knows no ending. Unfortunately, there are many believers who take the new-birth experience as the experience, as though this were the end, that there is nothing more. In other words, after we are born again, what more can we expect but to die and go to heaven? Yet the apostle Peter said: "You are begotten to a living hope." To be begotten of God is not the end, it is the beginning of something more. We have been begotten to a living hope.

We often say that Paul is the apostle of faith, John is the apostle of love, and Peter, the apostle of hope. Here, Peter tells us that we are begotten to a living hope. Oh, we have hope. People who do not have God have no hope. It is appointed for man to die and after that, judgment. What hope is that? But we, who are begotten of God, are begotten to a living hope: "To an incorruptible and undefiled and unfading inheritance, reserved in the heavens for you" (I Peter 1:4).

There is an inheritance reserved in heaven for you, but this does not refer to your new birth. It is because you are born again that there is an inheritance reserved for you. In other words, if you are not born to a certain family, then you have no promise and no right to any inheritance from the family. The reason why you have a hope to inherit the family's inheritance one day is because you are a child of that family; you are born into that family. The same thing is true in the family of God. Unless you are born into the family of God, you have no hope to inherit. It is because you are born again that there is the hope of inheriting an inheritance, and this inheritance is termed incorruptible.

Everything upon this earth is corruptible and corrupted. Everything upon this earth is able to be defiled and is defiled. Everything upon this earth is able to fade away and is fading. But we have an inheritance reserved in heaven that is incorruptible. It has never been corrupted, nor can it *be* corrupted. It is not only undefiled, it cannot *be* defiled. It is not only unfading, it will never fade, because it is eternal. There is an inheritance, and we are called to be heirs of God and co-heirs with Christ. An heir is one who is to inherit.

We have a living hope. We are to inherit an incorruptible, undefiled, unfading inheritance reserved in heaven. We have, as it were, a reserved seat there, but because it is something reserved, it is in the future. Therefore, we need to be kept lest we lose our inheritance. So Peter said here: "Reserved in the heavens for you, who are kept guarded by the power of God" (I Peter 1:5a).

We are unable to keep ourselves and be undefiled and uncorrupted. We in ourselves cannot, but there is One who is able to keep us. The power of God is so great that He is able to keep us and guard us so that we may inherit our inheritance. But on our part we need to believe it: "Kept guarded by the power of God through faith" (I Peter 1:5b).

We need to have faith, but the faith in view here is not our believing in the saving grace of the Lord Jesus Christ. For you already have that. The faith here is our believing in the keeping power of God. We not only believe He can save us; we also believe He is able to keep us. That is the perseverance of the saints. He is able to keep us from falling and to present us wholly and blameless before Him in glory. God is able to do that, and we believe He is able to do that. We, who are the Lord's, who are saved, believe He is able to keep us "for salvation ready to be revealed in the last time" (I Peter 1:5c). The salvation mentioned here is not the initial salvation which we all know about; rather, it is something kept and reserved for us at the last time; that is to say, it is something in the future. We are begotten to a living hope and this living hope has to do with an inheritance which is incorruptible, undefiled and unfading. And this inheritance is reserved in heaven for those who are kept by the power of God through faith unto salvation. It is salvation, but it is not salvation of the past; it is salvation yet in the future. In the process of obtaining it, we have to go through many trials and sufferings, but it is only for a little while. And the reason for this process is that our faith may be tested and purified and become more precious than gold in order that we may be found in the revelation of Jesus Christ to praise and glory and honor.

An inheritance is reserved for you in heaven but, today, God is making you worthy of that inheritance. If the inheritance is incorruptible, then anything which is corruptible in you has to be cast out. If the inheritance is undefiled, then anything which is defiled in you has to be taken away. If the inheritance is unfading, then whatever is passing or transient in your life has to be eliminated. And how can these things be removed so that you may be fit—may be suitable—to inherit your inheritance? It is by trials and testings so that your faith may be more precious than gold.

"Receiving the end of your faith, the salvation of the soul" (I Peter 1:9). Now I know we are treading in an area which has been overlooked throughout the centuries in Christianity, especially in the Protestant churches. Salvation is a broad term, but oftentimes we limit salvation by equating it with being born again, with being regenerated, with being saved to go to heaven. But if we read the word of God carefully we will discern that salvation is a large word. It includes a great deal. Salvation reaches not only to our spirit but it reaches to our soul and to our body. When salvation touches our spirit we call it being born anew, experiencing new birth, a regeneration. When salvation touches our soul we call it transformation. And when salvation touches our body, the latter is transformed from a mortal into an immortal body. Human beings are created with a spirit, a soul, and a body. So when salvation comes to us, it not only comes to our spirit, it also reaches our soul and body so that our whole being may be perfected and sanctified (see I Thessalonians 5:23).

When God does any work He always does it from within—

from the center to the circumference. Therefore, when God saves us, it is first our human spirit. It is the spirit which has the capacity or the ability to communicate with God and to receive Him. That spirit was dead in sins and transgressions. "On the day that you eat the forbidden tree you shall surely die" (see Genesis 2). Adam and Eve ate the forbidden fruit, but they lived on for hundreds of years. What had died? The spirit in them. As soon as sin entered into a life, that human spirit which has the ability to communicate with God and the capacity to receive Him is now dead. There is no more communication between man and God, and there is no more possibility of a union of God and man.

But when salvation comes to us, the Holy Spirit quickens our dead spirit and makes it new. In John chapter 3 we are told that he that is born of the Spirit is spirit. The Lord Jesus is talking there about new birth. The first spirit mentioned there is the Holy Spirit: he that is born of the Holy Spirit is spirit. The second spirit mentioned is a reference to the human spirit. The Holy Spirit touches our dead spirit, raises it to life, revitalizes it and makes it a new spirit. Then the Holy Spirit comes and dwells in our new spirit. Immediately, the communication with God is reestablished there. The ability is restored and the capacity—the capability—to do so is now functioning. God comes to dwell in our spirit and witness with our spirit that we are children of God. That is the experience of salvation, of new birth, and when that happens it happens in our spirit.

It does not happen in our body. We are still in this mortal body which has not been made immortal yet. It does not even happen in our soul, because we find we still have the old way of thinking, with our own will, likes and dislikes, choices, and all such things. We are still ourselves. It does not happen in our body, nor in our soul, but in our spirit. We each know we are a child of God. But bear in mind that that is only the beginning of salvation.

After God has put His Spirit in our new spirit and has put

the life of Christ in us, the Holy Spirit dwells in us as the Spirit of life. It is the life of Jesus Christ in us, and this life in us is to be lived out. This eternal life that is given to us and that is now in our spirit is not there as though it lies in a safe deposit box, and that when we die the safe deposit box is opened and we use the premium to go to heaven. This life of Christ in us is to live in us and through us. Christ is not to be confined in our spirit; He is to come forth from our spirit in order to penetrate and occupy our soul and to use our body.

In Ephesians 3 Paul's prayer is that Christ may dwell in your heart by faith. Christ dwells in your spirit but He wants to dwell in your heart, too. He wants to displace and replace the occupant in your soul, and this occupant is your self. Self is the life of the soul; flesh is the works of the fallen soul. So Christ lives in your spirit, and thus you are a new creation; and now you are supposed to live a new life just like Christ's, because it is He who is to live and not you anymore. Unfortunately, your soul has been inhabited by self for so long that the self wants to continue to dwell there. The self does not want to give up his rights. In other words, even though you are born again, you are still under the tyranny of your self. Deep down in your spirit you know what you should do; yet your soul refuses to cooperate, and not only refuses to cooperate but even opposes the spirit. "This old Adam," as the Reformer, Philip Melanchthon, once said, "is too strong for young Melanchthon." This soul has to be saved. Self has to be displaced and replaced by Christ.

The soul is the seat of one's personality. Your soul represents or expresses yourself, which is your personality: "This is the way I think; this is the way I feel; this is the way I want." It represents you. But God said: "The goal and purpose of My salvation is to reach your soul so that all which is expressed from your soul will represent Me instead of you." The issue here is: not my will but God's will be done, not my mind but the mind of Christ, not my love and hate but the hate and love of God. How does this happen? You find that the self lives in your soul and will not give up, and that this is the reason why you have to go through some trials. Trials, pressure and sufferings are all measured out by God in your life for one reason, that your soul-life may decrease and the spirit-life of Christ may increase in you. Your soul is given to you by God. He is not going to destroy your soul; for were He to destroy your soul, you would no longer be there; your personality would cease to exist. No. God does not want you to be a soulless person; instead, He wants to save your soul.

The Commitment

Do we realize our soul needs to be saved? Do we realize that after we are born again, what troubles us most is our self? Our worst enemy is not Satan; our worst enemy is our very self. Romans 7 describes for us the conflict—the civil war—which rages within a person: "I know what is right and yet I do not have the power. What I want to do, I cannot; what I do not want to do, I do. O wretched man that I am, who can deliver me from this body of death? Thank God, through Jesus Christ." This is not a description of the experience of an unbeliever; this is the experience of a believer. A believer who is saved needs to be constantly saved, and will yet be saved.

When our Lord Jesus was on earth, He often said to the disciples: "If you want to come and follow Me, if you want to be My disciple, you must deny yourself, take up the cross, and follow Me. He who wants to save his life shall lose it; and he who is willing to lose his life for My sake shall save it to eternity" (see Luke 9:23-24). The word *life* here is the same Greek word as "soul." He who desires to save his life is he who desires to save his soul and he shall lose it, but he who is willing to lose his soul for the sake of the gospel shall save it to eternity. If you try to save your soul today, you will lose it. Such is obviously not the salvation of the soul. The salvation of the soul is that today you are willing to lose it; but then you will save it.

Emotions

What is meant by trying to save your soul today? The soul is where your personality is; it is you yourself. Your emotions express you. You love because you feel good, you hate because you feel hurt. It represents you. Oh, how we believers still cater to our emotions! Our emotions still represent our self. We love when we feel good. We hate when we are hurt. In short, our soul does not represent Christ, and it is because of this that the Lord Jesus said, "If you love your father and your mother and your wife and your children and your own life more than Me you cannot be My disciples" (see Luke 14:26). And in one or two other places where Jesus' words are quoted in the Gospels, He even said: "If you do not hate …" This statement of Jesus does not refer to the natural human love or the natural human hate. No, the Lord is explaining what you need to do to save your soul. In your emotional life you have to be willing to lose your soul: you love, yet not because of yourself; you hate, yet not because it hurts you; rather, you love because God's love constrains you and you hate because God's hatred constrains you. Love and hate are very strong emotions; yet they are morally neutral in and of themselves: if you love what should be loved, that is good, but if you love what you should hate, that love is wrong; or, if you hate what you should love, then again it is wrong. Love and hate are simply words; they are neutral. God loves sinners but He hates sin. In your emotional life you need to be saved. You need to be dealt with by the cross to such an extent that you will not react according to your own feeling, you instead will react according to how God feels, and so you can love the brethren. Otherwise, there is no way to love the brethren.

How can we love the brethren? What is brotherly love? It simply means that you love him because he is a brother, whether a male brother or a female brother. It is not because of what he or she is or because of what he or she does to you. It is not because he is lovely or unlovely, lovable or unlovable, or because he suits you or does not suit you. No; loving the brethren means you love every child of God notwithstanding anything. How can you possibly do that unless your emotional life has been dealt with? If it has not been dealt with, you will love only what you naturally love and will hate what you naturally hate. Then your soul is satisfied. But when you do something to satisfy the self in your soul, you shall lose it. You may gain your soul for awhile, but in the end you will lose it. On the other hand, if you are willing to have your emotional life purified through the cross, then you will deny yourself.

Deny Self

What is meant by denying yourself? Some people think that to deny is control; self-denial is self-control. No; self-control is, you are still in control. To deny yourself, simply means you do not know yourself. The best illustration, though it is not a totally accurate one, is Peter the disciple of Jesus. Peter denied the Lord three times. He said, "I do not know Him." Now if Peter had denied himself, he would have said to himself, "Peter, who are you? I do not know you." But he denied the wrong person; he denied Christ.

Oftentimes, we make the same mistake. We ought to deny ourselves. When our emotional life comes forth, we should say this: "Now, who are you? I do not know you. I have no reason to gratify you. I have no reason to yield to you. I do not know you at all." When we deny self, then the Lord Jesus says, "Take up the cross and follow Me." Denying self is a matter of the will; taking up the cross is a daily experience. All which God requires us to do is to be willing to deny self. If we are willing to do that, then the Holy Spirit will arrange our circumstances to give us crosses to take up and bear. Let us not try to create our crosses. Let us also not try to create crosses for our brothers and sisters. They have enough! There are too many people in the world who are manufacturing crosses—either for themselves or for others; let the Holy Spirit manufacture the crosses. However, it is on one condition, that we must deny self. May I boldly say that if we do not deny self, we have no cross to bear. Why? Because if there is a cross in front of us, we will by-pass it. I think a road by-pass is a wonderful thing because we are able to by-pass all the traffic. Unfortunately, too many Christians are on the by-pass.

The Mind to Suffer

"Christ, then, having suffered for us in the flesh, do ye also arm yourselves with the same mind" (I Peter 4:1).

It is very true that to deny self involves suffering. Who of us wants to deny self so that we may suffer? No one naturally will want to do that. Therefore, we must have the mind to suffer; we must be willing. If we are willing, then the Holy Spirit will arrange the crosses for us to bear, and the grace of God will be given to us to bear these crosses.

Sometimes you may hate a person. Do not think that Christians do not hate. I am afraid Christians are not completely delivered from hatred. Suppose you hate a person, perhaps with reason or the reason is yourself. (We always have a reason.) Then the Spirit of God begins to point this hatred of yours out to you. What will you do? Are you willing to go to the Lord and confess that it is beyond you not to hate? If it is His will for you to love (and it certainly is), then ask God to take away that hatred from you and fill your heart with love so that you may love that person instead of you hating him. When you do that, in reality, you are giving up something of your right because heretofore you believed you had the right to hate. If you are willing to be dealt with in that way, then instead of your heart becoming narrower and narrower, more bitter and more bitter, and totally consuming you, your heart will be enlarged. You at that moment have entered the process of saving your soul.

Indeed, the salvation of the soul has come upon you.

Suppose you love a person and the Spirit of God begins to point His finger at you and He says, "This love is not right. This is not who you should be loving." You struggle before the Lord but you nonetheless continue to love that person. Are you willing to deny the self and say, "Lord, if this is who I should not love, then give me grace to give up that person for You"? By doing so, do you think you will lose your soul? Yes, but you gain your soul because the love of God now fills your heart. Our emotional life needs to be purified in order that our soul may be saved.

Intellect

The same thing is true with our mental life—our psychological, intellectual life. There are many strongholds the enemy has raised up in our minds. These strongholds are standing there opposing God in order that the light of God and the word of God cannot penetrate. Paul said, "All these strongholds have to be torn down and be led into captivity to the obedience of Christ" (see II Corinthians 10:5). Among believers there are so many mental blocks and so many thoughts and prejudices which much of the truth of God simply cannot penetrate. These are the strongholds of the enemy, the reasonings of man. The Lord once said to Peter: "You mind the things of the world, not the things of God." Peter thought he was minding the things of God because he had told the Lord Jesus, "Take care of yourself; do not go to the cross." He thought he was being good and caring. But the Lord said in response, "That is a fleshly mind, not the mind of the Spirit." We need to have our mental and intellectual life purified.

Volitional Life

We are all strong-willed persons. Some are stronger than others in this regard; nevertheless, we are all strong. Sometimes we hear people say, "God only uses strong-willed persons." Is that true? If we are persons whose wills are weak, what can God do with us? But let me say one thing here: a person can be strong-willed in everything else, but when it comes to the will of God, no person's will is strong. Our wills must therefore be purified. Sometimes, God has to bring us to a point when we have to make a choice: "Not my will, but Thy will be done." It hurts not to have our will prevail in a given moment of choice. Nevertheless, the salvation of the soul at that very moment has come upon us.

Shepherd and Overseer of our Souls

The letter of I Peter is telling us that there is a process of salvation going on today. It is the salvation of our souls, and it is to this we need to commit ourselves. We need to return to the Shepherd and Overseer of our souls, Christ Jesus. Christ is our Shepherd. We all love Psalm 23, but do we know that this psalm has a condition attached to it? This psalm opens with: "The Lord is my shepherd." But for someone to say, "The Lord is my shepherd," signifies that I, as a sheep, am committed to Him to let Him lead me. Do we know the Lord as the Shepherd of our souls? He is the Savior of our spirit, but He is also the Shepherd of our souls.

You need to commit yourself to Him, give yourself to Him, so that He can lead you. He will lead you to green pastures. He will let you lie down by still waters. He will restore your soul, and sometimes He will lead you through the valley of the shadow of death. His rod and His staff, they comfort you. And the word *comfort* here means more than simply patting you on the back and saying, "It is ok;" such comfort simply strengthens your soul-life. Do realize that the Lord is our Overseer. He is the Supervisor of your soul. Do you daily commit your soul to Him and let Him supervise it? Or are you still taking care of your soul? If you are still attempting to do that, you will lose your soul; but if you commit your soul to Him, He will supervise it, He will see to it in every way, and take good care of it.

Consummation

The consummation of the whole matter is this: Christ suffered, and then He entered into glory. Therefore, for a little while we, too, shall suffer, but the grace of God will strengthen us, ground us, and establish us so that we, too, may enter into eternal glory. The salvation of the soul is going on today. Our souls are undergoing transformation from glory to glory until one day we are conformed to the image of Christ. He will lead many sons into glory, and there we will inherit the kingdom with Him. That is the consummation. And let us continually remember this one thing which Peter wrote in his letter: "This is the true grace of God in which you stand." There is nothing wrong in your decision to follow the Lord; we are on the right course; let us keep on going, trusting His grace. Yes, His grace has given us all these trials; and yet His grace is sufficient for our every need.

Shall we pray:

Dear heavenly Father, we do thank Thee because thou dost always have a word for us. We do pray that Thy word may register in us and will thus be like a seed which has sprouted and is growing up until it bears fruit unto the praise of Thy glory. We ask in Thy precious name. Amen.

II PETER

Seeing Christ in His Everlasting Kingdom

II Peter 1:1-11—Simon Peter, bondman and apostle of Jesus Christ, to them that have received like precious faith with us through the righteousness of our God and Saviour Jesus Christ: Grace and peace be multiplied to you in the knowledge of God and of Jesus our Lord. As his divine power has given to us all things which relate to life and godliness, through the knowledge of him that has called us by glory and virtue, through which he has given to us the greatest and precious promises, that through these ye may become partakers of the divine nature, having escaped the corruption that is in the world through lust.

But for this very reason also, using therewith all diligence, in your faith have also virtue, in virtue knowledge, in knowledge temperance, in temperance endurance, in endurance godliness, in godliness brotherly love, in brotherly love love: for these things existing and abounding in you make you to be neither idle nor unfruitful as regards the knowledge of our Lord Jesus Christ; for he with whom these things are not present is blind, short-sighted, and has forgotten the purging of his former sins. Wherefore the rather, brethren, use diligence to make your calling and election sure, for doing these things ye will never fall; for thus shall the entrance into the everlasting kingdom of our Lord and Saviour Jesus Christ be richly furnished unto you.

II Peter 3:17-18—Ye therefore, beloved, knowing these things before, take care lest, being led away along with the error of the wicked, ye should fall from your own stedfastness: but grow in grace, and in the knowledge of our Lord and Saviour Jesus Christ. To him be glory both now and to the day of eternity. Amen.

Shall we pray:

Dear heavenly Father, as we continue in Thy presence, we do ask Thee to shine Thy light upon our hearts that we may not only hear Thy word but we may hear Thy voice and see the glory of the Lord in the face of Jesus Christ. We commit this time into Thy hands and ask Thee to bless it. In the name of our Lord Jesus. Amen.

As II Timothy is the last will and testimony of the apostle Paul, so II Peter is the last will and testimony of the apostle Peter. Peter loved the Lord, and he was willing to give up his life for Him. Unfortunately, he did not know himself, and because of this he failed. He denied the Lord three times, but through his failure his love towards the Lord was actually purified. Therefore, after the Lord was risen from the dead, He appeared to Peter by the Sea of Tiberias. The Lord told him that when he was young he girded himself and went wherever he desired, but when he would be old he would stretch out his hand and another would gird him and lead him to the place he did not desire. In saying that, the Lord signified by what death Peter would die.

After the ascension of the Lord Jesus the apostle Peter, being a very active person, had been busily engaged in the Master's business until he reached an old age. It is commonly acknowledged that Peter was older in age than the Lord Jesus Christ, and possibly, he was the oldest among the twelve apostles. If this is so, then by the time he wrote this second letter, he must have been in his seventies or possibly early eighties. He served the Lord many long years and this, itself, was a miracle, a wonder, because Peter was such an impetuous and changeable person. Yet, he was kept by the Lord through all those years until his advanced age. He became almost like an unmovable stone. That is the grace of God. That shows the keeping power of the Lord.

It does not say here to whom he wrote this letter, but as we read it, we come across this statement: "I have [now] already written two letters" (see II Peter 3:1). In other words, he had written a previous letter and here is the second one. So we believe this second letter is addressed to the same people to whom he had written in his first letter. He was writing again to the sojourners of the Dispersion in Pontus, Galatia, Cappadocia, the province of Asia, and Bithynia. Even though the word dispersion was especially used for the Jews who were dispersed outside their Palestinian homeland, Peter—as was the case in his first letter—was not writing to the Jews in the Dispersion in general; he was again writing to those Jews scattered among the Dispersion who had become Christians. They were strangers and sojourners upon this earth, and he not only was writing to the Jewish believers but he also mentioned in this letter the Gentile believers; for the church is composed of both Jews and Gentiles. So we believe this second letter is addressed to the same people as previously; and that being so, we believe it is addressed to us also.

Peter wrote this letter because he knew the day of his departure from this life was approaching as the Lord had predicted, and he wanted to write a letter before he took his leave. In this second letter of Peter's there are at least three instances wherein he mentions why he wrote this epistle. He wrote it for one purpose only: to stir up their pure mind that they might remember what the holy prophets had said and what was the commandment which the Lord Jesus had said by His apostles (see II Peter 3:1-2). It is a letter written to bring to their remembrance that which the people had already heard. It was not something they had never heard before or something they had never known. They had known these things and had heard these things and were established in the truth; nevertheless, Peter felt it was his responsibility to remind them, to stir up their pure mind so that they would not forget.

Now if a person is probably going to be taking his leave

forever, and if this will be his very last message, he cannot afford to say or write something trivial; he will not engage in small talk. He cannot do that. He has to pour out what is uppermost, deepest, dearest and closest to his heart and share it with those whom he loves. We will recall that before the Lord Jesus was to leave His disciples and go to the cross to die, His last words to them were important words, words which were uppermost in His heart (see John 14—16). The same thing was true when Paul wrote II Timothy. So when Peter was trying to convey to those whom he loved his last departing thoughts, it must have been something very precious and very dear to him.

Purpose of this Letter

What were the things which Peter had tried to share in this second letter with those whom he loved? What was uppermost in the heart of Peter—not only at this time, but throughout the years in which he had followed and served the Lord—was the everlasting kingdom of his Lord and Savior, Jesus Christ. When He was upon the earth, He had spoken a great deal about the kingdom. We would like to have heard Him talk about heaven; yet strangely, when our Lord was on earth, He talked much more about the kingdom. At the very beginning of Jesus' ministry His message had been: "Repent for the kingdom of the heavens has drawn nigh" (Matthew 4:17). There on that mountain He had instructed His disciples about the kingdom. And when He came down from the mountain, He had demonstrated the power of God's kingdom by casting out demons and healing the sick. Jesus had told the disciples that from John the Baptist until now the kingdom of the heavens was to be seized by violence, and the violent seize upon it (see Matthew 11:12). This did not mean doing violence to other people; it simply meant that you will do violence to yourself, to deny yourself so that you might gain the kingdom. And in Matthew 13 we find recorded Jesus' parables concerning the mysteries of the kingdom of the heavens.

Jesus had been born to be King and that was His testimony before Pilate (see Matthew 27:11). He died as the King of the Jews. And after He was resurrected, for forty days He talked to the disciples about the kingdom of God (see Acts 1:3). So we see that the kingdom was something very much on the heart of the Lord Jesus. Therefore, when the apostle Peter, who had followed the Lord for three years and had heard much from Him about the kingdom, began to work for the Lord, the kingdom became something very dear and very close to him, too.

Preview of the Kingdom

The Lord had said, "My kingdom is not of this world" (John 18:36). It is a different kingdom, but it is a kingdom which the Lord Jesus is to establish upon the earth. He is gathering a people to that kingdom to make them sons of the kingdom, that one day these sons of the kingdom may inherit the kingdom with Him. To the apostle Peter the kingdom was a reality. It was ever before his eyes; it was always in his mind. This was something he had labored for; and he said about this kingdom in this last letter of his that he had not been duped into following a cleverly imagined scheme, but declared that he had been an eyewitness to that kingdom (see II Peter 1:16).

In Matthew 16 we learn that the Lord Jesus had told His disciples one day that some of them would not die before they saw the Son of Man coming in His kingdom. Immediately afterwards, as related in chapter 17, the Lord Jesus took with Him three of His disciples, Peter, James and John, up a mountain where He was transfigured. His face shone like the sun and His clothes were so very bright and white. Moses and Elijah appeared, and they even talked with the Lord Jesus concerning His exit from the earth: "How would He leave the world?" But these three disciples had gone to sleep. Probably, the glory was so great they could not stay awake. Suddenly,

Peter woke up and saw that Moses and Elijah were leaving, so he cried out: "Lord, it is so good to be here. Let us stay here forever. I will make three tabernacles, one for You, one for Moses and one for Elijah, and we will just sleep here in the open, but that is good enough." While he was still speaking, the heavenly Father intervened and stopped him and declared: "This is my beloved Son, in whom I have found my delight: hear him" (Matthew 17:5). And a bright cloud, the Shekinah glory of God, immediately covered everything; and when they opened their eyes they saw no one but Jesus only.

Now Peter was an eyewitness of this scene, which was a preview of the kingdom of God that is coming upon the earth. Peter had a foretaste of it, and for him it was so good and sweet. He could never forget it. Therefore, when he wrote this last letter as his last will and testimony, he mentioned and described this event in the following terms: "I witnessed the kingdom because I was there; I saw it. I beheld the Lord's majesty; I saw when Christ received honor and glory from the Father, and I heard a heavenly voice: 'This is my beloved Son: hear Him.' This is the kingdom. I was an eyewitness to it" (see II Peter 1:17).

We read in Scripture: "Thy kingdom come." One day, God's kingdom will be established upon this earth, but what is this kingdom? What is the kingdom of God? What is the kingdom of the heavens? The time of this kingdom is when the Lord Jesus shall receive honor and glory from the heavenly Father, and when the Lord Jesus will be the center of everything. We shall see no one but Jesus only. It is when we shall hear the voice from heaven: "This is my Son: hear Him." In a word, Christ himself is the kingdom.

In this letter Peter indicated that it was more than simply his personal testimony because there were also available many prophetic words about this matter (see II Peter 1:19). In God's word we find that both the Old Testament prophets and the New Testament prophets were all speaking about this same thing. Wrote Peter: "These prophetic words are like a lamp that shines into the obscure place until the day shall break and the morning star shall rise in our hearts" (see again II Peter 1:19). The world is dark, and we cannot see anything in darkness; but we are now approaching the darkest of the night. Everything is dark and obscure, but thank God, even though we live in a deeply darkened world, we have a lamp. The prophetic words of God are like a lamp that shines upon our path so that we are not in the dark. We know where we are going, and as we take heed of the prophetic words, something happens—the day begins to dawn in our hearts. Even though all around us it is still midnight, in our hearts the day has already dawned and the morning star has already risen. Please note that the morning star can only be seen by those who wake up early. If we are late sleepers we will never see the morning star because after the sun rises we cannot see it. But the morning star is there to behold before the sun arises, and it is a beautiful sight.

One day, the Lord Jesus will come upon this earth as the Sun of Righteousness (see Malachi 4:2). One day the Sun of Righteousness shall arise and the whole world will see Him, but before that happens He will appear in your heart as the morning star if you are awake. If you are waiting for Him, if you take heed to the prophetic words, then even though the Sun of Righteousness has not yet come, He has nonetheless already arisen in your heart as the morning star. How blessed it is for those who have seen the morning star in their hearts.

The kingdom of God is coming. It shall be established upon this earth. It is an assured fact, but among God's people there are many who do not even know about the kingdom; they only think of heaven: "One day when we die, we will go to heaven." Yes, you will go to heaven, but not that quickly because if you read the word of God carefully, you will find that if you are the Lord's and you die, you do not go to heaven right away; you go to Paradise. There you wait until you are resurrected, and then one day you will go to heaven. But unfortunately, many of God's people know only about heaven; they do not know concerning the kingdom. They do not know that before heaven shall be their eternal home there will be the kingdom coming upon this earth for a thousand years. That will be the time when those who are ready and waiting, those prepared ones who are following the Lord, those who are seizing the kingdom by violence, shall reign with Christ for a thousand years. There is not only heaven but also a kingdom for God's people. Heaven is a gift, but the kingdom is a reward. They are not only born again to inherit eternal life, but being born again, they are to enter abundantly into the everlasting kingdom of the Lord Jesus.

How to Obtain the Kingdom

However, there is a problem with people who know about the kingdom. There is a fear: "How can I obtain the kingdom?" The kingdom is of such glory and majesty, how can I possibly obtain it? Probably, it is so difficult to obtain that I will have to give up the idea; but the Lord Jesus has said, "Fear not, little flock, for it has been the good pleasure of your Father to give you the kingdom" (Luke 12:32).

Fear not. Why do we fear? "Fear not, little flock." This is the only time this term "little flock" is used in the Scriptures and it refers to the church. So far as the church, in comparison with the world, is concerned, it is but a little flock. The world consists of multitudes upon multitudes, but the church by comparison is nothing more than a little flock. Yet the Lord has promised: "Fear not, little flock, it is the good pleasure of your Father to give you the kingdom." Our heavenly Father delights—nay, He loves—to give you the kingdom. It is true that this kingdom of the heavens, which is far, far better than the kingdom of this world, has such a higher standard, and God will not in the least lower that standard by compromising. The standard is indeed high for people to inherit and enter that kingdom; nevertheless, the Lord has said, "Fear not, fear not." In other words, the way is not so difficult that you cannot obtain the kingdom. On the contrary, it is so majestic and so glorious that you should have it. But how? Well, God has made every provision for you by which to obtain it. If He had not made provision, then most certainly no one would be able to obtain the kingdom because the way is just too difficult for us. But if God has in fact *made* provision for everyone of his children to obtain the kingdom, and yet you and I do not enter the kingdom to obtain and inherit it, it is our own fault.

Calling of God

"As his divine power has given to us all things which relate to life and godliness, through the knowledge of him that has called us by glory and virtue, through which He has given to us the greatest and precious promises, that through these ye may become partakers of the divine nature" (II Peter 1:3-4).

God has called us by glory and virtue. We are all called by Him, but our problem is that we think of our calling in terms of our own need. I need to have my sins forgiven, so I consider that God has called me to come and have my sins forgiven. Thank God for that. My need is to go to heaven; therefore, I consider that God has called me in order to give me eternal life as a passport with which to gain entrance into heaven. We consider our calling according to our needs, and because of this, our calling descends into being a low calling. But let us be mindful that God has called us by His tremendous glory and virtue. He does not call us according to a need, He calls us according to what He is. He calls us according to His glory. In the Scriptures glory is something indescribable, yet it is synonymous with God himself. He calls us according to His glory; He calls us according to His virtue—that is to say, His very character. He has called us according to His very self so that we may be like Him. Therefore, it is an on-high calling, not a small, low-level calling. God calls us to be like Him, to take upon ourselves His virtues, His character. He calls us to enter His glory. He calls us into His kingdom to be heirs and co-heirs with Christ, to inherit the everlasting kingdom of our God and Savior, Jesus Christ. Now that is our calling, it is no small thing.

Promises and Power of God

However, God has not only called us, He has also given us the greatest and most precious promises. He has promised us, and with these promises we can become partakers of His divine nature. Let us contemplate all the greatest and precious promises of God and we will see that all these promises are for one purpose, to make us partakers of His divine nature: "His divine power has given to us all things relating to life and godliness." By His divine power He has given us life, the life of His only begotten Son; and with this life, there is all the power for godliness—that is, to be like God, to take up the character of Christ, to be conformed to the image of Christ.

Here in this passage from II Peter we see all the provisions: the calling, the promises, the divine power. God has not called us and has then said, "Now I have called you, you work it out." Not at all, for who in himself can do it? Yes, God has called us with an on-high calling; but then He gives us promises to lay hold of by faith; and then His divine power is made available to enable us to enter into all which He has promised. Everything which we need for the kingdom has been provided for us.

Our Responsibility

Do we realize this? Do we realize that God has made every provision for you and me to enter the kingdom abundantly? And if He has made all these provisions, then it is our responsibility to lay hold of these greatest and precious promises by faith and to avail ourselves of all the divine power that is there with which to work out our full salvation. Therefore, we have a responsibility, and our responsibility is that we be diligent. The kingdom of God is not for the lazy; it is for the diligent.

If we are lazy, we shall remain as babes in Christ, and as babes in Christ we cannot inherit the kingdom because there is no suitability in us that is correspondent with the kingdom. To inherit the kingdom, we have to be part of the kingdom. The very character of the kingdom must characterize our life; therefore, it is not for babes in Christ. It is for the grown-ups in Christ; and in order to grow up in Christ, we have to be diligent.

"But for this very reason also, using therewith all diligence" (II Peter 1:5). We cannot afford to simply sit back, lie down, and wait to be carried to heaven. We have to apply ourselves.

The Octave of Spiritual Growth

"In your faith have also [or, add to it] virtue, in virtue knowledge, in knowledge temperance, in temperance endurance, in endurance godliness, in godliness brotherly love, in brotherly love love" (II Peter 1:6-7).

That is the octave of spiritual growth: taking us from faith to love. You begin with faith—faith in the Lord Jesus, and then you add to it. The words *add to it* simply mean "supplying cost for any purpose," "affording more than that which is barely demanded." You have faith; you believe in the Lord Jesus; but you need to add to it or place alongside it, virtue or character. This is the same thing which James talked about: "You have faith. All right, show me your faith and I will demonstrate my faith by works." In other words, if you really have faith, then it is not a vague thing or simply a good idea. Faith is concrete in its outworking, and thus it will produce works: faith will create virtue or character.

With virtue comes knowledge. That is, there is added to you discernment or understanding. And with understanding comes temperance or self-control. Actually, it is spirit-control; and with spirit-control there is added endurance; and with endurance comes godliness—to be like God in His character.

Add to that, brotherly love. You love the brethren, not because this one is lovely or that one is ugly, but you simply love them because they are brethren of yours in the Lord. Finally, it is not only the case of loving the brethren, but loving all.

So we see that in order to enter the kingdom, God has provided every means for us to do so; and thus, we need to make use of every promise and His divine power, and with diligence apply ourselves so that the character of Christ can be built up within us. And as the character of Christ is being built up in us, such work will make us suitable for the kingdom of God. Then, when we inherit the kingdom, we will not feel strange because the kingdom character is already in us. If the kingdom character is not in you and me, and even if we were somehow put into the kingdom, we would be like fish out of water. We would not feel comfortable in the least because we would not be fit.

I remember a story: Once there was an excursion event, and two boats left the port at the same time. One of these boats was for Christians, and all the believers were singing and worshiping the Lord and sharing with one another. The other was a pleasure boat for the worldly people, with all kinds of worldly music and other pleasures. Unfortunately, one Christian had gotten on the pleasure boat, and so he discovered, "This is not it; this is the wrong boat for me!"

The moral of this story is correct and most apt. If you get on the wrong boat—if you find yourself in the wrong environment—you will not feel comfortable. That is the reason why, in order to inherit the kingdom of the heavens you must have the kingdom character built in you. How can it be built up in you? On your part it will require diligence, pure and simple. Diligently lay hold of the promises of God and allow His divine power to work them out. It is He who works in you. It is still grace but it is grace which needs to be diligently received and diligently obeyed. Diligently cooperate, and that is all which He requires of you. If you do that, then you will be neither useless nor unfruitful as regards "the knowledge of the Lord Jesus Christ" (see II Peter 1:8).

Full Knowledge of God

The word *knowledge* here in the Greek original is *epignosis*, a true or full knowledge, a personal recognition. And thus a full knowledge of God is to know His calling, to know His promises, to know His divine power; and if you do that, then you will not be idle or useless, and you will not be unfruitful. If you do not have these things, then you are blind, shortsighted and have forgotten the purging from your former sins (see II Peter 1:9). We thank God that He has purged us from our sins, but after our sins have been purged and we are saved, if we do not use diligence and press on from faith to love, then we are blind and shortsighted. Today, there are many believers who are spiritually shortsighted. The Lord has said, "Buy eye salve from Me so that you may be able to see" (see Revelation 3:18). Perhaps the modern idiom would be to buy a pair of glasses so you may be able to see.

If we have these things, then, writes Peter: "Wherefore the rather, brethren, use diligence to make your calling and election sure" (II Peter 1:10).

The calling is sure, the election is certain, but whether we are chosen is a matter which we must make sure. The Lord Jesus said, "Many are called but few are chosen" (Matthew 22:14). We are all called because it is the good pleasure of the Father to give us the kingdom. We are called, we are elected, but whether we will be chosen depends on our diligence to make our calling and election sure, "for in doing these things you will never fall" (II Peter 1:10). Again I say that this does not refer to eternal salvation, it does not refer to the gift of eternal life, it does not refer to our going to heaven. Thank God, that gift has been given to us, and once given it is never taken back, because God is faithful. But all of these things of which Peter writes here are concerned with the everlasting kingdom.

"For thus shall the entrance into the everlasting kingdom of our Lord and Saviour Jesus Christ be richly furnished unto you" (II Peter 1:11).

The Lord is coming and He is going to establish His kingdom upon this earth. However, when that time comes, whether you are able to inherit the kingdom with Him, whether you are to reign with Him, whether you are to be a co-heir of Christ at that time, is something which you have to decide. It is given, but whether you will take it or not is up to you.

May I illustrate this by citing again the Lord's preview of His kingdom? Of the twelve disciples, He only took three with Him up the mountain. In other words, only three of the disciples were able to see the kingdom. The other nine were left down below on the plain. Does this picture not give us a kind of hint? May I say the following? It may sound harsh, but it is the truth. We are all believers, we are all disciples; and thank God, because we are all believers and disciples, one day we will all go to heaven. The gift of God knows no repentance, but this does not mean that because we are believers and disciples we will all enter the kingdom and reign with Christ. The Lord Jesus said: "Many will come to me and say, Lord, Lord, in your name I cast out demons; in your name I did this and that." And the Lord will say: "I do not know you because you do not do the will of the Father" (see Matthew 7:21-23). Let this be a warning: let us not think that because we are believers that therefore the kingdom is ours. Yes, it is given to us, but whether we are qualified to inherit it is up to us. It is the good pleasure of the Father to give us the kingdom, and He wants us to enter it abundantly. He has made every provision for us to do so, but if we do not, it is our own fault.

The Heresy of False Teachers

Peter has the kingdom before him all the time, but as he is writing about the kingdom, immediately he senses the wiles of the enemy. The enemy of mankind, Satan, the devil, does not want us to gain the kingdom. He will attempt by every means to deceive and distract us to keep us out of God's kingdom. So in chapter 2 Peter began to speak about false teachers. "As there were false prophets in the old days with the children of Israel, so now there shall be false teachers with you. False teachers will come in and teach destructive heresies" (see v.1). Now what exactly is meant by heresy? This word is used today so freely that we do not really understand what it means; but actually, in the Greek original, it means "school of opinion." That is the reason why the word *sect* in Scripture in Greek is "heresy." In other words, instead of submitting one's self to the inerrant word of God, a person begins to have his or her own opinions. We are all opinionated people, and unless we learn discipline we will hold on to such opinions. There will be false teachers who come forth teaching their opinions about the word of God. They do not submit themselves to God's word and instead, they take His word and give their opinion about it. Eventually, they will begin to deny the Master who has bought them (see again v.1).

The English word *master* here means in Greek, "despot." We do not like the word *despot* because it means "absolute monarch." In other words, the Lord Jesus, who has bought us with a price, is our absolute Monarch. He is our Sovereign, and we are to obey Him to the uttermost. This is what we ought to do, but instead of doing that, these false teachers denied Him and rejected Him as their absolute Sovereign because they wanted to have their own opinion. Because they denied the Master, it was destructive. These false teachers used cleverly construed words, double talk and high-flown words in an attempt to deceive people; for their purpose was to make merchandise of people and take advantage for themselves. They led many people astray. They promised liberty, but they themselves were under bondage. It is very destructive but God's judgment upon them will be quick and thorough.

In I Peter we are told that the problems the believers had were the persecutions, the trials and the sufferings, and that these had come from outside. But the enemy of the Christians, as described in II Peter was not from outside the church but came from within. Within the church there were these false teachers, and they were enticing people away from Christ unto themselves, and in doing so they took away from the people their kingdom.

Mockers Within the Church

When we carefully inquire into the third chapter of II Peter, we learn that there were not only those false teachers but also there were mockers, and those mockers were not of the world: they were in the church. These mocking believers were very materialistically-minded; for they were judging everything by outward phenomena; and hence, they looked at the world and said: "Where is the promise of the coming of the Lord? Is not the world the same as when it was created?" (see II Peter 3:4) They had willfully ignored the fact that the world in their day was not the same as the world was at the beginning of creation. If you read very carefully you will find that this passage is not a reference to the flood in the time of Noah but to Genesis 1:1-2: "In the beginning God created the heavens and the earth. And the earth became waste and empty, and darkness was upon the face of the deep." Once upon a time at the very beginning, this world had been destroyed by water; but, then, God repaired it in order to make it habitable, and He shall preserve it until that day when it shall be destroyed by fire. But let us not forget that a day is as a thousand years with the Lord and a thousand years is as a day. The Lord has not yet come; He delays His promised return only because He is longsuffering: He does not want any to perish but that all may come to know Him. However, the day of the Lord's return and His judgment is definitely coming. One day the heavens will pass away and the earth will be burned and consumed by fire; and if this is so, how godly we need to be (see II Peter 3:5-12)! These mockers were trying then, and they are trying today to take away the people's kingdom. Their attitude was and is: "Let's eat and drink; let's enjoy the world; we will be here forever." Not so; the present world will certainly come to an end, and the kingdom of God shall be established upon this earth and in which shall dwell righteousness (see II Peter 3:13).

Hasten the Coming of the Lord

Finally, Peter exhorts us. "Beloved, knowing these things before, take care [be careful], lest, being led away along with the error of the wicked, ye should fall from your own stedfastness: but grow in grace, and in the full knowledge of our Lord and Savior Jesus Christ" (II Peter 3:17-18).

We are here not only to wait for the coming of the Lord with His kingdom, but we are here also to hasten His coming. The timetable of the Lord is flexible, for it is spiritual. It is not mechanical. We can delay it; but we can also hasten it. It depends on when the bride has made herself ready, suitable to Him, and fit for the kingdom. We have a great incentive. By the grace of God we can actually hasten His coming; we can actually hasten His kingdom. Do we want to hasten His coming or do we want to delay His return? If we grow in grace and in the full knowledge of Jesus Christ the Lord, we shall not only be waiting for His coming, we shall also actually be hastening His coming. So may the Lord help us.

Shall we pray:

Our heavenly Father, do put before us Thy kingdom that we may not be idle about it, but be diligent towards it. Enable us to avail ourselves of all Thy greatest and precious promises and all Thy divine power unto godliness so that the kingdom character may be built in us and Thy kingdom come. We ask in Thy precious name. Amen.

I JOHN

Seeing Christ in Christian Fellowship

I John 1:1-7—That which was from the beginning, that which we have heard, which we have seen with our eyes; that which we contemplated, and our hands handled, concerning the word of life; (and the life has been manifested, and we have seen, and bear witness, and report to you the eternal life, which was with the Father, and has been manifested to us:) that which we have seen and heard we report to you, that ye also may have fellowship with us; and our fellowship is indeed with the Father, and with his Son Jesus Christ. And these things write we to you that your joy may be full. And this is the message which we have heard from him, and declare to you, that God is light, and in him is no darkness at all. If we say that we have fellowship with him, and walk in darkness, we lie, and do not practise the truth. But if we walk in the light as he is in the light, we have fellowship with one another and the blood of Jesus Christ his Son cleanses us from all sin.

Let us pray:

Dear heavenly Father, we have read Thy word and now we ask that Thy Holy Spirit will open Thy word to our hearts that we may hear Thy voice, that we may be drawn into Thy fellowship, that Thy name may be glorified. So, we just commit this time into Thy hands and ask Thee to do the work that Thou dost want to do. In the name of our Lord Jesus. Amen.

The apostle John wrote three letters—those which are known as the first, second and third letters of John. Chronologically speaking, these are the very last writings of the New Testament, since he wrote these letters after he had written the Gospel according to John and the book of Revelation. John's first letter is addressed to no particular church, the second and third letters are addressed to individuals. However, when we read these three letters we can very easily discern that all three have something in common—they all are dealing with one essential issue: fellowship.

This first letter of John is rather unusual. Normally, a letter will have a beginning address, a salutation, and a closing greeting or remark. But in this letter there is neither a beginning nor an ending in the formal sense of a letter; nonetheless, there is no mistaking that this writing is in the form of a letter because throughout there is such a personal, intimate atmosphere and tone about it.

This letter was probably written between the years 95 and 98 A.D. by the apostle John. Of course, in the original, the writer was not mentioned, just as was the case with the Gospel according to John. Even so, there is a definite connection between the Gospel and this epistle because of a similarity in content and style between the two writings. For instance, in the Gospel of John the author writes: "But these are written that ye may believe that Jesus is the Christ, the Son of God, and that believing ye might have life in his name" (20:31). And in the epistle we find this: "These things I have written to you that ye may know that ye have eternal life who believe on the name of the Son of God" (I John 5:13). So we find there is a connection between the fourth Gospel and this first epistle. It is commonly accepted, and I do not think there is any doubt now about it, that the one who wrote the Gospel is the one who wrote the letter, and we also believe that the one who wrote the Gospel as well as this letter is the apostle John.

John was among the first who followed the Lord Jesus. He was one of the disciples of John the Baptist, and one day while he and Andrew were with their master, Jesus passed by. John the Baptist said, "Behold the Lamb of God," and the two disciples left their master, followed the Lord Jesus, and stayed with Him that night. In the Gospel according to John Andrew's name was mentioned as one of the two disciples, but the other's name was not mentioned. However, we know that it was John himself. He was the one whom Jesus loved. He was the one who lay upon the breast of the Lord Jesus during the so-called Last Supper. He was the one who followed the Lord to the cross, the only one of the Twelve who was there when He was crucified. Among the twelve apostles he was the one who lived the longest. All the other eleven had died, but John lived almost to the close of the first century. So, we can say that his life spanned most of the first century.

A study of this man reveals that John was a most unusual person, because in him was a combination of temperaments which were truly opposite to each other. On the one hand, this apostle was a very reserved introvert. He was a deep thinker and one who was a contemplative who meditated a great deal. On the other hand, John possessed a fiery passion; and for this reason, the Lord Jesus bestowed upon him and his brother James the nickname: "the Sons of Thunder." These two opposing temperaments seem to have taken up residence in this man John; and under God's sovereign control and discipline, he was greatly used by the Lord.

Even though John did not write this letter to any particular church by name, we believe that because he had labored—during his last years—among the churches in the Roman provinces of Asia Minor (where Turkey is today), he had most likely addressed this first letter to those churches. Therefore, it would be helpful to know what was the condition of the early church at the close of the first century, since the apostle John wrote this letter during that time.

We know the church had its wonderful beginning on the day of Pentecost. When the Holy Spirit came down from heaven and one hundred and twenty believers were baptized into one body, that was the time the church formally came into being. It was such a glorious beginning! Within a generation, thirty years, the gospel was preached to the end of the world—from Jerusalem to all Judea and Samaria and even to Rome, because Rome at that time was considered the center as well as the end of the world. At the beginning, when God's people were together, they were in one accord, they loved one another, and they shared everything in common. That testimony was so strong that the Lord added to their number daily. That was the glorious beginning of the church.

Also at the beginning, the believers in Christ were opposed by the Jews and then by the Gentiles, and later on the Roman Empire persecuted the church. But at the time John wrote this epistle, evidently, there had occurred a lull in the Roman persecution of believers. It was now towards the end of the first century, and because of this, the Christians at that time were probably in the second or third generation. The glory of the new discovery of the gospel of Jesus Christ seemed to be gradually fading. The vision of the Lord Jesus seemed to grow dim, and because there was no persecution, people began to relax and their lives began to take on a more loose character. The enemy was able to use that kind of condition to creep into the church and thus, many false teachings commenced making their appearance.

If our understanding of Revelation chapters 2 and 3 is based on a prophetic approach, then we would describe the church at that time as having entered upon the Ephesian period. The first of the seven letters to the churches mentioned there is the letter to the church in Ephesus. What were the characteristics or features of that period in church history? Outwardly, everything continued on as usual. There was work, there was labor, there was endurance, knowledge and discernment. Everything seemed to go on as though nothing had changed; but the Lord said, "I am against you." Why? The explanation given them was that the believers had left their first love.

Outwardly, everything seemed to be ordinary, nothing wrong, but the inner spring had vanished. They did not love God with all their hearts. Their love towards the Lord Jesus was now divided. They loved God but they also loved the world, and because of this, their love for one another had also weakened. They did not love one another to the extent of being willing to give their lives for each other. They became more *self*-centered than Christ-centered, and the Lord called them to repent, to remember from where they had fallen, to return and do the first work. That was the situation of the church at that time and to that kind of situation John addressed himself in this letter.

Living Fellowship

This first letter of John is about Christian fellowship. First and foremost, the church (*ekklesia* in Greek) is a fellowship (*koinonia*): the *ekklesia is* the *koinonia*. The church, the called-out ones, whom God has called out from every tribe, tongue, nation and people, and has gathered together unto His name, becomes a fellowship. It is a living fellowship and is based upon the fellowship of the Father and the Son in the Spirit. Or we might word it another way: this fellowship of the believers is the extension of the fellowship of the Father and the Son in the Spirit. We know there is a fellowship between the Father and the Son, and the word *fellowship* itself means "sharing in common." In the Godhead there is perfect fellowship. The Father shares everything with the Son and the Son shares everything with the Father, and all such is done in the Spirit. The Father and the Son share everything in common—all the essence of the Godhead—and they are one.

In John chapter 17 we read that the Lord Jesus was addressing the Father in prayer, and He said this: "All that is mine is thine and all that is thine is mine" (v. 10). And later He said: "Thou, Father, art in Me and I in Thee" (v. 21). They share everything in common. All that is the Son's is the Father's and all that is the Father's is the Son's because they are one. One is in the other and the other is in the one. Their oneness is based on "in-ness." It is not an external thing but an inward reality; and because of this, their fellowship is perfect harmony and sweet communion. There is no shadow, no shade, no darkness. It is the fellowship in the entire universe.

We cannot imagine how joyful, how glorious that fellowship is between the Father and the Son. The Son always pleases the Father; the Father always finds His delight in the Son. That is the fellowship, the sharing in common, in the Godhead. But thank God, because of His great love, He desires to extend that fellowship to include mankind. Now we must remember that the fellowship the Father and the Son have with one another in the Spirit is something which no other person can ever demand or ask to join. We have no right to demand that we be accepted into that fellowship. We are completely unqualified and undeserving; but it is the good pleasure of the Father to extend that fellowship to mankind. "God is faithful, by whom ye have been called into the fellowship of his Son Jesus Christ our Lord" (I Corinthians 1:9).

We have no right whatsoever; nevertheless, we are called into the fellowship of God's Son, Jesus Christ our Lord. This fellowship of God's Son is that He is to share the Father with us. The Father is His exclusively from eternity. He is the only begotten Son and He is the only One who has the right to fellowship with the Father and to share with the Father everything in common. All that the Father has is the Son's and all that the Son has is the Father's; but thank God, today, He has called us into the fellowship of His Son. And the Son is willing to share His Father with us and all that the Father is. That is the reason why God can bless us with every spiritual blessing in the heavenlies in Christ Jesus. Our fellowship with the Father is through the Son, and as we fellowship with the Father we are likewise fellowshiping with the Son. It is to that unique fellowship we have been called.

Yet how did this fellowship come about? In order to extend Their fellowship to us the Persons of the Godhead had to do something. Fellowship is a very costly thing. It cost God the Father greatly, or to put it more plainly, it cost God His beloved and only Son in drawing us into Their fellowship. "For both he that sanctifies and those sanctified are all of one" (Hebrews 2:11).

He who sanctifies is the Lord; those sanctified are we, and we are all of one. How does that oneness come into being? He who sanctifies is the Son of God; those sanctified are fallen human beings. We in ourselves are certainly not one, but the Bible says, "He that sanctifies and those sanctified are all of one."

"Since therefore the children partake of blood and flesh, he also, in like manner, took part in the same, that through death he might annul him who has the might of death, that is, the devil; and might set free all those who through fear of death through the whole of their life were subject to bondage" (Hebrews 2:14-15).

We, His children, partake in blood and flesh. This English verb partake is *koinoneo* in Greek, that is, "sharing in common." We are born of flesh and blood, which is our common lot; but because we have flesh and blood, and are in bondage under sin, therefore, the Lord Jesus also, in like manner, took part in the same. In order to save us and draw us into being one with Him, He had to take upon himself flesh and blood. But that phrase, *took part in the same*, is not *koinoneo* (the verb form of koinonia); it is another Greek word, *metecho*. It means Christ Jesus took upon himself something which is outside of Him. He was not originally of flesh and blood as we are, but He deliberately took upon himself something which was outside of himself and it became His. He took part in flesh and blood. In His incarnation the Word became flesh. God the Father through His Son entered into flesh, and in His incarnation He identified himself with us who are flesh and blood. That was the first step.

The second step was that thus having been made a man, Jesus humbled himself and obeyed God; He died on the cross in our stead, taking upon himself all our sins so that we might be freed from death. Then, thirdly, in His resurrection the Lord Jesus released His own life to us; He gave His life to all who would believe in Him. In this manner, therefore, we are made one with Him. In other words, He identified himself with us at His incarnation and we are identified with Him in His death and resurrection. Christ's death is our death to the old creation, and His resurrection is our resurrection. We are raised into newness of life and are made one with Him. Let us realize that it cost God tremendously to bring us into the fellowship of His Son, and we can discern immediately that this fellowship which we are drawn into is not some outward thing; it is an inward reality; it is a matter of life. This fellowship is based upon the life which He has given to each one of us; and hence, we are now in that unique fellowship of the Son with the Father.

Principles of Fellowship

What is fellowship? Fellowship is based on life and is the sharing of life. Anything which is not life, which is not the sharing of Christ, cannot be considered as fellowship. Today, we too often think of fellowship as something outward. Just as many people today think of the church as an outward organization. But the church is the called-out ones gathered together to be a living fellowship, to share the life of Christ, to manifest Him together.

Sometimes we say, "Well, let's have some fellowship together." What do we do? We share our problems. Is that fellowship? The more you fellowship in this way, the more depressed you become. Worse than that, sometimes we gather together for fellowship and we talk about politics, social problems, and all such things. Is that fellowship? That is social interaction. Or we try to teach each other the teachings and the doctrines about the Lord Jesus and about all the different interpretations concerning the truth. Is that fellowship? It can be, if *Christ* is being shared; but too often it is only a matter of mind to mind being shared. Now, we may have a very clever, analytical and penetrating mind, and we may think we see something in the Bible which other people have not seen and so we share it. We share our mind with other people, but where is Christ? After we have shared such with others, their knowledge may be increased but their life has not been increased an inch. Can we call that fellowship?

Fellowship is the sharing of Christ, the sharing of His life. Anything that is not of life is not fellowship. Because of this, we realize how much fellowship we must have with the Father and with the Son! In other words, our fellowship with one another is measured proportionally by our fellowship which we have with the Father and with the Son. We cannot have interrupted fellowship with the Father and with the Son and expect to have uninterrupted fellowship with our brothers and sisters. That is impossible. Hence, the degree of our fellowship in sharing with our brothers and sisters is determined by the degree—by the depths with which—we have fellowship with the Father and with the Son. How much we have known and experienced of the Father and of the Son will determine the extent of our fellowship with our brothers and sisters, and no more. Thus, we shall discover that fellowship is a very disciplined matter.

Let me repeat: *koinonia, fellowship, a sharing in common* can only occur because we have something in common, and that something is the life of Christ. Therefore, when we fellowship, we fellowship in life; and because of this, this fellowship is all-inclusive among God's people. All who have the life of Jesus Christ are in that fellowship. Now, today, we may refer to this fellowship or that fellowship, but such is unscriptural since there is only one fellowship. It is the fellowship between the Father and the Son in the Spirit; it is the fellowship of God's Son, Jesus Christ the Lord; it is the fellowship of the apostles. "They continued in the teaching and the fellowship of the apostles" (Acts 2:42). The fellowship of the apostles is the fellowship of God's Son, Jesus Christ. So the fellowship of the apostles, as it is extended to us, is the sharing of Christ with us. It is the one fellowship in the universe, and there is none other; and because of this, it has its practical application. In other words, we who know the Lord must receive all who have the life of the Lord Jesus. We cannot be exclusive. If we exclude anyone who has the life of the Lord Jesus, we become a sect, a party, a division. And it displeases the Lord because this fellowship of His is all-inclusive; it includes all who know the Father and the Son, all who have the life of God in Christ Jesus.

On the other hand, this fellowship is extremely exclusive. Everything and anyone that does not have life, and no matter how good the thing or the person is, cannot be in the fellowship. We cannot draw certain people into the fellowship because they are very good, are very moral, have a good social standing or have a good name in the world. No; we cannot do that because this fellowship is based on life. Even Nicodemus had to be born again in order to belong to that fellowship. Thank God, we have been born again into this fellowship. There is no way to join it but to be born into it. The membership book for this fellowship is not on earth. We cannot find that book anywhere, not even in a safe. The book of life is in heaven, and that is where our membership is. All who believe in the Lord Jesus, all who have the Son, have eternal life, and they belong to this fellowship. We all have something in common. God has shared with us His beloved Son, His own life, and so we have fellowship with the Father, with the Son, and with one another.

Then, too, fellowship is not based on light but on life. By light is meant here that there may be some light which you have concerning the word of God. We believe all the word of God, but there are so many different interpretations. Some people say they have light on a certain portion of Scripture, and other people think they have a different light on that same portion of Scripture. Among God's people there are those, as it were, who have different light. I do not know whether it is light or darkness, but they profess they have light on God's word; yet because of their different interpretations, they divide God's people. Their attitude is: "If you do not believe in my interpretation on a certain portion of the Scriptures, you are out." Let us be reminded that even though you and I may have different light, different interpretations on the Scriptures, if you and I have the same Christ, we must have fellowship with one another. None of such differences should affect our fellowship, because church fellowship is based on life. Thank God, it is not based on light, it is not based on how much you or I know about the Scriptures, or how you or I know it; it is based upon the life of Christ which both you and I have received by grace through faith. Then we have fellowship with one another.

John's Report

The apostle John begins his letter with this matter of fellowship. "That which was from the beginning, that which we have heard, which we have seen with our eyes; that which we contemplated, and our hands handled, concerning the word of life" (I John 1:1).

Fellowship is very personal; it is experiential in nature because you cannot share or report to others what you have not seen or heard. Accordingly, fellowship is based upon what you have seen and what you have heard. Therefore, you can report and share it with others; and when you share it they will see what you see and hear what you hear. That is the joy of fellowship.

"That which was from the beginning ..." Who or what is that which was from the beginning? The Word. "In the beginning was the Word and the Word was with God and the Word was God" (John 1:1). John is trying to share with us Jesus, the Word of life. He is the beginning; He is from the beginning; He is God eternal.

"That which we have heard ..." Where did we hear? We heard from the prophets of old. That which was from the beginning was unknown, but God has spoken through the prophets to our fathers in pieces and fragments, in many parts and in many ways (see Hebrews 1:1). "That which we have seen with our eyes ..." when the Word became flesh and dwelt among us. "That which we contemplated ..." The word *contemplated* means "gazed upon." You gaze upon Him until you see something which other people do not see; in other words, there is a revelation. "The Word became flesh and tabernacled among men and we have contemplated or gazed upon Him and have seen the glory of Him as the glory of the Son with the Father" (see John 1:14). In other words, as you contemplate, the Spirit of God reveals what He really is to you. Hence, we learn here that the disciples have received revelation about this man Jesus. Next: "and our hands handled ..." When? After the resurrection of the Lord Jesus, the Lord told Thomas, "Touch Me. Put your finger into My wounded hand and feel that there is a hole there. You can handle Me" (see John 20:27). Resurrection.

Hence, here in summary is the entire history of the gospel story—His story: the Son of God becoming Man; how He then died for us; how He next was raised from the dead; how He is the Word of eternal life; how this life has been manifested in the flesh—in the Person of the Lord Jesus; how we who have followed Him have seen and borne witness to Him and now report to you this eternal life. This is life. Eternal life is not something outside of God; this life is not only something which God gives. Eternal life is God himself in the Person of His Son. He is the true God; He is the eternal life. This eternal life is more than simply a matter of living in endless time; eternal life is the first quality of living. And God in His Son is the eternal life.

"This eternal life," writes the apostle John, "we have seen and heard." Jesus' disciples had personal experience of this eternal life and, therefore, they report this to us, which means they share it with us. And as they share it with us we obtain it as well; we also receive eternal life; for we, too, now see and hear the Word of life. Then the apostle said this: "Let me tell you what this fellowship is. We are reporting this to you so that you may have fellowship with us. We are sharing with you what we have gained in order that you may have this in common with us; but do understand that what we share with you has its root somewhere else. Its root is verily with the Father and with the Son. We are not fellowshiping and sharing with you of ourselves. No. Peter, for example, is not fellowshiping or sharing himself with you; on the contrary, he is sharing the Christ who is in him with you. Our fellowship is with the Father and with the Son, and as you receive this fellowship—as you are drawn into this fellowship with us—you shall enter into the fellowship which is with the Father and with the Son."

"These things write we to you that your joy may be full." There is nothing which can bring us more joy than real spiritual fellowship. Through fellowship with your brothers and sisters, you are actually fellowshiping in the spirit with the Father and the Son. Can you find anything more full of joy than that fellowship? As you fellowship with your brothers and sisters, you are in reality fellowshiping Christ; and as you are fellowshiping Christ, you are fellowshiping with your brothers and sisters. How full must be this joy! Fellowship is heaven on earth.

Practice of Fellowship

Now, having laid down the principles of fellowship, let us next discuss the practice of it. As we have said, fellowship is based on life; therefore, when we practice fellowship, it has to be practiced in accordance with life. I think that is evident. We cannot practice fellowship outside of the nature of life, eternal life. This eternal life which we receive has its nature and its character; and it is only as we develop our fellowship according to life's character and nature will our fellowship increase. But if in any way we violate the nature of that life, then we will suffer and our fellowship will be hindered. And that is what I John is all about.

The church towards the close of the first century had begun to lose her first love because of her dimmed vision of Christ. Therefore, the believers' fellowship among themselves had been weakened to the point that it was often interrupted, hindered or damaged. So John tried to help them to see how their fellowship could be spiritually revitalized and increased.

By its very nature, true Christian fellowship is living. Anything which lives will grow. When it stops growing, that is a sign that the process of death has begun. Fellowship is the same thing. Christian fellowship is a growing process. We do not come to a point in its process wherein we can say, "Now we have arrived; we cannot grow anymore." To think or to utter this is death. The fellowship between the Father and the Son is ever growing and never ending; and our fellowship together is the same. Is that not wonderful?

God is Light (I John 1:5-2:28)

In I John the character or the nature of God is defined or described by three different statements: 1. God is light 2. God is righteous 3. God is love. Let us take up each of these in that order.

"This is the message which we have heard from him, and declare to you, that God is light, and in him is no darkness at all" (I John 1:5). Here it says, "God is light." The light in view here is different from the light which I mentioned earlier. That light discussed earlier had to do with the interpretation of the Scriptures. Of course, God's word is the lamp at our feet; it is the light for our steps (see Psalm 119:105). The word of God is light, but we are not talking about that because we are talking here about fellowship. Fellowship is not based upon what light you or I may have on the word of God in terms of interpretation. Fellowship is upon light, but what light? God is light. There is therefore a great difference here. God himself is light. That is His nature, His character. He is pure, brilliant, glorious, with no darkness nor shadow nor shade, and no change, He is full light. That is God himself. "In Him was life, and the life was the light of men" (John 1:4). In Christ is life; in the Son is life, and that life is the light of man. In chapter 8 of the Gospel of John, Jesus is quoted as saying: "I am the light of the world. He that follows me shall not walk in darkness, but shall have the light of life."

The life we receive is Christ, and this life has the nature of light. In other words, the life that we have in Christ is to be our light; for He is the light of life. This light in us will shine, and as it shines, we walk forward. We cannot walk in darkness because we will stumble. As Christians we do not walk by outside rules or regulations; we walk instead by the light of life in us. As we follow the Lord the light in us will blink, will shine, and will reveal one step ahead of us. The light of life will not give us the light for our whole life's journey, but it will provide us light for our next step. If we obey the light of life, then we can walk with the Lord. We go a step, and then the light of life will shine another step before us. That is Christian growth.

"If we walk in the light ..." The word if here in this passage is not meant to be saying that we may or we may not. "If we walk in the light …" We, as believers, must walk in the light. Where is the light? Again I say, the light is not the interpretations of God's word, because there are too many different interpretations. The light is the light of life—we follow life. Put it another way: for him who walks according to the Spirit it is life and peace (see Romans 8). In other words, if we follow the light in us as it shines upon our path and we obey it, then God is in the light. Now, of course, there is a huge difference here between ourselves and God as it pertains to light. We walk in the light; yet God is not only in the light but He himself is also the light. God lives in the impenetrable light and His light is full, perfect, a hundred percent. God is holy, pure, glorious. But we walk in the light of life as it shines on our path, and if we do, then the wonderful thing is, we have fellowship with God.

There is no fellowship between light and darkness (see II Corinthians 6:14). We may therefore ask how God, who is light and in whom there is no darkness, can fellowship with us, who, even though we have the light of life in us, have so much darkness around us and in us? The answer is that this is God's mercy and grace upon us. God is in the light, and He is light. We have the light of life in us and God says, "Now walk." As His light shines forth one step on our path, we walk out that step. So far as our experience is concerned, even though the difference is unspeakable and insurmountable between the extent of our light and that of God who is light, nevertheless, the quality or the nature of the light is the same. And hence, God can say to us: "As long as you walk in the light I will have fellowship with you." Even though we still have much darkness in us, that will not interfere with the fellowship between us and God because we have obeyed the light of life which we have today. Is that not an evidence of God's marvelous grace? On the other hand, if we do not walk in the light of life which has been given us, then we walk in darkness and there can be no fellowship between us and God until we confess our sins. In order that our fellowship with God the Father and with the Son remains uninterrupted, it is extremely important and most fundamental that every believer learns to walk faithfully in the light of life that is given him or her.

Of course, there will be a great difference in our experience, one from another. Some people are like little children in whom the life is still young, so the light shines only a little. But as long as you obey that light, you are all right; your fellowship with God is not interrupted. Then you grow to be young people. As your life grows, your light grows; and if you obey that, then you have fellowship with God. Then you grow to be fathers, and the light grows much brighter; and you need to obey. If you do not, you are in darkness and your fellowship will be interrupted. In other words, this fellowship with the Father is a living one; and that is the reason why you and I cannot judge one another. You cannot use your standard and put it upon another brother or sister because he or she may at that moment be a child in the faith and, according to him or her, he or she has obeyed. But you may be a young person or a father in the faith who knows more, and has received more of God's light, so you need to be more faithful. If you are not, you are worse than a child.

"If we walk in the light as He is in the light, we have fellowship with one another." The strange thing here is, this particular *one another* is not between us and the Father and the Son; strictly speaking, it refers to our fellowship with our fellow believers. If we walk in the light as He is in the light, we have fellowship with the Father and with the Son, and it is because of this that we have fellowship with one another. If we do not walk in the light, our fellowship with the Father and the Son is not right, and therefore we can have no fellowship with our brothers and sisters. I think this is clear.

"And the blood of Jesus Christ His Son cleanses us from all sin." Think of that! As you fellowship with your brothers and sisters, as you exchange light and life, the light grows. Perhaps I am one candlelight, and as I fellowship with my brother, he serves as another candlelight. Immediately, there are now two candlelights and the light grows. As the light grows, you realize your darkness that has never been exposed before. And thank God, the blood of God's Son Jesus Christ cleanses us from all sin, and so we increase in life. Is that not true? When you fellowship with your brothers and sisters and nothing happens, something is wrong with that fellowship. If you truly fellowship with your brothers and sisters, are you not convicted? Oftentimes, when you fellowship with brothers and sisters you are convicted because the light of life in him or her begins to shine upon you and in that particular area in your life you are in darkness. But then you begin to see; therefore, you confess and the blood of Jesus cleanses you, and your character is thus purified. This is the glory of fellowship.

Let us not think that fellowship is cheap and that it is nothing more than having a good time. No; sometimes, fellowship can be very costly; because if you dare to truly fellowship with your brothers and sisters, you will open yourself to being exposed, but also to being delivered. Do you dare to fellowship with God? Let us not think fellowship with God is all roses. There are many thorns there, numerous purgings, frequent emptyings, and many works to be done; but thank God, nothing is more glorious than what fellowship can give.

God Is Righteous (I John 2:29-4:6)

We have seen that fellowship is based on life, the life given to us in Christ Jesus. Fellowship has its origin in the fellowship of the Godhead, and this fellowship between the Father and the Son in the Spirit has been extended to us through Christ the Son. The degree or extent of our fellowship with one another is determined by the degree or extent of our fellowship with the Father and with the Son. In order to have our fellowship increased without hindrance we must learn to develop along the nature of God's life in us. First, God is light, so we must walk in the light of life in order to have fellowship and to grow from little children to young men to fathers. Next, we see that God is righteous (see I John 2:29). Whatever God does is righteous because He is righteous in His very character. It is not a matter of some righteous acts which God does, but it is a being righteous in himself. God cannot deny himself. That is, He will not and cannot do anything other than what is just and right.

Now we are the children of God. "See what love the Father has given to us" (I John 3:1). As children of God, we have His seed—that is, His life—in us (see I John 3:9). The life in us is a righteous life. This distinguishes us from the world—from the children of the devil (see I John 3:10). The latter sin, and cannot but practice sin, for this is the nature of their father. We as children of God, however, do not practice sin, for sin is lawlessness, that is, it is against the law of God (see I John 3:4). As children of God, we should not sin for that would be against the nature of the life in us, that would be unlike God. And we may not sin, because this life given to us is a righteous and sinless life: Christ was tempted in all things, but without sinning; for His life overcame all temptation and thus, He did no sin. Nevertheless, it is also true that we still have the possibility of sinning—sinning against our new nature—because we still have the flesh in us. However, we do not *practice* sin, that is to say, we do not "commit sin" as a habit (see I John 3:8-9 AV) nor do we "keep on sinning" nor "continue to sin" (both in I John 3:6 NIV). Instead of practicing sin, we practice righteousness, for God is righteous. The righteousness in view here is practical righteousness, not the righteousness of God which comes to us when we believe in the Lord Jesus Christ nor Christ our righteousness as the robe with which we are clothed. No, these give us acceptance and access to God. The righteousness in view here is the righteous acts of the saints (see Revelation 19:8: "it was given to her that she should be clothed with fine linen, bright and pure: for this fine linen is the righteousnesses of the saints"): we do the things which are right in the sight of God, such as loving the brethren: we do what Christ has done: He loved us and has laid down His life for us, so we too ought to lay down our lives for the brethren (see I John 3:16).

We often are concerned with not sinning, which we should; but we neglect the positive aspect of practicing righteousness. Many of God's children are careless in living a righteous life. They consider righteousness as a thing of the past, that is, they have become righteous in Christ, and that is good enough. They fail to see that God requires us to practice righteousness. This is one of the errors which John fights against. False and wrong teaching leads to loose and sinful living. If we do not practice righteousness, how can we prove that we are God's children? How can we fellowship with God and fellowship with one another? "For what participation is there between righteousness and lawlessness?" (II Corinthians 6:14)

How do we know we are doing the right thing? "And hereby we shall know that we are of the truth, and shall persuade our hearts before him—that if our hearts condemn us, God is greater than our hearts and knows all things" (I John 3:19-20). We know we do the right thing or not because God has given us a conscience of the heart purified by the blood of the Lord Jesus. A purified conscience is most important to have in our daily walk. For God is able to speak to us through our conscience. If our conscience condemns us, we know that God has condemned us because His heart is greater than ours and He knows all things. But if our conscience does not condemn us, we have boldness towards God because we have kept His commandments and have practiced the things pleasing in His sight (see I John 3:21-22). Our hearts are of course smaller than God's; our consciences condemn us far less than what God condemns.

So, then, how is it possible that if our hearts do not condemn us, we have boldness towards God? We not only can fellowship with God, but even have the confidence that He will hear our prayers. This again shows the condescending love of God. He is willing to fellowship with us so long as our consciences are clear before Him. This is the way to lead us on to more maturity. Our consciences will tell us that we must owe nothing to anyone except love (see Romans 13:8). We must love in deed and in truth (see I John 3:18), otherwise our hearts will condemn us. The reason why our hearts serve as a measure in fellowship is because God has given us His Spirit (see I John 3:24). The Spirit of God is the Spirit of the incarnate Son. He is concerned with our daily walk because the Son of God came in the flesh and also walked on earth in righteousness. Any spirit who does not confess that Jesus Christ came in the flesh is not of God but is of the antichrist (see I John 4:3). Such erroneous teaching corrupts righteous living. This is the spirit of the world, but He who is in us is greater than he who is in the world. Hence, we are able to overcome (see I John 4:4).

So, if we want to fellowship with God, we must keep our consciences void of offense. When the consciences of our hearts condemn us, we are unable to come to God. We know we are not what He is, therefore we are afraid to come. Thank God, the blood is always available. We must not allow the accuser of the brethren to take advantage of our unrighteous condition; rather, the brethren overcame him by the blood of the Lamb (see Revelation 12:11).

The same is it with respect to our fellowship with one another: if we have anything against our brother, or if we do not forgive concerning whatever our brother sins against us in; our fellowship with one another is hindered until reconciliation is made and forgiveness is given. This is why the Lord says, "If therefore thou shouldest offer thy gift at the altar, and there shouldest remember that thy brother has something against thee, leave there thy gift before the altar, and first go, be reconciled to thy brother, and then come and offer thy gift" (Matthew 5:23-24). Whether we practice righteousness or not affects our fellowship with God.

God Is Love (I John 4:7-5:12)

Fellowship is according to life, yet not our old life, but the new life of Christ given to us by God. Now the character or nature of this new life is love, for God is love. The love of God is more than an emotion, it is the very nature of God. He loves not because He is emotionally stirred by external circumstances but because love is what He is. This is a basic difference between God's love and our so-called love. Our love is emotionally based, since it is conditioned by external circumstances. It is basically selfish. It is quite limited in scope and duration. But the love of God is an inward character. It is active and spontaneous. It is self-sacrificing, and it knows no limit.

We are called into this fellowship of love. First, we are to see and experience God's love towards us; and, then, we are to love one another as He has loved us. What kind of love is this love of God which draws us into this fellowship? (1) It is a love which comes forth naturally; for God is love: He cannot help but love. There is no second thought or consideration in His love, He just loves. (2) It is a love that was manifested through God sending His beloved Son into the world that we might live through Him. It is therefore a practical love, a sacrificial love, a selfless love. God thinks of us and counts not the cost. (3) God loves us first, that is to say, His love is not a reaction but an action. His love is not governed by our love towards Him. By loving us first He opens the way of fellowship to us.

Having received such love from God, we ought to love one another with the same love. By loving one another, we manifest and prove our love to God. By loving those who are begotten of God, we show our love to Him who has begotten us. How can we say we love God yet we do not love our brethren? If we cannot show love to these whom we see, how can we prove we love God whom we do not see? (see I John 4:20) Our fellowship with one another is dependent on our abiding in God. It is the outcome and overflow of our connection with Him. The more we abide in God, the more He abides in us. Thus, His love begins to flow from us to the brethren.

A passage of Scripture in I John mentions "perfect love" (4:18). What is perfect love? It does not mean perfection in the sense that there is absolutely nothing which can be improved upon. Only God's love is perfect. In relation to us, perfect love is a love that is perfected by our abiding in God's love. "Abiding" means "making our home in." It is not an erratic experience but a permanent condition. As we abide in God's love we abide in Him, and He in us. We have fellowship with

God and we have boldness in the day of judgment, knowing that we have done what He has done. Such love casts out all fear. We love God with all our hearts. We love because He has first loved us.

Let us move forward in this matter of fellowship in accordance with the nature of life. God is light; so we walk in the light. God is righteous; so we practice righteousness. God is love; and hence we love one another, and as we do so, fellowship increases. May the Lord bless us.

Shall we pray:

Dear heavenly Father, what can we say? We have no right, we do not deserve anything; yet Thou dost extend Thy wonderful, glorious fellowship to us. Thou dost share Thy Son with us and Thy Son shares Thee with us. Oh, we do praise and thank Thee that today we are called into the fellowship of God's Son, Jesus Christ. Our fellowship is with the Father and with the Son and with one another. Father, we do pray that we may truly understand what this fellowship is, that we may treasure it, that we may be willing to pay any cost for it. And we do pray that our fellowship may increase and grow so that Thou mayest be glorified and our joy may be full. We ask in the name of our Lord Jesus. Amen.

II JOHN

Seeing Christ in Fellowship: Love and Truth

II John 1-13—The elder to the elect lady and her children, whom I love in truth, and not I only but also all who have known the truth, for the truth's sake which abides in us and shall be with us to eternity. Grace shall be with you, mercy, peace from God the Father, and from the Lord Jesus Christ, the Son of the Father, in truth and love. I rejoiced greatly that I have found of thy children walking in truth, as we have received commandment from the Father. And now I beseech thee, lady, not as writing to thee a new commandment, but that which we have had from the beginning, that we should love one another. And this is love, that we should walk according to his commandments. This is the commandment, according as ye have heard from the beginning, that ye might walk in it. For many deceivers have gone out into the world, they who do not confess Jesus Christ coming in flesh—this is the deceiver and the antichrist. See to yourselves, that we may not lose what we have wrought, but may receive full wages. Whosoever goes forward and abides not in the doctrine of the Christ has not God. He that abides in the doctrine, he has both the Father and the Son. If any one come to you and bring not this doctrine, do not receive him into the house, and greet him not; for he who greets him partakes in his wicked works. Having many things to write to you, I would not with paper and ink; but hope to come to you, and to speak mouth to mouth, that our joy may be full. The children of thine elect sister greet thee.

Shall we pray:

Dear heavenly Father, as we continue in Thy presence, we look to Thy Holy Spirit to reveal afresh to us Thy word that

Thy word may not be merely letters to us but it will be life and spirit. We do thank Thee for Thy word; we thank Thee for the living Word. We thank Thee for Thy Holy Spirit, and we just commit this time into Thy hands and ask Thee to grant us the spirit of wisdom and revelation in the full knowledge of God. In the name of our Lord Jesus. Amen.

The second and third letters of John are the last two writings in the New Testament. They were probably written between 95 and 98 A.D., at the close of the first century. These two letters are addressed to individuals. The second letter is addressed to a chosen lady and the third letter is addressed to the beloved Gaius—one to a lady and one to a gentleman.

We know that the purpose of God is corporate in nature. In other words, what God is after is a body, a church, a bride, a house; but because of the failure of the majority, God has to call individuals as overcomers of the church. It is through these individual overcomers, or the company of these overcomers, those individuals who respond to God's call, that God is able to perform what He wants the whole church to do.

As noted earlier, we know these writings of John are concerned with the principle of recovery. Therefore, it is in line with the principle of recovery that we take notice that the second and third letters of John are addressed to individuals.

The writer does not give us his name. He only says *the elder*. We know that the word elder basically means one who is older, who is of senior age; but this word is also applied to those people whom the Holy Spirit has set apart and appointed to be elders of the church. They are spiritually more advanced and so they are placed in responsibility over the assembly of the church.

Now there are different thoughts as to whether the word *elder* used here refers to a person who is older in age or to one who is an elder in an official position in the church. Personally, I feel this cannot refer to the elder officially, that is, to an elder of a church. This is because an elder of a church has jurisdiction or authority only over the people who are in the local assembly where he is. In other words, his jurisdiction or authority does not extend beyond the local assembly. But this author is writing to someone who is not in the same locality, and he writes with an authority which the reader can sense in this letter. Therefore, I feel the word *elder* is not used here in an official sense but in the more common sense of it referring to an older person, a person who is advanced in age, who is wise in experience, who has spiritual weight, and who has a long history with the Lord. And he is writing to a lady, sharing with her some of his advice, and offering encouragement and warning; hence, most likely, the elder is not in an official position but is instead engaged in a more intimate personal relationship.

Most people believe the writer of this letter is the apostle John. One of the characteristics about John in all his writings is that he does not mention his name, except in the book of Revelation. In his Gospel he simply identified himself as, "one whom the Lord loved" (see John 13:23). But everybody knows that the one whom the Lord loved was the apostle John, and he was therefore actually the one who wrote the Gospel. In the first letter of John his name is again not mentioned. We say it is the first letter of *John* because it is almost universally accepted that the writer of this first letter is the apostle John. There is such similarity between the Gospel and this epistle that they must have been written by the same person. There is the same atmosphere, the same approach, the same conviction, many of the same words being used, the same expressions. Everything about these two writings tells us that it is the same person who wrote both the Gospel and this first epistle.

And again, the second letter is so similar to the first. Once more, the atmosphere is the same in both letters, as well as the same expression and emphasis. There is such a similarity that most people believe this second letter was written by the apostle John also.

We see, of course, that the author does not begin this second letter by saying, "The apostle John writes to the elect lady." He could have written in that manner because he is an apostle; instead, he wrote as follows: "The aged, the elder, the older man, writes to an elect lady." We discern here the humility of this man John. He has the humility of Christ in him. You will recall that when our Lord Jesus was on earth He always referred to himself as the Son of Man. Jesus is the Son of God, and if He had called himself by that title, it would probably have given Him more dignity. Yet, instead of calling himself the Son of God, which He is, He called himself the Son of Man in deep humility; and this man John has the humility of Christ. Rather than using His spiritual authority as an apostle, he merely wrote as an older man who has received much from the Lord.

Elect Lady

Who is this elect lady to whom John writes? There are naturally all kinds of theories about it. The word *lady* in Greek is kuria, which is the feminine form of the word *kurios* meaning "lord" or "master." The Hebrew word for lady is *martha* which means "mistress," and in those early days this was a common feminine name—Martha. So in those early days there were women who were named Kuria. In this instance the lady—or Kuria—could be a common name for this woman or it could simply be a title—a mistress or a lady who is of noble character, well known and respected by people. This is one interpretation.

Another interpretation is that it refers to a church or to the church universal. You may remember that in I Peter 5:13 Peter had said, "Your sister in Babylon ..." (ASV mg.), and of course, he is referring here to the church in Babylon. Therefore, some people think this letter of John is written to a local church, because the church, in a sense, is feminine in nature: Christ is the man, the church is the woman: the church is the bride of Christ; therefore, it can be applied to either the church local or the church universal. We really do not know for sure whether this letter was written to a noble lady by the name of Kuria, a lady as a mistress, or to a local church or the church universal. Someone has observed: the writer could have very well told us who he was and he could have very well told us who the receiver of the letter was; but, he intentionally held back his own name and the name of the addressee. There must be a reason for it, and probably, it was because of the danger involved. If he had revealed his identity, there might have been some danger involved because there were persecutions at that time. But even though the names were withheld, of course, the addressee knew who the addressor was. There was no mistake as to who wrote it or who the receiver of this letter was. Even though we do not know with absolute certainty who wrote and who received, we nonetheless know it is part of the Scriptures. And whatever is in the Scriptures is written by the Spirit of God to us. So we do accept this from God as a letter to us individually as well as corporately.

The Church at the Close of the First Century

In order to understand this letter we have to reconstruct the conditions of the church in those days. Keep in mind that this is towards the close of the first century. After the death, resurrection and ascension of the Lord Jesus, and from the day of Pentecost to this closing point of the first century, there were Christians alive who belonged to the second and even the third generation of believers. Christianity had been on earth for quite a number of years. Within some thirty years following the ascension of the Lord Jesus, the gospel had been preached from Jerusalem to Judea, to Samaria, and to the end of the world which was Rome. By the year 62 or 63 the gospel had been preached everywhere, and then there ensued another thirty some years more. So most likely, by the first century's close the church belonged to the second or the third generation of Christians.

The first generation had come and gone, but this old man who wrote this letter belonged to the first generation and he was still living. We know that the apostle John was the very last of the twelve apostles to expire, and he lived to a very old age in his nineties. Although he belonged to the first generation, he was writing to the second or perhaps the third generation.

In the first generation people keep vision; they receive revelation directly from God, and they have no tradition to follow. They are the pioneers of the heavenly way, and in obedience to the heavenly vision they lay down their lives. They pay a tremendous cost in order to be obedient to the vision which God has given them. Everything with the first generation is living, real, fresh, vivid, powerful. But, then, the vision which the first generation had received is passed on to the second generation, and this vision becomes a tradition. The second generation does not have that direct revelation from God; they receive it secondhand. So it is really a tradition that they keep. Outwardly, it is the same thing; in that regard, there is no difference. But inwardly, there is a great difference; the inward revelation is no longer there. The outward form is kept, but the inward reality is not there anymore; and because of that, the testimony begins to be weakened. The tradition is a good and right tradition; but, even though it is orthodox, even though it is scriptural, even though it is right, something is missing. And when we consider the third generation the spiritual condition descends even lower than the second generation. Unfortunately, this is usually the case.

If one carefully reads church history, he shall find again and again how God makes a move, how God gives a revelation, a recovery of the truth of himself to some people. They rise up in response to what God has revealed and there is such power present, there is such life there; but, then, they hand it on to the second and third generation; but though the outward vessel is there, the inward life is missing.

This was the situation which obtained by the end of the

first century. Christianity had developed to the second and third generations. Persecutions had come and gone, but the real danger for the church at that time was the intrusion and advance of false teachings into the church. When the inward reality is lessened, then the intrusion of false teachings finds its way into the church. When the church is bathed in the light of revelation and vision, when the church has that spiritual reality, when there is that life relationship with the Lord, false teachings find it very difficult to creep in and enter the church. But when the church itself is weakened and the fellowship is confused, such is the time when the enemy will try to infiltrate the church with all kinds of false teaching; and, of course, this further weakens the testimony of the church.

John's Ministry

The ministry of the apostle John is of a very special kind because it is a ministry of recovery. When he was called by the Lord, he was mending nets. When Peter was called, he was casting the nets. Spiritually speaking, Peter's ministry was to gather in all the fishes: that is to say, all kinds of people—from both the Jews and the Gentiles—to gather them together and "net" them into the church. But John's ministry was of another kind—the kind that can be likened to mending a net. After a net has been used, there will be holes in it which need to be mended and strengthened so that it can be used again. Spiritually speaking, that is the special ministry of the apostle John.

It seems that John's ministry did not really begin until after Peter and Paul were gone. Peter was the one who had gathered people in, and Paul was the one who had built them together. After they had passed off the scene, then the ministry of John truly began. He is the one who was left to mend the torn places and the holes in the church, to strengthen the church so that the testimony of Jesus might be restored. In doing that kind of work, John always takes us back to the beginning; he always leads us back to the fundamentals—back to the essentials. And what is more basic, fundamental and essential than life at the beginning? So we can discern that the ministry of John is the ministry of life. When everything seems to be going wrong, this matter of life needs to be reemphasized; and that is the reason why this apostle always goes back to the very beginning—to life.

What is the church? The very beginning of the church is life, and this life has to continue on to the very end. If life is taken away, there is no church. The framework is there, but there is nothing within it. What is needful continually is life—fellowship; and fellowship is the fellowship of life. If there is life, there is bound to be fellowship; if there is no life, there is no fellowship. That is the reason why in all the writings of the apostle John he always leads us back to life and to fellowship.

Confusion in Fellowship

The Gospel of John is the gospel of life. Likewise, the First Epistle, Second Epistle and Third Epistle are all writings about fellowship, but the fellowship is based upon life. Therefore, John attempts to lead people back into what life and fellowship really are. When there are problems in life, there will be problems in fellowship. At the time he wrote this second letter there was confusion regarding this matter of fellowship. In other words, the believers at that time did not really know with whom to fellowship and with whom to refuse to have fellowship, whom to receive and whom not to receive into fellowship. There seemed to be such confusion at that time; and in a very real way, I believe we have the same problem today. Among God's people there is a real lack of understanding as to what fellowship is. We do not really know whom we should receive into fellowship and whom we should reject. There is such confusion today.

What is fellowship? Some people believe that the organized church is church and that the unorganized church is fellowship. They call mainline Christianity *church*; they call her offspring *fellowship.* Is this your concept of fellowship? Some people ask, "Why do you call yourself fellowship and not church? Is it because you are not organized? Is this what fellowship means?" Even worse, some people believe that fellowship is smaller than church. In the church in Corinth there was the Pauline fellowship, the Apollonian fellowship, the Petrine fellowship. Not at all! The word fellowship actually is the action word of the church. The church is a fellowship; the fellowship is the church. They are the same thing. If it is the church, it is bound to be a fellowship. If it is a fellowship, it is a church. There is only one church; there is only one fellowship. The scope of the church is the sphere of fellowship. In other words, as large as the church is, so large is the fellowship of the saints.

What is the church? The word *ekklesia* means "called-out-ones gathered together." God has called us out of every nation, tribe, people and tongue, and has gathered us together unto the name of the Lord Jesus. At the same time, we are called into the fellowship of God's Son, Jesus Christ the Lord. We are called to be the church of God. We are called into the fellowship of God's Son, and this is the fellowship of the Father and of the Son in the Spirit. It is also the fellowship of the apostles.

"They persevered in the teaching and the fellowship of the apostles, in breaking of bread and in prayers" (Acts 2:42). The fellowship of the apostles is none other than the fellowship of God's Son, Jesus Christ the Lord; and the fellowship of God's Son is none other than the fellowship of the Father and the Son in the Holy Spirit. There is only one fellowship, and this fellowship of the Father and the Son in the Spirit is extended to mankind. God has called us into the fellowship of His Son, Jesus Christ the Lord, in order that we may share with Him what He is.

As we learned earlier, the word fellowship means "having in common." Actually, it is the Lord who shares everything in common with us. We have nothing to share with Him. Whatever we are able to share later on is given to us by the Lord, and He is so gracious that He is willing to share everything with us. He is the Son of God, and yet as the Son of God He is willing to share His very life with us; He shares everything with us. That is what we are called into—the fellowship of God's Son, Jesus Christ the Lord. There is only one fellowship.

Principles that Govern Fellowship

When the elder wrote to this lady he said, "We love you in the truth." This elderly man loved this lady and her children in the truth, and he said: "Not only do I love you, but all who have the truth love you, the truth that abides in us." As you read this short letter you discover two words which stand out as key: one is love, the other is truth. Although this is a very short letter with only thirteen verses, the word *truth* is used five times and the word love is used four times. In other words, the writer tried to impress upon his readers that two principles govern fellowship—love and truth. You cannot have fellowship in truth and not in love. It will make you very hard and harsh and cold and exclusive. You cannot have fellowship in love but not in truth. It will make you very liberal, willing to embrace everybody, and your fellowship will become very loose and weak. Fellowship must be in love and in truth together.

What God has joined together let not man separate; but the problem is, we always separate these two. We think that if we have love we cannot have truth, and if we have truth we cannot have love. For instance, if we have love, then we try to love everybody and everything. We even love and condone sin; we are ready to indulge people because we want love. We cannot discipline anybody or be strict with anyone. We have to be so soft. We think that if we love, then we cannot have truth. On the other hand, if we want to keep the truth, we will think we cannot have love. We have to stand for the truth; we have to fight for it. And if we fight for the truth, we have to offend somebody; we have to hurt someone; we will have to step on somebody. If we want to have truth, we cannot have love—it is impossible, humanly speaking, to have both. Either we hold on to truth or we hold on to love.

Love

The problem here is that what we call love is not real love and what we call truth is not real truth. The Greek word for love which the apostle or the elder used here is not *phileo,* which means "friendship" or "affection." Naturally, we have so-called human affection which is a good thing because if we look into Romans chapter 1, "… without natural affection …" is one of the sins listed there. Some people have no human affection; they are inhuman. But human affection or friendship is very limited, and is conditioned by our circumstances. Why do you strike up a friendship with somebody? Usually, it is because you have the same temperament; you have the same interests; you can talk; you like each other. So you form a friendship. Why do you show affection? Again, it is because you find someone lovable, someone who does not go against your grain but somehow merges with you. So you cultivate or develop a kind of affection for that person.

However, the love the elder is speaking of here is not *phileo*; it is *agape*. Agape is divine love; it is selfless love; it is love which comes from within and is never affected by outward circumstances. "God is love." It is not that God loves us because we are loving or we are lovable or that He has something to love in us; but it is because He is love. He just loves. No matter what we are, no matter how we are, He loves us. Our condition does not change His love. And in the word *agape* there is that absolute, selfless love which initiates and never changes.

Truth

Sometimes we fight for the truth. In Christianity the most fierce fight is waged over the truth, not over falsehood. We do not fight for falsehood, but we often fight for truth, and it often is a very fierce fight. And we can fight over truth to such an extent that even the husband and the wife will not talk to each other. There are certain areas that husband and wife cannot meet together on because they stand for different truths. Yet what we call truth is not truth; it is actually interpretations. The truth is one, but there are many interpretations. We fight against each other because we think this or that is the truth, when actually it is one's interpretation. If it is truth there is only one, and we can be together. But, if it is interpretation, then we differ and that is why people are so divided.

What is the truth? Christ said, "I am the truth." Is Christ divided? Of course not! Then why is it that it seems that truth divides us? It is our interpretations. Let us recognize that the two primary principles of fellowship are love and truth. It is agape love, the love of God, in us that enables us to love one another. What is the truth? The truth is the commandment of God. "This is his commandment, that we believe on the name of his Son Jesus Christ, and that we love one another" (I John 3:23). The truth is Christ. We believe in the Lord Jesus; we believe in His Person and His work, and because we believe in Him we keep His commandment—that we must love one another. The Lord said, "As the Father has loved me, I also have loved you; abide in my love. If ye shall keep my commandments, ye shall abide in my love" (John 15: 9-10). Truth and love are not separate; they are together; and fellowship is based on both love and truth.

Encouragement

"I rejoiced greatly that I have found of thy children walking in truth, as we have received commandment from the Father" (II John 4). The writer tried to solve this confusion of fellowship, but we find that when he wrote, he began with the positive side. Oftentimes, when you try to fight against a heresy or a falsehood you get so involved with the negative that you lose your own ground. But in the Scriptures, invariably, whenever you are going to fight against an untruth or a falsehood you show what is truth, encourage what is the truth; then the false will be exposed. So in this letter the writer began with the positive. "I rejoiced greatly that I have found of thy children walking in truth, as we have received commandment from the Father."

It is very interesting that in this short letter we are shown something of the situation and the condition of the believers in those early days at the end of the first century. We do not know too much about the church in the first century, but in this small letter we do find some clue, some hint, as to what the church was like back then. John said, "I rejoiced greatly." In other words, it gave him great joy in his heart when he wrote: "I have found of thy children walking in truth." On the one hand, this shows us a Christian family. Probably, this lady was a widow with a number of children, even though some of them were not with her at that time. Evidently, some of her children were in the place where the elder was living, and he saw them walking in truth. Although these children were not at home, they were so trained and brought up with the discipline and the admonition of the Lord that even when they were in another city away from home and from their mother, they continued to walk in truth; they continued to be faithful in following the Lord and in loving the Lord. When the aged writer of this letter saw such a situation, it made him rejoice greatly. So in one sense, his letter does give us a clue that in the early days Christians' homes were truly built up in Christ. And this is a trait which we really need to have more and more of today. We need to bring up our children with the knowledge of the Lord, the love of Christ, and the truth which is in Christ, so that even if they are away from us in some other city or some other place, they can still stand for the Lord and continue on. That is something rare today. Oftentimes, in Christian families, when the children are with their parents they seem to be quite Christian, but when they leave their home it is a different story.

There is not that solidity nor stability nor foundation which are so essential. But we thank God that in the early church there was stability there, even though the church was already into the second and third generation. This was something which made the old man rejoice very, very much.

If this elect lady refers to the church, then this letter reveals that the church has truly laid down a good foundation for all the brothers and sisters of that day. Even though some young brothers and sisters may have gone to other places to study or to work, they were still standing and walking in the truth, following the Lord and loving the Lord. This shows that a good foundation had been laid in the church where they were brought up. This is also something which we need to be very careful about. We should bring up our young people in such a sound way that they will be solidly built up in love and in truth, so that wherever they go they will not get lost in the world but will continue in fellowship, walking in love and in the truth.

Continue in Fellowship

Then the writer encourages the lady: "And now I beseech thee, lady, not as writing to thee a new commandment, but that which we have had from the beginning, that we should love one another" (v. 5). In those earlier days the Christians had met in homes. They did not have a meeting hall as we have today, so some people opened up their homes for meetings. Most likely, this widow, who had such a noble Christian character, who had brought up her family in such a way and with such a good testimony, opened up her home for God's people to come together and fellowship and also for hospitality. (That is what they used to do in the olden days.) But because of the great confusion which had come into the church on this matter of fellowship, this lady needed some encouragement.

We will recall that our Lord Jesus said: "Because lawlessness shall prevail, the love of the most shall grow cold; but he that has endured to the end, he shall be saved" (see Matthew 24:12-13). When the church begins to lose its strength—its spiritual life—the love of the many will grow cold. So many things happen which should not happen that naturally you will think that you cannot love anymore. You will probably feel that you have to compromise in the truth. That is a natural reaction. So the writer here was trying to encourage this elect lady to have the attitude that no matter what confusion there may be, no matter how evil or what abnormalities she might see everywhere, she must continue maintaining fellowship in love and in truth. We today need the same encouragement. Let us not allow what we see around us, or what even may happen to us, to lead us away from the fellowship in love and the fellowship in truth. I believe this is something very needful for us today.

Warning

After the elder had encouraged the lady to continue in this fellowship in love and in truth, he moved on to the negative side. Once again, we need to know something of the background here. In those early days they not only had no meeting place, they also had no resident pastor. Today, however, wherever there is a church there is a building, and there is also a pastor who resides there to take care of all the teachings and all the so-called spiritual services for the people. This kind of pastor-system actually was developed later on, but in the beginning, all believers were priests—all believers served the Lord. Back then, it was not the case of having a small group of people, especially trained to serve the Lord, who took charge over the spiritual well-being of the whole church and who monopolized all the spiritual services. Not so. In those days the Christians learned to build up one another in love. They learned to minister to one another. That was the way the church was built. They did not look to one man as their pastor to take care of all their spiritual well-being. In the early church all the believers themselves had to build up one another in order to strengthen or help.

God does give to the church universal some apostles, some prophets, some evangelists, and some pastors and teachers (see Ephesians 4:11). They travel around visiting and ministering to the different assemblies in order to perfect, to mature and to equip the saints, so that the saints in turn can build themselves up together in love. That is the way we find in the Scriptures.

So, in the early days, there were people who traveled around—traveling apostles, traveling prophets, traveling evangelists, and traveling pastors and teachers. They would go about and try to strengthen and build up the church. They did not go around building up their own kingdom, as we too often see today. They built up the church of God. When, for example, Peter came to an assembly of believers, he would build up the church there; and when Paul also came there, he would build up the same church. These traveling ministers of the Lord were not building up their own kingdoms.

Some people, like Paul who was well known, did not need any letter of recommendation. He told the Corinthians that even though other people needed a letter, he did not, because he was their spiritual father and they ought to know him. But other people, like Apollos, when he first started out, needed a recommendation. He was in Ephesus, and it may be recalled that Priscilla and Aquila had received him and helped him in furthering his knowledge of the Lord Jesus. Then he wanted to go to Corinth, and these two introduced him to the brethren in Corinth because nobody there knew him. Hence, in the early church there were many traveling ministers (or, to borrow today's term, traveling preachers). They traveled around visiting different groups, assemblies and fellowships, attempting to build up God's people so that they could build up themselves.

FALSE TEACHING

At that time the church was not highly organized, nor is it God's will for today that she should be highly organized. Therefore, in these various fellowships or churches, the doors were wide open. They received anyone who came in the name of the Lord for the purpose of helping them and building them up. But because of this, some problems arose. There were false teachers and false prophets even in the first century, and they were bringing in false teachings. The doors to these churches were so open that they took advantage of the sincerity and innocence of the believers. The false teachers would say that they had been sent of the Lord to come and help. "Fine; please come in and help us." And so they would begin to minister, propagating their false teachings. Now, how could the local churches control that? Were they going to close the door to all these visiting ministers? If the church was highly organized, this problem would not exist because that church would only permit those in who were part of that organization. Whoever was outside of the organization would stay out; and hence, the situation would be easy to control. But if the church were not organized and remained wide open, and if, as was the case in the days of the early church, the Christians were quite sincere, ignorant, innocent and loving, then anybody could come in and take advantage and lead an entire church assembly astray. It was, and still is, a most serious matter.

What was the false teaching which the writer of this letter was writing about? In the back of John's mind when composing the Gospel of John, he was fighting against the false teaching that denied the deity of Christ. The proclaimers of this heretical teaching were denying the deity of the Lord Jesus. They said that the Lord Jesus was just a man; He was not God at all. They even taught that when Jesus was baptized, God came to him, but when he was crucified, God left him. He was only a man and not God. That was a serious heresy, and that is the reason why John wrote his gospel. At the back of John's mind was his desire to combat this heresy that the Lord Jesus was just a human being; that He was not God. Yet this heresy continues even till now. There are many today who are teaching this same false notion that the Lord Jesus was only a man and that He is not God.

However, in this letter of John's now before us, it was just the opposite heretical teaching which the apostle addressed. False teachers had begun enticing the churches and teaching that Jesus is God but that He was not a man at all; that God had never become flesh. This Gnostic teaching had gained entry into Christianity. According to the teaching of Gnosticism, matter itself is evil. Therefore, the body is evil. How, then, can God join himself to that which is evil? He cannot do that; therefore, there was no Incarnation. The body of the Lord Jesus was a phantom; it was not real. They rejected the truth that the Lord Jesus had come in the flesh. They did not believe in His humanity.

The heresies which we find in Christianity today are mostly centered upon the Person and the work of the Lord Jesus. Of course, there are other issues; but all these heresies have something to do with the Person and the work of the Lord Jesus, because if someone rejects the Person, he rejects the work. If someone does not believe that Jesus is God but was only a man, then Jesus cannot save anyone. All which anyone can do is save himself, try to behave like Jesus behaved. On the other hand, if Jesus is God and not human, then we have no mediator. Accordingly, when you reject the Person of the Lord Jesus, you automatically must reject His work. You cast away the faith which God has once delivered to us.

This that has been said is not a matter of interpretation. We can have different interpretations on many so-called truths, but when we come to the basic faith in the Person and the work of the Lord Jesus, it cannot be viewed as a matter of interpretation, it is a matter of truth or falsity; and this is what false teaching really is. These false teachers and prophets went out proclaiming they had advanced, because the words used by John, "Whosoever goes forward," actually convey the idea of "development." These false teachers claimed they had developed Christianity; that is to say, they had developed the Christian truth into something which could be accepted more intellectually. They thought they had advanced beyond the truth which had been revealed in the Scriptures; they had developed the Christian faith into a deeper system of thought. But in doing that, they had destroyed the very foundation of Christianity and the very foundation of fellowship. In view of that, John the writer of this short epistle shows us whom to receive and whom not to receive into the fellowship of the called-out ones.

Basis for Fellowship

"Wherefore receive ye one another according as the Christ also has received you to the glory of God" (Romans 15:7). How do we receive one another? We receive one another as Christ has received us. Christ receives us in agape love; not because we are loving, or that we are lovable, or that there is something in us that can be loved, but because He loves us. Therefore, He receives us. But Christ also receives us in truth. He does not just love us and then say, "It does not matter if you sin; it is all right." No. He receives us in truth, and because of that, He lays down His life for us. He who knew no sin was made sin for us that we may become the righteousness of God (see II Corinthians 5:21). The way He receives us is in both love and truth; and the Lord said, "Receive ye one another likewise." We need to receive one another in love and in truth; first of all, in love, because we are all begotten of God: I am begotten of God; he is begotten of God. Therefore, no matter who I am or what he is, we love one another. This is the love of the brethren. We love because there is that life there; there is Christ there. And second of all, we receive one another in truth. The truth is the Person and the work of the Lord Jesus. We believe He is the Christ, the Son of the living God. We believe He has come in the flesh: "the Word became flesh." That is the truth and that is the basis upon which we receive one another.

We also apply this principle, negatively, in the matter of not receiving someone into fellowship. We do not receive those who are not in love nor in truth. In other words, fellowship is having in common, and what we have in common is Christ. If a person does not have Christ, he is not begotten of God. If a person does not believe that Jesus is the Christ, the Son of the living God, and that He has come in the flesh, there is no truth there. So if there is neither truth nor love, there is nothing in common and because of that we find the writer instructing the lady as follows: "Do not receive him; do not even greet him." It is very serious.

Someone may think this is contradictory to love and contradictory to truth. Not at all, because what has been said here has to do with whom we receive into fellowship. We receive into the fellowship only those who have something in common, and that something in common is Christ. Those false teachers rejected the Son; therefore, they rejected the Father, and thus there was nothing in common. Light has no fellowship with darkness. Truth has no fellowship with falsehood. So that is where the line of separation is.

It does not mean that because we do not receive somebody into fellowship, we have to reject that person. It does not mean that at all. We should love those people who do not know the Lord. We should share the truth with them and tell them about the Lord Jesus so that they, too, may be received into the fellowship of the church. But before they are in love and in truth, they are not in the fellowship, but we reach out to bring them in through the way of love and truth.

Another aspect to all this is that some people may have different interpretations from your viewpoint on certain truths in the Bible. Therefore, you say you cannot receive such people. No, what has been said above does not mean that. Remember this: you cannot reject those persons who seem to hold false teachings because they do not know better or have never really been taught the truth. Such are not included in our discussion here. We have to help them to see and accept the truth. On the other hand, we have to keep ourselves away from those professionals and others who claim they have more light, who claim they have developed Christian truth. These we should not even greet lest we be partakers in their evil works. It is serious. Let us not think we are able to mingle with these people and not be contaminated or defiled. History tells us of some who have tried to mingle with these people. Even though they loved the Lord very much, gradually, they were turned away from the Lord because human reasoning is very powerful. What we learn here from John's letter is the way to keep those away who propagate false teachings, so that the church and her testimony may be kept pure.

Finally, John wrote: "I want to fellowship with you more, yet not with ink and paper but face to face" (see v. 12). In spite of the problems with fellowship, we still need to desire after it. Do not think that because there are problems with fellowship we should stop having fellowship. We need to desire it so that our joy may be full. There is nothing which brings us more joy on earth than fellowship.

Shall we pray:

Dear heavenly Father, we do praise and thank Thee for calling us into the fellowship of Thy Son, our Lord Jesus Christ. Oh, what a privilege, what an honor and what a joy that we can fellowship with Thee and with one another. Our Father, we do acknowledge that there is much confusion in fellowship today. We pray that Thou wilt open our eyes and understanding that we may be kept in the purity of fellowship, that we may not close ourselves to fellowship with people whom we should receive, nor open ourselves to fellowship with those whom we should not receive. Lord, we ask that Thou wilt give us discernment, that Thou wilt give us wisdom. In the name of our Lord Jesus. Amen.

III JOHN

Seeing Christ in Hospitality

III John 1-14—The elder to the beloved Gaius, whom I love in truth. Beloved, I desire that in all things thou shouldest prosper and be in health, even as thy soul prospers. For I rejoiced exceedingly when the brethren came and bore testimony to thy holding fast the truth, even as thou walkest in truth. I have no greater joy than these things that I hear of my children walking in the truth. Beloved, thou doest faithfully in whatever thou mayest have wrought towards the brethren and that strangers, (who have witnessed of thy love before the assembly,) in setting forward whom on their journey worthily of God, thou wilt do well; for for the name have they gone forth, taking nothing of those of the nations. We therefore ought to receive such, that we may be fellow-workers with the truth. I wrote something to the assembly; but Diotrephes, who loves to have the first place among them, receives us not. For this reason, if I come, I will bring to remembrance his works which he does, babbling against us with wicked words; and not content with these, neither does he himself receive the brethren; and those who would he prevents, and casts them out of the assembly. Beloved, do not imitate what is evil, but what is good. He that does good is of God. He that does evil has not seen God. Demetrius has witness borne to him by all, and by the truth itself; and we also bear witness, and thou knowest that our witness is true. I had many things to write to thee, but I will not with ink and pen write to thee; but I hope soon to see thee, and we will speak mouth to mouth. Peace be to thee. The friends greet thee. Greet the friends by name.

Shall we pray:

Dear heavenly Father, we are in Thy presence, and we do pray that the light of Thy countenance will shine upon our hearts. We pray that Thou wilt remove any veil which may be upon us that we may behold the glory of the Lord with unveiled face, that we may be transformed by Thy word through Thy Holy Spirit from glory to glory according to Thy image. Our Father, we just commit this time into Thy hands and trust Thy Holy Spirit to lead us into all truth. In the name of our Lord Jesus. Amen.

The second and third letters of John are very closely related. We know that both of these letters were written by John the elder, who is none other than the apostle John, now in his very advanced age. He is the aged John. He has known the Lord for many, many years, and he is writing this personal letter.

These two letters, II John and III John, were written approximately between the years 95 and 98 A.D. As to the second letter, we are not sure whether the elect lady is an individual or is representative of a local church, or represents the church in general. But so far as III John is concerned, we do not have such a problem because by name identification it was written to Gaius, the beloved.

We know that in the New Testament there appear a few Gaiuses because Gaius is a common name. For instance, in Acts 19 there is "Gaius, a Macedonian." Recall how, during the tumult in Ephesus, the people took hold of Gaius and Aristarchus and pushed them forward into the theater. Then in Acts 20 there appears another Gaius: "Gaius and Timothy of Derbe," and they were among those people who had traveled with Paul to Asia. Then, in I Corinthians there is another Gaius mentioned. He was the host of the apostle Paul; and not only the host of the apostle but he was also the host of the entire church; furthermore, he was among the few people whom the apostle himself had baptized. But most likely, the Gaius to whom John the elder addressed his third letter is not any of these three. Even though Gaius of Corinth was a very hospitable person, having the same trait as the Gaius in this letter, we believe he was not the same one. This is because the Gaius of Corinth was more related to the apostle Paul whereas this Gaius was more related to the apostle John. Furthermore, John mentioned in this same letter that he was extremely glad to learn that his—that is, John's—children were walking in truth; so evidently, this Gaius must have been one of the children of John in the faith. Therefore, we believe this must be a very different Gaius from the other three. But of whatever city he may have been, this Gaius is a brother in the Lord and a very hospitable person; and because he loved the Lord, he is loved by God and by the apostle.

The apostle John said he loved Gaius in truth. Yet this was not human love or any emotional type of love. The love which John had for Gaius is divine love; it is selfless love. It is a love that is based upon truth because we know the apostle John loved the truth, and he loved whoever walked in the truth.

Salvation of the Soul

Even though this is a very short letter, there is so much here. For instance: "Beloved, I desire that in all things thou shouldest prosper and be in health, even as thy soul prospers" (III John 2). This is a standard quote for people who preach the gospel of prosperity. We know, today, that there is a gospel which is being preached which is very popular in Christianity, especially in this country, and it is the "prosperity gospel." God wants you to prosper, to have wealth, to have health, and to have everything. And who does not want to be prosperous in all these areas of life? So this is a standard quote. Unfortunately, when people select this verse, they only quote the first part of it. They say, "I desire that in all things thou shouldest prosper and be in health." They ignore the last part of it: "... even as thy soul prospers." In other words, the reason why the apostle John wishes that Gaius be prospered in wealth and in health is because his soul is prosperous. You dare not pray that God would bless a person, make him rich, and give him good health if his soul is not prosperous because that would be most dangerous. That would lead him into many temptations and might even mean his destruction. But for a soul that is prosperous in the sight of God, wealth and health will be of great service to the Lord.

This man Gaius has a prosperous soul, he has a soul that is being saved. In the Bible we find that not only our spirit is being saved, but there is also in view the salvation of the soul. Our spirit is saved by believing in Jesus Christ as our Savior. He who is born of the Spirit is spirit. Hence, when we believe in the Lord Jesus and accept Him as our personal Savior, we are born again. Our spirit is renewed. That is the salvation of our spirit; but from the Bible we learn that salvation is for the whole being, not only for our spirit. Our soul needs to be saved—our personality, our very selves, this very person needs to be saved. In other words, our mind, emotion and volition need to be renewed so that Christ may be expressed through us.

How can a soul be prosperous? That is to say, how can a soul be saved? A soul can be saved by losing one's own self. We remember the Lord Jesus saying this: "Deny yourself, take up your cross and follow Me. He who loves his soul-life shall lose it, but he who loses his soul-life for my sake and for the sake of the gospel shall save it to eternity" (see Mark 8:34-35).

Our soul needs to be saved. It is only when our soul is saved that it is prosperous in the sight of God; and the only way to have our soul saved is to lose our soul-life. It requires our being willing to deny ourselves, take up the cross, and follow the Lord Jesus so that our soul-life can be purified. Christ will reside in our heart and rule in our soul. In that way our soul is prosperous.

Such a person no doubt would walk in truth, just like Gaius. Gaius walked in truth because his soul was prosperous before God. For such a person the apostle John could pray that God would prosper him in physical things and in health because the more God prospers him, the more he will serve God. A person whose soul is saved does not live for himself anymore; he lives for God. And this is the reason why one of the characteristics of this man Gaius was hospitality. He lived a selfless life; therefore, he was hospitable to people and served them. For such a person as this I believe we can pray that God would prosper him in all things and in health, so that with good health he may serve the Lord even more, and with many more resources he may use all for the glory of God. God does want us to prosper, but let us remember that, basically, the soul needs to prosper. That is more important than anything else, and with the prosperity of the soul, may God prosper us in all things and in health.

Hospitality

In the period of the early church there were many believers who traveled from city to city for various reasons. Some people traveled because of business; others traveled to visit relatives or friends, or for many other purposes, just as today. But more than that, in those earlier days, there were many servants of the Lord. God gave to the church "some apostles, and some prophets, and some evangelists, and some shepherds and teachers" (Ephesians 4:11). These people were sent by God to visit assembly after assembly in many places in order to perfect and help the saints. So back then, there were not only many believers traveling, there were also many so-called wandering preachers who were traveling around helping different assemblies. And in those days there were not many good hotels. Inns were not only few, they were also very poorly managed, and the atmosphere in them was not conducive to Christians. Because of this, hospitality among the believers was something quite necessary and very important for lodging these traveling brothers and sisters. It also provided a good opportunity for fellowship with visiting brothers or sisters or servants of the Lord, and through this fellowship people were built up and united in one spirit and in one soul. So in those earlier days hospitality was a big thing. It was also a necessary activity and practice among God's people.

Hospitality is God's Character

Our God is most hospitable; He is a giving, loving, caring God. Before He created man, God had first created other things; so that when man came into the world God had already made every provision for him. And even when man fell into sin, God provided salvation for mankind. Our God lets the sun rise over the evil as well as the good, and He sends rain upon the wicked as well as the good. Our God is such a generous God. He is so kind, so generous, so hospitable. Such is God's character. You cannot think of God as being at all stingy or selfish. No, He is selfless, generous, giving, hospitable.

Now because God's character is hospitable in nature, in the Old Testament period there were many instances when He commanded the children of Israel to be hospitable even as He is hospitable. For instance, we learn in Deuteronomy 15 that God said: "Let your hands be bountiful to your brethren, to the poor, to the needy, and to the strangers." In Deuteronomy 16 we find that God said the following: "When you go to the Feast of Tabernacles you should include the Levites, the strangers, the widows, the fatherless, and the poor in your city with you." Again, in Deuteronomy 24 we read that God said: "When you are harvesting and leave some sheaves behind, you cannot go back and pick them up because they should be left for the strangers, for the widows, and for the fatherless. And when you have shaken the olive trees, you cannot shake it again because whatever fruit remains is for the poor, for the strangers and for the fatherless. And when you are harvesting the grapes, whatever is left behind you cannot go back and pick because they are for the strangers, for the poor and for the fatherless."

Throughout the Old Testament God's commandments, statutes, and precepts exhibit and manifest His character. God's character is such that He is most hospitable. He is always thinking of the needs of His people. He is so selfless, and He wants His people to be like that.

When we come to the New Testament, we read that we are to be "... given to hospitality" (Romans 12:13); and this is a command to all of God's children. So far as gift is concerned, different people may have different gifts, but so far as grace is concerned, everybody has the same; and hospitality is not only a gift, it is likewise a grace. Here we learn that we need to be hospitable. In other words, we need to think of others, we need to care for others, we need to share with others.

Hospitality is Fellowship

Hospitality is a practical way of fellowship. It is a sharing with others whatever God has given to us. We read of this in Hebrews 13:1-2: "Let brotherly love abide. Be not forgetful of hospitality; for by it some have unawares entertained angels (messengers of God)." One of the qualifications of an elder is hospitality, and this is found in I Timothy 3:2 and Titus 1:8. So this is a trait which God truly desires His people to have: to be hospitable just as He is.

Hospitality is a Favor

The classic example of hospitality is found in Genesis chapter 18. In the heat of the day, Abraham was sitting at the door of his tent when three men suddenly appeared before him. The Bible says that Abraham ran to meet them, bowed down before them, and said, "Now Lord, if I shall find favor in your sight, do not just pass by; let me fetch a little water to wash your feet, let me bring a morsel of bread to refresh you while you rest by the tree."

And the Lord said, "All right."

Abraham hurried back and prepared not only the cake,

but he even took a tender and good calf. He put it all before them, and stood by and served them. During the time of eating they began to have fellowship, and the Lord said to Abraham, "Where is Sarah?" And God promised Abraham on that very day that Sarah would have a son.

The Bible says that when they finished the feast, Abraham conducted them on their way for a distance. In other words, he did not simply say, "All right, now you may go." He went along with them for a distance to see them off personally. That is hospitality. Because of that, God revealed to Abraham what He was going to do with Sodom and Gomorrah, and he was able to intercede for Lot. Thus, we can see from this that hospitality is not a burden; it is a favor.

Sometimes we view hospitality as a burden: "Brothers and sisters are coming, what should we do? We have to do something for them." It is as though it is a burden; but not so. Abraham said, "If I find favor in thine eyes ..." If anyone is willing to be entertained by you, if anyone is willing to be helped by you, it is a favor. They are doing *you* a favor. We should not consider hospitality a burden but a great favor from God. If we view the matter in that light, we will do it in the way God does: we will do it generously, and we will do it in such fashion as did Abraham. At first he had said, "I will fetch a morsel of bread;" but he actually brought a calf. That is hospitality. Neither will we simply tell guests when they have finished eating, "All right, you can go now, I have other things to do." No, we will go a distance with them; we will send them off in royal fashion. That is Christian hospitality.

Hospitality is Not Sociability

Hospitality and sociability are two different things. The word hospitality in Greek is *phileoxenia. Phileo* means "love," and *xenia* means a "stranger." So, hospitality actually means: "love a stranger."

What is sociability? Some people are very social by nature. They entertain a lot, but they entertain people of their own status, from among their peers, from among their rank. That is not hospitality. Hospitality is: "love a stranger." That is the reason why the Lord Jesus said that when you entertain, do not entertain those rich people who are able to repay you (see Luke 14). If you invite someone for a meal and expect that person to invite you back, that is sociability. But hospitality is different; it is inviting the poor, the blind or the crippled who have no way to repay you; but God will repay you.

Hospitality of Our Lord Jesus

The Lord Jesus was most hospitable when on earth. One day He was preaching, and the people had been with Him for three days because they loved to hear Him preach. They had eaten all the food they brought, and the disciples came and said, "It is towards evening; send them away so that they can buy food. But the Lord said, 'No, let us feed them.'" He could not allow people to leave His presence hungry. How hospitable was the Lord!

On the night when Jesus was betrayed, He had gathered with His own. He got up, girded himself with a towel, poured water into a basin and washed His disciples' feet. That is hospitality. The Lord Jesus was most hospitable.

When Jesus sent His disciples to preach the gospel, He commanded them not to go to the Gentiles but to the house of Israel. He told them to take nothing with them—neither gold nor silver nor brass nor script, neither two body coats nor staff nor sandals: for the workman is worthy of his work. When they entered a city, they were to inquire who in that place was a good man and to stay with him. When they went into that good man's house, they were to salute it, and if that man was worthy of peace, peace would come to that house. If he was not worthy, then peace would return to them (see Matthew 10). The children of Israel, being God's chosen people, were commanded to be hospitable; and that is the reason why the Lord told His disciples that when they went to the people of the house of Israel they did not need to provide anything for themselves. At the end of that same chapter we learn that the Lord Jesus said this: "If anyone receives you, he receives Me, and if anyone receives Me, he receives the Father. If anyone receives a prophet, he shall receive a prophet's reward. If anyone receives a righteous man, he shall receive the reward of a righteous man. And if anyone should give a cup of cold water to one of these little ones in My name, in the name of a disciple, he shall not go unrewarded." At this same time, the Lord had added this: "Expect rejection."

The Early Church Practiced Hospitality

In the time of the early church there did not exist the pastor system which Christianity has today. Every church now has a resident pastor, and by and large he takes care of the church's spiritual needs. But in the period of the early church, when God's people came together, there were elders who would govern, supervise, and shepherd them. In some churches, like the one in Antioch, there may have been prophets and teachers raised up for the local needs and the ministry, but much of the ministry was done by traveling preachers: those apostles, prophets, evangelists, and pastors and teachers whom God gives to the church. They did not reside in one place but traveled from place to place, visiting different assemblies and ministering the word of God to them. They went out in the name of the Lord Jesus and did not accept anything from the unbelieving Gentiles. So naturally, they would be entertained and helped by the brothers and sisters in various places. And I do believe that as we begin to return to what the word of God says, as we begin to recover the practice of the early church, the need for traveling ministers of God will increase. In other words, God will send His servants out more and more, traveling from place to place, in order to help the people of God; and in doing that, hospitality will be ever more necessary.

Problems with Hospitality

Whom to Receive

Of course, there are problems in this matter of hospitality. As people more and more begin to travel around, the problem arises: whom to receive and whom not to receive, whom to entertain and whom not to entertain. The apostle John in his II John letter makes it very clear: "If anyone comes to you and does not preach that the Lord Jesus has come in the flesh, if such a one does not believe that the Lord Jesus is the Son of God who has come into this world to be a man and thus be our Savior, do not receive him, nor even greet him. Do not receive him into your home, because if you do, you will partake in his evil." And in those earlier days there were indeed people who thought and spoke like that. The servants of the Lord who traveled around, in a sense, had a special position that carried with it a kind of prestige; and when they came to your place you received them and entertained them. But there were unscrupulous and bad characters who would take advantage of this trait of hospitality. Such bad characters could make a very good living out of it and thus had a very easy and comfortable life. They did not have to work but simply traveled from place to place taking advantage of this or that local assembly. There were evil people doing it at that time, and there are people still doing the same today. That is the reason why the apostle John wrote, "If anyone should come to you and does not preach 'Jesus Christ having come in the flesh,' nor believes that the Son of God has come to be a man, to be our Savior, then do not receive him." You do not need to be hospitable to such a stranger because if you do, you will be partakers of that evil. In other words, you will be influenced by that evil.

Letter of Commendation

Because of that, in the early church they engaged in the practice of providing what was called a *letter of commendation* or, *recommendation.* When brothers and sisters traveled to unfamiliar cities, usually they were given a letter of recommendation. For instance, in Paul's letter to the Romans he took the opportunity of recommending Phoebe. Phoebe was from Cenchrea and she was visiting Rome for business reasons. She did not know anybody in Rome, but Paul knew some of God's people in the assembly there, and so he wrote a recommendation: "This Phoebe has been a patroness to me, and she has helped many people; so if she needs help, please give help to her" (see Romans 16:1-3).

Apollos was also recommended—by Aquila and Priscilla. This man had great Biblical knowledge, and he went to Ephesus and preached Christ there; but he only knew the baptism of John. Aquila and Priscilla helped him in this regard; and when Apollos wanted to go to Corinth, this couple wrote a letter of recommendation to the brethren in Corinth. Accordingly, he was received by them, and he greatly helped the people there.

Again, from II Corinthians we learn that Paul recommended Titus. So we see that it was a common practice in the early days to write a letter of recommendation because of the abuse of hospitality by certain false teachers. However, even though there may be abuse, it does not mean we are to cease being hospitable. In every good thing there will be abuse, but we cannot be governed by abuse; we have to walk in truth and love. And if anyone should walk in truth and love, he is beloved of God.

In John's second letter he addressed the negative side of hospitality: If anyone should come among the believers who does not believe that Jesus Christ has come in the flesh, if he comes with a false doctrine, then do not receive him. But in III John he addressed the matter of hospitality in a positive way. He recommended Gaius because Gaius was hospitable. John had evidently written a letter to that church because he said, "I wrote to the assembly" (III John 9). He had probably written a letter for the purpose of recommending some brothers who were traveling and preaching the gospel at that time. Unfortunately, they were not received; but Gaius, who was in that church and walking in truth, received those brothers. He was hospitable to those brothers; so John wrote this letter to recommend him and to encourage him, and said: "You did what you should do and you can do more, not only to receive them, but even to send them onward because they did not receive anything from the nations, that is, the unbelieving Gentiles" (see III John 5-7).

Hospitality is for All

Hospitality is a virtue which we all need to show. It is not a matter of how able you are, it is a matter of love. It is not a matter of how sociable you are, it is a matter of your walking in truth. So here, in this letter, we see Christ in hospitality, because when God's people practice hospitality, Christ is being manifested. You do not do it for any other reason but for the love of Christ. You love a stranger because you love Christ, and in doing that Christ is being manifested.

I do believe this is something we need to learn together more. It is not just for a few to practice hospitality; it must be practiced by all. And it is not just providing lodging to people, because perhaps your house is too small and thus you cannot lodge people. I remember an incident back in China. Once a brother came to a certain place and another brother invited him to stay with him. He had only one room and one bed, but when night came he asked that brother to sleep in the bed. After the visiting brother had been asleep for awhile, after midnight he woke up. He heard a noise, like someone snoring, and he looked to see where the snoring was coming from. He saw the brother who had entertained him sleeping under the bed. He had very little with which to entertain the visitor; but he had done his best.

I remember another story, this one about J.N. Darby. Darby was a very important brother in the Brethren movement, and one day a poor brother asked Darby to come and have a meal with him. Darby consented to do that because he was a very humble person. And this brother had nothing to serve him; but his son had a rabbit. So, before Darby arrived, he killed the rabbit with which to entertain that great spiritual man Darby. Darby came to the house, and when the cooked rabbit was brought to the dining table, he noticed that the son was crying. He did not understand, and so he tried to talk with the son and discovered that the rabbit had been his pet. So Darby would not eat it.

I use these stories as illustrations. It is not only a matter of how able we are to be hospitable; it is also a matter of our heart. We need to have the character of God; God's people need to be hospitable. It is true that there will be abuses, but there are ways to control those abuses. For instance, if a person comes with a strange doctrine, we are not to receive him. Furthermore, if we read on in this letter, we find there is another criterion, which is, that we are to discern the character of that person. Not only his teaching but his character needs to be considered because, unfortunately, in this world there are those who take advantage. If we read church history, we will learn of many laughable, outrageous things and many abuses. Sometimes, churches back then even had the following saying: "If any preacher comes to you and stays over three days, he is a false prophet." Well, I am not endorsing that, but it does demonstrate that there were abuses. But as the Lord has said, "At the end, when lawlessness prevails, will He find love among His people?" It is very, very easy to close our hearts.

But God's character is to be hospitable, and God's people need to be characterized by the character of God.

This matter of hospitality is part of fellowship, and it is a practice everybody can participate in. This is an activity which is not limited to a few; and we do look to the Lord that He will stir up our hearts. Oftentimes, when strangers come into our midst, after the meeting is over, we let them go. We do not know whether they will go away hungry or not. Where is our sense of hospitality? It is true, in exercising or practicing hospitality, it needs some sacrifice; but our God is a sacrificial God, and He never draws back. He always gives, and He expects us, who have His very life in us, to do the same. Thank God for Gaius. He may have been a man of means because he was able to do quite a lot; and because his heart was right, John prayed that God would prosper him even more so that he could do even more for the Lord. Nobody lives for himself or herself. We all live for God.

The Problem of Ambition in the Church

In the church where Gaius was (and we do not know which church it was), there was another problem. There was a man called Diotrephes, who evidently was one of the elders there, one of the leading brothers. However, he was a man of ambition. He was not content merely to be one of the leaders. God has great wisdom. That is the reason why, in the New Testament, elders are always mentioned in plural number. God always wants collective leadership in the church because Christ himself is the Head, and no one person can represent Him as the Head of the church. It needs a collective eldership to represent Him so that no one man will take over the church. But all through the many centuries of church history, even as it was at the end of the first century, there have been people who were very ambitious. It is not only in the political world that we find ambitious people; there may even be more ambitious people in the religious world.

Unfortunately, this Diotrephes wanted to have first place in the local church. He was most ambitious, inasmuch as he had wanted to control the church. He was not content merely to be one of the leaders, but through his maneuvering he was able to control and hold the church in his hand. He made the flock of God his own private property, and he did it in such a way that when the apostle John wrote the letter to the church recommending some brothers who would be a help to them, Diotrephes rejected them. He would not receive the letter, nor would he receive those brethren. Furthermore, he said something slanderous against John and against those brothers. Even when other brothers and sisters were willing to receive those people, he forbade them and even cast them out of the church if they received them. We do not know whether that was excommunication or not; but people can so abuse their authority that they excommunicate whoever displeases them. There was such a person in that church. He deprived God's people of the privilege of the ministry of those whom God had sent to them. In short, Diotrephes was a dictator in the church.

True Spiritual Authority

How do we deal with such a problem? We are supposed to be hospitable, walking in truth, but here is a man who tried to control the church and would not allow this hospitality to be exercised for those who were worthy of it. Now how are we going to deal with this kind of situation? First of all, John said, "When I come I will deal with him face to face." In other words, it will be a matter of spiritual authority against abuse of authority. When authority is abused, then it can only be dealt with by true spiritual authority. In addition, John wrote this: "Do not imitate evil, but imitate good, because what is evil is not of God, but what is good is of God" (see III John 11).

So, perhaps Gaius was in great difficulty because Diotrephes forbade people to be hospitable and yet Gaius was hospitable. I do not know whether he was cast out or not; but most likely he was, and John was attempting to encourage him: "When you are in that kind of situation, you have to imitate good and not imitate evil" (see III John 11).

When authority is wrongly used, then your responsibility is to obey God rather than obey man. You are to be submissive, but you may not be obedient to man. We have to be one hundred percent submitted to God in attitude, and obey in practice. But with man, if we are under authority, we can submit in attitude but not necessarily obey if we must obey God in a given situation. Let us not misunderstand this and think that because it does not please us, we can say, "I do not need to obey." It is a matter of obeying God or obeying man. Gaius had to obey God. Even though in this instance he might be cast out, he had to obey God and not man. So this was another problem in the church there, and we do thank God for this letter because, otherwise, when we have such problems, we would not know what to do.

There is a third person mentioned in this letter—Demetrius. Evidently, Demetrius must have been one of those wandering preachers whom God had sent to the churches—perhaps a prophet, an evangelist, a pastor or teacher. Probably, he was the bearer of this letter written to Gaius and not to the church because the church under Diotrephes had rejected him. Notice the character of this servant of the Lord: he was recommended by all who met him, he was recommended by the truth to which he was faithful, and he was also recommended by John. With such a recommendation, I do not think anyone would have had any problem with being hospitable to Demetrius.

On the one hand, this matter of hospitality is our duty, our privilege and our honor to practice it. On the other hand, we do need to be discerning of not only the doctrine side but also the character side. And if there is no problem with either doctrine or character, then we should be hospitable to such people.

Fellowship in Practice

This letter shows us fellowship in practice. Fellowship is not a theory; fellowship is a life, a daily life. It is something which we can all practice. Of course, we do not limit hospitality only to providing lodging or food. Even if we give a cup of cold water to one of the little ones, it is extending hospitality. The Lord said, if we visit the sick, we are in reality visiting the Lord. If we visit the prison, we are visiting the Lord. If we are clothing the poor, we are clothing the Lord. Hospitality is something very broad. Therefore, let us not think it is merely limited to food and lodging. We can be hospitable in many, many different ways; just as it is already being practiced among us. Thank God for that! Perhaps a family has some problem; perhaps there is sickness—the wife or mother is sick—some of the sisters can therefore cook some food for the family. If they are in the hospital, we can send something there. We can help with baby-sitting or mowing the lawn for the elderly sisters. That is showing hospitality. All of these activities are included. We can find areas of hospitality everywhere. The thing is, do we have such a heart? With a heart like the heart of God, the opportunity for extending hospitality is never lacking. So may the Lord help us.

Shall we pray:

Dear heavenly Father, we do desire to have Thy character characterize us. Lord, we do acknowledge that we are small people. We need Thee to enlarge us that we may be kind, we may be generous, we may be hospitable, we may be all-embracing as Thou art. Oh Lord, do create in us a heart like Thine and also do give us discernment that we may know what to do and what not to do, that we may be a people who not only know the truth, but walk in the truth to the glory of God. In the name of our Lord Jesus. Amen.

JUDE

SEEING CHRIST THROUGH APOSTASY

Jude 1-25—Jude, bondman of Jesus Christ, and brother of James, to the called ones beloved in God the Father and preserved in Jesus Christ: Mercy to you, and peace, and love be multiplied. Beloved, using all diligence to write to you of our common salvation, I have been obliged to write to you exhorting you to contend earnestly for the faith once delivered to the saints. For certain men have got in unnoticed, they who of old were marked out beforehand to this sentence, ungodly persons, turning the grace of our God into dissoluteness, and denying our only Master and Lord Jesus Christ. But I would put you in remembrance, you who once knew all things, that the Lord, having saved a people out of the land of Egypt, in the second place destroyed those who had not believed. And angels who had not kept their own original state, but had abandoned their own dwelling, he keeps in eternal chains under gloomy darkness, to the judgment of the great day; as Sodom and Gomorrha, and the cities around them, committing greedily fornication, in like manner with them, and going after other flesh, lie there as an example, undergoing the judgment of eternal fire. Yet in like manner these dreamers also defile the flesh, and despise lordship, and speak railingly against dignities. But Michael the archangel, when disputing with the devil he reasoned about the body of Moses, did not dare to bring a railing judgment against him, but said, The Lord rebuke thee. But these, whatever things they know not, they speak railingly against; but what even, as the irrational animals, they understand by mere nature, in these things they corrupt themselves. Woe to them! because they have gone in the way of Cain, and given themselves up to the error of Balaam for reward, and perished in the gainsaying of Core. These are spots in your love-feasts, feasting together with you without fear, pasturing themselves; clouds without water, carried along by the winds; autumnal trees, without fruit, twice dead, rooted up; raging waves of the sea, foaming out their own shames; wandering stars, to whom has been reserved the gloom of darkness for eternity. And Enoch, the seventh from Adam, prophesied also as to these, saying, Behold, the Lord has come amidst his holy myriads, to execute judgment against all; and to convict all the ungodly of them of all their works of ungodliness, which they have wrought ungodlily, and of all the hard things which ungodly sinners have spoken against him. These are murmurers, complainers, walking after their lusts; and their mouth speaks swelling words, admiring persons for the sake of profit. But ye, beloved, remember the words spoken before by the apostles of the Lord Jesus Christ, that they said to you, that at the end of the time there should be mockers, walking after their own lusts of ungodlinesses. These are they who set themselves apart, natural men, not having the Spirit. But ye, beloved, building yourselves up on your most holy faith, praying in the Holy Spirit, keep yourselves in the love of God, awaiting the mercy of the Lord Jesus Christ unto eternal life. And of some have compassion, making a difference, but others save with fear, snatching them out of the fire; hating even the garment spotted by the flesh. But to him that is able to keep you without stumbling, and to set you with exultation blameless before his glory, to the only God our Saviour, through Jesus Christ our Lord, be glory, majesty, might, and authority, from before the whole age, and now, and to all the ages. Amen.

Shall we pray:

Dear heavenly Father, we do thank Thee for the privilege of remembering Thy Son together. Oh, how we praise and thank Thee that through Thy beloved Son we are now accepted by Thee, that we belong to Thee and to the family of God. We do praise and thank Thee that Thou hast given us holy boldness to enter into the holiest of all, even Thy very presence, to behold the glory of the Lord in the face of Jesus Christ. And our Father, we just ask Thee at this moment, that by Thy Holy Spirit Thou wilt enlighten Thy word to our hearts, that it may not just be letters but may be life and spirit to us, to the praise of Thy glory. We ask in the name of the Lord Jesus. Amen.

This little book of Jude is one that is very much neglected by God's people. Probably some of the Lord's people have never read it; and yet, it is most relevant to our day because this letter gives us some history of certain things which happened to the early church after the time of the book of Acts. The book of Acts gives us the beginning history of the church, but this little letter of Jude gives us some further history that happened in the church after the record of the book of Acts was finished. In a sense, it typifies what will happen at the end of the church period. Someone has said that the book of Acts, which gives us the beginning of church history, is the acts of the apostles; this little letter of Jude, which gives us the history of what will happen at the end of the church period, can be called the acts of the apostates. It is because through apostasy that the man of sin, the man of perdition, will be introduced to the world.

Prophetically speaking, the last period of the church age is the Laodicean period, as we find in the seven churches mentioned in the book of Revelation. The church in Laodicea, the last church mentioned, represents, prophetically speaking, the church in its last stage, and we are living at the end of the last days. Therefore, generally speaking, we are living in a Laodicean period. And what is the characteristic of Laodicea? One word—lukewarmness. The church is lukewarm; it is neither hot nor cold. And leaven, if it is going to leaven the whole loaf, needs a lukewarm temperature. We will recall that the Lord Jesus said the following: "The mystery of the kingdom of the heavens is like the woman who puts leaven into three measures of meal and the leaven begins to work until the whole loaf is puffed up."

As a matter of fact, even towards the end of the apostolic period, the leaven was already being secretly put into the three measures of meal. It continues to work until the Laodicean period of church history with its lukewarm temperature. It is just the right temperature for it to work to such an extent that the whole loaf, which represents the whole church, seems to be completely leavened. This is the period in which we are living. Therefore, it is of utmost importance for us to know what is happening today in the church, to recognize it, and by the grace of God, to avoid it, to keep away from it, and to keep on course towards the Lord. That is the reason why this little book of Jude is so relevant and so important to us.

This letter was written by "Jude, bondman of Jesus Christ, and brother of James ..." Jude or Judas, which is the same word, was a very common name at that time, and even in the New Testament there were five persons who had the name Jude or Judas. Of the twelve apostles of the Lord Jesus listed in Matthew 10, the last one, the one who betrayed the Lord Jesus, was Judas the Iscariote.

Also, among the twelve apostles there was another Jude: "Jude of James" (Acts 1). In Matthew 10 he goes by another name, Thaddaeus. In some of our Bible versions we will find the phrase, "the brother" of James, in parentheses after Judas or Jude. In the original it simply says, "Judas of James," but the translator probably thought that that was the brother of James. Furthermore, according to the common usage of that time, whenever it was said, "someone of someone," it meant he was the son of that someone. Hence, that would mean that Judas was the son of James, not the brother of James. Now it is that Judas or Jude who asked the Lord Jesus a question recorded in John 14: "Judas, not the Iscariote ..." So, among the apostles of the Lord Jesus, there were two named Judas.

In Acts 9 we are told that the Lord appeared to Ananias and instructed him to go see Saul who was living at the house of Judas in Damascus. This is the third Judas mentioned in the New Testament. Next, in Acts 15 we learn that when the church council in Jerusalem sent its letter of decision to the churches of the Gentiles, they sent two brothers with the letter, and one of them was named Judas, also called Barsabas. This is the fourth Judas. The fifth and final one was a brother according to the flesh of the Lord Jesus (see Mark 6). The Lord had a number of brothers and one of them was named Judas or Jude. Now which one of these five Judases or Judes was the writer of this little letter? It seems that all would agree that this Jude is the brother of the Lord Jesus according to the flesh. There are many reasons, but we need not go into them here.

This brother of the Lord Jesus according to the flesh called himself "bondman of Jesus Christ" instead of saying "brother of Jesus Christ." If we had been the brother of Jesus Christ according to the flesh, probably that would be what we would have written; instead of doing that, he said he was a "bondman of Jesus Christ." Perhaps it was because when the Lord Jesus was living on earth, Jude, as a brother according to the flesh, did not believe in the Lord Jesus. It was after the resurrection of the Lord Jesus that His brothers according to the flesh all came to know Him as their Lord. Because of that, Jude felt that he could not, or did not want to, use the brother designation because he was unworthy. But I think there is a better reason behind it, because our relationship with the Lord Jesus is never according to the flesh; it is always according to the spirit. Even though Jude was a brother to the Lord according to the flesh, it would not be that relationship anymore. It would be a relationship in the spirit and that spiritual relationship is: he is a bondslave to the Lord Jesus. The Lord Jesus is his Lord and Master and he is but a love-slave to Him. I think this is most appropriate; and this is what our relationship with the Lord is today.

However, for the sake of clarity, Jude wanted to identify himself in some way, so he wrote: "brother of James." Now everybody knew James at that time because he was the leading brother in the church in Jerusalem. Therefore, by calling himself "brother of James" everybody would know which Jude or Judas wrote this letter.

The letter does not tell us to whom he wrote, but most likely it was to the same people who received the letter of James and the letters of Peter. Instead of specifying which place or what people he wrote to he merely said, "To the called ones [to those who are called] beloved in God the Father, and preserved [or kept] in Christ Jesus." In reality, he specified the qualifications of those who were to receive the letter: the called ... the beloved ... and the kept. Now that includes all of us. Are we not the called ones? Thank God, we are. Out of every tribe, tongue, nation and people, God has called us unto His beloved Son. Even before the foundation of the world God has chosen us in Christ Jesus. He has called us by His mercy and grace. We are not volunteers. If we could volunteer ourselves in, we could volunteer ourselves out; rather, we are called, and once we are called, we are caught. Thank God, we are the called ones. But we are not only the called ones, we are the "beloved in God the Father." We are dear to our heavenly Father. He loves us dearly. And we are preserved in Christ Jesus; we are being kept by Him and in Him. This is the preservation work of God. Sometimes we hear the term, "the perseverance of the saints." Actually, the perseverance of the saints is the perseverance of Christ, because He is the one who has preserved us; He has kept us. Thank God, we are not only called, we are also loved, and we are also kept. It is to these people that the letter is addressed; which means it is addressed to us.

When Jude began to write this letter, he wanted to write about the common salvation which we all share in Christ Jesus because this was a subject very dear to his heart. But when he started to write, he was moved by the Spirit of God to write something else: an exhortation. Instead of describing our common salvation, he was constrained by the Holy Spirit to give us an exhortation. He was stirred in his spirit by what he saw coming to the church. Now we know an exhortation means two things. On the one hand, it is a warning; on the other hand, it is an encouragement. Exhortation always includes these two elements. It warns us against something which is not of God, and it encourages us into something which is of God.

Jude's Exhortation to the Church

"I have been obliged or, [I feel urged] to write to you exhorting you to contend earnestly for the faith once delivered to the saints" (Jude 3). What is "the faith once delivered to the saints"? This faith includes all the revelation and all the truth which God has given to the church through the apostles and the prophets. It is our heritage; it is our faith. It is that on which we build. It is the faith once delivered. It is described as "once delivered" because we know that all the truth of God which comprises our faith has been delivered to us by means of the word of God. In other words, all the revealed truth has once been delivered to us, and it is now in our New Testament or in the whole Bible. There is no more new truth or new revelation, as such, because all the truth which comprises the faith has been once delivered to the church.

This particular passage from Jude—"... contend earnestly for the faith once delivered to the saints ..."—has been used very wrongly. Because it says, "contend earnestly for the faith," some people have gotten very enthusiastic and quite zealous, arguing and fighting with people over what they consider to be the faith. For instance, some people fight with others over the truth they call rapture. "This is what rapture is, and if you do not believe the same way, we will cast you out." And they defend their actions because the Scriptures say they must contend earnestly for the faith. Over the two thousand years of Christianity, God's people have fought against each other over certain aspects of the faith because they thought that if they gave in or compromised they would be giving up their faith. Therefore, they had to fight and contend to the death. Actually, this verse has been incorrectly applied because to contend earnestly does not mean we have to fight to the death for whatever interpretation we hold as regards the truth. The phrase to contend means "to agonize" or "to strive." It simply means we need to agonize or strive in reference to the faith which has once been delivered to us.

Paul said, "I have fought the good fight, I have run the race, I have finished the course" (see II Timothy 4:7). In other words, there is the faith once delivered to the saints and this is the faith we must strive after. This is the faith we must achieve in our life on earth. This is the faith we must agonize over so that we may have the faith once delivered to the saints and not lose out in anything which God has given us by grace in Christ Jesus. It is not to employ what we call faith with which to fight with one another. Instead, seeing the faith, we strive after it; we diligently seek after it lest we miss out.

We live in the time of apostasy, and that is the reason why we must contend earnestly for the faith once delivered to the saints. Otherwise, we will fall away from it just as other people have. Let us not give up the faith once delivered to the saints. Let us live it, work for it, strive after it, agonize over it, until we achieve and gain it fully—until that faith becomes our heritage, our property, our possession. Now that is what is meant here.

The Apostates

Jude's epistle is a letter on apostasy. Although the word *apostasy* is not used in this letter, the substance is there. Apostasy in English has no meaning because it was not an English word in the beginning. It is a transliteration of the

Greek word, *apostasia*, and the English translators, instead of translating it, simply borrowed it whole. In other words, they turned a Greek word into an English word. So, in Greek it is *apostasia* and in English it is *apostasy*. *Apostasia* comes from a combination of two words in Greek: *apo* which means "from," *stasis* which means "to stand." When these two words are put together, it means "to stand away from." And hence, the word apostasy conveys the meaning of a "departure, a departing, a falling away, a standing away from where one stood originally." In short a person falls away from what he or she originally possessed, and that is what apostasy means.

II Thessalonians 2:3 tells us that there will be a falling away, an apostasy, before "the man of sin, the son of perdition," shall appear upon this earth; and we know that the man of sin, the son of perdition, is the antichrist. One day the antichrist will appear upon this earth, but before he appears there will be a general departure first, a general falling away in the church. Because the church begins to fall away from where it originally stood, because God's people begin to lose what they originally had, such a development prepares the way for the antichrist to appear.

We are living in the day of apostasy. The word apostates, strictly speaking, does not refer to unbelievers, for an unbeliever has never had to make that stand in the first place. If you have never stood on some ground, you cannot fall away from it. You cannot depart from something which you have never possessed. So, if you have possessed these things and then begin to fall away from them, that is apostasy.

In Hebrews 6, for instance, the writer there describes certain situations. He writes that the foundation which is laid includes: "repentance from dead works, faith in God, the doctrine of washings, imposition of hands, resurrection of the dead, and eternal judgment." He speaks to believers because they have already had such a foundation laid. They have repented from dead works; they have faith in God; they know the teaching of washing and baptism; they know the meaning of the laying on of hands which is identification; they know the resurrection of the dead; and they believe in eternal judgment. It describes them and says they have been "once enlightened ... have tasted of the heavenly gift ... made partakers of the Holy Spirit ... have tasted the good word of God and the works of the power of the age to come" (see Hebrews 6:4b-5). These are therefore not unbelievers. Not only have they heard of the Holy Spirit, they have the Holy Spirit, and have tasted the good word of God. They know all the works of the power of the coming age. These are believers, but they fall away, they have apostatized.

"For where we sin willfully after receiving the knowledge of the truth" (Hebrews 10:26). The word *knowledge* there in the Greek is *epignosis*, meaning "the full knowledge of the truth." After we have received the full knowledge of the truth—not just a little knowledge of it—we come to know even the purpose of God in Christ Jesus. Yet, if we sin willfully, it is as though we have "... trodden under foot the Son of God and esteemed the blood of the covenant, whereby he has been sanctified, common, and has insulted the Spirit of grace" (v. 29). These people have known the Son of God, but they have fallen away. They have trodden the Son of God under their feet. They have been sanctified by the blood of the covenant, but then they consider the blood as common, as nothing. They have the Holy Spirit, but they insult the Holy Spirit. Apostasy is not something in the world; apostasy is something in the church. These are people who have believed in the Lord Jesus, who have known the Lord, who have received from Him, and yet they fall away. They leave their early faith. It is a very serious matter.

There are different degrees of apostasy, because the apostasy in Hebrews 6 is not as serious as the apostasy of those mentioned in Hebrews 10 who apostatize. We can see from this that there are different degrees of falling away; but the central point to all of this is: we are to hold on to the faith once delivered to us—we are to strive after it and agonize over it—lest we fall away. It is most serious. As we look at the condition of the church today we observe how Christianity has fallen so far away from the faith once delivered to the church. We live in the time of apostasy.

"For certain men have got in unnoticed, they who of old were marked out beforehand to this sentence, ungodly persons, turning the grace of our God into dissoluteness, and denying our only Master and Lord Jesus Christ" (Jude 4).

There is much similarity between the book of Jude and II Peter chapter 2. The question has arisen: who copied whom? Naturally, there are different opinions, but personally, I believe that Jude used Peter's writings. This is because of the verb tenses used by these two writers. In II Peter 2 Peter wrote: "There shall be also among you false teachers, who shall bring in by the bye destructive heresies, and deny the master that bought them, bringing upon themselves swift destruction." Peter said that there will be false teachers among you, but Jude wrote: "Certain men have got in unnoticed, ... turning the grace of our God into dissoluteness, and denying our only Master and Lord Jesus Christ." In other words, Peter was saying that false teachers will be coming in whereas Jude declared that they have gotten in already. That is the reason why I believe that Jude made use of Peter's writings.

The Grace of God

Who are the apostates? They are those who turn the grace of our God into dissoluteness. These people know the grace of God—the grace of God in Christ Jesus. What is the grace of God? To put it very simply, it is His Son, the Lord Jesus Christ. "God so loved the world that He gave His only begotten Son." The Lord Jesus is the grace of God. It is through the Lord Jesus that we receive grace, the free and undeserved gift of eternal life. These people know the grace of God; yet, they turn the grace of God into dissoluteness.

We have all received the grace of God, and we need to stand upon His grace; we should not waste the grace of God; we should not turn it into dissoluteness. Some people have said: "Because God is so gracious and has so much grace, it does not matter if we sin. It does not matter if we live a loose life. After all, because God is gracious, He will forgive us. We can therefore live our life according to our self-will because the grace of God is so great." But in doing that, we are turning the grace of God into ungodliness. The grace of God is given to us that we may be holy. Without God's grace how can we be holy? How can we be separated from the world and unto God? How can we belong to Him completely? How can we be godly, like God, possessing that character of God in us? It is impossible. But the grace of God in Christ Jesus has been shown and granted to us so that we may be holy, so that we may be a separated and sanctified people, and that we may serve and glorify God. But often, people turn the grace of God into dissoluteness, into licentiousness and loose living, into self-will. That is apostasy.

Absolute Monarch

"And denying our only Master and Lord Jesus Christ" (Jude 4b). A person cannot deny what he or she has never confessed. Here, the apostates have not yet denied Jesus as their Savior. Some apostates do go so far as to deny the Lord Jesus as their Savior, and this is the spirit of antichrist which the apostle John wrote about in his first letter. But these apostates discussed in Jude have not yet denied the Lord Jesus as their Savior; they have only denied Jesus as Master and Lord.

The word *Lord* here is a special term in Greek; the word's English translation is "despot." This is a bad word in English today because an absolute monarch is deemed to be a despot. He does everything according to his wish; he can kill people and anything else he wishes to do—despotism. In Greek this is the same word, yet it does not have a bad connotation but a good one. The Lord Jesus, who has bought us with such a price—with His own blood—is to us our absolute monarch. In other words, you do not belong to yourself; you belong to Him absolutely. He can do anything He likes with you. He is your benevolent despot. He is your Lord and Master, and you are His. You should obey Him; you should surrender to Him; you should yield to Him completely and absolutely. Instead of doing that, these apostates denied the only Master and Lord, Jesus Christ. They may not have denied His name yet, but they denied Him as their absolute monarch. They wanted to live their own lives. They wanted to do their own thing. They did not care about the Lord's interests. They would not subject themselves under the authority of Christ. This is apostasy.

Should we not be warned about this, lest in carelessness we too turn the grace of God into dissoluteness, lest in carelessness we also deny the only Master and Lord, Jesus Christ? It is serious that we could be falling away from the faith once delivered to the saints. Oh, how we need to stand on the grace of God and let it so work in our lives that we may be sanctified wholly for God! How we need to confess the Lord Jesus as our absolute Lord and Master and surrender our life completely to Him, lest in any way we begin to do our own will and go our own way. How we need to be warned about this, and how the church needs to recognize that she has fallen away!

Walking According to the Flesh

"Yet in like manner these dreamers also defile the flesh, and despise lordship, and speak railingly against dignities" (v. 8). These apostates were dreamers. There are two kinds of dreamers. One kind is good. We need to dream, but these dreams come from above—they are visions. God has given us vision. He reveals His mind and His heart to us in our spirits. But there are also bad dreamers. Their dreams do not come from above but from these dreamers' own lusts. Such come from their own fleshly desire. When people think a lot about certain things, they begin to dream about such things. These things are not things given to them but they are created out from them. These are the bad dreamers. They are not people who receive heavenly vision but are those who dream up their own dreams. They defile the flesh. As is their dream, so they are.

What are we dreaming about? We will become what we dream about. If we dream about the Lord we will be like Him. If we dream about the world we will be like the world. These people walked according to the flesh, not according to the spirit. They despised lordship, and spoke railingly against dignities. In other words, they did not obey authorities but despised all authority. All authorities come from God; and if we despise authority, we despise God. They wanted to be their own master and their own authority. They spoke badly against things they did not even know, and in those things which they did know, they corrupted themselves.

"These are murmurers, complainers, walking after their lusts; and their mouth speaks swelling words, admiring persons for the sake of profit" (v. 16). They were murmurers. They murmured all the time. They complained and spoke swelling words—big words—about those people whom they admired, and all done for the sake of gain. These are the apostates.

How to Recognize the Apostates

In the church today there are many apostates, many false teachers and false prophets. The spirit of antichrist is already here in the church. We live in the days of apostasy. How do we recognize them? We know them by their ways, by their actions. First, "they have gone in the way of Cain" (v. 11). That takes us back to Genesis chapter 4. Cain had offered the produce of his land to God as his sacrifice. He thought that what *he* had produced was good enough for God. He did not recognize himself as a sinner who needed to be redeemed by the shedding of blood. Thinking that he was good enough, Cain tried to offer his good works to God, believing that he would be accepted. But he and his offering were rejected, and the result was that he became angry and killed his brother Abel. This is the way of Cain. We can recognize those apostates by the way they go. They do not go in the way of the Lamb of God but despise the blood of the Lord Jesus. They are so self-confident that they think they have enough good and merit in themselves to please God. They believe they can be accepted on their own merits. Such is the way of Cain.

Second, we observe that these apostates have given themselves up to the error of Balaam for reward. That takes us back to Numbers chapters 22-24. The Gentile prophet Balaam was employed by Balak the Midianite, to curse the children of Israel, but God would not allow Balaam to curse. Instead, God turned his curse into a blessing. Because of that, Balaam counseled the Midianite how to entrap the children of Israel into sin so that they might then be cursed. In other words, Balaam sold his prophetic power for money, for gain. We can recognize these apostates because they always enter into the error of Balaam. God may have given them prophetic gifts, but they use such for their own gain instead of faithfully uttering the oracles of God.

Third, they "... perished in the gainsaying of Core." That is a reference back to Numbers chapter 16. Core (that is, Korah) was of the tribe of Levi, and his co-conspirators—certain of the leaders among the children of Israel—conspired against Moses and Aaron because they all wanted to gain the top position and power over the people. They began to speak evil of Moses and Aaron—the gainsaying or denying of Core—and they perished. These apostates always try to gain some place or position, something which God has not given to them. They are ambitious, and they are not satisfied with what God has given to them; they want something more. And finally, they perish in it.

Scripture, here, uses several ways by which to describe these apostates. "They are like spots in your love-feasts." The word *spot* in the original can be translated "rocks," but when the translators wrote down "rocks in the love-feast," it did not make sense, so they translated it as: "spots in your love-feasts." We know that in the days of the early church the believers used to come together to have what they called a "love-agape." The word *agape* was coined for the feast. In other words, they came together to eat together as an expression of mutual Christian love. The early church used to do that, but these apostates who were in the church would come and they were like rocks in the love-feast. In other words, they were like sunken rocks with a little water over them, and when a ship passed over them, it sank.

The apostates were "pasturing themselves"—that is, everything was for their own.

They were like "clouds without water." When you see the rain-clouds, you will naturally think that there must certainly be rain, but there is no water; the apostates, like these rain-clouds, are nothing but a pretense, an hypocrisy.

They were like "autumnal trees, without fruit." There is no fruit; hence there is only an appearance with these apostates.

These apostates are like "raging waves of the sea, foaming out their own shames; wandering stars" who end up in destruction.

Such are the apostates, and their punishment will come quickly. The Lord will come and judge them. Let us be warned of apostasy, lest we too fall away from the faith once delivered to us.

Thank God, this letter does not end here. If it had ended here it would be a nearly total negative writing. Even though Jude had felt constrained to exhort his readers to contend earnestly for the faith once delivered to the saints, he did not have time to write about the common salvation; and yet, deep down in his heart there was still the desire to share about the common salvation. So from verse 20, he turns back to the positive side. You brothers and sisters who are called the "beloved in God the Father and preserved in Christ Jesus," what should you do when you live in such a time of apostasy? When people apostatize all around you and fall away, will you fall away also? No, but because you find apostasy around you, you need to strive more than ever before for the faith once delivered unto you.

Building Yourselves Up

"Building yourselves up on your most holy faith" (v. 20). When people around us are losing faith, when they are falling away from faith, that is a time when we should build ourselves up on the most holy faith. If we are not going forward, we are going backward; we are unable to stand. That is the reason why in Hebrews 6 it says we have to press on to perfection; we have to press on to maturity, because there are other people who are falling away or who are falling back. The only way for us to keep on is to press on and build ourselves up on the faith. If we do not build up, we shall be torn down. We cannot afford to stand still!

Let there not be an unholy contentment among us. There must be a holy *dis*contentment in us. Let us not be so contented with our spiritual condition, with our brothers and sisters, or with the meetings or the assembly in which we are. We can become so contented that we may think we have arrived, that we have everything now; that there is nothing more we need to contend for, to strive after. If we have that kind of attitude, let us beware lest we fall. The only way which can keep us from falling away is to build up. Oh, we need to continually build up on the most holy faith. There can be no letdown! We have to continue to press on, to strive after, to agonize over, and to build ourselves up on the most holy faith.

"But for this very reason also, using therewith all diligence, in your faith have also virtue, in virtue knowledge, in knowledge temperance, in temperance endurance, in endurance godliness, in godliness brotherly love, in brotherly love love: for these things existing and abounding in you make you to be neither idle nor unfruitful as regards the knowledge of the Lord Jesus Christ ... Wherefore the rather, brethren, use diligence to make your calling and election sure, for doing these things ye will never fall; for thus shall the entrance into the everlasting kingdom of our Lord and Saviour Jesus Christ be richly furnished unto you" (II Peter 1:5-8, 10-11).

We have to build ourselves up on the most holy faith, and it is a building up from faith to faith, from faith to virtue, from virtue to knowledge, from knowledge to temperance, from temperance to godliness, from godliness to brotherly love, and from brotherly love to love.

Praying in the Holy Spirit

The second thing we should do is pray in the Holy Spirit. Now praying in the Holy Spirit does not mean here a praying in tongues. Some people believe that praying in the Holy Spirit means praying in tongues, but if we read I Corinthians 14 carefully, we find that Paul says, "Praying with the tongue." It is praying with the tongue. Praying in the Holy Spirit—whether it is in tongues or whether it is in plain words—simply means that when we pray, we do not pray according to our own mind and words. We pray, relying on the Holy Spirit to help us, to teach us how to pray so that we may pray according to God. That is praying in the Holy Spirit.

Why do we need to pray in the Holy Spirit? Because if we want to build ourselves up on the most holy faith we shall discover how helpless we are. If a person does not try, he will think he is able; but if a person tries, he will find how difficult it is and that he can never make it on his own. We begin to realize our own weakness and feebleness, and thank God, the Holy Spirit is here to help us in our infirmities; and praying shows that we depend on Him. That is why we pray. As the Holy Spirit reveals to us our own weakness and feebleness, we will pray according to the mind of God.

Kept in the Love of God

"Keep yourselves in the love of God" (v. 21). How are we to be kept in the love of God? In John 15 we read: "If you keep My commandments then you love Me and you will be loved by Me." Besides building up and praying, we also need to keep ourselves in God's love. By the grace of God we are able to obey, and as we obey and keep the commandment of God, we are kept in His love.

Awaiting Mercy

"Awaiting the mercy of the Lord Jesus Christ unto eternal life" (v. 21). All the time we are waiting—waiting for the return of the Lord Jesus. When He shall return He will show mercy to us. It is all mercy. We do not deserve it; so let us not think we have accomplished something. It is all by His grace and mercy; and it is still by His mercy that we are waiting for His coming. This is the way that we have to strive after the faith once delivered to the saints.

"To him that is able to keep you without stumbling, and to set you with exultation blameless before his glory, to the only God our Savior, through Jesus Christ our Lord, be glory, majesty, might, and authority, from before the whole age, and now, and to all the ages. Amen" (vv. 24-25).

When everything is done, we must see that it is God who has kept us. We must acknowledge that we cannot keep ourselves, but thank God, we know He is able to keep us. He is able to keep us from falling; He is able to keep us from stumbling. Not only that, but with rejoicing He is able to present us without fault and blameless, even before His glory. This is our blessed hope; this is our confidence. Our confidence is not in ourselves: we cannot think that we are better than anybody else because we will fall just like anybody else. No; it is all because of Him who is able to keep us from falling and to present us faultless before the presence of His glory. Now to Him be glory, majesty, might and authority forever and ever. Amen.

Shall we pray:

Dear heavenly Father, Thou hast warned us that we live in the days of apostasy. Oh, we do acknowledge that if we are left to ourselves we will fall just as other people; but we do praise and thank Thee that we know Thou art our God, and Thou art able to keep us from falling, and not only from falling but even to present us blameless before Thy glory. Oh, our Father, we only desire to commit ourselves to Thee. We want to tell Thee, as Paul did, I know whom I have believed, and I am assured—fully persuaded—that Thou art able to keep that which I have committed to Thee until that day. So our Father, today we commit ourselves to Thee: spirit, soul, and body into Thy keeping. And we believe that Thou art able to keep us until that day. Oh, our Father, we do praise and thank Thee because Thou art our confidence, Thou art our perseverance. Father, we do pray that if there be those who have begun to fall away, Thou wilt restore, because Thou art the God of compassion and love. We ask in the name of the Lord Jesus. Amen.

REVELATION

Seeing Christ as the Heir of All Things

Revelation 1:1-3—Revelation of Jesus Christ, which God gave to him, to shew to his bondmen what must shortly take place; and he signified it, sending by his angel, to his bondman John, who testified the word of God, and the testimony of Jesus Christ, all things that he saw. Blessed is he that reads, and they that hear the words of the prophecy, and keep the things written in it; for the time is near.

Revelation 19:10b—For the spirit of prophecy is the testimony of Jesus.

Shall we pray:

Dear heavenly Father, how we do praise and thank Thee for giving us such honor and privilege to gather together unto the name of Thy beloved Son, our Lord Jesus Christ. How we praise and thank Thee knowing that Thou art with us even now. We ask that Thy presence shall be so manifest that we can only bow before Thee and worship Thee. We ask Thee, Lord, that we may hear Thy voice, that we may respond to Thee, that we may love Thee with all our hearts, with all our souls, with all our understanding, and with all our strength. In the name of our Lord Jesus. Amen.

We have come to the last book of the New Testament, the book of Revelation. In the Bible, Genesis is the beginning, and we know that in the beginning the purpose of God is revealed. Revelation is at the end of the Bible; it is the end. In other words, it is the realization of the purpose of God: all things are summed up in Christ.

This book of Revelation is a book of prophecy because we are told at its very beginning: "Blessed is he that reads, and they that hear the words of the prophecy, and keep the things written in it; for the time is near." But let us remember that the spirit of prophecy is the testimony of Jesus. In this book, there are many prophetic words written concerning coming events. Many things will happen, and happen soon, but these coming events are but the letter of God's word. The spirit of this prophetic word is the testimony of Jesus.

Now we are all curious by nature. We like to know what is coming in the future. In one sense, we feel more secure if we know what is coming. We are curious about coming events, but this is not the purpose of this book. It is true that this book gives us the coming events, things which must shortly come to pass; but its purpose is not that we may know *what* is coming but *who* is coming. It is the testimony of Jesus which is the spirit of prophecy. What if we know all the coming events and yet we are not ready for the Lord? What if we come up short in regard to the word of prophecy without inquiring into the spirit of prophecy? If we lack the latter, we will find that the letter kills; it is the spirit that gives life. In other words, if we have mental understanding of the coming events as recorded in the book of Revelation, and yet there is not a corresponding spiritual preparedness in our hearts, such knowledge will condemn us instead of save us. Hence, I believe it is very important, as we approach this book of prophecy, that we be very clear in our hearts that it is not the events we are interested in but it is the One who is coming whom we await. If we do that, then surely we shall be happy. Blessed are we who hear the words of the prophecy and keep the things thereof.

This book of Revelation is the revelation of Jesus Christ which God gave to Him to show to His bondmen what must shortly take place. John the apostle is not the author of this book, although his name is mentioned four times. We have noted already that in the Gospel according to John and the First Epistle of John his name is not mentioned, but here in the book of Revelation his name is mentioned four times: in 1:1, 1:4, 1:9 and 22:8. John is not the author of this book; he is merely a scribe taking down what is shown to him. The author of this book is none other than God himself, because at the very beginning we are told this: "The revelation of Jesus Christ which God gave to him ..." It is the revealing and unveiling of Jesus Christ, and this unveiling of Jesus Christ is given by God. To whom? To Jesus Christ. God unveils His beloved Son and what is going to happen to Him, to none other than Jesus Christ himself. Then, our Lord Jesus is going to show this to His bondmen—to all those who are His servants, His bondslaves—concerning the things which are coming. So, actually, this book of Revelation is God the Father revealing the Son to His Son, and then, in turn, His Son shows all the things which are coming to pass to His bondmen.

The immediate receivers of this book were the seven churches in Asia Minor, but let us remember that it is not only the seven churches in Asia who receive this book but it is also shown to the bondmen of Jesus Christ. Who are the bondmen or bondslaves of Jesus Christ? We will recall how Paul took pride in calling himself the bondman of Jesus Christ. We who are purchased by the precious blood of the Lord Jesus are His bondslaves. We are His love-slaves. He has purchased us and we do not want to go free because we love Him; we want to serve Him.

"And he said to me, These words are faithful and true; and the Lord God of the spirits of the prophets has sent his angel to shew to his bondmen the things which must soon come to pass" (Revelation 22:6).

This book is therefore written to us. We are His bondmen. Not only that, but we also read this in this book: "I Jesus have sent mine angel to testify these things to you in the assemblies. I am the root and offspring of David, the bright and morning star. And the Spirit and the bride say, 'Come'" (Revelation 22:16-17a).

These things are shown to the church of God, and as the church of God is shown all these things, "... the Spirit and the bride say, 'Come.'" We may thus say that this book is written to the bride of Christ. The church, the bondmen, and the bride are all one and the same. We are the bondmen of Jesus Christ purchased by His blood; we are also the church of Jesus Christ; we are His bride as well; and, accordingly, we are the people who receive this book.

Many do not read this book because they view it as a horror story. However, let us bear in mind that this is a love letter; it is not a horror story to terrify people. To us who are the church of God, who are the bondmen of Jesus Christ, who are the bride of Christ, this is a love letter. It is the last love letter our Bridegroom writes to us before the marriage. If we see this writing in that light, then we will see how precious this book of Revelation is. This is the last love letter we shall receive, and then the next thing will be: He our Bridegroom is here, and hence there will be the marriage. Wonderful!

The apostle John received this revelation on the island of Patmos where he had been exiled by the Roman Emperor Domitian. Some people think it was during the time of Nero, but this cannot be true because during the time of Nero the persecution of the Christians had not yet been extended to the province of Asia—it was centered only in Rome. Also, in Nero's reign the manner of punishment meted out upon the Christians was actually to be thrown to the lions or to be set afire in Rome's gardens as light; whereas exile was the method used by the Emperor Domitian by which to punish believers. Hence, it was during the time of Emperor Domitian that John was exiled to the island of Patmos, a barren, rocky island off the coast of Asia Minor in the Aegean Sea. There, the apostle John received this book of Revelation.

This book, being the last one in the Bible, is the

consummation of God's revelation. What is the eternal purpose of God? His eternal purpose is centered upon His beloved Son. It is the will of God that His Son should be the heir of all things (see again Hebrews 1:2). In other words, all things shall be brought into subjection to Christ Jesus. And the central, most important thing to be brought into subjection to Christ is man, because man is the center of all things which were created, and it is through man that Christ is to inherit all things. So, first of all, He has to inherit us. After He has inherited us—that is, man—then through man He is to inherit all things. Therefore, we find that man plays a very important role in the economy of God.

"Out of the mouth of babes and sucklings thou hast established praise because of thine adversaries, to still the enemy and the avenger" (Psalm 8:2).

So far as man is concerned, he is like a babe and suckling in comparison with other created things, because God created man last, on the sixth day. It was in anticipation of this event that God said: "Let us make man according to our image and our likeness" (see Genesis 1:26a), and thus He made man in His own image. So far as the chronology of creation is concerned, if we compare mankind with the earth (the planet) and with the universe, then we are the latecomers, we are like babes and sucklings. Yet God said that out of the mouth of babes and sucklings He would establish praise; God will be praised through the mouth of babes and sucklings. Why? "... because of thine adversaries." God has an adversary—Satan; but He will use one who is made lower than the angels—man—to still the adversaries and the enemies. In other words, God is going to use man as His vessel and instrument in bringing all things into subjection to Christ. God is going to use man to defeat His enemy, Satan, to close the mouth of the enemy, to bring in the purpose of God, so that Christ may inherit all things. No wonder the Psalmist said, "What is man that thou art mindful of him?" (Psalm 8:4).

It truly humbles us to think that God should be mindful of us who are nothing but dust and ashes, the latecomers of the universe, mere babes and sucklings; that God should come to us for the purpose of having Christ, first, inherit us, and then through us have Christ inherit all things; that God should use us as His vessel and instrument to defeat His adversary and to bring in His eternal purpose. It does humble us very deeply and causes us to worship God.

In this book of Revelation we learn how God deals with mankind in these last days. It is the final revelation of Jesus Christ in relation to mankind, how God will bring mankind and all things under Christ's feet. According to I Corinthians 10:32 mankind is divided into three groups: the Jews, the Greeks (or, Gentiles) and the church of God. Or to put it another way, this is how mankind is classified: the church, the Jews, and the nations. We will approach this book of Revelation from these three different perspectives. We will see how Christ is to inherit the church as His bride in His capacity as the Bridegroom, how Christ is to inherit the Jews in His capacity as the Lion of the tribe of Judah—the root of David, and how Christ is to inherit the nations in His capacity as the King of kings and Lord of lords.

The Church

In the eternal purpose of God concerning His beloved Son there is the church. The church is a mystery hidden in God throughout the ages and generations, until, in the fullness of time, God revealed and opened up this mystery by the Holy Spirit through the apostles and the prophets, so that today we may know what the church is. The church was an unknown matter in the past. It was hidden in God because it could not be known. It had to be hidden until, first of all, Christ came into this world, because without the coming of Christ into this world there could be no church. It is through His coming, His incarnation,

His life on this earth, and through His death and resurrection that the church came into being. We will recall that the Lord Jesus was crucified on the cross and died, one of the Roman soldiers had thrust a spear into His side. Out of His side came blood and water, and the church was built with that which came out of the side of the Lord Jesus. Through His death there came out His blood for the remission of our sins. Through His death there was poured out His life like water that we may receive life. It was by this blood and water which came out of His side that the church was born, and on the day of Pentecost the Holy Spirit came forth, and one hundred and twenty individual believers were baptized into one body, one church.

The history of the early church is given to us in the book of Acts. Roughly speaking, we may say the Lord Jesus lived on earth for some thirty-three years, and then the book of Acts covers some thirty-three more years. This would have been the period from the day of Pentecost after Jesus' ascension to heaven up to the time when Paul is seen at the end of Acts as a prisoner in chains living in hired quarters in Rome preaching the kingdom of God and teaching the Lord Jesus—this latter development having occurred in approximately 62 or 63 A. D. So we find that the history of the early church covered by the book of Acts is roughly thirty-three years. Then the book of Revelation continues with a history of the church. In the first three chapters of Revelation there are mentioned seven historical churches. These churches actually reveal to us the condition and characteristics of the church towards the end of the first century, because we know that by this time all of the apostles had passed away except John. He is the one who lived the longest and it was during his latter years that he received this revelation. Thus, Revelation chapters 2 and 3 continue the book of Acts and give us the history of the church at the end of the first century.

What is the purpose of the church? In the book of Revelation the seven churches are represented by seven golden lampstands. Now a lampstand is not an end in itself; it is a means to an end.

The lampstand is to uplift the light. In other words, the church is not an end in itself; it is a means to an end, and the end is to uplift the testimony of Jesus. That is the light. And if the church fails to shine forth the testimony of Jesus, then she has failed in her mission. The church is not to draw people to herself; it is to point people to Christ. So these seven churches of Asia Minor are represented by seven golden lampstands.

The Seven Churches

At the end of the first century there were actually these seven churches in Asia Minor—in the Roman province of Asia, not Asia the continent as a whole. As a matter of fact, the apostle John, in his latter years, had labored in these seven churches and then he was taken away from them and placed in exile on the isle of Patmos. It is no wonder, therefore, that he would be thinking of them on the Lord's day, and that is how he received the revelation. This revelation revealed their spiritual condition before God. That is true; that is historical. (Actually, there were more than seven churches in Asia Minor at that time—for instance, there were the churches at Colosse and Hierapolis as well.) However, this book being a book of prophecy, we believe that the Holy Spirit selected these seven churches specifically because they could prophetically represent the whole history of the church until the return of Christ.

Ephesus

The first church, the church in Ephesus, represents the church towards the end of the first century and even somewhat into the early part of the second. The word *Ephesu*s itself in Greek means "desire" or "loosening." In the beginning, this church in Ephesus did have a desire for the Lord. "Whom do I have in heaven but thee? Whom do I desire on earth but thee?" (see Psalm 73:25) This should be the continual attitude of the church. The desire of the church is the Lord—to love the Lord with all her heart. The history of the early church as recorded in the book of Acts demonstrates that there was such a desire towards the Lord, there was that first love towards Him. The same had been true in the church in Ephesus, for we can discern from the letter to the Ephesians that the reason the Ephesian believers had received such revelation as is given in that letter was because they loved the Lord. They had loved the Lord greatly, but this desire gradually weakened; and towards the end of the first century they had left their first love. There is nothing the Lord looks for more than responsive love. The church at that time had labors, works, knowledge, and understanding, and they had also not deviated from the teaching of the Lord Jesus; and yet, they had lost their first love. So the Lord said, "This I have against thee ... repent."

Smyrna

The second church mentioned was that of Smyrna. The name Smyrna comes from the root word of myrrh, and *myrrh* means "bitterness." In other words, when the church began to lose its first love towards the Lord, the Lord reacted by sending persecutions to the church. Persecution is not all bad. God used persecution to awaken the church out of her loss of first love. Hence, in the second and third centuries the church was deeply persecuted, but out of these persecutions there came forth a reviving towards the Lord, a rekindled desire and love for the Lord once more.

Pergamos

The third church listed was Pergamos, and *Pergamos* means "high tower." At the very beginning of the fourth century, 303 A.D., to be exact, Constantine the Great became the Roman Emperor. The story was told (and I do not know whether it is true or not) that he was one of the Roman generals. When the emperor of that day had died, many of the generals vied to become the next emperor and fought with each other. Constantine was a general in the land of Gaul, which is France today; and many of his soldiers were Christians. The story was told that one night he dreamed a dream. In his dream he saw a banner with a cross that said: "In this sign, conquer." He therefore used that as his rallying banner. He marched to Rome and obtained the empire.

After Constantine gained the empire, he tried to patronize Christianity. Christianity was no longer persecuted; it was patronized by the emperor himself. Immediately, from being persecuted, Christianity became the most popular religion in the world. Many people flocked into the church. The emperor told his soldiers that if they would be baptized he would reward them with a certain amount of silver and two suits of clothing. Hence, many of his soldiers got baptized, not only for material gain but also to win favor with the emperor. Immediately, the church became a high tower. The church had fallen into the world, and as a consequence there was a mixture of the church and the world. The teaching of doctrine other than the truth of the Bible began to be accepted. So, Pergamos can represent the history of the church from the beginning of the fourth century to the end of the sixth century.

Thyatira

After Pergamos came Thyatira in Revelation's list of churches. *Thyatira* means: "sacrificing untiringly, full of sacrifices." And that represents the Roman Catholic system commencing at the end of the sixth century and extending up to the time of the beginning of the Reformation in the early sixteenth century. To be more exact, it began with the pontificate of Gregory I in 590 A.D. The Roman system had become firmly established, and with that there came in the special priesthood and idol worship. All these things began to come into the church.

Sardis

After Thyatira came Sardis. *Sardis* means, "revival or restoration." In the sixteenth century God raised up such reformers as Martin Luther, John Calvin, and others. There was a reviving, a restoring; but unfortunately, nothing is perfect, and it thus became a matter of names instead of reality. It gradually died out. There is a name, but there is no life inside; and that is what Protestant churches are even today. There is a name there; but where is the reality? Where is the life? But thank God, again, God reacts, and that brings in Philadelphia.

Philadelphia

Philadelphia means "brotherly love." Approximately one hundred and fifty years or so ago, at the beginning of the nineteenth century, God began to raise up what we today call the Brethren movement. There were brothers all over the world who began to come out of sects, and they simply called themselves brothers. They loved one another and they kept the word of God. Many truths which had been buried for centuries were recovered by these dear brothers. It was a tremendous movement in Christianity, but sadly it gradually became Laodicea.

Laodicea

Laodicea means "people's opinion." The church has become very democratic instead of being theocratic. Then, when such things happen, there develop both lethargy and false pride. These believers think they have everything, not realizing that they are naked, wretched, poor and blind. The Lord calls them to repent; otherwise, He will spew them out of His mouth. Laodicea represents the church in our day and age. We are living in the Laodicean era.

Conclusions Drawn from Church History

In going through the history of the church, to what conclusions do we come? There are at least two. The first one is that whenever God entrusts the testimony of His beloved Son into the hands of man, man fails very soon. When God reacts, when He gives revelation, there will be a revival and there will be a restoring. In the first generation all seems living and vibrant, but then it begins to be organized. Man seeks to preserve it. In the second generation the organization becomes strong; and by the third generation all one can find is an organization without the life within. This pattern seems to be repeated and repeated and repeated throughout church history. Whenever God entrusts His revelation to man, man loses it as quickly as possible. That is one conclusion we learn from church history.

But thank God, there is another conclusion, and it is this: that God never gives up. No matter how man fails, no matter how many times man repeatedly and always fails, God never falters; He never gives up. He is always stepping in to recover whatever can be recovered; and He does indeed recover. That is the reason why in chapters 2 and 3 of the book of Revelation, at the end of every letter to every church, there is the call for overcomers. "Yes, it is true, I have entrusted My testimony into your hands, but you have failed. Yet, in spite of your failure, I am calling overcomers in your midst."

Overcomers

Who are the overcomers of the church? Let us clearly understand that they are not people outside the church, they are in the church; nevertheless, they are the normal Christians—they are not some super saints. Everybody is subnormal, abnormal; but God is calling for normal Christians—those who will respond to His grace and be faithful to His testimony. We find that at the end of the first century in these seven churches, invariably, God called for overcomers; and He obtained His overcomers. In Revelation chapters 2 and 3 we can see the overcomers of the church at the end of the first century. It was by these overcomers that the testimony of Jesus was maintained at that time and that they did it as representing the whole church.

In the second part of Revelation chapter 7 we are given to see countless people standing before the throne of God and they have in their hands palm branches. They are clothed with white robes and they cry with a loud voice, saying, "Salvation to our God who sits upon the throne, and to the Lamb." Who are they? We know that the overcomers are rewarded with white robes—the righteousnesses of the saints. And we know that palm in the Scriptures—palm trees, palm leaves, palm branches—always signifies victory. So what we see here is a vision of the overcomers of the church from the end of the first century to the last days. So as we look back through church history as represented by these seven churches in the book of Revelation, we find that from the end of the first century up through to the last days, God has always had His overcomers throughout the centuries and throughout the generations everywhere—and they are countless. We may see failure upon failure upon failure everywhere; but thank God, He likewise has always had His band of overcomers upon overcomers upon overcomers everywhere. They may be hidden from the eyes of men but they are known to God, and it is by these overcomers that the testimony of Jesus has been preserved through the centuries. Thank God, for these countless overcomers!

Now when we come to Revelation chapter 12 we find another vision—the vision of the woman bearing a child. What does this tell us and what does it represent? It tells us of what is going to happen in the last days. Let me simply say this: we are living in the last days. The woman in the vision represents the church in the last days. She is clothed with such glory. That is what the church ought to be—a glorious church; nevertheless, surprisingly, she is neglected by the dragon. Think of that! This woman is clothed with such glory, yet the dragon willfully ignores her. In other words, the dragon knows that she is of no use, that she has no effect in the spiritual realm. The church ought to be a glorious church. She is gloriously saved, gloriously endowed, and yet in spiritual reality, Satan, represented by the red dragon, knows very well there is no power there. The church will not in the least affect his kingdom. He will leave that woman alone, for what he pays very close attention to is the manchild within that woman. That woman is in labor to bring forth a male child, and the dragon is waiting there to devour him because he realizes that that male child is powerful: indeed, that male child will mean his downfall. Satan therefore wants to swallow the male child as soon as he comes forth; yet we learn from chapter 12 that when the male child comes forth, he is immediately raptured to the throne.

This manchild is a collective term, for as we read on in the chapter we find that the brethren overcome the enemy, the accuser, "... by the blood of the Lamb, by the word of their testimony, and have not loved their life even unto death" (see 12:11). The manchild represents the overcomers in the last days. God will still have His overcomers even in the last days, and these overcomers will be raptured alive to the throne. Let us understand that we are not waiting for death; we are waiting to be raptured alive! We are living in the end-times. We have the opportunity; we have the privilege; these are thrilling days! We are looking forward to the overcomers being birthed, and as soon as it is completed, they will be taken to the throne, and the enemy will be thrown down from the air.

"... by the blood of the Lamb." The overcomers in the last days are those who overcome him "by the blood of the Lamb." It is not because they are perfect. They are just as weak as anybody else; but they confess their sin, they trust in the blood of Jesus, they are being washed continuously, and hence their robe is kept white all the time.

"... and by the word of their testimony." What is the testimony of these overcomers? Their testimony is: Jesus is Lord. Jesus is Lord of their life and they speak out, and with a life at the back of what they say, their word—their testimony—has power.

"... and [they] have not loved their life even unto death." They are willing to lay down their life, their soul-life, for the Lord. These are overcomers in the last days. These are the people who have maintained the testimony of Jesus in the last days. Oh, that we, by the grace of God, may be among them!

We learn from the beginning part of Revelation chapter 14 that there are one hundred and forty-four thousand standing on Mount Zion with the Lamb, and they are singing a new song which nobody else could sing. Who are they? No doubt, they are the overcomers who shall be manifested towards the end of the Great Tribulation, for as we read on in the chapter we learn that there is the harvest which shall be gathered in at the end of the Great Tribulation. So these who stand on Mount Zion with the Lamb represent the overcomers towards the end of the Great Tribulation period.

In chapter 19 we are told of a man riding on a white horse who is none other than the Lord himself, the Word of God. He has an army following Him, and this army represents the overcomers at the second coming of Christ. They will be the bride of the Lamb.

And in chapters 21 and 22 of Revelation we learn of the consummation. In other words, the whole church will be in that new city, the New Jerusalem, because the foundation is the twelve names of the apostles. The Lord will inherit His church, and she will be His eternal bride.

The book of Revelation tells us that in spite of man's failure, God will have the bride for His Son, and His Son will eventually have a glorious church that is without spot or wrinkle or any such thing, holy and without blemish. There will be that eternal union with Christ. Thank God for that! HE IS WORTHY. Now that is the book of Revelation as approached from the perspective of the church.

The Jews

The second perspective in our approach to this book of Revelation is the Jews, whom Christ is also to inherit, in this instance, in His capacity as the Lion of the tribe of Judah. Like the church, the Jews are another mystery. God chose the Jews because of their father, Abraham. Hence, the Jews are a chosen people of God. The apostle Paul tells us concerning the Jewish people: "Whose is the adoption, and the glory, and the covenants, and the lawgiving, and the service, and the promises; whose are the fathers; and of whom, as according to flesh, is the Christ, who is over all, God blessed for ever. Amen" (Romans 9:4-5).

Because of their father Abraham, the Jews were selected as a chosen race: and to them belong adoption, sonship, glory, covenant, lawgiving, service, and all the promises; and theirs also are the patriarchs; and even the Lord Jesus came from the Jews. What a privileged people they were! But because of their blindness, when the Messiah came, they rejected Him, and they were temporarily set aside as a nation. Now we must be clear about this: it does not mean that all Jews have been set aside, but the nation as a whole was set aside temporarily—not permanently. For through the centuries there have been many Jews who were saved. As a matter of fact, in the first century, at the church's beginning, all the believers therein were Jews who had believed in the Lord. Paul said, "I myself, being a Jew, was of the Lord." Throughout the centuries Jews as individuals have been added to the church because she is made up of Jews and Gentiles—"There is neither Jew nor Greek [Gentile], … for you are all one in Christ Jesus" (Galatians: 3:28 NASV). But as a nation, because of their blindness in part, the Jewish people have been temporarily set aside by God as a chosen nation until the fullness of the Gentiles (that is, of the nations) be come and then all Israel shall be saved (see Romans 11:25-26).

Because of their blindness, the Jews were scattered all over the world. While He was on earth, our Lord Jesus cursed only one thing—a fig tree. That fig tree had leaves but no fruit, and the fig in Scripture is a symbol of the Jewish nation. God had been good to them. Christ had come to them and labored among them for three years, but they bore no fruit. They only had leaves—a good appearance and form of godliness without the power of it. So the Lord cursed it, and it was withered from the root. For centuries the Jewish people were scattered all over the world without a land, government or country. But, strangely, they had never been assimilated into the various host countries and peoples. Not only that, but in many ways they controlled the world. They were persecuted without cause but, then, what the Lord had said while on earth began to come true: "When the fig begins to be tender and sprout, to bud, then you will know that the summer is near; then you will know I am at the doors" (see Matthew 24:32-33). For to the surprise of the politicians and statesmen of the world, and as though out of nowhere, in 1948 the nation of Israel was reestablished. But let us be clear that this was a political recovery. There has not yet occurred a religious restoration.

Even though the nation of Israel was established once again, they were surrounded by enemies. They have never felt secure. Security has become the biggest problem to the Israeli nation. How could it find peace and security? There is none, for the Prince of Peace has not yet come. They have had no peace ever since 1948 and because of that, their greatest desire is for security; and according to Daniel chapter 9, towards the end of this age, one day there will arise someone who will declare that he can guarantee their security. One day the antichrist will make a peace pact with the nation of Israel promising to guarantee peace and security for the nation for seven years. They therefore shall fall into his trap because their greatest concern will be how they can obtain peace. In the middle of that seven-year period the antichrist will show his true colors and will break the covenant. Then the Jewish nation will enter into what Jeremiah 30:7 calls "Jacob's trouble."

Surely, God has the Jews in His mind because if we read in the book of Revelation 1:7 it says this: "Behold, he comes with the clouds, and every eye shall see him, and they which have pierced him, and all the tribes of the land shall wail because of him. Yea. Amen."

"Behold, he comes with the clouds ..." That is the Messiah. Christ will come with the clouds, and "... every eye shall see him and they which have pierced him and all the tribes of the land ..." "The tribes of the land" is the literal translation, and such always refers to the Jewish nation. "They shall wail because of him. Yea. Amen." This is actually a quotation from Zechariah (see below). In that day, the nations will surround Jerusalem and break into it.

"And I will pour upon the house of David and upon the inhabitants of Jerusalem the spirit of grace and of supplications; and they shall look on me whom they pierced, and they shall mourn for him, as one mourneth for an only son, and shall be in bitterness for him, as one that is in bitterness for his firstborn" (Zechariah 12:10). As we read on in Zechariah we learn that a fountain will be opened to cleanse the Jewish people from all their iniquities (see 13:1).

At the very beginning of the book of Revelation we can discern that the Lord gives us a hint that at the end He shall return again to the Jewish nation. God has never forgotten His promise; He has never forgotten His covenant with Abraham, Isaac and Jacob. For in the first part of Revelation 7 we find that there are a hundred and forty-four thousand who shall be sealed with the seal of the living God, and these refer to Jewish people. Let us not mix these up with the one hundred and forty-four thousand mentioned in chapter 14; because these two numbers refer to two different groups of people. In chapter 7 the group of one hundred and forty-four thousand cited there are the Jewish people from out of the twelve tribes of the Jewish nation, and they will be sealed with the seal of the living God. Bear in mind that they are not sealed with the seal of the Lamb but with the seal of the living God. In other words, before "Jacob's trouble" comes, God prepares His chosen people. There will be among the Jewish nation a goodly number of pious Jews. They are not Christians because the name of the Lamb is not associated with this group; nevertheless, they are pious Jews who shall be sealed with the seal of the living God, for they believe in the living God. Therefore, even though the revival of the Israeli nation today is a political one, towards the end, God will have a people among them who are sealed with the seal of the living God. These will be godly, pious Jews. And though, when Jacob's trouble comes they will be greatly persecuted, God will have already sealed them and they shall be preserved by the power of God.

We are told in chapter 11 that God will send two men into their midst. These are two prophets who will strengthen them because they are in Jacob's trouble. To the Christians this period is known as the Great Tribulation; to the Jews it is called Jacob's trouble. Actually, they are one and the same period of events that will occur at the same time. For instance, when the antichrist wants his image made with everybody worshiping it, of course, the faithful Christians will never do that and the pious Jews will also never do that. So these will be persecuted during these three and a half years; but God will send two men to strengthen the pious Jews (see again Revelation 11). Most likely, these two men whom God will send back are Moses and Elijah, because they are the most respected among the Jewish people—the lawgiver and the prophet.

And from Zechariah chapter 14 we learn that the nations will be gathered and surround Jerusalem. They will break into it; but, then, Jehovah—the Lord Jesus himself—will come down and place His feet on the summit of the Mount of Olives. At that very moment the Mount will break asunder into two, and one-third of the Jewish people in Jerusalem who are left will flee through that passage, and thus the Lord will come to deliver His people. The Jews will see Him with their own eyes, and they will greatly weep because they had rejected Him. They will repent and be washed clean, and all Israel shall be saved.

After the battle of Armageddon the millennial kingdom is established. During the millennial kingdom all the promises of God to Abraham, Isaac and Jacob, including the covenant of God with the forefathers of the Jewish people, will be fulfilled. And during the millennial age the Jewish nation will be the center of the nations. They will be a nation of priests. They will go out to teach all nations concerning the ways of God. Finally, in the New Jerusalem the Jews will have a place there since the city's twelve gates will bear the names of the twelve tribes of Israel. It will be the consummation of all the work of God throughout the centuries. Both the Old and the New Testament saints will all be gathered together to be the eternal bride of the eternal Son. Christ will inherit the Jewish nation. He will be accepted as King David, the Lion of the tribe of Judah.

The Nations

How about the nations, which constitute the third and final perspective in our approach to the book of Revelation? They, too, shall Christ inherit in His capacity as the King of kings and Lord of lords. Revelation chapter 5 reveals the Lamb as standing before the throne and receiving from the One who has in His hand a little book, and that little book is the title deed to the earth. Heretofore, Satan has been the usurper of the earth. He has been the squatter on the earth. Nevertheless, he has never been the owner; God only is the owner, for He never gave up His ownership; so now, God is giving the ownership to His beloved Son who has overcome. And hence, the Lamb begins to open the seals and to execute the counsel of God in bringing the earth and the nations thereof back into subjection at His feet. But when God, through His beloved Son, begins to bring the earth and the nations back to Him, there is resistance. That is why, as the seals are being opened and the trumpets are being sounded, all kinds of disasters are seen coming forth upon the earth's nations. These disasters are caused as a result of the resistance which comes from the enemy. Satan and the world are trying to resist Christ from inheriting the earth, and because of that, there shall occur all these disasters and woes upon the world. Yet let us not blame God for that. As a matter of fact, all these woes and disasters are said to be the beginning of birth pangs. In other words, God is able to effect something most positive from these dire events which will answer to His heart. Such is the wisdom of God.

With the coming of the end, Satan puts forth his last attempt to resist the kingdom of God, but the Lord will come and slay all His enemies with the word of His mouth (see chapter 19). Satan himself will be bound and sealed in the bottomless pit; the antichrist and the false prophet will be thrown into the lake of fire, and all those who resist the Lord will be killed. There will next be the judgment of the nations—the goat nations and the sheep nations (see Matthew 25), and then there will be the commencement of Christ's millennial rule on the earth over the nations.

The Millennium

The millennium is what the philosophers and the idealists have always been looking for—the utopia of their dreams; and finally, the true utopia comes. When Christ shall reign upon this earth, He will reign with righteousness; He will also reign with a rod of iron.

"And righteousness shall be the girdle of his reins, and faithfulness the girdle of his loins. The wolf also shall dwell with the lamb, and the leopard shall lie down with the kid, and the calf and the young lion and the fatted beast together, and a little child shall lead them. And the cow and the she-bear shall feed; their young ones shall lie down together; and the lion shall eat straw like the ox. And the sucking child shall play on the hole of the adder, and the weaned child shall put forth its hand to the viper's den. They shall not hurt nor destroy in all my holy mountain; for the earth shall be full of the knowledge of Jehovah, as the waters cover the sea. And in that day there shall be a root of Jesse, standing as a banner of the peoples: the nations shall seek it; and his resting-place shall be glory" (Isaiah 11:5-10).

Also, in Micah 4:3 the prophet tells us that people will beat their swords into plowshares, their spears into pruning knives. There will be no more war and people will not learn war anymore. Peace shall be upon this earth because the Prince of Peace has finally come. That is the millennium.

Final Judgment

After the millennium there shall occur the last Satanic rebellion, and after the last rebellion comes the final judgment (see Revelation 20). All the dead will be raised and they will be judged according to the works they did on earth. Anyone whose name is not in the book of life will be judged at that time and will be thrown into the lake of fire, and the old earth and old heaven will be burned. A new earth and a new heaven will come. The New Jerusalem will descend upon this new earth, and the nations shall walk in the light of the holy city, New Jerusalem, and they will bring their glory to God.

Christ shall be the King of Kings and Lord of Lords. Such, in brief, is the book of Revelation containing the testimony of Jesus: God testifying that His Son shall be the heir of all things—the church, the Jewish people, and the nations.

Now, then, what should be our response? Our response as the bride should be to say, "Come, come!"

The Lord said, "Behold, I come quickly."

"Come quickly, Lord Jesus." That should be our constant attitude and our response.

Shall we pray:

Dear heavenly Father, we do praise and thank Thee that through these prophetic words Thou hast revealed Thy beloved Son to us. He is the center of Thy purpose; He is the heir of all things. Oh, how we consider it a great privilege that He should inherit us, that we should be His bride. Oh, Lord, we pray that by Thy grace we may be faithful to Him, that we may be overcomers, that we may be useful in His hands, that we may glorify His name. And Lord, in spite of what we see around us, and even what we see within us, we do praise and thank Thee because Thou art faithful. Thou dost never fail. Thou wilt get what Thou hast ordained from the beginning for Thy beloved Son. So Lord Jesus, our cry to Thee today is: Perfect us for Thy glory. In the name of our Lord Jesus. Amen.

OTHER TITLES AVAILABLE

From Christian Fellowship Publishers

By Watchman Nee

The Basic Lesson Series

Volume 1 - A Living Sacrifice
Volume 2 - The Good Confession
Volume 3 - Assembling Together
Volume 4 - Not I, But Christ
Volume 5 - Do All to the Glory of God
Volume 6 - Love One Another

CD Rom — The Complete Works of Watchman Nee as Published by CFP

Aids to "Revelation"
Back to the Cross
A Balanced Christian Life
The Better Covenant
The Body of Christ: A Reality
The Character of God's Workman
Christ the Sum of All Spiritual Things
The Church and the Work – 3 Vols
"Come, Lord Jesus"
The Communion of the Holy Spirit
The Finest of the Wheat - Volume 1
The Finest of the Wheat - Volume 2
From Faith to Faith
From Glory to Glory
Full of Grace and Truth - Volume 1
Full of Grace and Truth - Volume 2
Gleanings in the Fields of Boaz
The Glory of His Life
God's Plan and the Overcomers
God's Work
Gospel Dialogue
Grace for Grace
Interpreting Matthew
Journeying Towards the Spiritual
The King and the Kingdom of Heaven
The Latent Power of the Soul
Let Us Pray
The Life that Wins
The Lord My Portion
The Messenger of the Cross
The Ministry of God's Word
The Mystery of Creation
Powerful According to God
Practical Issues of this Life
The Prayer Ministry of the Church
The Release of the Spirit
Revive Thy Work
The Salvation of the Soul
The Secret of Christian Living
Serve in Spirit
The Spirit of Judgment
The Spirit of the Gospel
The Spirit of Wisdom and Revelation
Spiritual Authority
Spiritual Exercise
Spiritual Discernment
Spiritual Knowledge
The Spiritual Man
Spiritual Reality or Obsession
Take Heed
The Testimony of God
Whom Shall I Send?
The Word of the Cross
Worship God
Ye Search the Scriptures

By Stephen Kaung

Discipled to Christ
The Songs of Degrees - Meditations on Fifteen Psalms
The Splendor of His Ways - Seeing the Lord's End in Job
God Has Spoken – Vol. II, Seeing Christ in the New Testament

Order From: 11515 Allecingie Pkwy Richmond, VA 23235

www.c-f-p.com